Shirley Jackson and Domesticity

Shirley Jackson and Domesticity

Beyond the Haunted House

Edited by
Jill E. Anderson and
Melanie R. Anderson

BLOOMSBURY ACADEMIC
NEW YORK • LONDON • OXFORD • NEW DELHI • SYDNEY

BLOOMSBURY ACADEMIC
Bloomsbury Publishing Inc
1385 Broadway, New York, NY 10018, USA
50 Bedford Square, London, WC1B 3DP, UK
29 Earlsfort Terrace, Dublin 2, Ireland

BLOOMSBURY, BLOOMSBURY ACADEMIC and the Diana logo are trademarks of
Bloomsbury Publishing Plc

First published in the United States of America 2020
This paperback edition published in 2021

Volume Editors' Part of the Work © Jill E. Anderson and Melanie R. Anderson
Each chapter © Contributors

For legal purposes the Acknowledgments on p. ix constitute an extension
of this copyright page.

Cover design: Eleanor Rose
Cover images: (top) Vintage photograph of 1950s woman in kitchen against pile of
photos © catscandotcom / iStock / Getty Images Plus; (bottom) Haunted House
© Andy McGowan / Getty Images

All rights reserved. No part of this publication may be reproduced or transmitted
in any form or by any means, electronic or mechanical, including photocopying,
recording, or any information storage or retrieval system, without prior permission in
writing from the publishers.

Bloomsbury Publishing Inc does not have any control over, or responsibility for, any
third-party websites referred to or in this book. All internet addresses given in this
book were correct at the time of going to press. The author and publisher regret any
inconvenience caused if addresses have changed or sites have ceased to exist, but can
accept no responsibility for any such changes.

A catalogue record for this book is available from the British Library.

Library of Congress Cataloging-in-Publication Data
Names: Anderson, Jill E, editor. | Anderson, Melanie, editor.
Title: Shirley Jackson and domesticity : beyond the haunted house /
edited by Jill E Anderson and Melanie R Anderson.
Description: New York : Bloomsbury Academic, 2020. |
Includes bibliographical references and index. |
Summary: "This collection explores the ways domesticity
weaves through, interferes with, and influences Shirley
Jackson's writing"– Provided by publisher.
Identifiers: LCCN 2019051467 | ISBN 9781501356643 (hardback) |
ISBN 9781501356667 (pdf) | ISBN 9781501356650 (epub)
Subjects: LCSH: Jackson, Shirley, 1916–1965–Criticism and interpretation. |
Domestic relations in literature. | Housekeeping in literature. |
Home in literature. | Families in literature.
Classification: LCC PS3519.A392 Z8525 2020 | DDC 818/.5409–dc23
LC record available at https://lccn.loc.gov/2019051467

ISBN: HB: 978-1-5013-5664-3
PB: 978-1-5013-7001-4
ePDF: 978-1-5013-5666-7
eBook: 978-1-5013-5665-0

Typeset by Newgen KnowledgeWorks Pvt. Ltd., Chennai, India

To find out more about our authors and books visit www.bloomsbury.com
and sign up for our newsletters.

To Daddy, always by my side.
— Jill
For my parents.
— Melanie

CONTENTS

Acknowledgments ix

    Introduction 1
    Melanie R. Anderson

1 Hideous Doughnuts and Haunted Housewives: Gothic Undercurrents in Shirley Jackson's Domestic Humor 7
   Bernice M. Murphy

2 Enemies Foreign and Domestic: Shirley Jackson's *New Yorker* Stories 27
   Ashley Lawson

3 "You Didn't Look Like You Belonged in This House": Shirley Jackson's Fragile Domesticities 43
   Michael J. Dalpe Jr.

4 "Sharp Points Closing in on Her Throat": The Domestic Gothic in Shirley Jackson's Short Fiction 59
   L. N. Rosales

5 Endless House, Interminable Dream: Shirley Jackson's Domestic Architecture and the Matrophobic Gothic 77
   Luke Reid

6 Casting a Literary Spell: The Domestic Witchcraft of Shirley Jackson 97
   Alissa Burger

7 Homemaking for the Apocalypse: Queer Failures and Bunker Mentality in *The Sundial* 113
Jill E. Anderson

8 Domestic Apocalypse in *The Sundial* 133
Christiane E. Farnan

9 "I May Go Mad, but at Least I Look Like a Lady": The Insanity of True Womanhood in *The Sundial* 149
Julie Baker

10 Insisting on the Moon: Shirley Jackson and the Queer Future 169
Emily Banks

11 Shirley Jackson's Merricat Story: Conjugal Narcissism in *We Have Always Lived in the Castle* 189
Richard Pascal

12 My House Is My Castle: On the Mutually Enabling Persistence of Familial Devotion and Defunct Economies in Shirley Jackson's *We Have Always Lived in the Castle* 205
Allison Douglass

13 Flipping Hill House: The Netflix Renovation of Shirley Jackson's Landmark Novel 223
Jessica R. McCort

Notes on Contributors 243
Index 245

ACKNOWLEDGMENTS

The editors of this volume must thank the contributors who shared our love of Shirley Jackson and graciously provided the following critical analyses of her fiction. Without their ideas, meticulous work, and patience with us and the process, this collection would not exist. We also wish to thank the team at Bloomsbury for shepherding this manuscript through the process of publication and into readers' hands. This appreciation extends to the anonymous readers, whose feedback, in the early stages especially, was valuable in the development of the collection and its scope.

Jill E. Anderson wishes to thank Melanie, her coeditor, for going along this ride with her, communicating effectively, and being consistently understanding, supportive, and witty. Thanks also to Lisa and Katie, her perennial cheerleaders who've supported this work along its way. Most importantly, she is grateful to her daddy, for instilling a love of the written word in her, and to her mama, who is supportive though she pretends to not understand any of it. Also to Hans and Alistair, whose insistent loyalty is sometimes a little too steadfast but always true. And finally, a million thanks to Jonathan who always haunts their home and cooks the meals when domesticity is a burden.

Melanie R. Anderson must thank her coeditor Jill for being a hardworking and understanding partner in this process that involves paying attention to many different details from beginning to end, usually all happening at once. Thanks also are due to her family, particularly her parents, for their support. And finally, much appreciation must go to Bobbie, whose patience is immense and who is one of the best of man's best friends.

Introduction

Melanie R. Anderson

Fans and scholars of Shirley Jackson's fiction have witnessed a resurgence of interest in her work in the past ten years, and, recently, two of Jackson's most well-known novels have been adapted for the screen. In October 2018, Netflix released Mike Flanagan's ten-episode series *The Haunting of Hill House*, and in the same year, the full-length movie *We Have Always Lived in the Castle*, directed by Stacie Passon, had a limited theatrical release and appeared on streaming services. These two iterations of Jackson's work followed the release of previously unpublished stories in the collection *Let Me Tell You* (2015)—edited by two of Jackson's children, Laurence Jackson Hyman and Sarah Hyman DeWitt—and Ruth Franklin's biography *Shirley Jackson: A Rather Haunted Life* (2016). The Netflix series and the movie constitute clear evidence of a continued interest in Jackson. They also, however, show how she has been remembered as a writer of gothic horror tales, often centered on a haunted home.

While the Netflix series *The Haunting of Hill House* was a well-constructed and popular television program with talented actors, it may have overshadowed Jackson's own contribution to the source material. There were new editions of the 1959 haunted house novel tied into the streaming program, but, for the most part, the show used the novel as the bare bones for a larger and much different saga, albeit with similar themes. Flanagan borrowed the names of characters and the eponymous house and brilliantly sprinkled Easter egg references to Jackson's oeuvre throughout the episodes, but Shirley Jackson was referenced only in the first name of one of the Crain siblings. Furthermore, even though there was a book titled *The Haunting of Hill House* in the show, it was written by Steven, Shirley

Crain's brother. This relegation of Jackson's authorship to the background was not lost on critics.[1]

Adaptation is not an exact science and is dependent on interpretation; thus, Netflix's Hill House taking on a life of its own in the twenty-first century is not surprising. I do think, though, that the manner in which the Netflix program departed from Jackson's work and the very choice to adapt *The Haunting of Hill House* indicate her popular and critical legacy. This focus on Jackson's predilection for the gothic has eclipsed the actual variety of her writing and led to critics examining her work through a limited number of texts: "The Lottery" (1948), *The Haunting of Hill House* (1959), and *We Have Always Lived in the Castle* (1962). There are two previous edited collections of essays on Shirley Jackson's work, Bernice M. Murphy's *Shirley Jackson: Essays on the Literary Legacy* (2005) and my *Shirley Jackson, Influences and Confluences* (2016), edited with Lisa Kröger. Each of the introductions to these collections has repeated the lament of Jackson scholars that, until the years leading up to the twenty-first century, and particularly by 2010 when the majority of Jackson's work came back into print, academic writing on Jackson's work was sparse. Beyond journal articles, classroom use of her writing was usually limited to "The Lottery." While the number of articles on Jackson's work has increased, much more attention could be paid to her rich and varied fiction beyond the most cited novels and stories. Of her six completed novels, *The Road through the Wall* (1948), *Hangsaman* (1951), *The Bird's Nest* (1954), and *The Sundial* (1958) have yet to be fully explored. We offer in this collection three takes on *The Sundial*, which seems to be emerging as the novel to watch for in current critical literature. Additionally, a staggeringly large number of her short stories published in popular magazines of the time and in her collection *The Lottery and Other Stories* (1948) have, thus far, eluded sustained scholarly attention. Bernice M. Murphy addressed this situation in 2005, writing, "Critics have not quite known what to make of [Jackson], a problem caused by the fact that she operated in two popular and yet frequently marginalized genres: those of horror and the gothic and the so-called domestic humor that appeared in women's magazines during the 1950s."[2] The popular perception of Jackson has focused on her influence on the horror genre without taking into consideration her diverse output, which includes nonsupernatural meditations on life for women in the home and her penchant for linking the position of women in 1950s America to gothic themes of the uncanny and entrapment.

Jackson was so much a part of 1950s American letters that Linda Wagner-Martin described the 1950s as "the decade of Jackson."[3] New writers of the 1950s and 1960s were often compared to her. Because of her writing and her husband's critical and professorial career, she ran in literary circles that included Ralph Ellison, Howard Nemerov, Bernard Malamud, and Kenneth and Libbie Burke, to name a few luminaries. In addition,

Jackson was aware of the social changes surrounding her. Biographer Ruth Franklin describes the atmosphere of growth and paranoia that prevailed at the time Jackson was writing, from rampant conspicuous consumerism to the House Committee on Un-American Activities to the justified, but simultaneously inconceivable, fear of nuclear apocalypse to the beginnings of desegregation and the stirrings of the coming second wave of feminism. Franklin writes, "All these tensions are palpable in Jackson's work, which channels a far-reaching anxiety about the tumultuous world outside the home even as it investigates the dark secrets of domestic American life."[4] Jackson may have written about haunted spaces, but she had her finger on the pulse of contemporary women's experiences in America. In her fiction, she negotiated the tension between women's obligations to home and family and the possible desire to avoid marriage and family altogether or to pursue a career outside the home. As a writer who was a wife and mother, she knew from her own experiences the internal and external conflicts faced by individuals who did not fit into the socially scripted roles of the 1950s. Jackson's stories often focus on a woman facing the social issues of her day, whether she was writing gothic fiction or domestic sketches loosely based on her family's everyday life. Moreover, she did not shy away from humanity's inhumanity to individuals perceived as the Other, as seen in stories like "The Lottery," "A Fine Old Firm," "After You, My Dear Alphonse," and "Flower Garden." The aim of this collection of essays is to continue to move beyond the focus on Jackson's haunted houses and horror motifs to excavate the concerns that are present in her more realistic fiction and that may lie beneath her Gothicism.

This collection begins with essays that explore short stories by Jackson that may not have received much attention up to this point. The first chapter is Bernice M. Murphy's "Hideous Doughnuts and Haunted Housewives: Gothic Undercurrents in Shirley Jackson's Domestic Humor." Murphy connects Jackson's traditional gothic works and her domestic sketches of family life collected in *Life among the Savages* (1953) and *Raising Demons* (1957). She points to the confusion critics felt over what they interpreted as a dissonance between Jackson's novels and her humorous sketches that initially appeared in popular magazines, such as *Good Housekeeping*. In her chapter "Enemies Foreign and Domestic: Shirley Jackson's *New Yorker* Stories," Ashley Lawson takes us back beyond the point often read as the beginning of Jackson's career—the 1948 publication of "The Lottery" and all the confusion it caused among readers of the *New Yorker*. Lawson carefully traces how changing trends and readership at the *New Yorker* affected Jackson's work as she attempted to place stories in that august publication, ultimately leading her to use some of the trademark characteristics of a *New Yorker* story, while still developing her own style and concern for female protagonists. Michael J. Dalpe Jr.'s "'You Didn't Look Like You Belonged in This House': Shirley Jackson's Fragile Domesticities" explores how Jackson used her short fiction to invert the social expectations and power dynamics of the American home in the 1950s and 1960s. He posits that Jackson interrogates ideas of "belonging" and "normalcy" to show how polite society polices social order, which results in oppressive control for women who cannot quite fit in. In "'Sharp Points Closing In on Her Throat': The Domestic Gothic in Shirley Jackson's Short Fiction," L. N. Rosales, like Murphy earlier, joins the gothic to Jackson's domestic concerns. Rosales argues that Jackson makes the domestic space seem fragile and dangerous as familiar aspects of the home, such as children, become strange and threatening. Rather than the home being a safe, nurturing space, it is a site of invasion and fragmentation. Rosales shows how Jackson views the expectations of the traditional role of the housewife as fraught with peril and demanding perfection no one could possibly achieve.

In a shift to an analysis of domestic spaces, Luke Reid focuses on mothers and houses in his article, "Endless House, Interminable Dream: Shirley Jackson's Domestic Architecture and the Matrophobic Gothic." He investigates the gothic poetics of space and architecture, linking gothic spaces to horrific domestic situations involving mothers and their families. He expands this idea of the haunted house and the maternal in Jackson's fiction to encompass *The Haunting of Hill House* and the under examined story "The Bus." "Casting a Literary Spell: The Domestic Witchcraft of Shirley Jackson" by Alissa Burger likewise links space to gothic themes. Burger takes the theme of magic often associated with Jackson, because of her purported interest in witchcraft, and expands it to show how Jackson's fictional women use magic outside her supernatural stories to seize power, create protection, and navigate the possibilities of everyday experience. She includes Jackson's domestic sketches in her analysis alongside *Castle*.

At this point in the collection, there is a turn to Jackson's apocalyptic novel *The Sundial*. In Jill E. Anderson's "Homemaking for the Apocalypse: Queer Failures and Bunker Mentality in *The Sundial*," she argues that this novel plays out against the nuclear concerns of Jackson's age, including the anxieties surrounding the preparation for a nuclear war and the unknown implications of such an event for human society. She identifies in the Halloran's preparation for the end of the world aspects of what she terms "homemaking for the apocalypse," or the actions taken in the 1950s to prepare homes and bunkers for the faint hope that life could continue beyond the nuclear inferno. Christiane E. Farnan, in her "Domestic Apocalypse in *The Sundial*," focuses on the multiple murders in *The Sundial* as women seek to acquire power, first from men and then from each other. She argues that Jackson illustrates how women may wield power just as absolutely and cruelly as the patriarchal icons they attempt to overthrow, thus disrupting the 1950s ideal of the peaceful refuge of the family home. Julie Baker takes on the continuation of the Cult of True Womanhood into this novel in "'I May Go Mad, but at Least I Look Like a Lady': The Insanity of True

Womanhood in *The Sundial*." She reads Aunt Fanny's power struggle against Orianna and her developing madness as a picture of the damage wrought by traditional stereotypes of feminine behavior.

The next three chapters explore themes in the *Castle*. In Emily Banks's "Insisting on the Moon: Shirley Jackson and the Queer Future," she places *Hill House* next to *Castle* to illustrate how women may resort to destructive and violent actions to dismantle and escape the patriarchy. Banks posits that the heroines in each book go to extreme lengths to avoid entrapment in traditional family structures. In "Shirley Jackson's Merricat Story: Conjugal Narcissism in *We Have Always Lived in the Castle*," Richard Pascal argues that in Merricat Blackwood, Jackson created an adult child consumed by solipsism. He connects this isolation and narcissism to the same focus on self often encouraged in post–Second World War American descriptions of home and family life. In "My House Is My Castle: On the Mutually Enabling Persistence of Familial Devotion and Defunct Economies in Shirley Jackson's *We Have Always Lived in the Castle*," Allison Douglass also focuses on isolation. She, however, links the stasis and containment of the experience of the Blackwood family survivors to gothic portrayals of families in castles with inherited wealth and bloodlines and then traces this motif through the expansion of consumer capitalism into the domestic spaces of 1950s and 1960s America.

Jessica R. McCort's essay "Flipping Hill House: The Netflix Renovation of Shirley Jackson's Landmark Novel" ends the collection where I began this introduction: with Netflix's Crain family in a twenty-first-century Hill House. McCort compares and contrasts Jackson's representation of motherhood and home with the Netflix show's more recent interpretation of such themes. She identifies what she calls the "monstrous feminine" in both incarnations. She teases out how women still, even though we are approaching the third decade of the twenty-first century, struggle between the roles expected of them by family and society and their life choices, ranging from marriage to family to career that echo Jackson's meditations from 1959.

Jill E. Anderson and I hope that this collection of essays continues the work of opening the scope of Jackson studies to explore beyond the gothic haunted house to find the domestic themes and conflicts that the home contains. In her fiction, Jackson was reacting to and questioning the social issues of 1950s American culture: the fear, the paranoia, the conflicts stemming from discrimination based on race and gender, and enforced conformity and heteronormativity. She looked at the American family, the small town, and the suburbs, and she saw the cracks within them. She saw how the expectations and mandated behaviors that made up these American institutions harmed individuals who wanted to choose or act differently. At the same time, as a wife and mother who wrote, published, and delivered lectures on writing, Jackson not only was aware of the cracks, but she saw the possibilities as well. Quite possibly, we may have her knowledge of that paradoxical position to thank for the lasting power of her imagination.

Notes

1. See Jason Zinoman, "*The Haunting of Hill House*, on Netflix, Is a Family Drama with Scares," *New York Times* (October 11, 2018), n.p.
2. Bernice M. Murphy, ed., *Shirley Jackson: Essays on the Literary Legacy* (Jefferson, NC: McFarland and Company, 2005), 11.
3. Ruth Franklin, *Shirley Jackson: A Rather Haunted Life* (New York: Liveright Publishing, 2016), 5–6.
4. Ibid., 6.

References

Anderson, Melanie R., and Lisa Kröger, eds. *Shirley Jackson, Influences and Confluences*. London: Routledge, 2016.

Franklin, Ruth. *Shirley Jackson: A Rather Haunted Life*. New York: Liveright Publishing, 2016.

Murphy, Bernice M., ed. *Shirley Jackson: Essays on the Literary Legacy*. Jefferson, NC: McFarland, 2005.

Zinoman, Jason, "*The Haunting of Hill House*, on Netflix, Is a Family Drama with Scares." *New York Times* (October 11, 2018), n.p. (accessed on September 22, 2019) https://www.nytimes.com/2018/10/11 /arts/television/netflix-the-haunting-of-hill-house-review.html.

1

Hideous Doughnuts and Haunted Housewives: Gothic Undercurrents in Shirley Jackson's Domestic Humor*

Bernice M. Murphy

It may initially seem surprising that Shirley Jackson, the author of unnerving, ruthless tales such as "The Lottery" (1948) and *The Haunting of Hill House* (1959) spent much of her career penning humorous anecdotes about life as an apparently conventional mother and housewife. The contrast certainly baffled contemporary critics, many of whom found themselves unable to understand the gulf between these two superficially divergent facets of Jackson's writing. This puzzlement, as Lynette Carpenter notes, contributed to Jackson's long-standing critical neglect: "... traditional male critics could not, in the end, reconcile genre with gender in Jackson's case; unable to understand how a serious writer of gothic fiction could also be, to all outward appearances, a typical housewife, much less how she could publish housewife humor in *Good Housekeeping*, they dismissed her."[1]

---

*This chapter is a revised and slightly updated version of a book chapter that first appeared *The Ghost Story from the Middle Ages to the Twentieth Century* ed. Helen Conrad O'Briain and Julie Anne Stevens (Dublin: Four Courts Press, 2010), 229–59. It is reprinted here with the kind permission of Four Courts Press as well as the author.

The relationship between Jackson's "housewife" humor and her gothic fiction is more compelling (and revealing) than first impressions suggest. If a casual browser were to simply survey the titles of Jackson's domestic memoirs, *Life among the Savages* (1953) and *Raising Demons* (1957), they would probably assume that the texts are concerned with subjects of a horrific nature. Though indicative of Jackson's sardonic sense of humor, it seems odd that, as more than one previous commentator has noted, the most outwardly "gothic" and suggestive of Jackson's eight book titles should belong not to an intense exploration of madness and multiple personality like *The Bird's Nest* (1954) or family annihilation such as *We Have Always Lived in the Castle* (1962) but the most apparently innocuous texts in her entire oeuvre.

As Darryl Hattenhauer notes, Jackson's money-spinners were among the most lucrative of her time: "Her novels were bestsellers. There were movie deals on two of those novels (*The Bird's Nest* and *The Haunting of Hill House*) … Jackson got a minimum of one thousand dollars for each short story and article appearing in a mass market magazine: the average fee was probably much more."[2] Much of Jackson's financial success arose from her frequent appearance in women's magazines in the 1950s. "The editors … knew that Jackson's name on the cover meant higher sales" and were willing to pay premium prices to secure her writing. Jackson's 1949 contract with *Good Housekeeping* ensured her a large fixed fee for eight stories a year. The deal was so lucrative it enabled her family to move from New York to New England. It also confirmed her status as one of the decade's leading writers of so-called housewife humor.[3] As Nancy Walker has observed, Jackson's generation of female humorists "wrote about the domestic life of the woman in terms that were strikingly similar to those of their nineteenth century counterparts."[4] The postwar suburban ideal that led many middle-class women out of the cities, "the labor saving devices that merely elevated the expectations for women as homemakers, and the virtual isolation of women from commuting husbands all helped promote that particular sub-genre of domestic humor that shows women interacting more often with girl scout cookies and matchless socks than with ideas."[5]

The subgenre Walker dubs "the domestic saga" is generally characterized as "an account of a female persona in a domestic setting struggling to cope with the many demands of her role as homemaker."[6] The domestic saga originated in the early nineteenth century, in the work of Caroline Kirkland and Fanny Fern but "reached its fullest flowering in mid-twentieth century works such as *The Egg and I* by Betty McDonald, Jean Kerr's *Please Don't Eat the Daisies* and Shirley Jackson's *Life among the Savages*."[7] In each of these memoirs the heroine and her family are transplanted from the big city to an unfamiliar rural environment. Both Jackson and Kerr begin by detailing moves from New York City to rural New England, while McDonald details her husband's decision to swap a city existence for life as a chicken farmer.

These moves away from the city paralleled the flight toward suburbia that many readers of such volumes would have themselves experienced.

Life among the Savages (1953) was bookended by two intense explorations of psychological breakdown, *Hangsaman* (1951) and *The Bird's Nest* (1954). It is a revealing juxtaposition, demonstrating Jackson's range and the close relationship between two of her favorite subjects: mental instability and domesticity. *Savages*, like *Demons*, is a series of extended anecdotes previously published as magazine stories. "Charles," Jackson's most frequently anthologized humorous piece, first appeared in *Mademoiselle* in July 1948 and "My Son and the Bully" debuted in *Good Housekeeping* in October 1949, while several other stories were initially featured in *Harper's*—all popular women's publications of the time.[8] For the book, the stories were arranged chronologically, given added descriptive passages, and worked in alongside previously unpublished pieces.[9]

Jackson was often scathing about the literary quality of her domestic sketches: she was "appreciative of their salability, but considered them potboilers."[10] A strong note of self-deprecation frequently surfaces in her thoughts on this facet of her career. Responding to a letter from her parents that criticized the quality of these pieces, Jackson responded: "I quite agree with you ... they are written for money and the reason they sound so bad is because these magazines won't buy good ones, but deliberately seek out bad stuff because they say their audiences want it."[11] At a rate of at least a thousand dollars a story, Jackson felt that she "could not afford to try to change the state of popular fiction today, and since they will buy quite as much of it as I write, I do one story a month and spend the rest of the time working on my new novel or other stories."[12] Jackson's self-deprecation also may have been due to her suspicion that success in this female-led field would have a negative impact upon critical responses to her "real" writing.

This suspicion was well founded. As Joan Wylie Hall notes, "Jackson's discovery of an appealing formula and a lucrative market distracted critical attention from the balance of her short fiction, which was much more important to her."[13] For many years, it was relatively easy for critics to dismiss or ignore *Savages* and *Demons*. Yet, as Walker has demonstrated, "Women's humor is an index to women's roles and values; and particularly to their relationship with American cultural realities."[14] While Betty Friedan may famously have seen "housewife humor" as collaboration with a system oppressing American women (because, in her analysis, it belittled the desperation of the women who read it), David Van Leer notes, "even highly conventional literary treatments of the housewife functioned unintentionally to increase female awareness."[15] From this perspective, "housewife humor" is not, as Friedan argues in *The Feminine Mystique* (1963), a cynical exploitation of female desperation by women who are themselves anything but "typical"; but rather, as Walker argues, a highly significant chronicle of the American woman's "self-perceived inability to meet a set of culturally determined standards for her role as homemaker."[16]

The titles of the most popular domestic humor texts of the postwar period reflect the impossibility of meeting rigid societal expectations. Jackson implies that her own children are *Savages* and *Demons*; Jean Kerr's *How to Be Perfect* is "an ironically titled account of just the opposite," and most overt of all is Peg Bracken's *The I Hate to Cook Book*.[17] Such titles encapsulated the contrast that existed between the "official" ideal of a woman's life and the more realistic attitude that many women had toward their own circumstances.[18] In Jackson's family chronicles, as in those of her contemporaries, the daily frustrations of motherhood and housekeeping are raised to the self-conscious absurdity of slapstick comedy, yet, Walker continues, "throughout the book(s) are strong suggestions that the life of the average housewife is repetitive and demeaning."[19] Indeed, as David Van Leer notes:

> All suburban novels reinforced clichés about the importance of the family and of the mother's role as nurturer and moral exemplar. Yet their comic tone established a conspiratorial relationship to their audience ... in so defining "Housewife" as a job and as an object of literature, these novels set the stage for Friedan's subsequent critique of society's evaluation of that job. Only after readers recognized that they were housewives could they decide whether or not "housewife" was something that they wanted to be.[20]

Contrary to Freidan's impassioned indictment of "housewife humor" therefore, it is more accurate to characterize such writing as the means toward highlighting the absurd gap between the way women were supposed to be and the way things were. The desperation and dry humor depicted in their pages were arguably indicative of many deeper social and domestic problems, and a reflection, as Walker suggests, not of "'the individual failure of an individual woman' but rather a 'symptom of a society wide structure of power and powerlessness.'"[21]

For several decades after Jackson's death, analysis of the family chronicles has tended to confine itself largely to a single extract: the story "Charles," which was first published as a stand-alone tale in 1948, but later included in *The Lottery and Other Stories* (1949) and then integrated into *Savages*. This is perhaps because it is the most obvious example of Jackson's gothic sensibilities being given expression in her domestic humor. It also showcases Jackson's interest in the dramatic possibilities provided by "split" personalities, a topic also explored in *Hangsaman* and *The Bird's Nest*.

"Charles" begins unassumingly enough, as the narrator (a version of Jackson) is watching her eldest son Laurie leave for his first morning at school, "seeing clearly that an era of my life was ended, my sweet-voiced nursery tot replaced by a long-trousered, swaggering character who forgot to stop at the corner and wave good bye to me."[22] It begins as a conventional account of a child's first morning at school, and in the narrator's sadness at the end of this stage of her child's development, there is also a sense of foreboding regarding the inevitable consequence of the postwar era's emphasis upon motherhood and childbearing. Even an apparently innocuous milestone such as that recorded in "Charles" serves as a reminder that a woman's days of fertility, and "usefulness," would soon end. As Glenna Matthews notes of the era, "There could be no more cruel reminder of the essential uselessness of the older woman in the culture of consumption than the reduction of the last several decades of a woman's life to a 'desert of wasted time.'"[23]

Laurie soon starts arriving home with tales of a classmate named Charles who is constantly getting into trouble. Charles hits the teacher, throws chalk, and makes a classmate cry. By the third week of kindergarten, stories of his misdeeds have become so familiar that, "Charles was an institution in our family."[24] Laurie's parents naturally become extremely curious about this disruptive child's parents, so at the PTA. meeting, the narrator sets out to encounter his poor mother: "At the meeting I sat restlessly, scanning each comfortable matronly face, trying to determine which one hid the secret of Charles. None of them looked to me haggard enough."[25] The denouement comes after the meeting, when, having failed to find Charles's mother, the narrator converses with her son's kindergarten teacher. To her immense surprise, the narrator is told that Laurie has had some problems in adjusting to school. The narrator nervously tries to laugh this off by saying, "I suppose this time it's Charles's influence"—and is shocked when the teacher responds, "We don't have any Charles in the kindergarten."[26] The twist in the tale—Laurie and Charles are the same person—is played for laughs: but in Jackson's gothic fiction, this kind of discovery is always chilling. *Hangsaman* even features essentially the same twist: Natalie Waite's new friend Tony is a figment of her disturbed imagination.

Houses and the concept of "home" also constitute one of the most important preoccupations in Jackson's gothic fiction. *Savages* begins with the line that immediately highlights Jackson's interest in living space: "Our house is old, and noisy, and full."[27] Next, there is a move from New York City to the New England countryside that would be replicated on many occasions in Jackson's fiction. *Hill House* begins with Eleanor's fateful drive from the city to the titular rural mansion, while "The Flower Garden," "The Renegade," and "The Summer People" (all published in *The Lottery*) also depict city dwellers adjusting to life in the unwelcoming countryside. *Savages* opens with the implication that the narrator and her husband have become enmeshed in a life of apparently cozy, but cheerfully chaotic, domesticity— without ever really intending to. Jackson tellingly invokes a metaphor that suggests entrapment rather than contentment: "This is the way of life my husband and I have fallen into, inadvertently, as though we had fallen into a well and decided that since there was no way out we might as well stay there and set up a chair and a desk and a light of some kind ...."[28]

Even with the apparently humorous opening, there is a definite hint of the panic that so often infects Eleanor in *Hill House*. This sense of domestic anxiety also afflicts the protagonists of stories such as "The Demon Lover" and "The Tooth." It is a feeling intensified by the circumstances by which the family has had to move from New York—the landlord simply rented their apartment to someone else. Having decided upon a move to Vermont (biographical sources suggest that Jackson had become prone to severe panic attacks exacerbated by the stress of city life), the newcomers are maneuvered into leasing a large, old house by canny locals.

When Eleanor first views Hill House, she experiences a jolt of visceral dislike, and immediately declares it "vile." Eleanor's accurate first impressions are almost the same as those of the narrator in *Savages* when she first enters *her* new home. As she and her husband view a kitchen "where a monumental ironwork stove threatened to fall on us,"[29] the narrator is suddenly stricken with a desperate desire to flee. "'I'm sorry we stayed,' I said to my husband earnestly, my hands shaking as I looked at the two hideous doughnuts." The narrator's reaction is described in terms suggestive of the dread that characterizes a panic attack, as is Eleanor's instinctual response to Hill House:

> I should have turned back at the gate, Eleanor thought. The house had caught her with an atavistic turn in the pit of the stomach, and she looked along the lines of its roofs, fruitlessly trying to locate the badness, whatever dwelt there; her hands turned nervously cold so that she fumbled, trying to take out a cigarette, and beyond everything else she was afraid, listening to the sick voice inside her which whispered, *Get away from here, get away* .[30]

Yet, just as Eleanor resists her initial instincts, so too does the narrator of *Savages*. It seems that the Fielding house is the last suitable place in town; moreover, the elderly leaseholder presumes, without being asked, that the family will move in and offers them absurdly cheap rental terms. The narrator, still shaken, blames her husband for deciding to stay: "'You seem to have taken the house,' I said unjustly to my husband. 'It's probably because we went inside,' he said. 'No one else has ever gone inside and that probably constitutes a lease.'"[31] Despite the narrator's misgivings, when the family returns a few weeks later, they find that the house has been transformed: "literally scraped clean; down to the wood in the walls, straightened up, painted and repaired." Upon seeing the residence on this occasion, the narrator voices a completely different opinion: "It's beautiful"—a remark that anticipates Eleanor's similar volte-face in Hill House and her remark, "I don't think we could leave now even if we wanted to."[32] This sense of ambivalence is, of course, a major recurrent theme of Jackson's work: but here, as is so often is the case in her fiction, the home space is simultaneously enthralling and terrifying.

What is most interesting about the opening of *Savages* is that Jackson personifies her new home as a kind of living, thinking entity. The residence has rooms that seem to choose where furniture should go and instinctively prefers old things to those brought from the city: "All these things, the ones that had been in the house before, and other things which had been in similarly old houses and knew their ways, fell naturally into good positions in the rooms, as though snatching the best places before the city furniture could crowd in."[33] It's a description that further underlines the extent to which Jackson adhered to long-established gothic conventions, even in her nonfiction. As Fred S. Franks has noted of the importance of Horace Walpole's *The Castle of Otranto* (1764), by making the castle the centerpiece of his gothic tableaux, Walpole ensured that "the principal engine of the gothic plot would be an inlaid system of architectural contraptions, acoustical effects installed throughout the gothic castle … where inanimate objects behaved in human ways."[34] Like the classic eighteenth-century gothic castle and its successors, Jackson's real-life residence is characterized as a semi-sentient entity furnished with objects that have decidedly human preferences and dislikes.

There is the sense here of an inevitable caving in to the demands of the countryside: the old furniture instinctively crowds out the family's newer city possessions. The narrator and her family soon learn the futility of trying to impose human will upon their new home: "After a few vain attempts at imposing our own angular order on things with a consequent out-of-jointedness and *shrieking disharmony* … we gave into the old furniture and let things settle where they would."[35] It is a statement that of course recalls the non-Euclidian geometry of Hill House, a place of "clashing disharmony." The Jackson family's eventual acceptance of the old furniture in *Savages* is also reminiscent of Eleanor's surrender to the will of Hill House. There is one key difference, however: the home Jackson and her family move into in *Savages* turns out to be "a good house, after all"—the benign flipside of her most notorious fictional edifice, with an intelligence that is ultimately welcoming rather than malevolent—once the new inhabitants accede to its wishes.

The relationship between the two houses also provides an important clue as to how we should view Jackson's domestic humor in relation to her gothic fiction. As Carpenter has noted, while the preoccupation may often be the same—in this case the personification of a family home—the *tone* constitutes the key difference. If an observation is framed within the explicitly comic context of her domestic writing, then it is clearly in that spirit that the reader is intended to take her remarks. Yet it remains the case that when removed from this reassuring context, or even considered in more detail, we often see Jackson discussing the same themes broached in her serious fiction with notably similar language. The seemingly cozy façade of her domestic humor is unsettled by this close relationship to her more explicitly gothic tales. If the reader has no knowledge of this side of Jackson's career, she will likely be mollified by the narrator's declaration that "It *was* a good house after all": but that significant use of italics opens up other chilling alternate possibilities. What if it *had* been a "bad" house? It is a question that Jackson obviously found intriguing enough to use as the premise for her most famous novel.

Demons opens with another move, this time from the house discussed in *Savages*. Here, the clutter that litters the household is said to be too much to deal with, so again without really making a conscious decision, the family is maneuvered by the local community into purchasing a new home, thus provoking in the narrator "an extraordinary sense of inevitability."[36] We are yet again told that the family's fate is not in their own hands: "I have not now the slightest understanding of the events which got us out of one big white house which we rented and into another, bigger white house which we own."[37] The narrator soon discovers the real reason why the local community was so eager to see them move: a member of the local family who originally owned their rental home has decided to reclaim her ancestral estate. When this erstwhile scion tours the property, she displays a sense of entitlement that shocks the narrator: "'I thought someone had told you,' she said, 'I was a Fielding before I was married ... we are coming home again.'" It is clear that a preoccupation of Jackson's fiction noted by Carpenter—her recurrent portrayals of the clash between city newcomers and long-established rural communities—is also present in her domestic humor.

In *Savages* and *Demons*, however, the network of gossip that fuels small town discourse is treated in comedic fashion. Although the local people encourage the move for their own reasons, they help the narrator's family find a new home quickly: "I was to learn later that the grocer not only knew our housing problems, but the ages and names of our children, the meat we had served for dinner the night before, and my husband's income."[38] Though here played for laughs, the very same reservoir of local knowledge can, with just a slight change of emphasis, become deeply disturbing. Consider, for instance, the shopping trip which opens *Castle* (1962). Merricat Blackwood's final foray into the local village is a virtuoso exercise in paranoia and resentment. The scene was anticipated by the relationship between the arrogant Halloran clan and hostile locals in *The Sundial* (1958), and then Eleanor's uncomfortable stop at a local coffee shop in *Hill House*.[39]

However, her most accomplished exploration of the clash between rural New England and urban newcomers takes place in her 1950 story "The Summer People" in which an elderly couple unwisely overstays their welcome in the countryside and come to an uncertain end. Similarly, in *Demons*, the narrator's family briefly takes up residence in a summerhouse in another part of the state while their new home is being renovated. As the narrator tells us, "Our neighbors were almost all summer folk like ourselves, and agreeable, informal people."[40] Though the family soon moves into their own residence, there is always this sense, as in Jackson's fiction, of never truly belonging. It is a preoccupation that would reach its ultimate expression in her final novel *Castle*.

Unsurprisingly, given that *Savages* and *Demons* take the form of what Friedman has aptly described as "family chronicles," Jackson's children often take center stage. While mothers with small children crop up frequently in Jackson's short stories, not one of Jackson's six novelistic heroines is a mother. The mothers who do appear in Jackson's novels are either ineffectual (*Hangsaman*), dead (*The Bird's Nest*, *Hill House*, *Castle*), or domineering (*Sundial*). Indeed, the closest we get to a benign maternal figure in Jackson's novels is a sister, such as Constance Blackwood, or, at a stretch, *The Bird's Nest*'s brusque but well-meaning Aunt Morgen. Jackson's only sustained portrait of loving motherhood therefore comes in the domestic humor. Nevertheless, we are left in little doubt that the maternal role is highly challenging one. The children here, as in many of her fictional works, are simultaneously magical and frightening, a tendency that imbues these ostensibly lighthearted sketches with a revealing undercurrent of maternal ambivalence (even if that ambivalence is usually softened by humor). For instance, one particularly revealing passage in *Savages* finds the narrator reflecting upon the fundamental unknowability of her offspring: "Sometimes, in my capacity as a mother, I find myself sitting open mouthed and terrified before my own children, little individual creatures moving solidly along in their own paths and yet in some mysterious fashion vividly reminiscent of a past which my husband and I know we never communicated to them."[41]

Like the mothers in fictional stories such as "The Witch" and "The Renegade," the narrator is suddenly able to perceive her own children with more than a hint of fear. For instance, the little boy on the train in "The Witch" laughs delightedly as a strange old man talks about beheading his sister. Jackson's children can also be diverted away from their parents by outside ("local") influences. In *Demons*, the narrator worries that "The children were changing in the new house: they belonged to the town now."[42] The same thought strikes the protagonist of "The Renegade" as she listens to her children excitedly discuss gruesome methods of preventing the family dog from stealing chickens: "Mrs. Walpole looked at them, at her two children with their hard hands and their sunburned faces laughing together, their dog with blood still on her legs laughing with them."[43]

Children also provide Jackson with the opportunity to explore another of her favorite thematic preoccupations: identity slippage. Besides "Charles," there are plenty of other such instances; as Friedman and Hall note, Jackson's children in the family chronicles are constantly changing their names and adopting new, fantastical identities. For example, in *Savages* we are told that the narrator's eldest daughter Jannie has an imaginary friend named "Mrs. Ellenroy." This conceit, like that recounted in "Charles," recalls Natalie's imaginary friend in *Hangsaman*.[44] The narrator's wry comment on this perpetual shifting of identities encapsulates the warning given in so many of her more obviously fictional creations: "Nothing is stable in this world."[45] There are also clear resonances with Jackson's fiction to be found in the narrator's observation that her youngest daughter Sally spends her days "wandering perpetually in a misty odd world where familiar signs merged and changed as she passed."[46] After all, what is the typical Jackson story but the tale of a wrong turn taken on a familiar road, where the line between madness and reality is crossed in an unwary instant? The singsong doggerel uttered by Sally has clear echoes in the unconventional syntax of Merricat Blackwood and Natalie Waite. At one point in *Demons*, Sally suddenly comes out with a statement that the narrator finds as disturbing as it is nonsensical, "'In my river,' Sally remarked once, chillingly, 'we sleep in wet beds and hear our mothers calling us'—giving me a sudden, terrifying picture of my own face, leaning over the water, and my voice far away and echoing.'"[47] Sally also chants the question asked by nearly every Jackson heroine at some point, if only of herself: "'Do you know who I am?' Sally was singing on her head in the backseat, 'Do you know who I am?'" In this case the answer is both surreal and baffling: "'I'm a rat and you're a fish,' Sally said, 'and now you know who I am.'"[48]

One of the other most significant preoccupations of Jackson's literary fiction is her dramatization of female anxiety about the limited roles middle-class white women were being forced into during the postwar era. Jackson's obvious frustration toward the life expected of a 1950s housewife does not surface explicitly in *Savages*. By contrast, in *Demons*, the narrator's deep-seated anger frequently comes to the surface. The book, though relatively successful, did not achieve the commercial popularity of its predecessor. Jackson attributed its poorer reception to inadequate publicity;[49] but, as Judy Oppenheimer suggests, there may have been another reason: "Though funny and enjoyable, the book as a whole did not come off as well as *Savages*—the tone was more harried, at times even irritable, with more than a few rough edges. Occasionally a harsher reality broke through: Shirley's jealousy of Stanley, for instance, cropped up in no less than three episodes."[50] In other words, her readers may well have been deterred by these hints of seemingly genuine bile. This tendency emerges as early as chapter Two, when the narrator, who is feeling under the weather during a bitter New England winter, explodes in anger:

> I got to feeling that I could not bear the sight of the colored cereal bowls for one more morning, could not empty one more ash tray, could not brush one more head or bake one more potato or let out one more job or pick up one more jacket. I snarled at the bright faces regarding me from

the breakfast table and I was strongly tempted to kick the legs out from under the chair on which my older son was teetering backward.[51]

The narrator's frustration is aimed at the unrelenting tedium of domesticity—the constant round of minor tasks to be completed. Yet there is no obvious way for her to escape. Unlike many of the housewife protagonists in her short stories, who often flee "normality," she pragmatically accepts her situation: "This state of mind is not practical in a household which continues to move relentlessly on from breakfast to mail to school to bath to bed to breakfast, no matter how *I* feel."[52] Jackson characteristically softens the extract by ending on a note of comedy, but the daily routine continues uninterrupted, and the machinery of domesticity grinds on. Nancy Walker has stated that Jackson's primary technique in *Savages* and *Demons* is "raising the daily details of motherhood and housekeeping to the absurdity of slapstick comedy."[53] However, there are also, she continues, "strong suggestions that the life of the average housewife is repetitive and demeaning."[54]

Intimations of unease continue to appear in *Demons*. Jackson's narrator goes on to sarcastically describe the existence of a particular substratum of housewife: "the faculty wife."[55] "On Being a Faculty Wife," which first appeared in the Bennington College alumnae magazine, was slightly extended for publication in *Mademoiselle* and was finally incorporated into *Demons*.[56] In this story, the narrator describes how her husband's job has begun to encroach upon her own identity: "I was slowly becoming aware of a wholly new element in the usual uneasy tenor of our days: I was a faculty wife."[57] Jackson then wryly explains what this position means: "A faculty wife is a person who is married to a faculty. She has frequently read at least one good book lately, she has one 'nice' black dress to wear to student parties, and she is always just the teensiest bit in the way, particularly in a girl's college such as the one where my husband taught."[58] The faculty wife's assumed pastimes, Jackson continues, are all typically "feminine" tasks such as "knitting, hemming dish towels, and perhaps sketching wildflowers."[59] They certainly do not include a successful career of her own.

Jackson's sarcastic listing of these qualities was anticipated in *Hangsaman*, which was largely set in an all-girl college based on Bennington. As well as being Jackson's first sustained depiction of mental illness and identity slippage, *Hangsaman* further explores the sentiments expressed in "On being a Faculty Wife." The faculty wife in *Hangsaman*, Elizabeth Arnold, is protagonist Natalie Waite's only real friend. Elizabeth is 20, just a few years older than Natalie, a former college student who married her professor. She has achieved the supreme goal of every young woman of the time, at least as defined by society: marriage to a professional man. But although Elizabeth has conformed to societal expectations, she is deeply unhappy. Her husband is unfaithful, and she is isolated, bored, and possibly suicidal, with alcoholic tendencies. Like Jackson's narrator in *Demons*, Elizabeth is all too aware of the temptation posed by the hordes of bright young women that hang upon her husband's every word (after all, she was, until recently, one of their number). These young women have been brought up to believe that their prime objectives in life are to marry, reproduce, and keep a beautiful home. "On being a Faculty Wife" comes to a climax which details the narrator's strained conversation with one of these women, who asks, with jarring insensitivity: "Listen, when you were young—I mean, before you kind of settled down and all, when you were well *younger*, that is—did you ever figure you'd end up like this?"[60] The narrator's withering response is wasted upon her naïve interrogator: '"Certainly,' I said, 'My only desire was to be a faculty wife. I used to sit at my casement window, half embroidering, half dreaming, and long for Professor right.' 'I suppose,' she said, 'that you *are* better off than you would have been. Not married at all or anything.'"[61]

The result of such conversations, the narrator says, is that "By the end of the first semester, what I wanted to do most in the world was invite a few of my husband's students over for tea and drop them down the well."[62] When asked by her young hostess, "How come you just ended up doing housework and stuff? Couldn't you get a job?" the narrator conspicuously fails to mention her thriving literary career and asserts instead the importance of her work as a homemaker: "I have a job," she says, "I cook and sew and clean and shop and make beds and drive people places and—."[63] This response is all part of the calculated pose adopted by Jackson in these family stories. Here, she is a defensive housewife, not a successful author. Her irritable justification of the lot of the ordinary housewife would surely have struck a chord with her readers and further highlights the difference between the no-nonsense and relatable narrator and the arrogant younger women who judge her uncharitably but want to end up in the same position. It would have imbalanced the piece if Jackson-as-narrator had pointed out that she was a critically respected author, even though her reaction contradicts the defiant stance taken in "The Third Baby's the Easiest," one of very few occasions in which the narrator of Jackson's domestic stories declares herself a writer, or even mentions writing at all. However, as in that story, Jackson-the-author still gets the last laugh, by immortalizing these empty-headed, self-important young women in her prose.

If the true complexity of Jackson's status as a working creative force in her own right *and* a busy mother and housewife had been emphasized to her readers, it would surely have punctured the sense of solidarity her work inspired in the "ordinary" middle-class housewives who constituted her main audience (many of whom, much to Jackson's dismay, wrote to her looking for advice on the running of their own homes). So, Jackson continued to portray herself as a harried "average" housewife, even though the very fact these sketches were initially published in major mass-market magazine outlets suggested that she spent as much time at a typewriter as she did at the sink. Nevertheless, despite Jackson's considerable success, there were further suggestions throughout her domestic humor, but most particularly toward the end of *Demons*, that all was not well in "happy housewife land."

Three-quarters of the way though *Demons*, the typically stressed narrator, again snowed under by the demands of home and family, considers running away from it all—a fantasy that frequently occurs to Jackson's fictional housewives. She first considers making her escape to "'Mexico, maybe,' I said. 'Some place where it's hot and I don't need to talk to anyone because I can't understand a word they say.'"[64] Her wish soon comes true, sort of, in an episode that is strikingly reminiscent of one of Jackson's most overtly gothic short stories. The narrator's deliverance from domestic routine comes courtesy of a broken tooth: "I took my tongue out of the hole in my tooth and said to my husband, 'What I would like more than anything in the world is about three days in a hotel in New York City. Where it's quiet.'"[65]

Her wish is partly humorous, since New York City is not a quiet place at all, but it *is* away from home and family. However, her dreams of a peaceful, solo visit to the city are soon derailed; the children overhear her comment and demand to come along as well. There follows an extended account that has intriguing similarities to her story "The Tooth," in particular, and in "Pillar of Salt," which both appeared in *The Lottery*. Indeed, the incident recounted by Jackson in *Demons* bears such a striking resemblance to these stories (which were both published several years earlier) that it at first seems as if this piece is a humorous pastiche of her earlier, more obviously fictional tales. The profound anxiety that rapidly surfaces soon suggests that Jackson has written about a real-life episode in such a way that, despite the ostensibly lighthearted context, it contains resounding echoes of two of her most disturbing short stories.

In "The Tooth," Clara, a dowdy rural housewife, travels alone to New York on the night bus so that she may visit the visit the dentist and get rid of her rotting tooth (something which her concerned but dull husband notes has long been a problem: "You had a toothache on our honeymoon,"[66] he suggestively observes). Doped up on codeine, lack of rest, and whiskey, Clara falls into a "fantastic sleep" during the journey and ultimately escapes the tedium of her everyday life by surrendering her old identity all together and running away with a man who may or may not exist (another version of Jackson's "Demon Lover" figure). Jackson's account of a housewife's trip to New York in *Demons* has exactly the same starting point as "The Tooth"—the urgent need to visit the dentist—but, ultimately, her narrator ends up more in a situation more like that of the protagonist of "Pillar of Salt," a wife and mother from rural Vermont. As the story begins, she is bursting with enthusiasm at the thought of her trip to New York, but while in the city becomes paralyzed by panic, and ends up rooted to the spot on a busy street. The city has inspired a catastrophic panic attack and/or nervous breakdown.

Jackson's account of the family trip to New York in *Demons* begins with the narrator's observation:

> It has long been my belief that in times of great stress, such as a four-day vacation, the thin veneer of family unity wears off almost at once, and we are all revealed in our true personalities: Laurie, for instance, is a small town mayor, Jannie a games mistress, Sally, a vague, stern old lady watching the rest of us with remote disapproval and Barry a small intrepid foot soldier.[67]

Even as the other family members appear to be reverting back to some "truer," more essential version of themselves, the first subtle hint of the sense of profound mental disintegration which will soon afflict the narrator has already appeared: "These several personalities began to emerge in the car driving to Albany, and Sally's hat began to unravel."[68] Were it to appear in one of Jackson's fictional stories, Sally's unraveling hat would serve as a powerful symbol of psychological breakdown. Though the tone of this anecdote differs, it likely serves much the same purpose in *Demons*. It is an observation strengthened by Jackson's description of the narrator's reaction to the trip. It is implied that, like Constance Blackwood in *Castle* (and the author herself, in her final years), she suffers from agoraphobia. On the surface, Jackson tries to play the scene for laughs, but the humor is spiked with genuine disquiet:

> So long as we were within familiar territory, the circle of about ten miles which we cover regularly and of which I know every path and house, I was fairly comfortable ... When we got out into the world, and the hills were no longer at the same angle and the road turned past bewilderingly strange trees and houses, my hands began to tremble.[69]

Despite her desperate desire for escape, the narrator fears change to her usual domestic routine. Like Merricat and Constance Blackwood, she is terrified of anything that takes her out of her customary surroundings. Aptly enough then, she is also seized with obsessive anxieties related to the family home. Will they be burgled, she wonders, has something important been left behind, did she leave on the lights in the basement? Despite Laurie's blasé attempts to ease these concerns, the narrator's uneasiness persists. And all the while, her daughter's hat unravels. Her last clear impression of the trip takes place on the train: "We were going to New York. That was, I believe, my last clear, coordinated thought. From that moment until I came back through our own front door again, four days later, nothing happened in any kind of reasonable or logical order: nothing made sense."[70]

For the narrator of *Demons*, as for the protagonists of "The Tooth" and "Pillar of Salt," the city is a deeply disorientating locale that frustrates attempts to impose order or logic. Just as the family arrives in Grand Central Station, Sally's hat collapses completely: "the last knot disappeared out the taxi window when we were about half way to the hotel."[71] Once in the city, days run together in a haze of restaurants, sightseeing, children's tantrums, and excursions to old haunts. But soon, everyone is notably underwhelmed by these experiences: the family ends up coming home several days earlier than planned, and it is only when they have returned to normality that the narrator suddenly realizes, "I didn't get to go to the dentist after all." There really is no place like home, it seems, and the family, she concludes, "came off pretty lightly."[72] The episode further demonstrates that Jackson's domestic humor replicates the sense of desperation that so often afflicts her fictional heroines. The initial desire for escape into the city culminates in a relieved return to the countryside and to domestic routine. Like the protagonist of "Pillar of Salt," Jackson's narrator was woefully unprepared for the "blasting reality" of New York, where "Everything was imperceptibly quicker every minute."[73] In "Pillar of Salt," protagonist Margaret's disintegration is hastened when she and her husband visit a local beach, and escape, for a moment, seems possible.[74] Her reverie is brutally interrupted by the discovery of a dismembered human leg. Margaret cries, "'What starts to happen?' she said hysterically, 'People starting to come apart.'"[75] When the couple return to New York, she notices even more "perceptible cracks" in the fabric of the city. Her breakdown is hastened by the realization that even the place of escape she fantasizes about has been sullied by brutal reality: there is no "golden world," just ordinary life, and the "everyday dreariness" it encompasses.

Until relatively recently, Jackson's domestic humor has often been categorized as an interesting but relatively minor adjunct to her more "serious" work. Jackson's own often rather dismissive attitude toward this aspect of her creative output arguably encouraged this perception. Nevertheless, her domestic sketches constitute a vital component of her oeuvre, and engaging with them remains essential if one is to achieve a truly comprehensive understanding of her work. The portrait of family life painted in *Savages* and *Demons* may be (mostly) a happy and loving one, but this does not negate the multiple occasions where hints of the darker side of family life and its effect upon women surface. These sketches indict the failure of the American social system rather than belittling the anxiety and unhappiness of the women trapped within it. The themes, distinctive preoccupations, and even the language of her gothic fiction are all frequently replicated in her domestic sketches, and even the most apparently cozy evocation of conventional family life is often just a hair's breadth away from the desperation of her fiction. As Jackson's most recent biographer, Ruth Franklin, also notes, "Her horror stories, which always take place primarily on a psychological level, are grounded in the domestic ... Meanwhile, the domestic tales need only the gentlest tap to slide in to the dark."[76] Furthermore, that identification with themes related to madness and entrapment that so often manifest themselves in her later fictional works is also present, albeit framed in less sinister fashion, in *Demons*.

Like her gothic fiction then, Jackson's humorous writing for a mass-market readership dramatized the anxieties of her age. Jackson knew only too well that she was no "ordinary" housewife, and her writing consistently suggests that she was all too aware, even before Betty Friedan articulated much the same sentiment in 1963, that the "happy house wife heroine" was a comforting, but controlling, myth. Certainly, there is plenty of warmhearted humor to be found in *Savages* and *Demons*, but there is also the subtle, insistent suggestion that beyond the antics of the narrator's lovably boisterous children and the safety of repetitive tasks there is a nagging desire for something ... *more*. That same, often vague, longing for change also infects many of Jackson's fictional heroines. We should not be surprised then that the laughter in her family stories sometimes seems a little forced, or even slightly hysterical. As Jackson's writing so often reveals to devastating effect, there was always a great deal more going on than first impressions may have suggested.

Notes

1. Lynette Carpenter, "Domestic Comedy, Black Comedy, and Real Life: Shirley Jackson, Woman Writer," in *Faith of a Woman Writer*, ed. Alice Kessler-Harris and William McBrien (New York: Greenwood Press, 1988), 143–8.
2. Darryl Hattenhauer, *Shirley Jackson's American Gothic* (New York: SUNY Press, 2003), 19.
3. Ibid.
4. Nancy Walker, *A Very Serious Thing: Women's Humor and American Culture* (Minneapolis: University of Minnesota Press, 1988), 48.
5. Ibid., 49.
6. Ibid., 51.
7. Ibid., 48.
8. Ibid.
9. As detailed by Joan Wylie Hall in *Shirley Jackson: A Study of the Short Fiction* (New York: Twayne, 1993).
10. Lenemaja Friedman, *Shirley Jackson* (Boston: Twayne, 1975), 145.
11. Judy Oppenheimer, *Private Demons: The Life of Shirley Jackson* (New York: G.P. Putnam's Sons, 1988), 145.
12. Wylie Hall, *Shirley Jackson*, 75.

13 Ibid., xiii.
14 Walker, *Serious Thing*, 6.
15 David Van Leer, "Society and Identity," in *The Columbia History of the American Novel*, ed. Emory Elliott and Cathy N. Davidson (New York: Columbia University Press, 1991), 506.
16 Walker, *Serious Thing*, 95.
17 Ibid., 31.
18 Ibid.
19 Ibid., 11.
20 Van Leer, "Society and Identity," 507.
21 Walker, *Serious Thing*, 12.
22 Shirley Jackson, *Life among the Savages* (London: Michael Joseph, 1954), 25.
23 Glenna Matthews, *Just a Housewife: The Rise and Fall of Domesticity in America* (New York: Oxford University Press, 1989), 208.
24 Jackson, *Savages*, 28.
25 Ibid., 30.
26 Ibid.
27 Ibid., 7.
28 Ibid.
29 Ibid., 17.
30 Shirley Jackson, *The Haunting of Hill House* (New York: Penguin Books, 1984), 35 (emphasis in the original).
31 Jackson, *Savages*, 19.
32 Jackson, *Hill House,* 75.
33 Jackson, *Savages,* 21.
34 Frederick S. Franks, "The Early and Later Gothic Traditions, 1762–1886," in *Fantasy and Horror: A Critical and Historical Guide*, ed. Neil Barron (Lanham, MD: Scarecrow Press, 1999), 7.
35 Jackson, *Savages,* 21 (emphasis mine).
36 Shirley Jackson, *Raising Demons* (London: Michael Joseph, 1957), 12.
37 Ibid., 7.
38 Ibid., 12.
39 Jackson also explored the damage that local gossip can do in stories such as "The Flower Garden," "The Very Strange House Next Door," and "The Possibility of Evil."
40 Jackson, *Demons*, 15.
41 Jackson, *Savages*, 45.
42 Jackson, *Demons*, 85.
43 Shirley Jackson, "The Renegade," in *The Masterpieces of Shirley Jackson* (London: Robinson, 1996), 62.

44 Jannie, at one point, also pretends to have forgotten her own name, a form of identity loss anticipated by short stories such as "The Tooth," "The Beautiful Stranger," and "Nightmare."
45 Jackson, *Demons*, 70.
46 Ibid., 148.
47 Ibid.
48 Ibid., 149.
49 Friedman, *Shirley Jackson*, 150.
50 Oppenheimer, *Private Demons*, 208.
51 Jackson, *Demons*, 64.
52 Ibid. (emphasis in the original).
53 Walker, *Serious Thing*, 33.
54 Ibid., 33.
55 Hall, *Shirley Jackson*, 76.
56 Ibid., 77.
57 Jackson, *Demons*, 124.
58 Ibid.
59 Ibid., 125.
60 Ibid., 130 (emphasis in the original).
61 Ibid. (emphasis in the original).
62 Ibid., 131.
63 Ibid.
64 Ibid., 180.
65 Ibid., 189.
66 Shirley Jackson, "The Tooth," *The Masterpieces of Shirley Jackson*, 197.
67 Ibid., 192.
68 Ibid., 192.
69 Ibid.
70 Ibid., 194.
71 Ibid., 195.
72 Jackson, *Demons*, 198.
73 Shirley Jackson, "Pillar of Salt," *The Masterpieces of Shirley Jackson*, 181.
74 Ibid.
75 Ibid., 183.
76 Ruth Franklin, *Shirley Jackson: A Rather Haunted Life* (New York: Liveright, 2016), 5.

References

Carpenter, Lynnette. "Domestic Comedy, Black Comedy, and Real Life: Shirley Jackson, Woman Writer," in *Faith of a Woman Writer*, ed. Alice Kessler-Harris and William McBrien, 143–8. New York: Greenwood Press, 1988.

Egan, James. "Sanctuary: Shirley Jackson's Domestic and Fantastic Parables." *Studies in Weird Fiction*, no. 6 (Fall 1989): 15–24.

Franklin, Ruth. *Shirley Jackson: A Rather Haunted Life*. New York: Liveright, 2016.

Franks, Frederick S. "The Early and Later Gothic Traditions 1762–1986," in *Fantasy and Horror: A Critical and Historical Guide to Literature, Illustration, Film, TV and Radio*, ed. Neil Barron, 5–44. Lanham, MD: Scarecrow Press, 1999.

Friedman, Lenemaja. *Shirley Jackson*. Boston: Twayne, 1975.

Hattenhauer, Darryl. *Shirley Jackson's American Gothic*. New York: SUNY Press, 2003.

Jackson, Shirley. *Life among the Savages*. London: Michael Joseph, 1954.

Jackson, Shirley. *Raising Demons*. London: Michael Joseph, 1957.

Jackson, Shirley. *The Magic of Shirley Jackson*. New York: Farrar, 1966.

Jackson, Shirley. *The Haunting of Hill House*. New York: Penguin Books, 1984.

Jackson, Shirley. *The Masterpieces of Shirley Jackson*. London: Robinson, 1996.

Matthews, Glenna. *Just a Housewife: The Rise and Fall of Domesticity in America*. New York: Oxford University Press, 1989.

Oppenheimer, Judy. *Private Demons: The Life of Shirley Jackson*. New York: G.P. Putman's Sons, 1988.

Van Leer, David. "Society and Identity," in *The Columbia History of the American Novel*, ed. Emory Elliott and Cathy N. Davidson, 485–512. New York: Columbia University Press, 1991.

Walker, Nancy. *A Very Serious Thing: Women's Humor and American Culture*. Minneapolis: University of Minnesota Press, 1988.

Wylie Hall, Joan. *Shirley Jackson: A Study of the Short Fiction*. New York: Twayne, 1993.

2

Enemies Foreign and Domestic: Shirley Jackson's *New Yorker* Stories

Ashley Lawson

Shirley Jackson began her professional writing life by learning to adapt her literary vision to fit one specific publication's exacting standards: the *New Yorker*. Though biographers and critics typically treat the publication of "The Lottery" in the June 1948 issue of the magazine as a breakthrough moment in Jackson's career, this infamous story was not the first piece that Jackson placed there: between her debut in 1943 and including that 1948 issue, she published a total of eleven stories in the *New Yorker*. Once she made it past the magazine's notoriously fickle editorial staff, Jackson's work likely found a more receptive audience than previously acknowledged by descriptions of her career that emphasize the backlash from readers against "The Lottery."

Indeed, two key and often overlooked facts about the *New Yorker* during this period show why this venue was a fitting platform. At this point in its run, the magazine's readership was first equally and then majority female. In 1949, 45 percent of readers were women; by 1954, it was 54 percent. Surveys from the period also indicated that women were more likely to read the magazine in its entirety, especially the fiction.[1] Thus, by the time Jackson was submitting there in the 1940s, the magazine had a middle- to upper-middle-class female readership in common with some of the women's magazines where Jackson would later publish. Yet despite the shifting gender demographics of its readership—as well as a large number of female staff members and contributors before, during, and after the Second World War—the *New Yorker* seemed to envision a male reader as its ideal, and it demonstrated a critical, even scathing attitude toward both the real and fictional women depicted in its pages. Indeed, the magazine's contempt for a certain type of femininity was built into its mission statement. In 1925, Harold Ross wrote that his new publication would be "what is commonly called sophisticated, in that it will assume a reasonable degree of enlightenment on the part of its readers," meaning it would be a magazine "which is not edited for the old lady in Dubuque." To promote the bold, youthful, cosmopolitan nature of his new baby, Ross defined what it was not—old, female, and rural—and these same qualities, not coincidentally, were denigrated within the publication's content in its first decades.[2]

Jackson's work sought to subvert this blatant contempt for femininity in a manner subtle enough to allow her submissions to pass editors' approval, and the process of fine-tuning her approach to walk this precarious line helped her to hone an early version of a trademark style that seamlessly merges the real and unreal. More specifically, Jackson took advantage of the *New Yorker*'s ambivalent feelings about the domestic realm and utilized these spaces as her most effective tool for developing her trademark sense of unease, a sense of "the intrusion of the irrational into the rational, or the unfamiliar into the familiar," which, as Joan Wylie Hall has argued, is a primary theme that ties together Jackson's larger body of short fiction.[3] The displacement of the familiar in these stories predicts two central themes of Jackson's larger body of work: a frustrated search for the domestic idyll and the fragmentation of women's individual identity inside and outside of the home. Jackson's early *New Yorker* fiction is thus valuable for the way it brings to light subtle complications in the dynamics between the genders during the period before, during, and after the Second World War, not only within the larger American culture but also within the pages of the very magazine in which it first appeared.

Furthermore, while these works may predate her better-known pieces, they are significant because they represent Jackson's first attempts at addressing what would become trademark themes. Yet these stories should not simply be treated as a kind of polished juvenilia or an early reflection of brilliance to come; rather, they should be regarded as disrupters that upset a dominant strain of critical consensus about Jackson's work. Such theories tend to treat Jackson as the sole arbiter of her distinctive style and ignore her long record of periodical publication, a mode in which editors mandate and enforce specific conventions. While critics have offered useful and necessary analysis of how the family life sketches she wrote for various women's magazines may fit in with, rather than contradict, her larger literary output,[4] we have paid less attention to this early short fiction and the context in which it appeared, and we have been neglecting a key period of Jackson's literary development. The historical framework of this period has been similarly ignored. Though most analysis of Jackson's diverse body of writing typically considers it within the historical context of the "the problem that has no name" and the Cold War era of the 1950s and 1960s,[5] highlighting these *New Yorker* stories as a distinct period within her career reminds us that her earliest fiction was actually written and published during the 1940s, during and after the Second World War. By taking these stories and their publication context into account, we can gain a fuller picture not only of Jackson's varied body of work but also the influence that periodical publication, and the *New Yorker* more specifically, had on her development as a professional author.

Jackson's early *New Yorker* fiction brings to light subtle complications in the dynamics between the genders, not only within the larger American culture but also within the pages of the very magazine in which it first appeared. While the *New Yorker* editors might have believed that Jackson's work shared their critical and often dismissive view of both women and the home, her stories are less likely to take a simplistic "war of the sexes" approach to gender that would have been typical of the magazine. In order to understand how Jackson's stories swerved from the norm, we must first describe the kind of conventions with which Jackson would have been grappling. As Mary F. Corey explains, "Although the magazine's editorial voice was unerringly egalitarian and democratic, its short stories and cartoons detailing upper-middle-class domestic life were charged with a snarling contempt for women and a unequivocal disinterest in equality."[6] From its first issues, the magazine took a critical view of marriage, a stance that would persist even into the era of domestic glorification in the 1950s and 1960s. And in the editions published during the war, anxiety about women's increased participation in the public realm only compounded the magazine's negativity. Both humor and contempt were derived from a new American order in which women took on more prominent roles. Cartoons perpetuated the archetypes of "nags, bitches, courtesans, and dimwits" with which it had such success in previous decades[7] but now humor could be generated simply by placing female stereotypes within masculine contexts. This occurs in one August 1943 cartoon that played on the common conceit of "ladies who lunch" by depicting one woman in uniform asking the other, "Did I tell you the terribly cute thing my platoon did the other day?"[8] Just as before and after the war, women are mostly depicted gossiping and spending money, though in wartime the topic of conversation often extends to subjects like blood drives and the Red Cross, and their shopping is now dependent on ration coupons. This derisive attitude toward femininity made its way into the fiction section as well, even in stories written by female authors, as Jackson surely would have noticed. For example, in Irma Brandeis's humorous "Ladies in the Dark," two female Civilian Defense volunteers rely on the help of an exasperated male driver to get them home after they get lost walking back to their rural encampment. The story seems to ask: if women cannot be trusted to retrace their own steps down a country lane, how can they make a legitimate contribution to the war effort?[9] Even the few fictional portrayals that took a more serious approach to the suffering of their female characters tended to depict single women making futile, often pathetic attempts to create meaning in their lives, as if the absence of men has left them completely without purpose. For example, the ravenous hunger of the protagonist of Mollie Panter-Downes's "The Hunger of Miss Burton" is framed not as a depiction of the sacrifices made by those who kept the home front running during wartime; rather, it is a physical symbol of a larger sense of existential lack that life without men has created for the women left behind.[10] The *New Yorker* thus promoted an image of women as shallow and incapable, and such qualities, when considered within the larger sociopolitical context, could be seen as a liability to their countrymen's efforts to win the war.

The magazine's view of women also necessarily affected its portrayal of domestic ideals. During the strife of war and then in the restored tranquility of peacetime, the American home became an increasingly important and idealized symbol of stability. Both Jackson and the *New Yorker* diverged from common views of this era by questioning the purity of these symbolic spaces, though in very different ways. During this period, the *New Yorker* equated marriage with the concept of home, but not in a positive sense. Corey describes the way the publication treated the domesticity that came with marriage as "a feminine plot designed to emasculate men."[11] Whether it appeared as a house in the suburbs or as a city apartment, the domestic space was presented as a woman's realm, which admittedly was not atypical during this time period. What did differ was the way the *New Yorker* suggested that such a place was a trap or a cage for men, a source of emasculation rather than a sanctuary. If the war was a masculine proving ground, then the home was the counterpoint space that inhibited or diminished American men, and women—not the national political dynamics, nor the conventions of marriage—were somehow to blame for this.

Beyond the veneer of light humor, a concerning pattern emerged. Women were not just adorably ditsy; they could also be a source of domestic danger equivalent to the one that loomed abroad. This theme is taken more literally by the magazine's cartoons such as one from January 1943 in which a woman asks a bookstore clerk, "Do you have one in which a wife murders her husband in a *very* ingenious manner?"[12] Another from February 1943 shows a housewife offering to give her husband a "surprise" as she holds a gun behind her back.[13] A similar take on the oppressive nature of domestic life for viable young men showed up in the magazine's fiction. For example, in the story "Continued Humid" by Mark Schorer a bored French professor would rather be sent to war to face combat than continue to plod through a dull existence that circles around his job and his home life with his wife and child. The story seems ambivalent about whether it wants to mock the man or to commiserate with his sense of entrapment within this staid domestic tranquility.[14]

This is the context in which Jackson sought to publish her stories in the *New Yorker*, and her work should be viewed as a corrective to the magazine's more misogynist take on women, the home, and the home front. These stories are set during the clear and present danger of wartime life, yet they focus less on international politics than on interpersonal ones. In her ten pre-"Lottery" stories, Jackson proves especially adept at depicting the alienation of modern domestic life. As demonstrated, this approach was typical of *New Yorker* stories into the 1940s, but Jackson gives this theme a distinctive spin by showing this destabilized world through women's eyes. Indeed, while the *New Yorker* represented the private domestic space as an essentially female setting that stifles men alone, Jackson's stories show that it is actually women, subjected to repressive codes of behavior and the isolation of the private realm, who suffer most. Thus, Jackson subverts readers' expectations that not only the domestic space but women as well should be the primary symbols of the "rational" and the "familiar," and she dissolves the protected division between the private and public by transforming domestic spaces into uncanny symbols of the new world order that war and modernity have wrought. This disturbing point of view successfully highlights that the home is no adequate protection for women from the dangers of the world, and a pervasive sense of looming danger implies that further destabilization is soon to come.

In other selections from her *The Lottery and Other Stories* (1949), Jackson utilizes more overtly gothic techniques to create that sense of threat. These stories, best described as "psychological fables of the disunified subject," feature plots that pit female protagonists against specific oppressive male authority figures who stand in for the larger cultural dominance of women, and the resulting psychological unraveling of the female characters allows Jackson to deploy elements of fantasy within the everyday.[15] Jackson's *New Yorker* stories, by contrast, stayed firmly rooted in the real world, and they tend to focus on a less fantastical and more abstract sense of threat. Jackson infiltrates and defamiliarizes spaces associated with the home to skillfully craft a sense of uncanny menace that comes from within this supposedly safe and protecting domestic space.[16] These stories are, therefore, early evidence of a theme that James Egan has characterized as typical of Jackson's brand of domestic gothic: "the creation, maintenance, and destruction of the family idyll" and a frustrated search for "domestic sanctuary."[17] So while the stories may not be typically or fully gothic, as the *New Yorker* never would have tolerated even a hint of the supernatural within its pages, the larger sense of instability depicted through the female characters' perspective does reflect what we might call a gothic consciousness—that is, a sense of menace fills the character with fear and destabilizes her comfort in domestic spaces—yet the source of that instability is never implied as originating beyond the boundaries of reality. The *New Yorker's* mandate for unobtrusive narrators means Jackson neither confirms nor denies her characters' paranoia; however, she never allows readers to believe that these women are simply unstable or mentally ill, as a more typical *New Yorker* story would. Rather, the terror of these pieces comes from their absolute plausibility and the mundane nature of the perceived threat, and Jackson forces readers to dwell in and perhaps identify with the characters' growing sense of anxiety. She would, of course, deploy this dread with mastery in her allegorical breakthrough story, "The Lottery," but these earlier stories show a writer who refined her vision in the *New Yorker* over the course of five years within the boundaries of the magazine's strict guidelines. When viewed in this way, these stories can be more clearly regarded as important precursors of Jackson's later work.

Eight of the ten pre-"Lottery" stories are told in the third person from the point of view of one or more female characters, and in each of these stories, Jackson unexpectedly deploys this feminine perspective to criticize the domestic conventions that trap, rather than protect, American women. Whether these tales are placed within domestic spaces, in the public realm, or a space that falls somewhere in between, Jackson's female characters seem to feel "haunted" by the obligations of their domestic responsibilities in addition to the growing awareness of the way their domestic obligations trap and isolate rather than satisfy them. The exigencies of wartime changed the nature of domestic spaces as well as the construct of the family; the first group of Jackson's stories examines these changes by focusing on women whose husbands are away at war, those for whom their domestic space is a home only in the technical sense. They inhabit boardinghouses and apartment buildings that are an off-kilter amalgamation of the private and the public, the personal and the impersonal. In such a space, surveillance and invasion of privacy are practically expected, and, though they are surrounded by a multitude of neighbors who are literally within arm's reach, the female inhabitants of such spaces restrict themselves to the boundaries of their assigned rooms because, despite the similarity of their accommodations, they lack a sense of identification with their cohabitants. The common setting of these stories serves to demonstrate the way that the new, wartime vestiges of the cult of domesticity cannot protect women, who are always subject to the mandates of the public realm.

Take, for example, "Trial by Combat." At first glance, the premise of the story seems typical of the *New Yorker*'s portrayal of gender dynamics. Its focus on a low-stakes domestic conflict between two women could easily read as a "cat fight" to less attentive readers, but Jackson artfully uses the skirmish to represent a deeper crisis of female identity. Emily Johnson, a young woman living in a boardinghouse while her husband is at war, suspects her upstairs neighbor, a widow called Mrs. Allen, of sneaking into her room and stealing her possessions. At the beginning of the story, Johnson is meek and reluctant to defend her territory. Whether unwilling to cause a scene or unable to assert herself directly to an authority figure, she cannot bring herself to report the theft to her landlord; instead, she takes matters into her own hands. Johnson goes to the suspect's room to confront her, but she is thwarted by an uncanny realization about the similarity of their private spaces that implies a corresponding psychic parallel. The more time Johnson spends in the other woman's room, the more she recognizes herself in Mrs. Allen's loneliness and desperation. Ultimately, she does not accuse the woman of stealing her things, and she cements her transformation into the woman's doppelganger when she, whether out of curiosity or from a desperate need to confirm her suspicions, breaks into her counterpart's room and locates the missing items. Her vindication is cut short when Mrs. Allen returns to find her trespassing, though—returning the favor the younger woman previously bestowed upon her—she pretends to buy her flimsy excuses. Each woman's awareness of the other's transgression alleviates the title's "combat" and replaces it with an unspoken pact that bonds them to one another. The boundary between their domestic spaces becomes fluid in a way that could be either a source of comfort or of danger, indeterminacy that Jackson purposefully leaves unresolved to emphasize the double-edged nature of female bonds within a patriarchal society.[18]

The story "When Things Get Dark" similarly pits an isolated, uncertain young woman against an older female stranger. In this story, the recently married Mrs. Garden is unhappy to discover that she is already pregnant. Whether the young woman's ambivalent reaction to this news is because her new husband is away at war or because of some larger discomfort with her newly proscribed domestic role is left unclear, but the extent of her desperation is not. Though other women surround her in the boardinghouse, she is not close enough to any of them to seek their advice. Instead, she leaves her home to search for an elderly female stranger who once had showed her unexpected kindness on a public bus and later sent her an encouraging letter. Because of these limited and brief interactions, Garden, in her moment of need, has projected an idealized notion of maternal support onto the woman, and she seeks her out, believing that her sage advice will help her figure out how to respond to her dilemma.

Like "Trial by Combat," the older woman's space is not a source of comfort but rather a zone of destabilized identity. Garden is shocked and discomfited by the decrepit boardinghouse where she finds her supposed savior, and the disruption of the familiar domestic signifiers is the first sign that this interaction is not going to play out as planned. The older woman's furniture is old-fashioned and ornate, as is her clothing, and the room is unkempt, as is her state of mind. Because the pair has had only one cursory interaction in a neutral public space, Mrs. Garden is not prepared for the intimate details of this woman's life displayed in her home. The ironically named Mrs. Hope cannot help her—she does not even remember their meeting—and Garden quickly realizes that her presence in the woman's private space is not welcome. Mrs. Hope's only counsel is to hang on to her letter to make her feel better "when things get dark," and she all but physically pushes the young woman out her door. Garden discovers that their previous intimacy was a well-meaning but hollow social performance, a deception that she accepts because she is in desperate need of connection. Disgusted and disappointed, she then flees the dank room for the temporary relief of the sunny public street. She finishes the story as she began it: alone and confused.[19] In this first grouping of stories, shallow gestures breed shallow connections, and both protagonists finish worse off than they began, because they realize how alone and unprotected they really are. These isolated women seek solace in the social formalities that constitute a code of feminine interaction which also ties women back to the domestic context, but such conventions, like the domestic space itself, cannot provide real answers or genuine solace because these codes are not meant to satisfy the needs of women but rather to perpetuate a larger social order that relies on women's silence and complicity.

The more traditional housewife types depicted in the second group of stories also find themselves without their husbands, but these stories are set in seemingly stable domestic spaces that approximate the ideal home of this period rather than in boardinghouses. Yet even their perfect homes cannot protect them from the fear and dissatisfaction that tend to plague Jackson's characters. Like the characters in the first group of stories, they too struggle with feelings of domestic isolation, but theirs is born of their own prejudices. Though they seem to find comfort in the sense of security that comes from having achieved everything they are told they should want—a husband, children, a home of their own—this well-being is disrupted by the intrusion of Otherness into the homogenous sanctity of their highly controlled and carefully protected spaces. The more obvious forms of Otherness—a young African American boy in "After You, My Dear Alphonse" or the Irish drunkard in "Come Dance with Me in Ireland"—actually seem to be lesser threats, because their physical presence is a glitch and thus easily fixed by ejecting the interloper, even if the discomfort of the encounter lingers.[20] The more menacing interactions are those with other women who are supposed to be just like them—a gender dynamic that aligns these protagonists with those of the first set of stories.

For example, "Afternoon in Linen" is a story that seems, on the surface, to poke fun at children's predilection for rebellion at inconvenient moments. Jackson portrays a young girl who is intimidated by the presence of a male classmate in her grandmother's parlor and consequently rejects the conventions that such a social call requires. She mortifies her grandmother by refusing to play the piano or recite her poetry for the boy's mother, and her reticence aligns her with the more acceptable willfulness of her male classmate. While this young male interloper may have been the impetus for the conflict, it is the girl and her newly willful attitude that becomes the real threat to the home's stability. Now that her granddaughter has become her adversary and equal, the older woman has lost control over her domestic domain, and the story implies that small, private humiliations will soon be the least of her worries.[21]

"A Fine Old Firm" also is based around a conventional social call. A mother and her daughter receive a surprise visit from a Mrs. Friedman, who identifies herself as the mother of a young man who has become their beloved son's and brother's best friend while fighting abroad. An outsider who is relatively new to town and—as her name subtly implies—Jewish, she laments the trouble they have had "[getting] acquainted," but the Concord women are clearly well established and thus unsympathetic to Mrs. Friedman's advances. To signify her difference from the visitor, Mrs. Concord brags that her husband is a native of the town, and she rejects Mrs. Friedman's offer to help her son get a position at her husband's law firm because they have already made arrangements for him to work with a family friend at "the fine old firm" of the story's title. Literally on their own home turf, the Concords have a comfortable advantage over their guest. Yet the talk of war and the future beyond it that is instigated by Mrs. Friedman's unwelcome visit hints that a new world is dawning outside of their door, and the reader assumes that their smug certainty that their safe home represents may soon crumble thanks to interlopers like the Friedmans.[22]

The third group of stories takes place outside of the domestic realm but comments on it nevertheless, thereby showing the way domesticity regulates women's freedom even outside of clearly defined private spaces of the home. "Colloquy" and "Whistler's Grandmother" are set in a doctor's office examination room and a train, respectively, but both continue the theme of the dissolution of cultural certainty in the home as a stable symbol. Both stories center on women who attempt to find solace within a new world order. In "Colloquy," Mrs. Arnold seeks a doctor's help to find out whether she is as "crazy" as she feels. She complains, "I don't understand the way people live. It all used to be so simple," but she continually points not to specific current events but to the befuddling statements and actions of her husband's private reactions to modernity and her inability to do anything about it as the true source of her distress.[23] This symbolizes the way in which the encroaching threat of the new world will disrupt the sanctified and orderly space of the domestic realm and women's supposed control over it. Similarly, in "Whistler's Grandmother," the story starts conventionally as a seemingly harmless old woman proudly shows off a photo of her soldier grandson to her fellow train passengers. But her tone abruptly shifts to nastiness, cruelty, and suspicion when she tells them about his new wife, whose behavior she regards as promiscuous and thus evidence that the modern world is falling apart. The secondary characters are shocked when she reveals to the group that, in order to punish the badly behaved interloper to their family, she is on her way to rat out the new wife to her grandson now that he has returned from combat. The transformation of the grandmother figure from a conventional symbol of love and acceptance to one of judgment and punishment becomes the true source of threat in the story.[24] In both these pieces, the uncertain world outside the home has ruptured women's faith in the domestic space and its corresponding signifiers as symbols of comfort and stability. This demonstrates the way cultural security is similarly dependent on the steadfastness of women's conventional role in supporting the immutability of that space.

Whether the *New Yorker* story is regarded as a definite literary genre or "a specific kind of aesthetic lens on experience," an awareness of the conventions of the magazine most certainly affected writers like Jackson who wished to appear in its pages.[25] In an attempt to be published, they would need to make what Fiona Green has called "a range of reciprocal adaptations, conscious or otherwise, between writer and periodical context."[26] Or, as stated by one critic of the magazine's stylistic preferences in 1949, a more unfavorable view of this process is that writers "are edited (or edit themselves) almost out of existence so that everything in it appears to be by an anonymous body called the *New Yorker*."[27] Jackson both yielded to and resisted that heavy editorial hand. Though her publication of "The Lottery" has become a defining part of her literary biography, hers was no overnight success. She had to work hard to earn her status as a "*New Yorker* writer." She began submitting her work during a period that historians of the *New Yorker*, including Mary F. Corey and Ben Yagoda, have deemed the magazine's golden age, its "greatest period of cultural potency"[28] when it was the "most sought after literary showplace in the country."[29] Editors at the magazine had developed their own exacting guidelines for what kind of work would fit within the covers of their publication, and Jackson had to continually work to adapt her approach to fit these requirements. In the words of her husband Stanley Edgar Hyman—who, though he worked for the *New Yorker* in various capacities at the same time she was submitting her work, seemed to have little influence in getting her work accepted—the magazine liked "tight, objective sketches with a strong undercurrent of emotion, aimed at capturing a mood, a feeling, or a situation."[30] Additional attributes that were typical to most *New Yorker* stories from the first half of the twentieth century included brevity, typically topping out at no more than 3,000 words; preference for dialogue over plot; a journalistic attention to quotidian detail; a preference for an ironic tone over emotional displays by either characters or narrators; and a twist ending that was usually meant to emphasize to the reader the cruelty of modern life.[31]

Editors enforced these established conventions and chastised Jackson any time she submitted work that strayed too far from their expectations, and the young author often struggled to find that perfect balance that also stayed true to her own literary vision. Between her first attempt in July 1942 and that June 1948 issue, Jackson had eleven stories published and at least thirty-one stories rejected, which means the editorial staff turned down about 70 percent of her submissions.[32] These rejects were sent back with harsh, sometimes befuddled comments from editors, who criticized her work variously as clichéd, abstract, and bizarre. For example, in one rejection letter, fiction editor Gus Lobrano turned down two stories with a candid assessment that seems terribly shortsighted considering the success of Jackson's later work: "My suspicion is that Miss Jackson is a good deal better when she stays close to reality. Seems to have not much flair for whimsy or fantasy."[33] In a later response, he reported that he was disappointed to have to return three stories, calling the lot "a pretty cryptic and loony batch."[34] Editors' comments reigning in her more fanciful tendencies surely pushed her to grapple with domestic spaces on more realistic terms, and Jackson learned how to represent her own brand of psychological unease by adapting an image of women and their domestic realm that magazine editors could endorse. Through this process of continual acceptance and rejection, *New Yorker* editors taught Jackson how to locate that thin line between "cryptic and loony" and the realistically surreal, and, in this way, she figured out how to portray a home space that felt realistic, familiar, and uncanny all at once.[35]

Considering the limitations of the *New Yorker* format—whether in terms of literary form or content—it may seem counterintuitive to suggest that such a restrictive publishing context was beneficial for the development of Jackson's distinctive voice, but I argue that she honed important skills during her *New Yorker* period that would influence her writing for the rest of her career. Jackson's decade-long struggle to fit her literary vision to the magazine's requirements should be regarded as a coming-of-age period in her professional life, through which she learned how to balance what mattered most to her in her work with making necessary compromises for a specific audience. More specifically, to be published in the *New Yorker*, Jackson had to learn how to keep her content just this side of "loony," and thus the magazine taught her to veil her criticisms of restrictive gender roles within more conventional settings and plots. As Joan Wylie Hall has argued, the *New Yorker* story type may have led Jackson to "de-emphasize action and stress a civilized confrontation of opposing characters."[36] She also became adept at harnessing the "twists" the magazine favored to shock the reader out of a sense of complacency, and she learned to make use of its obsession with quotidian detail to make domestic spaces feel unfamiliar and even threatening. All of these would become distinctive elements of her mature domestic gothic style. Though she eventually had the freedom to become as "loony" as she liked, even her most fantastical stories keep one foot firmly rooted in a realistic domestic world with which even *New Yorker* readers would have identified.

When considered within the contexts of her career and the magazine's history, Jackson's *New Yorker* stories can be seen as aligned with her more subversive and inventive work. She made necessary adaptations to her literary approach in order to become a "*New Yorker* author," yet she subtly transformed the magazine's critical view of women and domesticity into a broader, less reductive vision that, by regarding these issues through female eyes, made gender expectations—not women themselves—the primary offender. In doing so, Jackson presented an early depiction of the "problem with no name," a subject that would come to dominate cultural conversations about gender in the 1950s and 1960s. Furthermore, she honed her own literary vision of domestic spaces as an uncomfortable and inhibiting space for women, a notion that, when freed from the exacting demands of the *New Yorker*'s editors, would develop into a more gleefully "loony" and overtly gothic form in the domestic spaces of her novels.

Notes

1. Mary F. Corey, *The World through a Monocle: The New Yorker at Midcentury* (Cambridge, MA: Harvard University Press, 1999), 179. For more on the *New Yorker* as a "woman's magazine," see Janet Carey Eldred, *Literate Zeal: Literacy, Gender, and the Rhetorical Work of Editing* (Pittsburgh: University of Pittsburgh Press, 2012).

2. Quoted in Faye Hammill and Karen Lick, "Modernism and the Quality Magazines," in *The Oxford Critical and Cultural History of Modernist Magazines: Volume II: North America 1894–1960*, ed. Peter Brooker and Andrew Thacker (Oxford: Oxford University Press, 2012), 185–6.

3. Joan Wylie Hall, *Shirley Jackson: A Study of the Short Fiction* (New York: Twayne, 1993), 8.

4. See especially: Lynette Carpenter, "Domestic Comedy, Black Comedy, and Real Life: Shirley Jackson, a Woman Writer," in *Faith (of a Woman Writer)*, ed. Alice Kessler-Harris and William McBrien (Westport, CT: Greenwood Press, 1988), 143–8; Bernice M. Murphy, "Hideous Doughnuts and Haunted Housewives: Gothic Undercurrents in Shirley Jackson's Domestic Humor," in *The Ghost Story from the Middle Ages to the 20th Century*, ed. Helen Conrad O'Briain and Julie Anne Stevens (Dublin: Four Courts Press, 2010), 229–50; Anne LeCroy, "The Different Humor of Shirley Jackson: *Life among the Savages* and *Raising Demons*." *Studies in American Humor*, 4, no. 1/2 (Spring/Summer 1985): 62–73.

5. See: John G. Parks, "Chambers of Yearning: Shirley Jackson's Use of the Gothic." *Twentieth Century Literature*, 30, no. 1 (Spring 1984): 15–29; Eric Savoy, "Between *as if* and *is*: On Shirley Jackson." *Women's Studies*, 46, no. 8 (2017): 827–44; Angela Hague, "'A Faithful Anatomy of Our Times': Reassessing Shirley Jackson." *Frontiers: A Journal of Women Studies*, 26, no. 2 (2005): 73–96.

6   Corey, *The World*, 150.
7   Ibid., 180.
8   *New Yorker*, August 14, 1943, 22.
9   Irma Brandeis, "Ladies in the Dark." *New Yorker*, September 4, 1943, 70–72.
10 Mollie Panter-Downes, "The Hunger of Miss Burton." *New Yorker*, January 16, 1943, 15–17.
11 Corey, *The World*, 157.
12 *New Yorker*, January 16, 1943, 19.
13 *New Yorker*, February 20, 1943, 14.
14 Mark Schorer, "Continued Humid." *New Yorker*, September 4, 1943, 20–2.
15 Daryl Hattenhauer, *Shirley Jackson's American Gothic* (Albany: State University of New York Press, 2003), 29.
16 One key element that distinguishes the approach of the stories in this collection that were previously published in the *New Yorker* from those that were not is the recurring appearance in the latter set of the daemon lover/Jamie Harris figure. See Wyatt Bonikowski, "'Only One Antagonist': The Demon Lover and the Feminine Experience in the Work of Shirley Jackson." *Gothic Studies*, 15, no. 2 (November 2013): 66–88 and Hattenhauer, chapter 2.
17 James Egan, "Sanctuary: Shirley Jackson's Domestic and Fantastic Parables." *Studies in Weird Fiction*, 6 (1989): 17.
18 Shirley Jackson, "Trial by Combat." *New Yorker*, December 16, 1944, 72; 74–6.
19 Shirley Jackson, "When Things Get Dark." *New Yorker*, December 30, 1944, 40–3.
20 Shirley Jackson, "After You, My Dear Alphonse." *New Yorker*, January 16, 1943, 51–3; Shirley Jackson, "Come Dance with Me in Ireland." *New Yorker*, May 15, 1943, 43–6.
21 Shirley Jackson, "Afternoon in Linen." *New Yorker*, September 4, 1943, 39–9.
22 Shirley Jackson, "A Fine Old Firm." *New Yorker*, March 4, 1944, 64–7.
23 Shirley Jackson, "Colloquy." *New Yorker*, August 5, 1945, 45.
24 Shirley Jackson, "Whistler's Grandmother." *New Yorker*, May 5, 1945, 59–61.
25 Ben Yagoda, *About Town: The New Yorker and the World It Made* (New York: Da Capo Press, 2000), 12.
26 Fiona Green, "Introduction," *Writing for The New Yorker: Critical Essays on an American Periodical*, ed. Fiona Green (Edinburgh: Edinburgh University Press, 2015), 4–5.
27 Stephen Spender, "The Situation of the American Writer." *Horizon*, 19, no. 111 (March 1949): 173.
28 Corey, *The World*, x.

29 Yagoda, *About Town*, 215.
30 Stanley Edgar Hyman, "The Urban New Yorker." *New Republic*, July 20, 1942, 91.
31 For further dissection of *New Yorker* fiction conventions, see Yagoda, *About Town*, 153–4 and Ruth Franklin, *Shirley Jackson: A Rather Haunted Life* (New York: Liveright, 2016), 149.
32 Even after her success with "The Lottery," Jackson's acceptance rate at the magazine did not improve, though by this time she had shifted her more serious efforts to her novels and focused her shorter efforts on the family life sketches she placed at the better-paying women's magazines. By 1951, her correspondence indicates that Jackson grew frustrated with the continual rejections and decided to devote her energies to publishing her work elsewhere. Correspondence from Brandt & Brandt to Shirley Jackson, January 22, 1951, Box 43, Folder 6, MSS52522, Shirley Jackson Papers. Manuscript Division, Library of Congress, Washington, DC.
33 Correspondence from Gus Lobrano to Frances Pindyck, February 11, 1943.
34 Correspondence from Gus Lobrano to Frances Pindyck, November 22, 1943.
35 Unfortunately, Jackson's association with the *New Yorker* also had its drawbacks. Pieces rejected by the magazine became difficult to place elsewhere because the magazine's distinct stylistic preferences were not shared by other publications. And many of the critics who reviewed the 1948 collection of stories that was titled after her now infamous "Lottery" story could not help but weigh in on their views of the magazine, even though only seven of the twenty-six stories in the book were first published there. An anonymous reviewer from *Time* magazine dismissed Jackson's pieces as "brightly lacquered sketches trimmed to *New Yorker* specifications," ruing that if the author "could break out of this mold," she might become one of the best American short story writers. "Come On, Everyone." *Time*, 53, no. 21 (23 May 1949), 105–6.
36 Hall, *Shirley Jackson*, 37.

References

Bonikowski, Wyatt. "'Only One Antagonist': The Demon Lover and the Feminine Experience in the Work of Shirley Jackson." *Gothic Studies*, 15, no. 2 (November 2013): 66–88.
Brandeis, Irma. "Ladies in the Dark." *New Yorker*, September 4, 1943.
Carpenter, Lynette. "Domestic Comedy, Black Comedy, and Real Life: Shirley Jackson, a Woman Writer," in *Faith (of a Woman Writer)*, ed. Alice Kessler-Harris and William McBrien, 143–8. Westport, CT: Greenwood Press, 1988.
Cartoon. *New Yorker*, January 16, 1943, 19.
Cartoon. *New Yorker*, February 20, 1943, 14.
Cartoon. *New Yorker*, August 14, 1943, 22.
"Come On, Everyone." *Time*, May 23, 1949, 105–6.

Corey, Mary F. *The World through a Monocle: The New Yorker at Midcentury.* Cambridge, MA: Harvard University, 1999.
Egan, James. "Sanctuary: Shirley Jackson's Domestic and Fantastic Parables." *Studies in Weird Fiction*, 6 (1989): 15–24.
Eldred, Janet Carey. *Literate Zeal: Literacy, Gender, and the Rhetorical Work of Editing.* Pittsburgh: University of Pittsburgh Press, 2012.
Franklin, Ruth. *Shirley Jackson: A Rather Haunted Life.* New York: Liveright, 2016.
Green, Fiona. "Introduction," *Writing for The New Yorker: Critical Essays on an American Periodical*, ed. Fiona Green. Edinburgh: Edinburgh University, 2015.
Hague, Angela. "'A Faithful Anatomy of Our Times': Reassessing Shirley Jackson." *Frontiers: A Journal of Women Studies*, 26, no. 2 (2005): 73–96.
Hall, Joan Wylie. *Shirley Jackson: A Study of the Short Fiction.* New York: Twayne, 1993.
Hammill, Faye, and Karen Lick. "Modernism and the Quality Magazines," in *The Oxford Critical and Cultural History of Modernist Magazines: Volume II: North America 1894–1960*, ed. Peter Brooker and Andrew Thacker, 176–96. Oxford: Oxford University Press, 2012.
Hattenhauer, Daryl. *Shirley Jackson's American Gothic.* Albany: State University of New York Press, 2003.
Hyman, Stanley Edgar. "The Urban New Yorker." *New Republic*, July 20, 1942.
Jackson, Shirley. "After You, My Dear Alphonse." *New Yorker*, January 16, 1943.
Jackson, Shirley. "Afternoon in Linen." *New Yorker*, September 4, 1943.
Jackson, Shirley. "Colloquy." *New Yorker*, August 5, 1945.
Jackson, Shirley. "Come Dance with Me in Ireland." *New Yorker*, May 15, 1943.
Jackson, Shirley. "Fine Old Firm." *New Yorker*, March 4, 1944.
Jackson, Shirley. "Trial by Combat." *New Yorker*, December 16, 1944.
Jackson, Shirley. "When Things Get Dark." *New Yorker*, December 30, 1944.
Jackson, Shirley. "Whistler's Grandmother." *New Yorker*, May 5, 1945.
Shirley Jackson Papers, MSS52522. Manuscript Division, Library of Congress, Washington, DC.
LeCroy, Anne. "The Different Humor of Shirley Jackson: *Life among the Savages* and *Raising Demons.*" *Studies in American Humor*, 4, no. 1/2 (Spring/Summer 1985): 62–73.
Murphy, Bernice M. "Hideous Doughnuts and Haunted Housewives: Gothic Undercurrents in Shirley Jackson's Domestic Humor," in *The Ghost Story from the Middle Ages to the 20th Century*, ed. Helen Conrad O'Briain and Julie Anne Stevens, 229–50. Dublin: Four Courts Press, 2010.
Panter-Downes, Mollie. "The Hunger of Miss Burton." *New Yorker*, January 16, 1943.
Parks, John G. "Chambers of Yearning: Shirley Jackson's Use of the Gothic." *Twentieth Century Literature*, 30, no. 1 (Spring 1984): 15–29.
Savoy, Eric. "Between *as if* and *is*: On Shirley Jackson." *Women's Studies*, 46, no. 8 (2017): 827–44.
Schorer, Mark. "Continued Humid." *New Yorker*, September 4, 1943.
Spender, Stephen. "The Situation of the American Writer." *Horizon*, 19, no.111 March 1949.
Yagoda, Ben. *About Town: The New Yorker and the World It Made.* New York: Da Capo, 2000.

3

"You Didn't Look Like You Belonged in This House": Shirley Jackson's Fragile Domesticities

Michael J. Dalpe Jr.

In "The Honeymoon of Mrs. Smith,"[1] a concerned neighbor confronts a woman, Mrs. Smith, with the suggestion that Smith's husband may be a wanted murderer. The quote, as it follows, lays bare the central thesis of much of Shirley Jackson's work:

> "In the second place," she said, "you didn't look like you belonged in this house, or in this neighborhood, because you always had plenty of money, which, believe me, the rest of us don't, and you always acted sort of as though you ought to be in a better kind of situation. And in the *third* place," Mrs. Jones said, hurrying on to her climax, "it wasn't two days before people began to think they recognized your husband from the pictures in the paper."[2]

Throughout many of her short stories, Jackson explores themes of morality and society through the lens of "belonging," whether that is within the context of belonging in a house or belonging in a certain social arena. An aspect of her fiction that is often overlooked is how that sense of belonging twists the mundane, the familiar, and the homely into sources of discomfort and terror. The confrontation between Mrs. Smith and her neighbor, Mrs. Jones, is a kind of interaction that, for the reader, feels uncomfortable and is only amplified by the knowledge that Mrs. Jones had arrived in Mrs. Smith's apartment unannounced and uninvited. Like Mrs. Jones, Jackson uses domesticity in a way that not only reinforces gothic tropes of the familiar-turned-terrible, but she also adds a gendered urgency, which cannot be ignored due to its interruption of expected order. That order, and the undermining of it, is inherently linked in Jackson's stories to expectations of gender performance; the discomfort that these stories invoke depends on the expectation that the home is a private, and therefore publicly illegible, space.

The success of Jackson's stories stems from the corruption of expectations, whether it is the corruption of a normal private life or the inversion of expected power dynamics of the pre-1970s America within which Jackson lived, wrote, and raised a family. For Jackson, domesticity is a form of power; inasmuch as domestic spaces are powerful, they are also traps, both for those who live within the expectations of "normalcy," and for others who seem to be betrayed by the perceived security those spaces offer. That normalcy, in itself, is dangerous because it questions *whose* normalcy is acceptable, and, for Jackson's fiction, there seems to be an assumption of white, heterosexual, middle-class Americana. Domesticity is a performance, and as such, when performances go awry, the hegemonic systems these performances work within are challenged; Jackson's stories challenge these expected performances by showing what happens when the social rituals of "polite society" break down.

Jackson obscures important details throughout her texts. Often, she leaves what may be occurring at the end of the story, off-page. Is Mr. Smith a murderer, or are the people in town hungry for gossip? Whatever *does* happen to Miss Strangeworth's roses? These occurrences and elisions happen often in relation to a house or domestic space; within those spaces, which are often marked as semisacred and are assumed to be private, this occlusion of details provides that much more anxiety to the situations. This planned lack of detail is a necessary component of the stories I will examine in this chapter—"The Honeymoon of Mrs. Smith," "The Possibility of Evil," "Louisa, Please Come Home," and "The Sorcerer's Apprentice"—because, when read together, these stories not only challenge what the expectation of privacy entails, but they also question how, and to what end, domestic spaces function outside the realm of fiction.

These expectations of polite performances are a trap for Mrs. Smith. When she is out in public, such as at the grocery store, she is the subject of gossip: "When she came into the grocery she obviously interrupted a conversation about herself and her husband."[3] She is not in control of her own narrative when she is outside her home. Even when Mrs. Smith is within her own apartment, which could be deemed as the domestic sphere within which she could exercise her own autonomy, Mrs. Jones is constantly watching her activities and is apt to comment on them, too.[4] Visibility is a trap, but for whom? Jackson lays bare the contradiction of the assumption of privacy in one's own home and the realities of living in close quarters. The horror of "The Honeymoon of Mrs. Smith" is not the implication that Mr. Smith is a murderer: the horror is that Mrs. Smith's every action is subject to scrutiny and gossip. Mrs. Smith is indicative of the many women within Jackson's stories, and indeed, of America in Jackson's lifetime and today: they observe and are observed, and they are judged accordingly. This produces a sense of insecurity, in that if a woman cannot be free and without scrutiny, even within her own home, where truly can she be alone? This story provides a reference point for particularly feminine anxieties, which are further reinforced with the other stories Jackson produced. Jackson uses the horror genre to illuminate the societal limitations faced by American women, while also implicating the social and political landscape in the reproduction of the systems that produced—and continue to produce—those limitations.

So often, the domestic is not only discussed but also at stake in Jackson's texts, and gender plays a role in determining the safety of spaces. Gender is important here because it is, in Judith Butler's terms, performative.[5] By performing in ways that are expected or not expected, the women in Jackson's stories interact with what is deemed "acceptable" ways of existing, and are in turn punished for acting in ways that are unacceptable. The pieces examined here are looked at through the lens of critical gender theory. The stories are found within the Penguin Classics compilation *Dark Tales*, and the perspective that the stories establish together depicts a world in which spaces that should be safe are not, and a world where a woman's place is often threatened and undermined by the assumption of privacy and safety.

Miss Adela Strangeworth in "The Possibility of Evil"[6] builds from "Mrs. Smith": her outward appearances are very much in contrast to her inner life, which proves to be a defining characteristic of Jackson's women. In this story, Miss Strangeworth is responsible for sowing discord among the townspeople about whom she feels a kind of patrician ownership: "she sometimes found herself thinking that the town belonged to her."[7] This ownership extends beyond physical aspects of the town, though; it is revealed that she is sending letters to other citizens in order to, in her eyes, keep them on a moral path since "as long as evil existed unchecked in the world, it was Miss Strangeworth's duty to keep her town alert to it."[8] Strangeworth, like many of the characters in Jackson's short fiction, makes use of a "weaponized civility" which is a kind of horror: she takes advantage of social mores and standards in order to manipulate others, and it is with a kind of pleasure that the reader observes that her roses are destroyed by the end of the story. The irony of this, though, is that Miss Strangeworth does not prepare for her own moralizing turning against her. When the townspeople discover her role in sending anonymous letters, she is punished in a way that she does not foresee, and in a way that the reader never actually sees. In ending the story with, "*Look out at what used to be your roses*,"⁹ Jackson engages with successful suspense writing that leaves the material of the letter off the page. This leads to a question about the title of the story, "The Possibility of Evil": Is the possibility that Miss Strangeworth *herself* is the malicious force she deems necessary to guard against within *her* town? Or is it that the unknown, but implied, destruction—or desecration—of her roses and her private space shows the potential for violence in even the most seemingly innocent people?

As John G. Parks references in his 1978 essay "The Possibility of Evil: A Key to Shirley Jackson's Fiction," this story reveals "a fundamental problem ... in American culture: the revelation of the imagination that sees evil only *out there*, and which thus must be smashed at any cost. Miss Strangeworth does not see that evil is a component within [the readers] that can be transcended only through its recognition and acceptance."¹⁰ Parks suggests that the "evil" that is referenced here is Miss Strangeworth discovering her own penchant and aptitude for it. However, an alternative reading of Miss Strangeworth's situation suggests that the sudden results of Miss Strangeworth's actions are not necessarily evil, nor is Miss Strangeworth herself, but rather the systems which produced her expectation of ownership of her own solitude could be described as "evil." Parks's reading does not account for the roles produced by space and place within Jackson's stories; indeed, since this story could be set anywhere in place or time, the reader is "given just enough information to see the universality of the human problem involved."¹¹ Any person can have ownership of a place, and any person could feel security in one's seemingly private affairs, but the "evil" that is possible within this story is not that of the actions taken by and against Miss Strangeworth, but the hegemonic systems that divide her property from "her" town, and divide her way of thinking from the perspectives of other characters within the story. Parks suggests that Miss Strangeworth is "corrupted by her own narcissism";¹² a different perspective suggests that the narcissism is not localized to just Mrs. Strangeworth, but to every person, fictional or otherwise.

Miss Strangeworth's destruction produces an insight into the horror of the personal becoming public, which is also mirrored in "Louisa, Please Come Home."¹³ While "The Possibility of Evil" receives some analysis, "Louisa" is largely unexamined. Instead, critics focus more often on Jackson's more popular works, such as "The Lottery." In one such reading, Gayle Whittier suggests that "The Lottery" reproduces and reinforces misogynist worldviews.¹⁴ While reading a single story in isolation may lead to that presumption, what is missing is a consideration of the larger matrix of themes present in Jackson's collective body of short fiction. Whittier asserts that "the lottery's formality and inherited procedures, which may be lost but not voluntarily changed, extremize [*sic*] that order kept by men in explicit opposition to women";¹⁵ she does not take into account what this story does for the reader, and what the reader gains by being complicit in the story. This is emblematic of most Jackson stories. Isolated, they may be read as attempts to reinforce seemingly misogynist behaviors and worldviews, but in bulk, these stories depict a deeply feminine-oriented world in which safety is desired but unattainable, and that yearning is a kind of horror, in particular, for a female audience.

"Louisa, Please Come Home" highlights this domestic yearning, and the subsequent shattering of perceived safety in a way that contrasts "The Possibility of Evil" in that Louisa disrupts her own domesticity by running away from home, assuming a new name, and then attempting to reconcile with her parents only to find that they do not recognize her. Ottessa Moshfegh's introduction to *Dark Tales* provides a perspective for this story that cuts to the heart of what Jackson's short stories often convey: "Don't be hypnotized by the sanctity of the superficial rhythm of humdrum life, Jackson warns, for under the surface of things, people change, sometimes irrevocably, and yet they may appear unaltered."[16] Moshfegh identifies the perversion and corruption of the "normal" that is at the center of Jackson's stories, in particular, "Louisa, Please Come Home." This inversion of what is expected is core to this story. The central focus is not just the idea that Louisa's parents would accept her with open arms back into her old life, but also that Louisa would be reconciled with typical social expectations of femininity, such as docility and acceptable domesticity. Through first-person narration, which is unique among the stories examined here, Louisa is rendered *in*visible and *illegible* to her parents when she eventually decides to return to them, while having her motivations transparent on the page. By continuing to be a living, breathing person (within the story), she is paralyzed and rendered an object in both her parents' eyes. The resulting discomfort of the text comes with the realization that Louisa is reduced to a pervasive feminine fear: to be reduced to an object, instead of a subject. Louisa at the end of the story is not the Louisa her parents recall, and that moment of nonrecognition is the core horror of the story.

"Louisa" creates a mirror of domestic spaces and may be read as one of the most explicit examples of a certain kind of wish fulfillment that pervades Jackson's works which starts from the idea that Jackson's intended readership consists of women in domestic roles similar to the one she lived. The need for escape that Louisa embodies and acts on, especially for a woman in 1950s and 1960s America when Jackson was writing, is a relatable aspect of daily life for her intended audience. The real horror of the text comes with the revelation to Louisa that she can never go home, and that "home" is actually not solid, but is permeable and susceptible to psychic erosion. Much like the perceived "nostalgia for a simpler time" within "The Lottery," "Louisa, Please Come Home" engages expectations of how a home and community are defined. For Jackson, the concept of "home" is not blissful, but is emblematic of a woman's limitations in a hegemonic system that is fueled by masculine desires and feminine labor. It is worth noting, too, that Louisa does not return of her own volition. She is compelled by Paul. Even in her self-imposed escape and exile, she is subject to the desires and physical domination of men; her agency is limited by her gender, which is a sentiment that is apparent in many of Jackson's works.

In the text, Louisa tells of how she planned to leave—escape, abscond, disappear?—on "the day before Carol's wedding on purpose."[17] Carol represents what is expected of women, whereas Louisa, an aberration, represents the unspoken and punishable desires that Jackson may have felt regularly, but which must have been discouraged. After all, what does marriage represent if not a shackle to a house, a town, a man, and a family? What makes Jackson so transgressive is that, at the time she was writing, the expected role of a woman was to be firmly within the domestic sphere; Louisa literally escapes the *domus* and creates an untethered life. She also creates a space where she gets to act on the impulses that plague a person: What happens if a woman packs up and leaves her old life? What happens if she attempts to undo that action? Jackson extrapolates on these questions, and the result is a kind of unanticipated freedom. Ultimately, Louisa is unable to return (or to be forcefully returned) to her parental home, which produces more of a shock than her sudden disappearance does.

So many of Jackson's stories are told in the third person that it is important that Louisa tells her own story, since the first-person narration produces an almost conspiratorial intimacy with Louisa's reasoning. This also gives her efficacy when so much of the story deals explicitly with the perceived lack of it. Louisa is aware of her own invisibility as she recounts that she was made "even more invisible by doing just what I told my mother I was going to"[18] when she disappears, and further, by letting the reader in on the joke when it comes to her constructing a whole other life story for Mrs. Peacock, her landlady in Carson:

> By the time I had been in the house an hour, Mrs. Peacock knew all about my imaginary family upstate: my mother, who was a widow; and my sister, who had just gotten married and still lived at my mother's home with her husband, and my young brother Paul, who worried my mother a good deal because he didn't seem to want to settle down. My name was Lois Taylor, I told her. By that time, I think I could have told her my real name and she would never have connected it with the girl in the paper, because by then she was feeling that she almost knew my family, and she wanted me to be sure and tell my mother when I wrote home that Mrs. Peacock would make herself personally responsible for me while I was in the city and take as good care of me as my own mother would.[19]

Louisa takes joy in becoming Lois Taylor, and in keeping tabs on the turmoil her disappearance has on her family and community. Her glee squeezes between the lines as subtext—but from where does this pleasure manifest? It is in the idea of getting away with something—it is in her freedom. By the time she is done recounting the excerpt just mentioned, it feels as if she needs to take a gulp of air, and it seems to be out of exuberance, out of the idea that she has gotten away with something illicit. And she has. She makes an ideal world for herself in her escape, even going so far as to recast the troublesome neighbor Paul as her brother. She gains pleasure out of her own deceit; it is little wonder that this form of enlightenment must be brought low by the end of the story. Jackson cannot allow Louisa's duplicity to go unpunished. Louisa's exuberance in recounting her exploits is a kind of hubris. The story cannot end in a way that rewards Louisa for her transgressions.

Louisa *must* be punished, after all. In a panoptic sense, as Foucault describes it,[20] her actions threaten the greater good of the social order. If she were allowed to return home, she would upend a system to which everyone around her subscribes. Instead of rewarding Louisa with incorporation back into the family, which would be a cruelty, Jackson casts her out finally: "'We know what it's like for a family to worry and wonder about a daughter,' my mother said. 'Go back to the people who love you.'"[21] It is important, and ironic, that the mother turns Louisa away. By turning Louisa away once and for all, she is denying the domestic safety of her own home and thus becoming not-Louisa's-mother. Louisa is ultimately cut off and unrecognized by her family, and the question arises of which would be worse: Louisa's returning to the captivity of her old life, or being unable to return. By ending the story where she does, Jackson leaves it as a warning for her readers. To desire too much is to destroy one's own chances of returning to expected safety, thereby signaling that desire is, in itself, a kind of destruction.

Jackson creates in Louisa an inverted Orpheus, being dragged back to a living death and being sentenced, irreparably, to never return again. She is cast out of what was once her home and is made unrecognizable by her own machinations. She gets what she wants, and by the time it is too late, she realizes what she loses. This is a cautionary tale of how women's desires are to be sublimated. Jackson is providing a kind of escape; "Louisa" is a morality story with no happy ending, or no happy ending that a housewife or a happy mother—or, a doting husband—would see. What does Louisa have to show for her efforts? A rented room and a fabricated name—and possibly her freedom.

Pivoting away from Louisa, "The Sorcerer's Apprentice"[22] is, in a word, unsettling and unsettled. The story opens with a description of Miss Matt, an unmarried 34-year-old English teacher who lives alone in an apartment complex. While adventurous, or potentially exotic—"she had gone from New York to San Francisco through the Panama Canal with two other teachers from her high school"—she is unfulfilled—"Sometimes, when … the future looked unusually dark, Miss Matt would permit herself to cry luxuriously for half an hour."²³ She carves out a space for herself in her apartment, and while she drinks tea with her landlady, she realizes that "in the six years she had lived in her apartment, Miss Matt had not met any of her neighbors."²⁴ A small girl named Krishna Raleigh, who is one of the neighbors, proceeds to impose on Miss Matt's private space to play records that have her father's voice on them, her father who is "in the Army ... killing Nazis."²⁵ Krishna then proceeds to desire and subsequently break a doll of Miss Matt's; in retaliation, Miss Matt breaks Krishna's record of Krishna's father's piano playing and then flees to the movies.²⁶ The resolution of the story is minimal, and almost seems unfinished; the actual destruction within the story is more symbolic than physical, in that it stands not just for destroying something of Krishna's, and therefore regaining a kind of control for Miss Matt. This destruction is also the tipping point for Miss Matt, transforming her from a victim of Krishna to a destructive force in her own right.

However, this story takes on a darker tone when examined within the contexts of domestic spaces. Miss Matt is kept at a formal distance from other characters within the story. Jackson provides Matt's last name and her profession, and hints that she has traveled, but not much else. Miss Matt has an established routine regarding her home life, and she has an expectation of respect where she establishes her personal spaces. This expectation is similar to what Miss Strangeworth experiences in "The Possibility of Evil": it is the *expectation* of others respecting her personal—her domestic—spaces that eventually leads to the destruction of those very spaces. Unlike Miss Strangeworth, though, Miss Matt seems to have done nothing wrong, in terms of performing domesticity—on the surface, at least. Being an unmarried woman in her thirties, Miss Matt is a threat to the hegemonic patriarchal systems of the Second World War era in that she is a housewife without a house or husband, and she has her own money and private space, both of which are not tied to masculine supervision. As such, she has her own determinism and ability to make decisions without a man's influence to consider. Despite her scheduled sobbing, she is, much like Louisa, a woman who embodies a kind of escapist pleasure, in that she is the master of her own professional and domestic lives. Naturally, as for the other women who are masters of their own domains, such as Miss Strangeworth and Louisa, established comfort and security that are the end results of professional and domestic self-determinism *must* result in some punishment.

Miss Matt's punishment comes in the form of a little girl from the next floor down of the apartment building. Because Miss Matt is somehow aberrant in not knowing her neighbors, she does not recognize Krishna, the girl, when she intrudes into Miss Matt's space. Krishna knocks and then lets herself in. Miss Matt's first words to her, through her tears, are, "Were you looking for me?" to which Krishna responds, "Marian said I could come in here."²⁷ This exchange relies on assumed etiquette. Miss Matt assumes that Krishna is there for a legitimate reason, and Krishna is there to fulfill her desires. The issue, though, is that Miss Matt does not respond with outrage to Krishna's intrusion. There is none of the expected chastising of Krishna, and the authority that Miss Matt has over her own domestic space is suddenly shattered. Krishna does not ask if she can come in, and grammatically, the first phrase uttered by Miss Matt is a question—it is a request for information, not an affirmation of her control of the space. In that moment, her privacy and constructed safety are shattered, and power is transferred to the girl, whose own first words are not an apology, but a justification for her intrusion. Someone outside Miss Matt's purview had given Krishna permission to intrude on Miss Matt's space, and Krishna is given power by allowing her first statement to be a declaration. Miss Matt's expectation of her own safety lies within the knowledge that she would not be aberrant in her actions: she would not act out and disappear, like Louisa, nor would she incite intentional discomfort in others, such as Miss Strangeworth. By performing femininity correctly, in that she is a teacher, and that, though she is unmarried, she acts with a sense of propriety that only slips, in the form of her scheduled crying, when she is alone. There is safety in her actions because she does not *need* to be punished until Krishna appears. Krishna is catalyst and punishment in one, and Miss Matt's perceived security, naturally, must be destroyed.

There is a larger conversation here, too, about the nature of the power that Krishna has in Miss Matt's space. Similar to Louisa's constructed life, or Miss Strangeworth's rose garden, Miss Matt assumes that in her apartment her personal space is unassailable. To an outside force, though, Miss Matt's apartment is permeable, and not because the door is unlocked. Miss Matt's expectation of private impenetrability is ultimately what causes the subsequent destruction. She relies on being sovereign in her own space, and Krishna represents the destruction that occurs in social breakdown. Krishna is a kind of colonial force, entering Miss Matt's space in a way that is neither sanctioned nor, unfortunately, challenged effectively. Miss Matt's home, therefore, becomes a place where American anxieties run amok; "What would happen," one may ask, "if a child were to enter my own private spaces uninvited?" Note, too, that Krishna's name, especially to an expected audience of the 1940s, evokes the unusual and the exotic. Jackson's pieces seem to deal primarily with the domestic—both on a civic level and that of the household—but, as a woman who experienced the destabilizing events of the 1940s, 1950s, and 1960s, it would be more perplexing if the anxieties of social instability did *not* find their ways into her writing. As such, the way that this intrusion—this invasion, this violation—occurs to Miss Matt's spaces speaks much to the uncertainty faced by Jackson and other American women of her time in the form of global armed conflicts, shifting cultural expectations, and a changing American economy. By having Krishna, named in a sense for an unstoppable entity, force her way into Miss

Matt's sanctum, Jackson is surreptitiously showing how tenuous domestic spaces are, especially when they are made only by and for women.

Krishna's authority comes from Marian, her mother, whose absence from the story makes Krishna's invasion more peculiar:

> "I'm six years old and I live just downstairs and right underneath here." Both she and Miss Matt looked down at the floor, and then Krishna went on, "Marian said I could come and play with my records here."
>
> "Who is Marian?" Miss Matt asked, "and why should she give you permission to come up here?"
>
> "That's my mother, Marian," Krishna said impatiently.[28]

Miss Matt seems to accept this alien authority of Marian, but it is increasingly strange that Miss Matt herself does not fight against this invasion; she sees it, potentially, as something innocuous or out of place, but not dangerous. Krishna's records are of her father, James Raleigh, who plays piano and is, according to Krishna, in the army. The reader could infer that Miss Matt feels sorry for the girl; it could also be inferred that Krishna's remark of, "when he's killed all the Nazis he's going to come home and play the piano again"[29] is a rote common response from Marian. It would not be out of place to assume that John Raleigh is dead, and that the records of him playing and of his voice (and of the pictures that are in Krishna's mother's apartment) are all that is left of him.

There is a specter throughout this text of the absence of men. Miss Matt does not have a husband, and James Raleigh is most likely a dead man; apart from these references, this story focuses on the women that are left behind by war and international conflicts—the women who are forced into their domestic spheres as a way of self-preservation. Through an absence of men, women within the story take on traditionally masculine-coded actions, such as violence and destruction. In having women perform the perceived masculine behaviors of invasion and destruction that are found within this text, as with Krishna entering Miss Matt's space and Miss Matt destroying the records, this violence becomes a kind of mundane ghost story: the horror is not the invasion of privacy or the destruction of property, it is Miss Matt turning into a destructive force. The horror of this piece is the act of Miss Matt breaking Krishna's record and being transformed into the "crazy old woman,"[30] an epithet that Miss Matt *knows* she is not, but which Krishna calls her. Miss Matt will not make it out of this story unscathed, and unlike Miss Strangeworth's destruction or Louisa's abandonment, Miss Matt becomes the monstrosity that she was avoiding. She materially harms another person by destroying Krishna's record, but Krishna laughs at her instead, calling her a crazy woman rather than being outraged by the loss of another aspect of her father. It is understandable that critics and reviewers would call Krishna "evil"; however, what Krishna does is to provoke Miss Matt by breaking a doll that she owned, whereas what Miss Matt does has wider implications.

Digging further, there is an irony in Krishna's name. In the *Bhagavad Gita*, a cornerstone text in Hinduism and Vedic philosophy, Krishna is the name of one of the avatars of an all-encompassing deity. It is unclear whether Jackson had any familiarity with Hinduism, but to a reader in 1940s America, the little girl's intrusion would clearly be seen as an invasion; one can imagine that Jackson would be familiar with Hinduism, or at least of the cultural anxieties of European and American authors writing about Hinduism and other Eastern religions. Indeed, referencing Edward Said,[31] it is a kind of reverse-Orientalism, in which the Other imposes itself in a space that is not its own and proceeds to destroy what is unfamiliar. In naming the 6-year-old blonde child Krishna, Jackson is potentially juxtaposing the ideas of an all-powerful incarnation of a deity with the forcefulness and stubbornness of a child, while also hinting at the ingrained xenophobia of wartime America. Miss Matt is no one in particular, and her apartment is of no social or political merit, but her space, if read through Said, reads very much as every home in wartime-era American. Jackson has the destruction of voices on the record suggest that the end result of any invasion can only be destruction: destruction of people's voices, property, and safety. The intrusions of the Other lead to the destruction of safety and the home, and Jackson is speaking to the latent anxieties of the time by recasting them into a firmly domestic, if peculiar, interaction.

There is a kind of delicious waiting in the text when Miss Matt goes to break Krishna's record after Krishna rips Miss Matt's doll apart. The line is split between two pages in the Penguin *Dark Tales* edition. On the bottom line of page sixty-five, the damning sentence begins, "Miss Matt watched Krishna for a minute, her chin trembling, and then she went over to the phonograph and lifted the record off"—the turn of the page is excruciating. In that split second, just like at the end of "The Possibility of Evil," there is space to imagine all the possible outcomes. Will Miss Matt shove it in Krishna's hands and usher her out the door? Will Miss Matt fling the record out a conveniently open window? Will Miss Matt—

Just like that, though, with the turn of the page, Miss Matt is undone. Unlike "The Possibility of Evil," this story provides a concrete ending: "and smashed it onto the floor."[32] Miss Matt is ruined not by some outside force, but by her own unchecked violence toward a child. Miss Matt hurries Krishna out of the apartment, cleans up, and leaves for the movies. She will "Go to the movies where it's dark, she was thinking. ... Come back later, she thought, when they're all tired of looking for [her]."[33] In abandoning her apartment for a movie and in actively avoiding her neighbors, her domestic space is changed irreparably. Instead of a haven, Miss Matt now lives above someone whom she knows has no problem invading her space. Instead of safety, Miss Matt now must walk past Krishna and her mother's door every day—until Marian confronts her, until Krishna reappears, until someone comes looking for her. That is why she goes to the movies: in the dark, no one can see her—her expected refuge is about sight, is about having someone else's story reflected onto her, instead of having her violence reflected onto another. If she cannot be seen, she cannot be interrogated— by either Krishna, or Marian, or, as Jackson most likely did on purpose, any other characters that remain off-page. In the dark, Miss Matt is safe, since her home, her personal, private, and domestic space had, just like that of Miss Strangeworth or Louisa, been turned against her.

The "elephant in the room" is the title of this story. It is taken from the record Miss Matt has on when Krishna appears, but seems to have no ties to the story. Indeed, the questions then arise of who is the sorcerer in this situation, and who is the apprentice? Which character is learning something from the other? The question is more about power: Who has more? Is it Miss Matt, whose ownership of the space and whose violence and actions that seem overwrought give her legitimacy? Or is it Krishna, the destroying force whose authority seems to come from the ability to cause harm and to impotently invoke her absent mother and most-likely dead father? In naming the story vaguely, and by having the title be a reference to a piece of music, Jackson is adding depth to the text. Both pieces of music referenced at the beginning of the story are important: "The Afternoon of the Faun" and "The Sorcerer's Apprentice" are both "programmatic music," or music that is meant to evoke emotions while also being accompanied by a text.[34] The musical score was based on a ballad by Goethe of the same name, whose first stanza is as follows: "Gone's for once the old magician / With his countenance forbidding; / I'm now master, / I'm tactician, / All his ghosts must do my bidding. / Know his incantation, / Spell and gestures too; / By my mind's creation / Wonders shall I do."[35] Knowing this, the question then becomes, indeed, what wonders *did* Miss Matt or Krishna accomplish? Both Krishna and Miss Matt are unmoored: Miss Matt is an independent, unmarried woman, and Krishna operates seemingly on her own. The wonders that are wrought, then, are left off the page. Is it magic, indeed, to spy on this destruction? Is it sorcery to take a certain joy in Miss Matt's turmoil? It seems so.

Miss Matt is ruined by her own actions; Louisa's ultimate abandonment by her parents cuts deeper than her original disappearance; Miss Strangeworth's roses are forever turned static as annihilated symbols of unnecessary meddling; Mrs. Smith is observed, whether she consents or not. For Shirley Jackson, a house is not a home, and a space belonging to someone does not mean that someone belongs in the space—it is a core American anxiety, and Jackson imbues each of her works with the destabilizing realization that what was once deemed safe is anything but. The construction of domestic spaces in Jackson's works falls on women's shoulders, and it is often other women who, in turn, undermine and destroy those spaces. While some theorists, like Whittier and others, may read Jackson's works as antifeminist, this chapter highlights how Jackson provides both a means of escape for her female readers, while also reminding them of the realities of living in a hegemonic, patriarchal system. No matter what they do, their safety and security depend on the complicity of those around them to maintain that normalcy. Jackson shifts the central question from asking what these women did, to asking the uncomfortable question of why the destruction of these women is so enthralling.

These stories escalate societal dangers while relying more heavily on the perception of protection via domestic spaces. For Miss Strangeworth, who determines that she owns the town, any decisions made are within her purview. This misperception leads to her carelessness and to her eventual punishment. Louisa expects to be able to rejoin the society that she abandons; that act of abandonment is revisited on her by her mother, and the sting is so much worse than Louisa's original betrayal, an act that is so much more than a social cut. Louisa is transformed into a different person by her rejection of her assumed domesticity and her creation of her own social and personal spaces. Miss Matt expects her home to be a space of her own, but it is invaded and invalidated by a girl who represents so much more than simply being "evil." These stories, taken together, produce a narrative that shows not just Jackson's own anxieties about living in a pre-1970s America, but also her anxieties about being a woman in a house. At every turn in Jackson's fiction, the sanctity of personal space is interrupted and violated. These repeated interruptions and violations within these stories suggest that women's places in society are malleable and that dominant cultural and social hegemonic structures are integral to the consumption and reproduction of these destabilizing societal forces for both female characters and female readers.

Notes

1 Shirley Jackson, "The Honeymoon of Mrs. Smith," in *Dark Tales* (New York: Penguin, 2017), 41–52.
2 Ibid., 47.
3 Ibid., 41.
4 Ibid., 45.
5 Judith Butler, "Performative Acts and Gender Constitution: An Essay in Phenomenology and Feminist Theory." *Theatre Journal*, 40, no. 4 (December 1988): 519–31 (accessed April 2, 2008). www.jstor.org/stable/3207893.
6 Shirley Jackson, "The Possibility of Evil," in *Dark Tales* (New York: Penguin, 2017), 1–11.

7   Ibid., 1.
8   Ibid., 7.
9   Ibid., 11 (emphasis in the original).
10 John G. Parks, "The Possibility of Evil: A Key to Shirley Jackson's Fiction." *Studies in Short Fiction*, 15, no. 3 (Summer 1978): 322 (emphasis in the original).
11 Ibid., 321.
12 Ibid.
13 Shirley Jackson, "Louisa, Please Come Home," in *Dark Tales* (New York: Penguin, 2017) 12–29.
14 Gayle Whittier, "'The Lottery' as Misogynist Parable." *Women's Studies*, 18, no. 4 (January 1991): 353 (accessed September 8, 2018).
15 Ibid., 354.
16 Ottessa Moshfegh, "Forward," in *Dark Tales* (New York: Penguin, 2017), x.
17 Jackson, "Louisa," 13.
18 Ibid., 17.
19 Ibid., 22.
20 Michel Foucault, "Panopticism: from *Discipline & Punish: The Birth of the Prison*," trans. Alan Sheridan. *Race/Ethnicity: Multidisciplinary Global Contexts*, 2, no. 1 (Autumn 2008): 7.
21 Jackson, "Louisa," 29.
22 Shirley Jackson, "The Sorcerer's Apprentice," in *Dark Tales* (New York: Penguin, 2017), 61–7. Note: This is the second time the text has been printed.
23 Ibid., 61.
24 Ibid.
25 Ibid., 64.
26 Ibid., 65–7.
27 Ibid., 62.
28 Ibid., 63.
29 Ibid., 64.
30 Ibid., 65–6.
31 Edward Said, *Orientalism* (London: Routledge & Kegan Paul, 1978).
32 Jackson, "Apprentice," 66.
33 Ibid., 67.
34 Carolyn Abbate, "What the Sorcerer Said." *19th-Century Music*, 2, no. 3 (Spring 1989): 221–30 (accessed January 2, 2019). www.jstor.org/stable/746503.
35 Johann Wolfgang von Goethe, "The Sorcerer's Apprentice," trans. Paul Dyrsen. 1878. https://germanstories.vcu.edu/goethe/zauber_e4.html.

References

Abbate, Carolyn. "What the Sorcerer Said." *19th-Century Music*, 12, no. 3 (Spring 1989): 221–30 (accessed January 2, 2019). www.jstor.org/stable/746503.

Butler, Judith. "Performative Acts and Gender Constitution: An Essay in Phenomenology and Feminist Theory." *Theatre Journal*, 40, no. 4 (December 1988): 519–31 (accessed April 2, 2008). www.jstor.org/stable/3207893.

Foucault, Michel. "Panopticism: From *Discipline & Punish: The Birth of the Prison*," trans. Alan Sheridan. *Race/Ethnicity: Multidisciplinary Global Contexts*, 2, no. 1 (Autumn 2008): 1–12.

Goethe, Johann Wolfgang von. "The Sorcerer's Apprentice," trans. Paul Dyrsen. 1878. https://germanstories.vcu.edu/goethe/zauber_e4.html.

Jackson, Shirley. *Dark Tales*. New York: Penguin Classics, 2017.

Jackson, Shirley. "Louisa, Please Come Home," in *Dark Tales*, 12–29. New York: Penguin, 2017.

Jackson, Shirley. "The Honeymoon of Mrs. Smith," in *Dark Tales*, 41–52. New York: Penguin, 2017.

Jackson, Shirley. "The Possibility of Evil," in *Dark Tales*, 1–11. New York: Penguin, 2017.

Jackson, Shirley. "The Sorcerer's Apprentice," in *Dark Tales*, 61–7. New York: Penguin, 2017.

Moshfegh, Ottessa. "Forward," in *Dark Tales*, vii–x. New York: Penguin, 2017.

Parks, John G. "The Possibility of Evil: A Key to Shirley Jackson's Fiction." *Studies in Short Fiction*, 15, no. 3 (Summer 1978): 320–3. EBSCOhost, ebscohost.com/login.aspx? direct=true&db=aph&AN=7133425&site=ehost-live.

Said, Edward. *Orientalism*. London: Routledge & Kegan Paul. 1978.

Whittier, Gayle. "'The Lottery' as Misogynist Parable." *Women's Studies*, 18, no. 4 (January 1991): 353 (accessed September 8, 2018). EBSCOhost, ebscohost.com/login.aspx? direct=true&db=aph&AN=5808719&site=ehost-live.

4

"Sharp Points Closing in on Her Throat": The Domestic Gothic in Shirley Jackson's Short Fiction

L. N. Rosales

When the familiar is invaded, when it is made somehow unfamiliar, when it becomes a trap rather than a comfort, we find ourselves—as characters in Shirley Jackson's short stories frequently do—in a particular kind of gothic situation. I refer to these situations as occurrences of the domestic gothic. A true domestic gothic narrative places the action in settings as recognizable to readers as their own homes, subverting the ordinary by uncovering the possibility of terror within the everyday domestic sphere. The domestic gothic is characterized by domestic invasion, often committed by uncanny characters who grotesquely distort our expectations of what they are supposed to be—frequently (and most perversely perhaps) in the figure of one's own child. Moreover, the domestic gothic exhibits victims trapped in horrifyingly awkward, impossible situations that expose their anxieties of helplessness and ineptitude.

Often these fears of ineptitude are specifically tied to the dread of domestic failure, reflecting the intense pressure on women to thrive in that sphere in midcentury America. Like classic gothic, the domestic gothic preys upon our fears of the unknown. However, the unknown is no longer displayed metaphorically by dark hallways or foggy moors, but, instead, it exists situationally, as characters are uncomfortably at a loss as how to proceed, avoid, or even to escape. Diana Wallace and Andrew Smith describe "the Female Gothic as a politically subversive genre articulating women's dissatisfactions with patriarchal structures and offering a coded expression of their fears of entrapment within the domestic and the female body."[1] This tradition in particular truly permeates the domestic gothic. In the stories I examine in this chapter, Jackson utilizes the gothic mode to critique mid-twentieth-century idealized visions of domesticity. By reshaping the domestic as a frightening—rather than a comforting and familiar—sphere, she highlights the perilousness of the cult of domesticity prized at that time.

Critics have remarked extensively on Jackson's use of the domestic. The nonfiction domestic stories, appearing in women's magazines like *Good Housekeeping*, have been the focus of a few studies.[2] Though this chapter focuses on the fictional portrayals of domesticity, it is productive to acknowledge the thematic overlap with her autobiographical works. In both genres, a discerning reader can detect what S. T. Joshi labels "disturbing undercurrents,"[3] and these undercurrents are an integral component of Jackson's "critique of the era's domestic ideology," which are, Bernice M. Murphy touts, "almost always present."[4] Such undercurrents also inform a reading of Jackson's work as gothic. Indeed, Jackson's relationship to the gothic has not gone unnoticed.[5] However, the associations of Jackson with the gothic are largely limited to the novels, especially *The Haunting of Hill House* (1959) and *We Have Always Lived in the Castle* (1962). Occasionally, critics will label a stray short story here and there as gothic[6]—for example, in her comprehensive study of Jackson's short fiction, Joan Wylie Hall describes "The Visit" as adhering so closely to the gothic convention of the haunted mansion that the "decorating scheme [is] worthy of Poe."[7] Hall also designates "The Rock" and "The Bus" as particularly gothic stories, recounting how each "again centers in a single woman's visit to an isolated house that entraps her."[8] Domestic spaces, as Hall's analysis demonstrates, have long provided the setting for gothic novels. However, while she identifies the classic gothic trope of young women visiting foreign, unknown domestic spaces, I am interested more specifically in the gothic situations that occur within a *familiar* domestic context.

In this examination, I focus on stories from the collection *The Lottery and Other Stories* (1949), though an extended consideration of *Come Along with Me* (1968) and the uncollected short fiction would undoubtedly be appropriate in a larger project. The first story in the collection, "The Intoxicated," is not as blatantly gothic as some of the other texts I will address, but it does introduce several of the tropes and themes that can be found in those tales. When a nameless guest at a cocktail party escapes from the festivities in the living room into the kitchen, he has an unexpected and unnerving encounter with the hosts' high-school-aged daughter, Eileen. Eileen is an uncanny character in that she drastically—even grotesquely—garbles the familiar stereotype of a high school girl. The partygoer thinks, "In my day ... girls thought of nothing but cocktails and necking"[9] and wonders if he should "ask her about boys? basketball?"[10] He becomes increasingly horrified at how drastically Eileen differs from his assumptions after he asks an innocuous question about her homework. Eileen reveals that she is writing an essay on "the future of the world"—and her vision of that future is one of apocalyptic proportions, complete with churches, apartment buildings and schools crumbling, subway trains crashing through the ground, and newspaper stalls overturning in the streets.[11] Though the guest makes multiple attempts to assert his authority and dismiss her predictions as childish, it is Eileen who remains calm, cool, and articulate, while he becomes sullen and resentful. This absurd reversal of roles upsets the guest, who hasn't been able to appear as he intended; he admits defeat and exits the kitchen, self-conscious that he has allowed himself to become ruffled.

The guest's retreat into the kitchen was meant to be just that—a retreat. His expectations of safety are utterly undermined as he lands in a verbal battle, resulting in a coolly delivered premonition of his own demise ("'I see,' he said. 'I go with the rest. I see'").[12] Ironically, when he escapes this frightening situation, he passes a cheerful group at a piano who are singing "Home on the Range." But there is nothing to celebrate in *this* domestic situation: the man has experienced nothing homely in this story. The setting paints a familiar picture as the hostess speaks "earnestly" with one man, and small groups cluster, either standing around the piano singing or sitting in fashionable but "stiff" chairs, deep in serious conversation.[13] There is even a "good spot" for his glass on the patterned kitchen table, as if to suggest that everything is in its right place.[14] But Eileen's dark portents subvert this supposition in an encounter that is sprinkled with a hint of the gothic, trapping the unsuspecting partygoer in her sinister speculations, regardless of the comfortable and coordinated kitchen furnishings.

The disturbing and uncanny child is a recurring figure in Jackson's short fiction. "The Witch" depicts a young boy on a train with his mother and baby sister whose fanciful comments about seeing a witch are encouraged and even extended by an old man passing through the carriage. Though this story is set in a train rather than a private home, the familiar situation of the young family on the suburban commute can be considered an extension of the domestic. The young mother, her 4-year old son, and baby daughter form a domestic unit in transit; the old man, in sitting down next to Johnny, disrupts that unit and, eventually, threatens it. There is a subtle sense of foreboding in the unsteady baby, who, despite being "strapped securely to the seat"[15] repeatedly slips sideways and requires swift repositioning; in a prescient moment of chaos, she "fell over too far sideways and banged her head"[16] and, subsequently, bursts into a cacophony of tears. It is after this (literally) unsettling incident that Johnny transitions from the usual observations ("We're on a river," "We're on a bridge over a river," "There's a cow")[17] to the more macabre—"I saw a witch ... There was a big old ugly old bad old witch outside."[18] The mother largely ignores him, and he continues to create a narrative about the witch until the old man enters the coach. Described as having "a pleasant face" and wearing a "blue suit [that] was only faintly touched by the disarray that comes with a long train trip,"[19] the man does not seem sinister. The mother does not even look up from her book as the boy informs the man that he is looking for "Witches ... Bad old mean witches."[20] She only intervenes when the young boy wildly lies about his age and his name, as if the only threat is this farcical misinformation. When the man seats himself next to her son, the mother does look up "anxiously," but returns "peacefully back to her book" when he innocently offers to tell Johnny about his own little sister.[21]

But, as in "The Intoxicated," events take an unexpected turn. "I loved her more than anything else in the world," the man says, but then he continues: "I bought her a rocking-horse and a doll and a million lollipops ... and then I took her and I put my hands around her neck and I pinched her and I pinched her until she was dead ... And then I took and I cut her head off and I took her head—."[22] Though the mother is shocked and appalled—so shocked that she opens and closes her mouth, speechless—Johnny is enthralled. "Did you cut her all in pieces?" he asks "breathlessly."[23] Seemingly encouraged, the man proceeds, "I cut off her head and her hands and her feet and her hair and her nose ... and I hit her with a stick and I killed her ... And I put her head in a cage with a bear and the bear ate it all up."[24] At this point, the mother has found her voice and crosses the aisle to demand his departure. She appears to be the only character who judges anything to be amiss, though. The old man looks up at her "courteously" and asks, "Did I frighten you?"[25] Yet, even as he politely appeals to her, the man conspiratorially nudges Johnny with his elbow, and they both laugh. She cuts an increasingly ridiculous figure when she threatens to call the conductor, and her son chimes in, "The conductor will *eat* my mommy ... We'll chop her head off."[26] As the man departs, both he and the young boy laugh, and then, courteous until the end, he says, "Excuse me" to the mother and exits the carriage.[27]

The mother finds herself at a loss. She seems paralyzed; she stands motionless, "wanting to say something" about the encounter, but unable to find the words.[28] She settles on handing Johnny another lollipop, a gesture toward the previous peaceful picture of domesticity, a drive to return to normal. When her son asks if the man had really dismembered his little sister, the mother "urgently" repeats herself twice, "He was just teasing ... Just *teasing*."[29] She is trying to convince herself as well as Johnny, who is not in the least disturbed. He returns to looking out the window and has the last word in the story: "Prob'ly he was a witch."[30] In this tale, the mother is powerless, and like a classic gothic victim, she is trapped and stripped of her agency. It does not matter that the man left the carriage at her prompting, because the interaction still haunts her. She easily dismissed

Johnny's earlier prattle about witches, but due to the alacrity with which he questioned the man about the gruesome details of his sister's death and subsequent mutilation, his preoccupation appears in a much different light. Moreover, the lighthearted politeness of the man undercuts her authority throughout. He never seems vicious; she is the one who intensifies the moment by taking his words seriously and becoming alarmed. Her son, of course, does not *actually* feel glee at the thought of decapitating his mother. She appears absurd for becoming distraught. Johnny even makes fun of her when he tells the man, "My mommy will eat *you*."[31] She cannot gracefully recover from the proceedings and is trapped both with her son who seems to delight in suggestive violence and within the persona she has inadvertently created, that of a mother who let the ramblings of a 6-year-old and the polite elderly man who humored him cause her distress. Johnny appears uncanny, switching suddenly from the innocent little boy delighting in a lollipop to a person who is excited at the prospect of chopping a little girl's head into pieces. Assuredly, his mother will not look at him the same way again for some time—and the reader, too, is inevitably unsettled by the rapid tonal shift, the subverted image of the innocent (though bored) child.

Appearing just after "The Witch" in the collection, "The Renegade" repeats the gothic image of the child startlingly enthusiastic at the suggestion of violence. In this story, a young housewife's already hectic day is thrown into further and more threatening disarray when she receives a call from a neighbor accusing her family's dog, Lady, of killing a neighbor's chickens. The aptly named Mrs. Walpole (recalling that eighteenth-century author of classically gothic texts, Horace Walpole) answers the phone "forbiddingly."[32] Unable to make out the woman's name, she seems to be receiving the ominous communication from a nebulous unknown source that the narrator paints as increasingly villainous. After the caller accuses Lady of killing her chickens, the narrator reports, "The voice sounded satisfied now; Mrs. Walpole had been cornered."[33] Then the woman goes on to detail the circumstances surrounding the chickens' demise "with relish," as if enjoying the position in which she has entrapped her neighbor. Her glee seems particularly menacing when she reveals that she doesn't require financial compensation of any kind, but instead demands, "You'll have to do something about the dog."[34] The vague "something" echoes the almost sinister fogginess of her undisclosed identity. Mrs. Walpole doesn't know with whom exactly she is in combat; she only knows that "her morning had gone badly, she had not yet had her coffee, she was faced with an evil situation she had never known before,"[35] and, as her husband waves "briefly"[36] to her on his way out the door, she is in this situation alone.

Ironically Mrs. Walpole's feelings of isolation increase exponentially when she leaves the house. First, she already feels deeply insecure about her status as a former city dweller newly living in the country. Lady's escapade has only further contributed to this anxiety. Ruefully, she reflects how her family would always be the kind of "people who owned a chicken-killing dog, people who washed on Tuesday,"[37] and is "painfully aware of her own kitchen with the dirty dishes in the sink"[38] when she visits Mrs. Nash next door. She watches her fry doughnuts in a "shockingly clean housedress,"[39] and frets, as if her inability to preemptively control Lady is simply another domestic failing. As she walks into town to get a new chain for her dog, the man who first identified the dog as the culprit, Mr. White, "grinned broadly and shouted to her, 'Guess you're not going to have any more dog.'"[40] His uncomfortably inappropriate enthusiasm for the impending doom of the dog is reminiscent of that of the woman on the phone, and the same attitude follows Mrs. Walpole into the general store downtown. The grocer and the man chatting with him laugh uproariously when they warn her that someone is liable to "put a load of buckshot" into Lady if she is allowed to roam freely, killing chickens willy-nilly.[41] They laugh, too, at the idea of a frenzied mother hen pecking Lady's eyes out, and Mrs. Walpole begins to feel so faint that she must leave the store and retreat home to lie down. Her shame has followed her through the town, and everyone from whom she has earnestly sought advice has responded with malice and cruelty. None of the men she encounters have any sympathy for the dog or imagine her as an entity of any significance; they even repeatedly refer to the dog as "him" despite her having the most clearly feminine name imaginable. If it is a domestic failing for Mrs. Walpole to even own poor Lady, she feels further alienated by the marked contrast between her own feelings to those of the villagers.

But more disturbing than the reactions of her neighbors or the townspeople are those of her children, come home for lunch. The children are full of noise and energy, excitedly interrupting each other with the news of Lady's imminent doom. Judy addresses Lady directly, "You're going to get shot," and deflects her mother's solemn chastisement, "She *is*, Mom."[42] Jack then fights her to describe the particularly violent alternative suggested to them by Mr. Shepherd, "a genial man who lived near the Walpoles and gave their children nickels and took the boys fishing":[43]

"But the spikes ... Tell about the spikes."

"The *spikes* ... Listen, Mommy. He says you got to get a collar for Lady ..."

"A strong collar," Judy said.

"And you get big thick nails, like spikes, and you hammer them into the collar."

"All around," Judy said. "Let *me* tell it, Jack. You hammer these nails all around so's they make spikes inside the collar."

"But it's loose," Jack said. "Let *me* tell this part."[44]

The children go on to explain how a long rope is tied to this contraption and that, when Lady tries to chase chickens, a tug on the rope counter to her swift movement in the other direction would, in effect, decapitate her. They are both thrilled with this notion, which is, in itself, disturbing enough. However, what is most unnerving about the scene is the uncanny juxtaposition of the children's wildly violent narrative with their clear fondness for the dog. Even as Jack explains, "Then we put this real sharp spiky collar around your neck," he kisses the top of Lady's head while she regards him "affectionately."[45] Jack's loving gesture is not compatible with the glee he exudes when describing Lady's hypothetical gruesome death. The contrast is humorously grotesque, given its inappropriateness. Though Mrs. Walpole tries to persuade herself, "Children don't realize ... death is never real to them," her sensible thought is overpowered by the threatening unruliness of the children.[46] While she speaks to them "quietly," the children sit down "noisily"; they don't simply eat their lunch, as they are depicted as "attacking their food."[47] They laugh at the thought that "the spikes cut her head right off" and even Lady, "looking from one to the other, panted as though she were laughing too."[48] Overwhelmed, Mrs. Walpole looks away from them, outside. Yet, despite the view of everything "quiet and lovely in the sunlight, the peaceful sky, the gentle line of hills," she is unable to recover herself.[49] The story ends as "Mrs. Walpole closed her eyes, suddenly feeling the harsh hands pulling her down, the sharp points closing in on her throat."[50]

The ending is a testament to Mrs. Walpole's domestic gothic entrapment. She identifies with Lady, feeling as though everyone in the town—even those in her own family—are against her. She is boxed into an impossible situation. How does she keep the beloved family dog safe and, likewise, placate her new neighbors? Mrs. Walpole is also trapped in another sense. The story ends with her violently claustrophobic vision; it begins with the frantic morning machinations of the housewife. She "had only had time to pour herself a glass of fruit juice and no time to drink it," as she repeatedly urges her children to eat their breakfasts before the bus arrives.[51] Even as they rush out the door, she is already clearing their meal and serving her husband's. She knows "she would have to have breakfast herself later."[52] She is an afterthought even to herself. She "made an effort" to cheerfully greet Mr. Walpole and "patiently" sets his food before him, but he says "'Morning,' without glancing up" and "devoted himself" to his newspaper instead.[53] Even before the crisis of Lady's predicament is introduced, Mrs. Walpole is trapped in the domestic sphere, trapped in the idea of what a housewife is supposed to be. She is a gothic victim of the pervading social expectations of the time in which she lives, constantly and helplessly reflecting on her own struggle to function as seemingly ceaselessly as those around her.

The story "Charles" paints another picture of a weird child and entrapped mother. Laurie starts kindergarten, and when he arrives home, he is full of stories, on this day and each day following, about another boy in his class named Charles. Charles misbehaves extensively. His initial sins range from being "awfully fresh"[54] to "pounding his feet on the floor,"[55] but he becomes increasingly and disturbingly violent. According to Laurie, Charles "hit the teacher" and "bounced a see-saw on to the head of a little girl and made her bleed."[56] In one week, Charles seems to have reformed, but then he tricks a girl into saying a very naughty word and appears to be up to his old tricks again by the time the narrator, Laurie's mother, makes it to a PTA meeting and decides to scope out Charles' mother. However, when she asks the kindergarten teacher about Charles, the teacher reveals that there is no child named Charles in the class.

In "Charles" the domestic gothic is most clearly located in the uncanny threat of Laurie, who is the epitome of the familiar become unfamiliar. The story opens with the narrator-mother reflecting that she does not recognize the school-bound son leaving the house for the first time—she does not recognize him because he is symbolically grown up (or at least, grown older), and wears a different manner of clothing. But, as the story unfolds, she recognizes him less and less until, at the climax, she realizes that she does not know him at all. At home, Laurie begins to spew purposely bad grammar and disrespectful language; he says, "I didn't learn nothing,"[57] "Hi, Pop, y'old dust mop,"[58] and even once "began to laugh insanely"[59] after tricking his father into gullibly looking up, down, and then at his thumb. In retrospect, the reader sees these moments as indications of what's to come in the conclusion—Laurie is not exactly innocent. But the mother misreads these signs. For the larger course of the story, it is Charles who is an outside threat, though he does begin to invade the domestic space. Not only does every day bring fresh news of Charles's deeds and subsequent punishment, but, as the mother observes to the reader, "With the third week of kindergarten Charles was an institution in our family."[60] Even her husband, caught by the telephone cord and upsetting the items from atop a table, remarks, "Looks like Charles."[61] As it turns out, though, "Charles" was always already in the house. Laurie is the true threat. His easy lies, raucous disruptions, and delight in performing and reporting violence seem especially sinister in the expected innocence and childlike veneer of the kindergartner, and for the mother, exponentially so, as she gave birth to and raised him. How could someone that quite literally came from herself, be so utterly foreign?

In these stories, children are cast as uncanny aliens who reconfigure the familiar landscape of the home as a gothic setting, threatening its reliability and comfort. Characters are trapped in the situations created by these dark children, who transform the domestic into the macabre. Other stories threaten the security of the home differently, though the sense of invasion and entrapment remain the same. Most frequently discussed in this sense is "Like Mother Used to Make," a story in which a man who is obsessively domestic becomes displaced from his own home when the overtly masculine woman from down the hall comes over for dinner. She surreptitiously steals his apartment from him when she invites a male coworker inside and allows him to mistake the apartment for her own in a situation that might be comic if it weren't so utterly discomfiting.

The story opens with David Turner rushing home after work, trying to remember what he needed from the grocery on the corner: "Butter, he remembered with relief; this morning, all the way up the avenue to his bus stop, he had been telling himself butter, don't forget butter coming home tonight, when you pass the grocery remember butter."[62] The harried single-minded pursuit of the butter emphasizes its importance to David, who leaves the shop thinking that he really must find a new grocery, one where the clerks are more polite. He enters his apartment:

> Tonight, as every night when he came home, the apartment looked warm and friendly and good; the little foyer, with the neat small table and four careful chairs, and the bowl of little marigolds against the pale green walls ... beyond, the kitchenette, and beyond that, the big room where David read and slept and the ceiling of which was a perpetual trouble to him; the plaster was falling in one corner and no power on earth could make it less noticeable. David consoled himself for the plaster constantly.[63]

This passage aptly sets the domestic scene. David loves his apartment to an extent that "every night" it always looks "warm and friendly and good" to him. His table is specifically "neat" and the chairs are "careful"; he has arranged his space just so and is evidently preoccupied with keeping it that way. The reader can sense that for David, the stakes are very high with regard to the domestic space. The ceiling of his bedroom is "a perpetual trouble to him." It is not simply inconvenient that the plaster is falling, or unappetizing to the eye, but it is an unending problem that actually haunts him. That "no power on earth could make it less noticeable" suggests that David has gone to extreme lengths, as hyperbolic as the phrasing, to right this great wrong of his living space. The big room has been painstakingly arranged and decorated, because "he had always been partial to yellows and browns, ... he had painted the desk and the bookcases and the end tables himself, had even painted the walls, and had hunted around the city for the exact tweedish tan drapes he had in mind."[64] David lives for the domestic. His keenest desire is to obtain "a low translucent green bowl for more marigolds."[65]

The story foregrounds his love for his living space so that the reader can understand the true horror of its later invasion. When David begins to make dinner, we learn that he even coordinated the color of his plates with the couch cover. The feelings David experiences as he prepares the meal are described as almost hyperbolically good ones: "He settled down *happily* to making dinner"; "it was *pleasant* to him to arrange a salad"; "with his dinner cooking *agreeably*"; "he set *lovingly* to arranging his table."[66] David is not trapped by his domestic duties; he glories in them. Perhaps David is able to enjoy domesticity to such a degree precisely because it is his choice—and not a socially prescribed one—to excel in it.

The exaggerated extent to which he loves the domestic can also be read as a critique; the reader cannot imagine any person so adoringly performing domestic labor, and yet so many women were expected to do just that. David's genuine tenderness for homemaking parodies the attitude required of women at the time. Of all things, his silverware is his pride and joy. The narrator reveals:

> Gradually, tenderly, David was buying himself a complete set of silverware ... each morning, he gloried in a breakfast that started with a shining silver spoon for his grapefruit, and had a compact butter knife for his toast and a solid heavy knife to break his egg-shell, and a fresh silver spoon for his coffee, which he sugared with a particular spoon meant only for sugar.[67]

David lives alone; his tenderness is reserved for his silverware collection. He glories in his breakfast every morning, not because of the food, but because he utilizes highly specific utensils as part of his routine. These routines and the precision and familiarity of his space are precious to David. This is emphasized when the narrator explains that David has a key to Marcia's apartment, but she does not have a key to his, as "it pleased him to have only one key to his home, and that safely in his own pocket; it had a pleasant feeling to him, solid and small, the only way into his warm fine home."[68] The irony is that by the end of the tale, having only one literal key to his home will not keep it safe from trespass. As it turns out, there is more than one way to obtain admission. Though he invites Marcia over for dinner, it is without his consent that *she* invites her colleague inside, offers him pie, and allows him to believe that *she* is the hostess.

Marcia is David's complete opposite. Her apartment is "not agreeable for him to come into" as it is "bare and at random" and also "too cluttered."[69] Like her apartment, Marcia herself is rather chaotic. She arrives to dinner late with "a shout ... and disorder."[70] The evening takes a sudden turn when Marcia invites her coworker, Mr. Harris, into David's apartment. She takes control of the situation by suggesting that David serve Mr. Harris a cup of coffee and a slice of homemade pie—she even hints untruthfully that she made the pie. Though "David raised a hand to protest,"[71] he is impotent to reverse the course of events; he begins to panic, feeling "an urgency to be rid of them."[72] He becomes a stranger in his own home, standing awkwardly like a third wheel at someone else's dinner engagement. When Marcia urges him to sit down, "David recognized her tone; it was the one hostesses used when they didn't know what else to say to you, or when you had come too early or stayed too late."⁷³ He is robbed of his agency when he observes, "It was the tone he had expected to use on Mr. Harris."⁷⁴ When he stands up to reclaim his domestic authority, he finds himself instead announcing his intention to depart. He is utterly defeated, shaking Mr. Harris's hand "limply" and speaking "much more genially than he intended," as if he cannot even control what comes out of his own mouth.⁷⁵ The story ends with David "miserably" looking around Marcia's grossly unkempt apartment, just able to catch the sound of the traitor and the intruder listening to "his radio" as he begins to pick up the papers littering Marcia's floor.⁷⁶ David has become trapped in a situation that he can only perpetuate, not escape. His safe domestic space is invaded, and he loses it in a battle he is too polite to fight.

"Trial by Combat" features another protagonist paralyzed by politeness, overcome by a more courageously crass adversary. This story depicts a young woman, Emily Johnson, who discovers that one of her neighbors is removing small items from her apartment. She is unable to bluntly accuse the woman to her face and is caught when she tries to steal the items back. The story ends with her defeat. She retreats to her rooms knowing that Mrs. Allen will continue to invade her space. Emily, like David Turner in "Like Mother Used to Make," becomes entrapped within a bizarre but frightening situation. Once she discovers the identity of the thief, "she had hesitated about complaining to the landlady because her losses were trivial and because she had felt certain that sooner or later she would know how to deal with the situation herself."⁷⁷ Emily does not want to seem either ridiculous or helpless to her landlady. Like Mrs. Walpole, she desires to be seen as domestically competent. She is "certain" that she can take care of the matter, but, at the end of the story, it becomes clear to both Emily and the reader that this is not the case. Like David, she intends to act one way, but helplessly betrays herself. Mrs. Allen is guilty, but she still maintains control of the situation. When Emily introduces herself, Mrs. Allen responds: "'I've seen you, of course, several times, and thought how pleasant you looked. It's so seldom one meets anyone really'—Mrs. Allen hesitated—'really nice,' she went on, 'in a place like this.'"⁷⁸ Here, she flatters Emily, who also mentally bemoans "Mrs. Allen's daily view: the fire escape opposite, an oblique slice of the street below."⁷⁹ After Mrs. Allen also reveals, "I had no children, to my sorrow," Emily begins to lose sight of her adversary's guilt and instead feels sorry for her.⁸⁰ Though Emily is quite obviously in the right, she is the one speaking "pleadingly" because she cannot bring herself to confront "a nice old lady."⁸¹ But Mrs. Allen is a grotesquely twisted version of the nice old lady stereotype. Like the discomfiting uncanny children found in previously discussed stories, her inappropriate behavior is all the more unsettling (and gothic) because it does not fit the image projected. When Emily is caught rooting through Mrs. Allen's drawers for her belongings, she is painfully aware of her own wrongdoing and experiences an eerie role reversal that makes her unrecognizable to herself. On the one hand, she feels unendurably sorry for Mrs. Allen when she sees the old photograph of her handsome, now dead husband: "They must have had such a pleasant life together, and now she has a room like mine, with only two handkerchiefs of her own in the drawer."[82] But, on the other hand, she is also taken aback by Mrs. Allen's unflinchingly polite behavior, thinking, "What does she want me to say … What could she be waiting for with such a ladylike manner?"[83]

Emily is defeated neatly and quietly, returning to her apartment nursing her faked headache with Mrs. Allen's promise (or, perhaps *threat*) to "run up later" to check on her. In addition to the horror of being powerless against Mrs. Allen, the uncanny resemblances between the two apartments and their inhabitants further contribute to the gothic feel of the story.[84] When Emily first visits Mrs. Allen, she notices, "The room … was almost like her own—the same narrow bed with the tan cover, the same maple dresser and armchair; the closet was on the opposite side of the room, but the window was in the same relative position."[85] If rooms are revealing of those who reside within them, the cookie-cutter layout and the carbon copy furniture remind Emily that she is not as different from this older woman as she might imagine. At the beginning of their first encounter, Emily lightly remarks, "I feel as if I know the furniture so well. Mine's just the same."[86] But during her trespassing return, she "had a sudden sense of unbearable intimacy with Mrs. Allen, and thought, This is the way she must feel in my room."[87] One of the reasons that she cannot bring herself to explicitly accuse her foe is that she has begun to see herself in Mrs. Allen: an uncanny experience.

Domestic invasion takes on another form in "Men with Their Big Shoes." In this story, a young and very pregnant housewife, Mrs. Hart, finds herself completely at the mercy of the older woman who cleans the house, Mrs. Anderson. Like Mrs. Walpole in "The Renegade," Mrs. Hart has newly relocated from the city to the country. The first line of the story emphasizes just how unfamiliar this territory is to Mrs. Hart: "It was young Mrs. Hart's first summer living in the country, and her first year being married and the mistress of a house; she was going to have her first baby soon, and it was the first time she had ever had anyone … who could remotely be described as a maid."[88] Though the narrator describes her initially as a woman who, based on all of these promising "firsts" spends hours each day "congratulating herself,"[89] Mrs. Hart will end the story "with a sudden unalterable conviction that she was lost."[90] The mitigating factor in this transformation is Mrs. Anderson. Mrs. Hart has always felt "unreasonably afraid of Mrs. Anderson"[91] but originally dismisses her instincts because "she had heard and read so much about how all housewives these days were intimidated by their domestic help."[92] Like Mrs. Walpole, she desperately wants to appear domestically accomplished. Unfortunately, her feelings were prescient: "By the time Mrs. Hart discovered that Mrs. Anderson never got anything quite clean, never completely managed to get anything back where it belonged, it was incredible to think of doing anything about it."[93] Thus, Mrs. Anderson inserts herself into the household. It is simply too late to be rid of her politely.

Moreover, Mrs. Anderson expertly manipulates Mrs. Hart in an unceasing power struggle. She toots the horn of her own niceness, protesting in response to Mrs. Hart's insincere paeans, "I'm only thinking of you ... I don't want thanks ... You just come through all right, that's all I want to see."[94] But she also paints herself as a victim, deserving of Mrs. Hart's deepest sympathies. The relationship between Mrs. Anderson and her husband is intensely strained, and she remarks offhandedly, "I wish *I* could be cheerful these days," before beginning an uncomfortably intimate narrative about her husband's cursing and yelling, his demands that she leave the house.[95]

The awkwardness that Mrs. Hart feels in this situation is, however, nothing compared to the horror she begins to experience when Mrs. Anderson begins to make insinuations against her husband, Mr. Hart. When she insists that Bill is not a heavy drinker, Mrs. Anderson asks about other women—"Is *that* what it is?"—as if, surely, there must be something the matter with Mrs. Hart's marriage.[96] Poor Mrs. Hart becomes trapped in a conversation she never desired to have, and in which she is not permitted to truly participate. Though she denies that her husband is likely to chase other women, Mrs. Anderson dismisses her trust cruelly, reminding her, "You only been married a year ... and no one that's older around to tell you."[97] She seems to take a perverse pleasure in informing Mrs. Hart of the probable infidelity of her husband, going so far as to suggest that Mrs. Martin at the grocery has been asking questions. She "grimly" says, "You just don't want to let her figure out anything's wrong," and talks over Mrs. Hart's protestations that there *isn't* anything wrong: "I *told* her ... I said I was sure Mr. Hart never did any running around's far as I knew ... I said I felt like you might be my own daughter sometimes and no man was going to mistreat you while I was around."[98] Mrs. Hart is lost for words, partly because of the condescending reference to her as being like Mrs. Anderson's "own daughter," but also largely because of the fear that her neighbors are gossiping about her marriage.

Mrs. Hart—again, like Mrs. Walpole—greatly values what other people think. It is this facet of her character that most allows Mrs. Anderson to triumph. When Mrs. Anderson repeats the grocer's suggestion that she move in with the Harts, Mrs. Hart does her best to make polite, amiable excuses about why this would not work. But Mrs. Anderson shoots them all down. When Mrs. Hart says that Mr. Hart would not allow it, she responds, "Of course not ... The men never do, do they? I told Mrs. Martin down at the grocery, she's the nicest little thing in the world, I said, but her husband wouldn't let the scrubwoman come live with them."[99] The compliment for Mrs. Hart, followed closely by the self-deprecating remark, is a perfect formula. Mrs. Hart is "horrified" that Mrs. Anderson would refer to herself in such a lowly manner. With "her fingers tight on her teacup," she imagines the grocer complimenting her and the girls back home being jealous at her letters if she *did* agree to have Mrs. Anderson move into the house.[100] She knows that it would appear to her advantage; she *wants* to be the "nicest little thing in the world" that Mrs. Anderson has publicly painted her to be. And so, by infusing herself with the perspectives of others, it is that Mrs. Hart ends the tale so utterly "lost."[101] The gothic aspects of this chilling domestic story are manifold, but perhaps the most explicit gesture toward the mode is in Mrs. Hart's loss of agency. The narrator describes her as "mistress" of her house, but the ending makes it clear that she is not in control of the domestic sphere at all. This outsider who has physically invaded her home and who has existentially invaded her perceptions of herself expertly manipulates her.

The gothic victims in these stories are variously trapped and experience unexpected horror in traditionally innocuous domestic situations. These are not young, unmarried women being kidnapped in distant European countries and imprisoned, their inheritances and virginal bodies under threat—in other words, not the victims of the classic gothic genre born in the late eighteenth century. Instead, these victims are descendants of that mode. It is not the physical body that is threatened, but rather, peace of mind. Classic gothic novels depict women who are physically trapped by literal captors, thereby making the power struggle visible; in these stories, the gothic victims are trapped in a subtler, existential sense. If a gothic heroine ultimately escapes her captors, the domestic gothic shows us characters for whom escape is impossible because the horror is in that which makes up the home. Admittedly, the situations depicted in these stories are largely ridiculous in one way, shape, or form, but they also contain elements of the sinister, making them simultaneously comic and frightening. If earlier critics failed to acknowledge the "seriousness" of Shirley Jackson's work, perhaps stories like these—as well as her similarly humorous and disturbing popular nonfiction domestic sketches—banked on their comedic value to lure unsuspecting readers into surprise cultural critiques.

Notes

1 Diana Wallace and Andrew Smith, "Introduction: Defining the Female Gothic," in *The Female Gothic: New Directions*, ed. Diana Wallace and Andrew Smith (London: Palgrave Macmillan, 2009), 1–12; 2.

2 Eunjung Hwang posits the tales as significant windows into the post–Second World War middle-class American women's experience, of a time when the cultural value of domesticity was at its peak. James Egan, in turn, suggests that Jackson, even as she paints that picture as the new normal, questions its ordinariness. Bernice Murphy, too, argues that Jackson's domestic stories challenge the very idea of there being a normal housewife.

3   S. T. Joshi, "Shirley Jackson: Domestic Horror," in *Shirley Jackson: Essays on the Literary Legacy*, ed. Bernice M. Murphy (Jefferson, NC: McFarland, 2005), 183–98;186.
4   Bernice M. Murphy, "Introduction: 'Do You Know Who I Am?': Reconsidering Shirley Jackson," in *Shirley Jackson: Essays on the Literary Legacy*, ed. Bernice M. Murphy (Jefferson, NC: McFarland, 2005), 1–21; 19.
5   In *Shirley Jackson: Essays on the Literary Legacy*, Bernice M. Murphy and John Parks both note the gothic tone of much of Jackson's fiction. In his study on Jackson and the American gothic, Daryll Hattenhauer describes many of Jackson's characters as specifically gothic victims; whereas, drawing particularly on Jackson's novels and the nonfiction domestic tales, Eunju Hwang suggests that the gothic mode works to expose midcentury middle-class women's disenchantment.
6   Roberta Rubenstein cites "The Bus" in her study of mothers and daughters and the female gothic in Jackson's work, and James Egan, too, cursorily labels "The Bus" as gothic.
7   Joan Wylie Hall, *Shirley Jackson: A Study of the Short Fiction* (New York: Twayne, 1993), 65.
8   Hall, *Shirley Jackson*, 67.
9   Jackson, "The Intoxicated," 5.
10 Ibid., 4.
11 Ibid., 5.
12 Ibid., 7.
13 Ibid., 3.
14 Ibid.
15 Ibid., 63.
16 Ibid., 64.
17 Ibid., 63.
18 Ibid., 64.
19 Ibid.
20 Ibid.
21 Ibid., 65.
22 Ibid., 66.
23 Ibid.
24 Ibid.
25 Ibid.
26 Ibid., 67 (all emphases in the original unless otherwise noted).
27 Ibid.
28 Ibid.
29 Ibid.

30 Ibid.
31 Ibid.
32 Ibid., 70.
33 Ibid., 71.
34 Ibid., 72.
35 Ibid.
36 Ibid., 73.
37 Ibid., 74.
38 Ibid., 75.
39 Joan Wylie Hall also notes Mrs. Walpole's feelings of "helplessness" and "inadequacy," though does not tie them to the gothic mode (24).
40 Jackson, "The Renegade," 77.
41 Ibid., 79.
42 Ibid., 82.
43 Ibid., 82.
44 Ibid.
45 Ibid., 83.
46 Ibid.
47 Ibid.
48 Ibid., 83.
49 Ibid.
50 Ibid.
51 Ibid., 69.
52 Ibid., 70.
53 Ibid.
54 Ibid., 91.
55 Ibid., 92.
56 Ibid.
57 Ibid., 91.
58 Ibid., 93.
59 Ibid., 92.
60 Ibid.
61 Ibid., 94.
62 Ibid., 29.
63 Ibid., 30.
64 Ibid.
65 Ibid.

66 Ibid., 32 (my emphasis).
67 Ibid.
68 Ibid., 31.
69 Ibid.
70 Ibid., 33.
71 Ibid., 36.
72 Ibid., 37.
73 Ibid., 38.
74 Ibid., 39.
75 Ibid., 39.
76 Ibid., 40.
77 Ibid., 41.
78 Ibid., 42.
79 Ibid., 43.
80 Ibid.
81 Ibid., 44.
82 Ibid., 46.
83 Ibid., 46–7.
84 Ibid., 47.
85 Ibid., 42.
86 Ibid.
87 Ibid., 46.
88 Ibid., 255.
89 Ibid.
90 Ibid., 264.
91 Ibid., 255.
92 Ibid., 256.
93 Ibid.
94 Ibid., 258.
95 Ibid.
96 Ibid., 261.
97 Ibid.
98 Ibid., 262.
99 Ibid., 264.
100 Ibid.
101 Ibid.

References

Egan, James. "Comic-Satiric-Fantastic-Gothic: Interactive Modes in Shirley Jackson's Narratives," in *Shirley Jackson: Essays on the Literary Legacy*, ed. Bernice M. Murphy, 34–51. Jefferson, NC: McFarland, 2005.

Hague, Angela. "'A Faithful Anatomy of Our Time': Reassessing Shirley Jackson." *Frontiers: A Journal of Women's Studies*, 26, no. 2 (2005): 73–96.

Hall, Joan Wylie. *Shirley Jackson: A Study of the Short Fiction*. New York: Twayne, 1993.

Hattenhauer, Darryl. *Shirley Jackson's American Gothic*. New York: SUNY Press, 2003.

Heiland, Donna. *Gothic and Gender: An Introduction*. Hoboken, NJ: John Wiley & Sons, 2008.

Hwang, Eunju. "'Writing Is the Way Out': Shirley Jackson's Domestic Stories and *We Have Always Lived in the Castle*." *Feminist Studies in English Literature*, 17, no. 2 (2009): 103–29.

Jackson, Shirley. *The Lottery and Other Stories*. New York: Farrar, Straus and Giroux, 1948.

Joshi, S. T. "Shirley Jackson: Domestic Horror," in *Shirley Jackson: Essays on the Literary Legacy*, ed. Bernice M. Murphy, 183–98. Jefferson, NC: McFarland, 2005.

Murphy, Bernice M. "Introduction: "Do You Know Who I Am?" Reconsidering Shirley Jackson," in *Shirley Jackson: Essays on the Literary Legacy*, ed. Bernice M. Murphy, 1–21. Jefferson, NC: McFarland, 2005.

Parks, John G. "Chambers of Yearning: Shirley Jackson's Use of the Gothic," in *Shirley Jackson: Essays on the Literary Legacy*, ed. Bernice M. Murphy, 237–50. Jefferson, NC: McFarland, 2005.

Rubenstein, Roberta. "House Mothers and Haunted Daughters: Shirley Jackson and the Female Gothic," in *Shirley Jackson: Essays on the Literary Legacy*, ed. Bernice M. Murphy, 127–49. Jefferson, NC: McFarland, 2005.

Wallace, Diana, and Andrew Smith. "Introduction: Defining the Female Gothic," in *The Female Gothic: New Directions*, ed. Diana Wallace and Andrew Smith, 1–12. London: Palgrave Macmillan, 2009.

5

Endless House, Interminable Dream: Shirley Jackson's Domestic Architecture and the Matrophobic Gothic

Luke Reid

The critical reception of American gothic has focused on domestic architecture as metaphoric and metonymic, understanding the space of the home as the locus of psychic displacements and repressions. However, the house is more than a metaphor. It is a material presence in its own right, its architecture not merely an analogical backdrop or static setting. Despite having productively explored the house as a representational figure, gothic scholarship has "almost never considered [it] for what it basically is—a spatial presence."[1] One way to reconsider the gothic house is to bring narrative poetics into explicit dialogue with spatial discourse and architectural history. In this chapter, I reconsider two of Shirley Jackson's gothic houses as they appear in her short story "The Bus" and her novel *The Haunting of Hill House* (1959). Using spatial theory and architectural history, I explore a convergence between domestic architecture, the maternal body, and the gothic uncanny. I argue that Jackson depicts the house as complicit in the strategic domestication of women and the reproduction of mothering. In particular, I contend that her haunted house narratives use a gothic poetics of space in order to acknowledge and critique the ways in which domestic architecture spatially organizes the female body's uncanny estrangement from itself. Jackson excavates these often hidden dynamics, using the genres of the gothic and "the supernatural to represent the horror of reality for women trapped in a patriarchal system."[2] Her work suggests that, in the American gothic tradition, the house persists as an enduring object of fascination not only because it represents the uncanny but because it actively participates in this "horror of reality," producing uncanny architecture in itself.

Writing in the matrophobic tradition, a subgenre of female gothic, Jackson uses the haunted house to explore the ambivalence of the mother–child dynamic, the twin impulses to separate and connect. In its literal sense "matrophobia" simply denotes a fear of mothers. But as Deborah D. Rogers points out, the "dramatic heart ... of the Matrophobic Gothic ... is the daughter's conflict with maternal figures from whom she cannot totally separate."[3] This inability to let go, either on the part of the mother or of the daughter, can lead to a varied set of phobias and anxieties that noticeably recur throughout gothic narratives, which include: the fear of becoming a mother oneself; the fear of specifically becoming one's *own* mother (a persistent trope in cultural production); or what Rogers describes as a "phobic response to the maternal body ... a reaction to the possibility of repeating a passive, dependent existence."[4] Throughout Jackson's work, the ambivalence of the mother-child relation is tied to what Roberta Rubenstein calls Jackson's "ambiguous houses,"[5] with the house fulfilling and resisting the associations between maternalism and domestic space. As Rubenstein argues, Jackson's fiction often merges maternal figures with domestic architecture, such that it is precisely by fulfilling the motherly expectations of comfort and succor that her houses become threatening and even terrifying.[6]

Exploring matrophobia in relation to domestic space, Jackson not only renders the house gothic in order to represent matrophobia; she also reveals how the matrophobia of spatial theory and architectural history has made the house gothic all along. Through his concept of "the architectural uncanny," Anthony Vidler elucidates the cultural and subjective meanings that have been projected onto the space of the home. And yet his conception of this space as neutral insists "there is no such thing as uncanny architecture."[7] As Vidler writes: "If actual buildings or spaces are interpreted through th[e] lens [of the uncanny], it is not because they themselves possess uncanny properties, but rather because they act, historically or culturally, as representations of estrangement."[8] Jackson's fiction, however, depicts built space as more than a representation of estrangement. Her work brings to light the often-repressed histories of spatial and architectural discourse, revealing how specific modes of historical suffering have specific poetics of space. Feminist architectural theory, for example, has demonstrated how, throughout the Western tradition, "the role of architecture [has been] explicitly the control of sexuality,"[9] rendering the home for some inhabitants decidedly *un*homely. The house is not merely the site of this control; it is also the technology or mechanism of control. As architectural historian Mark Wigley argues, the house's "primary role [has been] to protect the father's genealogical claims by isolating women from other men."[10] In this way, the house privatizes female sexuality, producing what Wigley calls a "new body,"[11] the female body as reconceived and redefined within the architectural imaginary.

The house, therefore, cannot be considered a neutral backdrop, let alone a protected site of agency and self-development. Exemplifying this reality, Jackson's houses consistently enact a phobic response to the female body in general and the maternal body in particular. Such matrophobia is not simply the expression of the gothic and supernatural genres. Rather, it is an explicit reflection of the culture and architecture of Jackson's time. Her domestic spaces demonstrate how architectural discourse and physical design actively take part in the policing of female sexuality and the essentialization of the maternal. If her houses are supernatural or gothic, this is because these modes enable Jackson to make legible that which the patriarchal imagination has obfuscated within spatial discourse and architectural practice. Recuperating the female subject position, Jackson's presentation of domestic space is a resistant intervention within this paradigm.

In a story such as "The Bus," for example, published in 1965 just months before Jackson's death, the depiction of the childhood home reveals and critiques the restrictive gender norms of postwar domestic ideology. The story recalls the work of philosopher Gaston Bachelard, whose 1958 study *The Poetics of Space* includes a phenomenology of the childhood home and its effects on identity formation. I revisit Bachelard here in part because his theories were contemporaneous to Jackson and in part because they remain so applicable to her fiction. More saliently, I see his work as emblematic of an emerging discourse of intimate space which, as Elizabeth Grosz argues, would go on to use "the endless metaphorization of femininity"[12] in order to co-opt the female body for the purposes of the patriarchal imagination. "The Bus" confronts this "endless metaphorization," using the gothic and the uncanny to present a counter-poetics of space. In the story, Old Miss Harper falls asleep on a night bus traveling home. Abruptly, the driver wakes her and kicks her out at a barren crossroads, telling her it's her stop even though it's not. After hitching a ride to a Victorian house that doubles as an inn, Miss Harper has the uncanny sense that the house is in fact her childhood home. Following a series of confrontations involving childhood and the maternal, she is chased from the house, only to wake up back on the bus, the driver shaking her and kicking her out all over again. The story ends with Miss Harper at the same crossroads as in her "dream," apparently stuck in a nightmarish loop.

In *The Poetics of Space*, Bachelard characterizes the childhood home as "furnish[ing] the framework for an interminable dream."[13] Jackson's story turns this dream into a nightmare, recuperating the female perspective and providing a sinister twist on Bachelard's gendered assumptions about domestic space and subject formation. Rather than the "protected intimacy"[14] which, according to him, allows the individual to dream herself into existence, Miss Harper encounters a space of confusion and alienation, experiences caused by her ambivalence about motherhood and sexual desire. Jackson depicts the childhood home as gothic and uncanny precisely because maternal ambivalence and the sexual desire of women are, within the patriarchal imagination, *excessive*. That is, they exceed the accepted categories of femininity as determined by patriarchal society and, as such, they produce anxieties about womanhood in relation to how men define their own identities.

These anxieties translate to the house in Jackson's story, which, more than a symbol, is a material presence reminding us of spatial discourse's co-optation of the female body and its sexual functions. It is no accident, for example, that Bachelard delineates his most notable concepts through a proliferation of maternalistic metaphors. These figurations position the house as a replacement for the womb, enumerating a series of qualities and functions associated with the latter but then systematically attributed to the former. The house is thus what he calls the "human being's first world," a "cradle" that allows the subject to begin life, as he puts it, "enclosed, protected, all warm in the bosom of the house," "envelop[ed]" and "bathed in nourishment."[15] In this way, the childhood home becomes "physically inscribed in us,"[16] the comfort and security of this "oneiric house" carried within our very beings, such that we are forever sheltered when conceiving and developing our subjecthood. Bachelard goes on to describe how, when returning to the house of childhood, we effortlessly "recapture the reflexes" of its physical spaces, climbing the stairway, for instance, without "stumbl[ing] on that rather high step," the house's "entire being ... open[ing] up, faithful to our being."[17]

A similar "opening up" occurs for Miss Harper in "The Bus," and yet one which, as Jackson suggests, is not exactly "faithful to her being." When Miss Harper retires for the night, she leaves the inn's saloon "kn[owing] where the staircase would be,"[18] and, as she reaches the stairs, she anticipates the "stained-glass window on the ... landing."[19] "Without thinking," Jackson continues, "[Miss Harper] turned at the top of the stairs and went to the front room on the left; that had always been her room. The door was open."[20] To use Bachelard's phrase, Jackson presents the house as "a group of organic habits,"[21] a series of muscle memories Miss Harper slips into "without thinking." On the one hand, there is the sense of an intimacy shared with the house, allowing her to move with ease and comfort through its rooms and corridors; on the other, something more sinister is at work, the sense that these spaces move through Miss Harper, directing and positioning her, such that she knows where to go and where to be but is prevented from thinking about it. In her room, she admits she has been "following [along] docilely" and vows that in the morning she will "show them" she can "make decisions for [her]self."[22] It is not clear who the pronoun "them" refers to here, but this childlike daydream of adult autonomy is immediately interrupted by the sound of Miss Harper's mother supernaturally singing from the drawing room downstairs. Here, Jackson merges the domestic space with a haunting maternal voice, juxtaposing Miss Harper's docility with an authority at once spatial and parental.

As the scene unfolds, the house reacts to Miss Harper's sexual desire with eruptions of the supernatural, estranging her from herself and suggesting the patriarchal home's domestication of female desire. Returned to a chastened, childlike state, Miss Harper associates her sexuality with disgust and fear, succumbing to the house's moralizing control. The maternal voice infantilizes Miss Harper, who, as if reversing the vow she has just made, submissively follows it to listen more closely at the top of the stairs. On the way, she is interrupted by a loud rustling in the closet which turns out to be her toy snake from childhood come to life, its erect "head lifted," its "wooden" body "rattling itself against the other toys."[23] With its decidedly phallic overtones, the snake unleashes a sexually charged chaos that drowns out the maternal voice and upends the ordered domesticity of the family home. Inside the closet, the snake "clatter[s] against a doll house where the tiny people inside stirred, and against a set of blocks, which fell and crashed."[24] Complicit in this warping of sexual desire into a destructive force, the spatial organization of the room places the closet—Miss Harper's secret "hiding place"—on the "wrong side" of the bed, this "oddness of construction"[25] suggesting the way in which Miss Harper's sexuality is a secret she must hide lest it reveal the oddness of *her* construction. Alone on the bed, she is "frightened at the faint smell of dark couplings and a remote echo in the springs,"[26] admonishing herself for even having such thoughts: "I will not let myself dwell on any such thing."[27] Miss Harper's castigation betrays the internalized logic of the patriarchal home: her thoughts are indecent and disallowed because, as she puts it, "this might be the room where I slept as a girl."[28]

The scene recalls Wigley's observation that, in the history and discourse of Western domestic architecture, female sexual desire is a "pollut[ant]"[29] threatening the operative purpose of the house, namely "the chastity of the girl, the fidelity of the wife."[30] Domesticating rituals are meant to neutralize such a threat to the house's "spatial integrity," whereby, as Wigley writes, the "virtuous woman becomes woman-plus-house or, rather, woman-as-housed, such that her virtue cannot be separated from the physical space."[31] Woman's sexuality, furthermore, is perceived as out of place precisely when it is not tied to reproduction and motherhood. The story's climactic scene, which sees Miss Harper not only rejected but also physically threatened by her demonically possessed childhood doll, enacts this logic. Arms outstretched, she pleads for acknowledgment from the doll ("Rosabelle, it's me"), only to have the doll's "flat slapping mouth" dismiss her as an unrecognized "old lady" who must "go away."[32] Miss Harper exemplifies a recurrent archetype in Jackson's fiction. Introduced in the story's opening words with the qualifying prefixes "Old" and "Miss,"[33] she represents the placelessness with which normative society punishes women who remain childless and unmarried. In the story's concluding moments, the bus driver again leaves Miss Harper at a stop that is not her stop, telling her "This is as far as you go,"[34] a line now inflected by the limitations placed on unattached women and thematically interrogated throughout the story.

The childhood home ultimately refuses to house Miss Harper because it cannot read or interpret her as either chaste or maternal, the only terms by which it recognizes and accommodates the female body. Following Bachelard, the house activates a group of bodily habits engraved within Miss Harper. And yet, rather than signaling an "opening up faithful to her being," these reflexes instead suggest the scripted roles and tracks proscribed by a patriarchal notion of womanhood, one determined and imposed by cultural imperatives and expectations. The house's spatial positioning of Miss Harper then works in tandem with a broader social conditioning. As Miss Harper notes, "there must be a thousand houses all over the country built exactly like this."[35] What Bachelard characterizes as a dream house conducive to self-development is here presented by Jackson as all too real, an architecture both physical and social which directs and commands, defines and constrains. When Miss Harper's ambivalence resists the constraints of this social and psychological "architecture," the house responds with its patriarchal logic, revealing the way in which her conflicted feelings of motherhood render uncanny both the house and Miss Harper. The "interminable dream" of subject formation promised by Bachelard takes on an altogether different meaning: reconceived within the projected fantasy of a proscriptive culture, Miss Harper is left within the limbo of a never-ending estrangement from herself. In contrast to contemporaneous theories of spatiality and domesticity, Jackson's story exemplifies a resistant poetics of the house. Exploring an eerily similar set of concepts and associations to those of Bachelard, her work radically questions the normative notions of house, home, and self to be found in traditional spatial discourse.

Jackson's most famous novel, *The Haunting of Hill House*, engages several of the same tropes, examining these concerns in fuller detail. If "The Bus" uses the female subject position to reorient a phenomenology of intimate space, then *Hill House* continues this approach, while also mounting a more elaborate critique, one that sees Jackson's focus expand from spatiality to architectural theory and history. Most notably, the novel maintains the legitimacy of a matrophobic reaction to a toxic maternal relation while, at the same time, interrogating the figure of the "monstrous mother" as a phallocentric construct—what Richard Pascal has characterized as "a manifestation of what modernity has transformed motherhood into."[36] Near the end of the novel, Luke Sanderson, the heir to the house, perpetuates this construct when he complains about Hill House's furniture and décor.

"It's all so motherly," he says. "Everything so soft. Everything so padded. Great embracing chairs and sofas which turn out to be hard and unwelcome when you sit down, and reject you at once."[37] His comments crystallize the contradictions of a ubiquitous notion of motherhood. For Luke, "motherly" is shorthand for an emotional ambivalence at once nurturing and withholding. This shorthand applies not only to his own mother, whom Luke has earlier decried as absent and inadequate, but also to all mothers as an essential attribute of the role.

Here, Jackson contextualizes her depiction of the unhomely within her historical moment, referencing the motherhood debates of her era.[38] To the postwar reader, Luke's comments would have been discernible echoes of the "momism" critiques then consuming the parenting culture of the time. Excoriating the figure of the so-called smothering mother, while, at the same time, vilifying mothers for not being protective and loving enough, these debates blamed the American "mom" for a host of social, cultural, and political ills. As historian Rebecca Jo Plant has argued, the rhetoric behind "momism" became so contradictory that it effectively legitimized a phobic response to *any* form of maternal affectivity.[39] Jackson's novel dramatizes this paralyzing logic. Rather than simply depicting the toxic mother as monstrous, she uses the gothic genre to excavate the cultural scapegoating of this figure. In the process, her novel brings to light the social imperative to silence the ambivalent and even hateful feelings that arise on both sides of the maternal relation, a repression which is itself toxic and, at least for her protagonist Eleanor Vance, gothically uncanny. Jackson furthermore demonstrates how the repression of mother-child ambivalence is reinforced by the idealizations of mothers and mothering which are not only foisted onto women but are also used to vilify and keep in place women and mothers who inevitably fall short of these impossible expectations.

The novel depicts internalized patriarchy as passed down between mothers and daughters, gothically portraying it as a form of haunting and suggesting the way in which it socializes women into alienating notions of "femininity" and "motherliness." Interrogating domestic architecture's complicity in this socialization, Jackson links Hill House and its spatial organization to normativity and matrophobia. Luke's comments, for example, testify to the kind of thinking which places women within the double bind of a culturally sanctioned patriarchal logic, one that intentionally constricts female identity. The spatial logic of Hill House is equally contradictory, and Jackson connects the house's closed doors and winding tower with the dead ends and circular thinking which preempt and misdirect Eleanor's efforts at self-development. For Eleanor appears stunted and disoriented precisely through the traditional notions of female selfhood and sexuality which have been handed down to her—that is, the kind of thinking in which she was raised and through which her mother continues to "haunt" her. Having been forced to read "[l]ove stories"[40] to her mother for two hours every afternoon, Eleanor's daydreaming now almost exclusively involves princes and lovers ripped from the pages of heteronormative culture's most hackneyed narratives. As Judie Newman points out, these fantasies nearly always include Eleanor's longing for a home, intertwining domestic space with conventional visions of marriage and mothering.[41] In turn, the novel's most glaring examples of maternal haunting are the inscriptions found on Hill House's walls which, first in chalk and then in blood, repeatedly implore Eleanor to "COME HOME."[42] Like the singing voice of the mother in "The Bus," these messages merge the space of the home with a maternal presence at once alluring and terrifying.

More pointedly, they tease out Jackson's motif of the haunting parent as a form of writing or narrative from which the child cannot break away or separate. Remembering how much time she spent reading to her mother, Eleanor says she "never could bear to read" anything for herself, an admission immediately followed by the thought: "But that's not all ... that doesn't tell what it was like even if I wanted to tell; why am I talking?"[43] Her mother's stories produce in Eleanor what might be called a crisis of narration, impeding her from either discovering or telling a story of her own. Jackson maps this trope onto the space of Hill House when, a few pages later, Eleanor is physically unable to enter the library. Associating her mother with the room's moldy books, she is at once physically preempted in her movements and psychologically preempted in her account of what is happening. She begins to explain her experience, saying "My mother—," only to back away from the door and abruptly fall silent, "not knowing what she wanted to tell."[44] The scene enacts a convergence between maternal haunting, suppressive normativity, and domestic architecture. As the novel progresses, this convergence exacerbates the uncanny split between who Eleanor is and who she has been told to be. This psychological disjunction leads Eleanor to a profound and gothic depersonalization; in turn, the novel exemplifies this disjunction in the purposeful elisions and perplexities of its own narration.

Indeed, Jackson's narrative poetics become gothic by way of Eleanor's oblique, repressed feelings, which, throughout the novel, evade the catharsis of traditional plotting. The novel pits Eleanor and Theodora against one another as they vie for the attentions of two archetypal male figures, Dr. Montague (the father) and Luke (the eligible bachelor). And yet the reader has the sense that neither woman is interested either in Dr. Montague's approval or Luke's advances. Instead, their tension seems to arise out of a mimetic desire for each other. Jackson dramatizes female competition, not as an indication of female desire but as a testament to the way in which internalized patriarchy and heteronormativity condition female identity and sexuality. The attraction between Eleanor and Theodora is rendered gothic not merely because of its potential queerness but, more specifically, because it would divert both women from the socially fixed tracks of marriage and motherhood. In a later scene, Jackson illustrates how fixed these tracks are. Walking along the garden path while moving "delicately along the outskirts of an open question," Eleanor and Theodora appear on the verge of confessing their feelings when the surrounding landscape suddenly turns horrifically surreal, the grass "colorless," the sky "black," the trees "transparent" and "white."[45] Now the "screaming blackness of the path" begins to widen and unwind before them, becoming more terrifying precisely because it "curve[s] out of sight"[46] into the unknown. Confronted with the prospect of this unknown, Eleanor experiences a "nausea of fear [that] almost double[s] her."[47]

Jackson's intentions are clear. For women, heteronormativity and motherhood constitute the only "path" available within a patriarchal society. To veer away from this "path" is to court a dissociative state, a split between one's own desires and the desires of a proscriptive, dominant culture. Jackson uses the gothic to remind us that such depersonalization is every bit as horrific as anything supernatural or uncanny. The scene culminates in a blinding vision of a family picnic, replete with laughing children, a checked tablecloth, and, revealingly, a mother leaning over to proffer a plate of ripe fruit.[48] Both women end up "crying and gasping and somehow holding hands,"[49] but, as the novel reaches its inevitable conclusion, Hill House succeeds in driving them apart. The deflections of their desire nonetheless energize much of the story's tension and plot. Whatever it involves, Eleanor and Theodora's relation constitutes yet another locus of excessive ambiguity—what, for my purposes, might be characterized as a "closeted" set of affects which cannot be integrated fully into the conventional "architecture" of the novel form.

In turn, *both* Hill Houses—the novel and the house within its pages—are uncanny sites of interpretive indeterminacy. Throughout the text, Jackson denies the reader any authoritative certainty about whether the phenomena in the house originate from a supernaturally gothic space or whether they stem from Eleanor's increasingly unstable mind. As a physical space, Hill House defies conventional scale and organization—the plan of the house is off, skewing and foreshortening its perspective and proportion such that it becomes a warped space of multiple architectural logics. Jackson links the house's "oddities"[50] of construction to its original owner and architect, Hugh Crain, an obsessive, authoritarian parent who, in the novel's backstory, is said to have built the house for his wife and two daughters. The house is "chillingly wrong in all its dimensions,"[51] everything is "on a very slight slant,"[52] the stairs are "not level,"[53] rooms are "entirely inside [other] rooms,"[54] and every angle is "actually a fraction of a degree off in one direction or another."[55] These "tiny aberrations of measurement" add up to "a fairly large distortion."[56] What the house distorts, it becomes clear, is self-identity, its architecture a system of control by way of disorientation and estrangement.

Such alienation, Jackson suggests, is caused by the symbiotic relationship between a controlling form of parenting and the house's controlling form of architecture. If, as Montague says, Hill House is "a masterpiece of architectural misdirection,"[57] then it is also a "monstrous monument to patriarchal parenting."[58] As one character puts it, Crain "made his house to suit his mind."[59] The reader is given a glimpse into this mind when a book is discovered in the library written in Crain's own blood and intended to teach one of his daughters the virtue of humility. Illustrated with ghastly representations of the deadly sins, the book reminds the girl not only of an "unceasing duty" to remain pious and chaste, but also to "Honor thy father and thy mother ... authors of thy being."[60] The book codifies in writing what is already the tacit law of Hill House—namely, the regulation of female individuality.

Crain's book also parallels the moralizing and prohibitive parenting style of Eleanor's mother, a woman who apparently instilled within her daughter a visceral association between self-expression and self-disgust. Eleanor cannot buy a pair of slacks[61] or leave a table uncleared[62] without seeing the scolding specter of a maternal presence. Saying her mother would disapprove, she characterizes the red toenail polish Theodora applies to her feet as "wicked"[63] and recoils from Theodora's physical closeness out of a body-shame she associates with her mother, fixating on the filthiness of her fingernails and hands, which, she feels, were marred during her years of caregiving and are now "awful" and "badly shaped."[64] Near the end of the novel, as Eleanor dances madly through the halls of Hill House, she calls out not only to her mother but to Hugh Crain as well. Within her addled mind, these two figures have fused into a parental unit. If Crain, the architect of Hill House, is also the architect of its laws, then Eleanor's mother is what Wigley describes as the "guardian of the laws."[65] That is, the wife and mother "responsible for [the] elaborate system"[66] of the patriarchal home while, at the same time, being oppressively domesticated by it. In the context of Western architectural discourse, Wigley argues that this figure "internaliz[es] the very spatial order that confines her,"[67] policing her daughter in the same way that the house polices her. Hill House may be a "housemother" or "mother house,"[68] as Luke describes it, but these appellations testify just as much to a patriarchal notion of motherhood as to any actual monstrous mother.

Seeing domestic architecture as more than a metaphor, Jackson excavates this patriarchal notion within architectural theory and the specific design movements of the postwar era. As an architect, Hugh Crain exemplifies what Diane Agrest has characterized as architecture's repression of the maternal body.[69] From Vitruvius to Alberti to Le Corbusier, architecture has all but ignored sexual difference, taking the human figure to be "synonymous with [the] male figure."[70] As Agrest contends, it has also co-opted the female body and its sexual functions in a "move of cultural transsexuality whereby man's ever-present procreative fantasy is enacted."[71] Hugh Crain embodies this "procreative fantasy." The backstory of Hill House suggests that the Crain girls, bereft of their biological mother, have been raised in some sense *by* the house. Eventually leaving his daughters, he positions Hill House as a replacement for a parental presence; moreover, this presence is one informed by his own notions of motherliness and designed intentionally to inhibit female identity. In this way, Crain recalls a specific movement in architecture which rose to prominence as Jackson was writing her novel—namely, biomorphism. Just as the "momism" debates were airing fears about mothers failing to provide the security and comfort necessary to curb aggression and violence, biomorphic architects were advancing designs and theories that invoked the maternal body as a space of protection and nurture. Essentializing femininity as maternal, biomorphism appropriated the womb as a design principle, developing an architecture that was then presented as both a replacement for the maternal body and an antidote to perceived maternal failings.

Throughout the novel, Jackson identifies Hill House as Victorian, but her descriptions of its effects on Eleanor evoke several of biomorphism's designs and theories. These correspondences may be simply an indication of how profoundly biomorphism had permeated the postwar zeitgeist, rather than Jackson's personal awareness of it. And yet, as her lectures and letters attest,[72] she was actively researching architecture in preparation for *Hill House* during the late 1950s, by which time biomorphism had become a pervasive presence within everyday American life, appearing "with unusual simultaneity in everything from ceramics to town planning."[73] Emerging as a repudiation of modernism's machinelike rectilinearity, biomorphic design reacted to Cold War anxiety, calling on openness and flexibility to inaugurate a more humane architecture. To do so, it emphasized natural shapes and biological forms which cast back to the earliest spaces of inhabitation, tapping into a visceral sense of security and protection. Several architects took this concept to its logical conclusion, designing explicitly womblike interiors. This maternal emphasis was foregrounded in the popular representations of the movement at the time. Eero Saarinen's Womb Chair was marketed heavily throughout the 1950s, often in the same publications for which Jackson frequently wrote,[74] while his TWA terminal at Idlewild Airport—its stairwells likened to fallopian tubes, its departure tunnel to a birth canal[75]—was seen as "the mainstream high-water mark of [postwar] biomorphic architecture."[76] Such designs testify to a widespread discourse of the era, one that responded to Atomic Age fears by investing the womb with "cultural fantasies of protection and shelter."[77]

Jackson depicts these fantasies as matrophobic horror. Whereas biomorphism's evocation of the womb was intended to facilitate self-development, Hill House's intrauterine allure precipitates Eleanor's depersonalization. The novel suggests that by appropriating the womb as a necessarily nurturing space, the culture of the time essentialized and idealized the maternal relation, repressing mother-child ambivalence and disallowing mother-child separation. Placed in dialogue with biomorphic design, Jackson's depiction of domestic space is not merely metaphoric, nor is Hill House simply a "voracious mothering force."[78] Producing in Eleanor a guilt-ridden inability to separate from her mother, Hill House gothically enacts the alienating effects of Jackson's own architectural moment.

In particular, it brings to mind a project by the Austrian American architect Frederick Kiesler called "Endless House," profiled in *Life* and *Time* magazines in 1952[79] and exhibited at the Museum of Modern Art in 1960.[80] Envisioning a domestic architecture wherein "all ends meet, and meet continuously,"[81] Kiesler developed a structural principle that "reduce[d] joints by unifying walls, ceilings, and floors," creating the rounded effect of "one continuous environment."[82] He called this design "tension-shell construction" since it was based on the form of an eggshell and was meant to nurture the subject's "inherent life processes."[83] The maternal associations are intentional. As Kiesler put it in his own words, inside "Endless House" "you could womb yourself into happy solitude."[84] By comparison, the central floor plan of Hill House is what Dr. Montague describes as a "concentric circle" comprised of inner and outer rings of rooms, the former without windows or a "direct way to the outside."[85] The house envelops Eleanor within this encircling space, its architecture variously portrayed as coming "around her in a rush,"[86] coming "back all around her,"[87] or "press[ing] down from all around."[88] Rather than producing Kiesler's "happy solitude," Hill House mobilizes its engulfing interior, not to nurture or protect Eleanor, but to position and isolate her. Waiting and watching, it is consistently described as surveilling Eleanor, following her movements, locating her, and even invading her thoughts and dreams.

The novel inflects the house's surrounding and supersensory space with an explicitly intrauterine terror, as though Eleanor were being physically and psychically reabsorbed into the maternal relation. Alone in her room, she feels consumed by the house, "a small creature swallowed whole by a monster," the monster feeling her "tiny little movements inside."[89] Following the broader culture of the time, biomorphism pursued an architecture expressly associated with "an obsessive neurotic return to the womb."[90] Using the gothic and the uncanny, Jackson illustrates how monstrous and horrific such a return would be. Kiesler, for example, openly endeavored to "recreate the sensual environment of continuity with the mother,"[91] by enveloping the inhabitant within the "warm palpable depths"[92] of an "elastic skin."[93] His designs sought a responsive alloplasticity between subject and house, as it were, merging the two in a womb-like symbiosis. Eleanor achieves just such a symbiosis. By the end of the novel, she has been sensually fused with Hill House, "feeling and hearing and smelling" everything that happens on its grounds and between its walls, from the scent of a "flowering bush" in the garden to an "eddy of wind" in the nursery.[94] While Kiesler believed such continuity would foster the subject's dreamlike self-actualization, for Eleanor it catalyzes a fatal dissociation. Haunted by a cultural imaginary that estranges female desire, Eleanor struggles to distinguish between her reality and the fantasies she has been taught to dream. The same imaginary haunts Jackson's narrative poetics. Just as Eleanor is destabilized by dreams that are not her own, the reader must contend with a narrative perspective that all but merges with Eleanor's unconscious, so much so that, as Melanie R. Anderson writes, "[t]he entire novel could be read as a series of [Eleanor's] waking dreams."[95] The continuous environment of "Endless House" was meant to transform domestic space from what Le Corbusier called a "machine for living" into what Kiesler envisioned as a "machine for dreaming."[96] As with Bachelard's "oneiric house," the dream metaphor is seductive until one remembers the fantasies to which the culture and architecture of Jackson's time were subjecting women and their bodies.[97] It is precisely in this sense that Hill House is a dream house. Rather than an oneiric space that facilitates identity formation, Jackson depicts a gothically rendered patriarchal home that "invad[es] human consciousness ... [and] preys on Eleanor's lonely hopes."[98] In the end, Eleanor effectively dreams herself out of existence.

By "disappearing inch by inch"[99] into Hill House, Eleanor gothically exemplifies how the phallocentric imaginary consumes female subjectivity. What is truly monstrous and voracious to Jackson is not the so-called toxic mother. Rather, it is the discourse that spawns this figure as its necessary negative: the culture that reproduces mothering as a feminine imperative; idealizes the maternal relation; represses mother–child ambivalence; and vilifies mother–child separation. It is this culture that, according to Jackson, is toxic and, ironically, matrophobic. Given the context of postwar architecture, Hill House is not merely a metaphor for this culture. The specifics of its design are the physical mechanisms of this culture's control. Much of Jackson's novel concerns a young woman's struggle for identity while trapped in a spatial and architectural paradigm that does not acknowledge sexual difference, denying Eleanor the ability to find her own place within the society and culture of the time. As Wigley argues, it is in this way that domestic architecture has traditionally rendered "the feminine position ... precisely not a position."[100] Early in the novel, Eleanor formulates her individuality in spatial terms, marveling at "what a complete and separate thing [she is]."[101] "I am here," she says, "and I have a place in this room."[102] At the end of the novel, as she deliriously climbs Hill House's tower, such emplacement appears all but lost, subsumed within the surrounding space. Her previous formulation is reconfigured: "Here I am,"[103] she says. Hill House now asserts its agency and primacy, repositioning and redefining the subjecthood Eleanor had briefly taken as her own. Turning her around and around, the tower becomes a phallic symbol for the circularity of male self-representation, a circularity furthermore demonstrated in the novel's final paragraph, itself a repetition of the first. As in her story "The Bus," the conclusion of Jackson's novel leaves us at a stop that is not a stop. Instead, it is the nightmare of an "interminable dream" and an "endless house," the unbroken loop wherein all "ends meet, and meet continuously."

Notes

1. Andrew Hock Ng Soon, *Women and Domestic Space in Contemporary Gothic Narratives: The House as Subject* (New York: Palgrave Macmillan, 2015), 5.
2. Melanie R. Anderson, "Perception, Supernatural Detection, and Gender in *The Haunting of Hill House*," in *Shirley Jackson, Influences and Confluences*, ed. Melanie R. Anderson and Lisa Kröger (London: Routledge, 2016), ProQuest E-book, 36–7.
3. Deborah D. Rogers, *The Matrophobic Gothic and Its Legacy: Sacrificing Mothers in the Novel and in Popular Culture* (New York: Peter Lang, 2007), 9.
4. Ibid., 6.
5. Roberta Rubenstein, "House Mothers and Haunted Daughters: Shirley Jackson and Female Gothic," *Tulsa Studies in Women's Literature*, 15, no. 2 (Autumn 1996): *JSTOR*, 311.
6. Ibid., 309.
7. Anthony Vidler, *The Architectural Uncanny: Essays in the Modern Unhomely* (Cambridge, MA: MIT Press, 1992), 12.
8. Ibid., 11–12.
9. Mark Wigley, "Untitled: The Housing of Gender," in *Sexuality and Space*, ed. Beatriz Colomina (New York: Princeton Architectural Press, 1992), 336.
10. Ibid.
11. Ibid., 346.
12. Elizabeth Grosz, "Woman, *Chora*, Dwelling," in *Gender Space Architecture: An Interdisciplinary Introduction*, ed. Jane Rendell, Barbara Penner, and Iain Borden (London: Routledge, 2000), 219.
13. Gaston Bachelard, *The Poetics of Space*, trans. Maria Jolas (Boston: Beacon Press, 1994), 15.
14. Ibid., 3.
15. Ibid., 7.
16. Ibid., 14.
17. Ibid., 14–15.
18. Shirley Jackson, "The Bus," in *Come Along with Me: Classic Short Stories and an Unfinished Novel*, ed. Stanley Edgar Hyman (New York: Penguin Books, 2013), 212.
19. Ibid., 213.

20 Ibid.
21 Bachelard, *Poetics of Space*, 14.
22 Jackson, "The Bus," 214.
23 Ibid., 215.
24 Ibid.
25 Ibid., 214.
26 Ibid., 213–14.
27 Ibid., 214.
28 Ibid.
29 Wigley, "Untitled," 337.
30 Ibid., 336.
31 Ibid., 337.
32 Jackson, "The Bus," 215.
33 Ibid., 203.
34 Ibid., 216.
35 Ibid., 214.
36 Richard Pascal, "Walking Alone Together: Family Monsters in *The Haunting of Hill House*." *Studies in the Novel*, 46, no. 4 (Winter 2014): Project MUSE, 470.
37 Shirley Jackson, *The Haunting of Hill House* (New York: Penguin Books, 2006), 154.
38 These debates can be traced to a much broader cultural shift, one that started decades earlier. At the turn of the century and into the 1930s, social commentators began to recast the Victorian ideals of maternal self-sacrifice and unconditional love as forms of unhealthy codependence. In 1942, Philip Wylie's bestselling book *Generation of Vipers* criticized the overbearing presence of American mothers, coining the term "momism." Although Wylie had intended his book to be a recognizably exaggerated repudiation of the overprotective mother, by the end of the decade several prominent psychiatrists were publicly lending professional sanction to his critique. Most notably, the psychiatrist Edward A. Strecker's 1946 book *Their Mother's Sons* classified seven different types of "mom," essentially pathologizing "momism" as a legitimate diagnosis. For further reading, see Rebecca Jo Plant's *Mom: The Transformation of Motherhood in Modern America* (2010) and Roel van den Oever's *Mama's Boy: Momism and Homophobia in Postwar American Culture* (2012).
39 Rebecca Jo Plant, *Mom: The Transformation of Motherhood in Modern America* (Chicago: University of Chicago Press, 2010), 12.
40 Jackson, *Hill House*, 62.
41 Judie Newman, "Shirley Jackson and the Reproduction of Mothering: *The Haunting of Hill House*," in *Shirley Jackson: Essays on the Literary Legacy*, ed. Bernice M. Murphy (Jefferson, NC: MacFarland, 2005), 172.

42 Jackson, *Hill House*, 107 and 114.
43 Ibid., 62.
44 Ibid., 75.
45 Ibid., 128–9.
46 Ibid., 129.
47 Ibid.
48 Ibid., 130.
49 Ibid.
50 Ibid., 46.
51 Ibid., 28.
52 Ibid., 77.
53 Ibid.
54 Ibid., 46.
55 Ibid., 77.
56 Ibid.
57 Ibid., 78.
58 Anderson, "Perception, Supernatural Detection, and Gender," 43.
59 Jackson, *Hill House*, 77.
60 Ibid., 124.
61 Ibid., 29.
62 Ibid., 89.
63 Ibid., 86.
64 Ibid., 63–4.
65 Wigley, "Untitled," 340.
66 Ibid.
67 Ibid.
68 Jackson, *Hill House*, 156.
69 Diane Agrest, "Architecture from Without: Body, Logic and Sex," in *Gender Space Architecture: An Interdisciplinary Introduction*, ed. Jane Rendell, Barbara Penner, and Iain Borden (London: Routledge, 2000), 358.
70 Ibid., 362.
71 Ibid.
72 See Ruth Franklin, *Shirley Jackson: A Rather Haunted Life* (New York: W.W. Norton, 2016), 400–16 and Shirley Jackson, "Experience and Fiction," in *Come Along with Me: Classic Short Stories and an Unfinished Novel*, ed. Stanley Edgar Hyman (New York: Penguin Books, 2013), 227–8.
73 Martin Filler, "Building Organic Form: Architecture, Ceramics, Glass, and Metal in the 1940s and 1950s," in *Vital Forms: American Art and Design*

in the Atomic Age, 1940–1960, ed. Brooke Kamin Rapaport and Kevin L. Stayton (New York: Harry N. Abrams, 2001), 122.

74 See Franklin, *Shirley Jackson* and Cammie McAtee, "Taking Comfort in the Age of Anxiety: Eero Saarinen's Womb Chair," in *Atomic Dwelling: Anxiety, Domesticity, and Postwar Architecture*, ed. Robin Schuldenfrei (London: Routledge, 2012).

75 Richard Lacayo qtd. in Caroline Rupprecht, *Womb Fantasies: Subjective Architectures in Postmodern Literature, Cinema, and Art* (Evanston, IL: Northwestern University Press, 2013), Project MUSE, 4.

76 Filler, "Building Organic Form," 130.

77 Rupprecht, *Womb Fantasies*, 7.

78 Pascal, "Walking Alone Together," 469.

79 Steven J. Phillips, *Elastic Architecture: Frederick Kiesler and Design Research in the First Age of Robotic Culture* (Cambridge, MA: MIT Press, 2017), 250.

80 Ibid., 257.

81 Frederick Kiesler qtd. in Phillips, *Elastic Architecture*, 258.

82 Phillips, *Elastic Architecture*, 219.

83 Ibid., 258.

84 Frederick Kiesler qtd. in Phillips, *Elastic Architecture*, 260.

85 Jackson, *Hill House*, 73.

86 Ibid., 25.

87 Ibid., 29.

88 Ibid., 42.

89 Ibid., 29.

90 Phillips, *Elastic Architecture*, 260.

91 Ibid., 237.

92 Ibid., 263.

93 Ibid., 264.

94 Jackson, *Hill House*, 179.

95 Anderson, "Perception, Supernatural Detection, and Gender," 47.

96 Phillips, *Elastic Architecture*, 264.

97 My phrasing here borrows from a formulation by Manohla Dargis that recently appeared in a *New York Times* article entitled, "What Movies Taught Me about Being a Woman" from November 30, 2018. Writing on her reevaluation of cinema in the wake of #MeToo, Dargis revisits the fantasies and dreams that movies promote and sell to women in particular. She writes: "The dream metaphor is seductive unless you remember what women are often told to dream."

98 Anderson, "Perception, Supernatural Detection, and Gender," 48.

99 Jackson, *Hill House*, 149.

100 Wigley, "Untitled," 385.
101 Jackson, *Hill House*, 60.
102 Ibid.
103 Ibid., 171.

References

Agrest, Diane. "Architecture from Without: Body, Logic and Sex," in *Gender Space Architecture: An Interdisciplinary Introduction*, ed. Jane Rendell, Barbara Penner, and Iain Borden, 358–70. London: Routledge, 2000.

Anderson, Melanie R. "Perception, Supernatural Detection, and Gender in *The Haunting of Hill House*," in *Shirley Jackson, Influences and Confluences*, ed. Melanie R. Anderson and Lisa Kröger, 35–53. London: Routledge, 2016. ProQuest E-book.

Bachelard, Gaston. *The Poetics of Space*. Trans. Maria Jolas. Boston: Beacon Press, 1994.

Filler, Martin. "Building Organic Form: Architecture, Ceramics, Glass, and Metal in the 1940s and 1950s," in *Vital Forms: American Art and Design in the Atomic Age, 1940–1960*, ed. Brooke Kamin Rapaport and Kevin L. Stayton, 122–61. New York: Harry N. Abrams, 2001.

Franklin, Ruth. *Shirley Jackson: A Rather Haunted Life*. New York: W.W. Norton, 2016.

Grosz, Elizabeth. "Woman, *Chora*, Dwelling," in *Gender Space Architecture: An Interdisciplinary Introduction*, ed. Jane Rendell, Barbara Penner, and Iain Borden, 210–21. London: Routledge, 2000.

Jackson, Shirley. "The Bus," in *Come Along with Me: Classic Short Stories and an Unfinished Novel*, ed. Stanley Edgar Hyman, 203–16. New York: Penguin Books, 2013.

Jackson, Shirley. *The Haunting of Hill House*. New York: Penguin Books, 2006.

McAtee, Cammie. "Taking Comfort in the Age of Anxiety: Eero Saarinen's Womb Chair," in *Atomic Dwelling: Anxiety, Domesticity, and Postwar Architecture*, ed. Robin Schuldenfrei, 3–25. London: Routledge, 2012.

Newman, Judie. "Shirley Jackson and the Reproduction of Mothering: *The Haunting of Hill House*," in *Shirley Jackson: Essays on the Literary Legacy*, ed. Bernice M. Murphy, 169–82. Jefferson, NC: MacFarland, 2005.

Pascal, Richard. "Walking Alone Together: Family Monsters in *The Haunting of Hill House*." *Studies in the Novel*, 46, no. 4 (Winter 2014): 464–85. Project MUSE.

Phillips, Stephen J. *Elastic Architecture: Frederick Kiesler and Design Research in the First Age of Robotic Culture*. Cambridge, MA: MIT Press, 2017.

Plant, Rebecca Jo. *Mom: The Transformation of Motherhood in Modern America*. Chicago: University of Chicago Press, 2010.

Rogers, Deborah D. *The Matrophobic Gothic and Its Legacy: Sacrificing Mothers in the Novel and in Popular Culture*. New York: Peter Lang, 2007.

Rubenstein, Roberta. "House Mothers and Haunted Daughters: Shirley Jackson and Female Gothic." *Tulsa Studies in Women's Literature*, 15, no. 2 (Autumn 1996): 309–31. *JSTOR*.
Rupprecht, Caroline. *Womb Fantasies: Subjective Architectures in Postmodern Literature, Cinema, and Art*. Evanston, IL: Northwestern University Press, 2013. Project MUSE.
Soon, Andrew Hock Ng. *Women and Domestic Space in Contemporary Gothic Narratives: The House as Subject*. New York: Palgrave Macmillan, 2015.
Vidler, Anthony. *The Architectural Uncanny: Essays in the Modern Unhomely*. Cambridge, MA: MIT Press, 1992.
Wigley, Mark. "Untitled: The Housing of Gender," in *Sexuality and Space*, ed. Beatriz Colomina, 327–89. New York: Princeton Architectural Press, 1992.

6

Casting a Literary Spell: The Domestic Witchcraft of Shirley Jackson

Alissa Burger

Shirley Jackson's short stories, fiction, and domestic writing have long cast a spell over readers, though significant debate continues over Jackson's actual belief in and use of magic. The most oft-cited evidence of Jackson's practice of witchcraft is drawn from a biographical statement written by her husband, Stanley Hyman, prior to the publication of her first novel, *The Road through the Wall* (1948). According to the blurb, Jackson "is an authority on witchcraft and magic, has a remarkable private library of works in English on the subject, and is perhaps the only contemporary writer who is a practicing amateur witch, specializing in small-scale black magic and fortune-telling with a tarot deck."[1] Published in the 2015 collection *Let Me Tell You* as "The Real Me," Jackson's autobiographical note for *Raising Demons* (1957) offers her own account of her use of witchcraft, as she notes, "the first thing I did when we moved in was to make charms in black crayon on all the door sills and window ledges to keep out demons, and was successful in the main." She also reveals that she "[relies] almost entirely on image and number magic."[2] Jackson's reputation as a witch was further bolstered by anecdotes from friends about Jackson's tarot card readings,[3] interviews the author gave with numerous reporters, and the legendary story that she used witchcraft to break publisher Alfred A. Knopf's leg following a disagreement between Knopf and Hyman.[4] Despite these entertaining anecdotes, "Jackson claimed to be embarrassed by the witchcraft talk"[5] and acknowledged in an interview with Harvey Breit that "she believed in magic but also said that it was 'a silly thing to talk about.'"[6]

Real or not, Jackson's reputed witchcraft has become an enduring part of her literary legacy, a consideration that resonates through a wide range of her writing and reflects the mystery, power, and enigmatic nature of Jackson as both a writer and an individual. This theme of magic is also inextricably intertwined with domesticity in Jackson's novels and nonfiction, where within the home, almost anything is possible. Representations of magic in a range of Jackson's work, including *Life among the Savages* (1953), *Raising Demons* (1957), *The Witchcraft of Salem Village* (1956), and *We Have Always Lived in the Castle* (1962) illustrate the various ways Jackson employed magical discourse in her life and writing, from literal spells to magic as metaphor, as well as Jackson's perception of writing as a form of magic in and of itself. Jackson's perspective on the role of magic in daily life resonates throughout her domestic writing in *Savages* and *Demons*, her accounts of her unconventional approach to homemaking, and the daily magic of her family life. Magic is also central to her nonfiction children's book *Witchcraft*, in which Jackson shifts from the personal to the objective, providing children with a historical and cultural context for the witchcraft hysteria in Salem, while also positioning this narrative firmly within the domestic sphere. Supernatural themes are present in much of Jackson's fiction, and protective magic plays a central role in *Castle*, shaping the lives and establishing the power of the Blackwood sisters. Taken together and read through the lens of magic and witchcraft that has shaped Jackson's life and legacy, these works examine the intersection of the domestic and the magical, the impact of the inexplicable on the everyday, and the myriad ways in which women claim power, whether directly or subversively, culminating in a unique perspective on life, literature, and magic that could only come from Jackson. Reading Jackson's life and work through this lens of witchcraft and magic illuminates the ways in which Jackson's engagement with the magical both encompass and transcend the domestic concerns central to so much of her writing, thereby highlighting Jackson's dynamic identity as wife, mother, homemaker, writer, and witch.

Some critics, like Darryl Hattenhauer, are dismissive of the witchcraft claim and its consideration, arguing that "Jackson did not experience the supernatural … [Rather] her consciousness was often in the ambiguous place between the seemingly supernatural and the real, where it seems hard to classify events as either supernatural or real because there seems to be evidence both ways."[7] The question of magic and witchcraft could also be read more metaphorically as an expression of subversive female power in the mid-twentieth century, a symbol of "female strength and potency."[8] As a result of these competing accounts and interpretations, the truth of Jackson's use of witchcraft remains difficult to pin down even decades later.

Contemporary headlines like Emily Temple's "Shirley Jackson: Possibly a Witch, Definitely Played the Zither"[9] and W. W. Norton's "Shirley Jackson Wasn't Actually a Witch, or Was She?," the title of a promotional excerpt for Ruth Franklin's biography, *Shirley Jackson: A Rather Haunted Life*, continue the question.[10]

The debate over whether or not Jackson was actually a witch is unlikely to ever be definitively settled, but its very endurance points toward a foundational truth of Jackson, her literature, and her legacy: her steadfast rejection of firm definition or categorization. Balancing her roles as author and homemaker, writing with equal effectiveness and authenticity about haunted houses and the everyday domestic scenes of her own home and family, Jackson refused to be limited to a single, defining focus. This refusal has posed a challenge for many critics and scholars, who have "tended to focus upon two rather disparate but revealing representations of Jackson— *either* as 'New England's only practicing amateur witch' *or* as a matronly housewife."[11] Bernice M. Murphy explains the limitations of this either/or construction, noting, "There was a grain of truth in each depiction, but ultimately neither revealed the true Jackson, and each would diminish the writer and her work."[12] Throughout Jackson's personal and professional lives, this same attempt at categorization was repeated, and was one to which Jackson never capitulated, refusing to define herself as one or the other, or to simplify her complex self for the consumption and understanding of others. This impulse toward defining Jackson continues to shape readings of and criticism surrounding her work, and while Jackson can be productively read from a variety of different angles—as a witch *or* a housewife, for example—the richest and most rewarding approach to reading Jackson is to embrace her complexity and seeming contradictions by appreciating the interconnections between Jackson's multiple roles and how each informed and influenced the others.

This defiance of easy categorization and understanding echoes the anxieties that surround witchcraft as well, with Malcolm Gaskill explaining, "People prefer clear-cut definitions to blurred ones, order to chaos. We want existence to be comprehensible and governable, and so habitually classify it using simple 'binary oppositions': night and day, life and death, good and evil, human and beast."[13] Witches flout this impulse to classify and define, and so does Jackson. In considering the question of whether or not Jackson was a witch, biographer Judy Oppenheimer suggests that the truth may lie somewhere in the middle, and this notion that that there is no definitive answer or single unassailable truth is one that seems to echo through much of Jackson's own work. As Oppenheimer writes,

> [Jackson] liked to pretend she was a witch; she liked to make people believe it; at the same time she liked to poke fun at the entire business, and at the very people who believed her so literally. ... She was a simultaneous

believer and debunker, psychic traveler and removed, amused onlooker. It was the same duality that made it easy for her to move between humor and fear in her work. She would not cut any of her options; she would not be cubbyholed, no matter how much easier it would make things for others.[14]

The context of magic and witchcraft is undeniably a valuable perspective through which to read and understand a wide range of Jackson's work. While witchcraft here refers to Jackson's reputed performance of specific magical practices, as well as similar powers with which she invests some of her most memorable characters, magic can also be more diffusely defined throughout Jackson's work and life. One clear example of this is Jackson's belief that storytelling had its own unique kind of magic, a perspective she frequently shared in her lectures on writing. A version of these lectures was posthumously published by Hyman as "Experience and Fiction" in the collection *Come Along with Me* (1968). Jackson begins this piece with her observation that in writing fiction "nothing is ever wasted; all experience is good for something; you tend to see everything as a potential structure of words .... That is what I would like to talk about now—the practical application of magic, or where do stories come from?"[15] Blurring the lines between the real and the imaginary, Franklin explains that "on some level writing was a form of witchcraft to Jackson—a way to transform everyday life into something rich and strange, something more than what it appeared to be."[16] This sense of magic, the inexplicable, and Jackson's witchcraft inform and animate her writing, from her daily accounts of housework and family life to her most chilling gothic novels, communicating Jackson's worldview by reminding the reader that anything is possible and reality may never quite be what it seems.

Jackson wrote extensively about her home and family life, published in the domestic collections *Savages* and *Demons*. While the subject matter of Jackson's domestic writing varies significantly from that of her novels, there are several characteristics that resonate between these two disparate types of writing. Jackson's power of observation and sharp humor are central to both her novels and her domestic writing, whether she is chronicling her protagonist's slipping grip on reality or family conversations around the dinner table. The uncanny is also a central characteristic of both types of writing. No matter what Jackson writes about, the daily course of events could easily and unexpectedly veer off in an instant, transforming the everyday into the unsettling or horrific. As S. T. Joshi notes, in considering the connections between Jackson's domestic writing and her larger body of work, its significance

> rests in its manipulation of very basic familial or personal scenarios that would be utilized in her weird work in perverted and twisted ways: things

like riding a bus, employing a maid, taking children shopping, going on vacation, putting up guests, and, in general, adhering—or seeming to adhere—to the "proper conduct" expected of her as a middle-class housewife.[17]

In Jackson's life, as in her fiction, the potential for magic and the unexpected was always just around the corner, and her use of such magic allowed her to transcend the confining "proper" conduct and expectations of her housewife role.

A full understanding of Jackson's embodiment and negotiation of her roles as wife, mother, and caregiver demands to be read through this lens of the magical, marking the ways in which Jackson claimed power and agency within these often restrictive roles, as "To figure housework *as* witchcraft ... allows Jackson to mobilize it as an oppositional category,"[18] with Jackson fulfilling her necessary domestic duties while also maintaining her own unique perspective and identity. Rather than choosing between or minimizing her domestic or authorial identities, Jackson instead "subversively rewrites the housewife role."[19]

Houses in Jackson's fiction have complex and contested meanings as refuge and prison, "a place of warmth and security and also one of imprisonment and catastrophe."[20] This representation seems to echo Jackson's own experience as a housewife, where she "chafed within the constraints of domesticity even as she genuinely delighted in motherhood and family life."[21] Jackson's use of witchcraft allowed her to be a housewife in her own unique way, as even the mundane annoyance of finding the right kitchen tool has, for Jackson, its elements of the magical. Oppenheimer recounts how "[a]ll the small kitchen tools—the peelers, can openers, knives, and so on—were crammed into one drawer on top of each other. Whenever Shirley wanted one, she would slam the door hard, call out the name of the tool, and open the drawer. The desired implement would always be on top."[22] As the anecdotes about crayon charms and kitchen utensils demonstrate, Jackson's understanding of and interaction within the space of her home was seemingly informed by discourses of magic and witchcraft, a perspective which highlights the ways in which Jackson claimed power within the traditional housewife role and exercised that power to enrich the lives of her family.

This tone of magic animates the lives of Jackson's children and their relationship with their mother as well, as they "became her enthusiastic collaborators."[23] Some of this camaraderie follows the familiar pattern of children's imaginative play, as when Jackson's daughter Sally "took on her storytelling face" to tell her father about how she had "put together the land of Oz and the country of the hobbits and Rootabaga and Mother Goose Land, because they were all scattered all over and I kept forgetting which book I had to take to get to each country," instructing him to "watch out ... or else make the magic sign."[24] At other times, the children become active accomplices in Jackson's domestic magic, as when Sally attempts to help her mother by magically unsticking the refrigerator door, using "Mommy magic."[25] When the refrigerator door comes off its hinges altogether, Sally laments "*Jeekers* ... I went and unstuck the wrong *side.*"[26]

Following in her mother's footsteps, Sally's use of magic seems designed to undermine traditional power structures and create her own meaning within the domestic space and the expected behaviors of small girls. As Jackson writes of Sally's magical exploits, following her father's admonition that refrigerators must be fixed by repairmen and not magic:

> Her father permitted her to come down for lunch, and when she came to her chair at the table she stopped to whisper in my ear. "I fixed *him*," she said, with an evil scowl at her father. "I'm going to show *him* about how magic is better. He can just *wait.*" ... I thought of Jerry Martin afraid to go to bed with a spell on him and of little Cheryl whose doll's head was on backward now because she had pushed Sally in the snow.[27]

Even once the repairman has fixed the refrigerator, Sally is unwilling to give up her own power and agency, refusing to capitulate to her father's expectations: "She announced at dinner one night that when she grew up she was going to be a mean mean old lady who lived in a forest and people came to her for advice and spells, except, she added, turning to look directly at her father, except wicked trolls."[28] This belief in magic creates a domestic world unique to Jackson and her children, separate from the outside world, in which—much like many of Jackson's most memorable fictional protagonists—they are able to imagine, fantasize, and exercise their own power and a small measure of control over the forces that shape the larger world. Jackson blurs the lines between the magical and the pragmatic in her own recollection of this incident in her lecture on "Experience and Fiction," saying, "I left the refrigerator where it was and went in to my typewriter and wrote a story about not being able to open the refrigerator door and getting the children to open it with magic. When a magazine bought the story, I bought a new refrigerator."[29] As this event, Jackson's story of it, and her recollection of the storytelling itself demonstrate, the boundaries between the magical, the domestic, and the everyday within Jackson's home and life were permeable and negotiable through the power of imagination and storytelling.

Given the intersection of Jackson's interest in witchcraft and her domestic, maternal perspective, she was well positioned to write a children's book on the Salem witch trials, which she was asked to do in 1953 for Bennett Cerf's Random House Landmark series. Children's literature is often central to the domestic sphere, as parents read to their children for both education and entertainment. Jackson's *Witchcraft* is a comprehensive historical treatment of the witch hysteria, the sympathies of which are firmly aligned with the accused, as in Jackson's description of "poor Tituba."[30] *Witchcraft* remains a rather minor work in Jackson's larger canon and is not among her strongest or most influential writing. Franklin remarks that the book has a "somewhat stilted tone,"[31] and Oppenheimer acknowledges: "straight, unadorned history had never been her métier, even if the subject was witches."[32] However, Jackson was ahead of her time in interrogating the complex causes of the witch trials, starting with her opening pronouncement: "It is difficult to understand the seeming madness which swept Salem Village in 1692 without first considering the many factors which had been building for long centuries before."[33] In considering this larger context, Franklin notes, "the women who were targeted were not accidental victims, but social outcasts or others outside the mainstream. [Jackson's] emphasis on these themes, novel at the time, anticipates a number of more recent treatments of the witch trials."[34] Jackson explains this context in detail, highlighting the complexity of the historical moment and its myriad causes, while also remaining accessible to the book's young audience, which is no easy feat. In positioning her consideration of the Salem witch trials firmly within the domestic sphere of individual homes and women's roles within them, Jackson offers an intimate and revealing analysis that merges the cultural and the personal.

Regardless of genre, one of Jackson's greatest strengths lies in her storytelling ability: taking individual moments and observations, whether imaginatively invented or of the daily household variety, and creating an engaging narrative filled with lively, believable characters. Rather than retelling the established historical narrative, bursting with a catalog of facts and figures, Jackson tells a story, foregrounding the significance of the domestic space and taking readers into homes as well as courtrooms, humanizing the individuals who played a part in the trials and bringing both the accusers and accused to life in vivid detail. Jackson provides detailed descriptions of the accused witches, including their disbelief and horror as they were imprisoned, tried, and in nineteen cases, executed. Similarly, Jackson describes one of the lead accusers, Ann Putnam, in personal detail as "the kind of little girl who is always very polite and sweet when grownups are around, and very rude and cruel to other children,"[35] a description that was likely to resonate with her young readers. In addition to these descriptions of the key players, Jackson provides a chronological account and details of the accusations, trials, and executions, crafting a compelling narrative for young readers drawn from the historical record. She also includes a list of the executed witches,[36] provides a chapter detailing the waning of the hysteria and its aftermath, and concludes with a final lesson that "spectral evidence, guilt by association, and a belief that the prisoner was guilty before he was tried, are not means to be used in fighting any evil, no matter how frightening it may seem,"[37] a message that resonates well beyond the specific historical moment of the Salem witch trials.[38]

Through this approach, Jackson endeavors to make each of the individuals and the events of the trials understandable and relatable, foregrounding the educational and empathetic potential of children's literature.

Just as Jackson's own home was central to her domestic writing, in *Witchcraft*, the domestic space is central to the narrative itself, as Jackson features scenes within individual homes and the perceived threat to home and family that fueled the witchcraft trials. Jackson traces the beginnings of the hysteria to the most innocuous and seemingly safest of places, as "Nearly every day [the girls] would gather in the big cheerful kitchen of Mr. Parris's Indian slave, Tituba ... If any of their elders noticed this, or cared, it must have seemed to them that the girls could get in very little trouble in the home of the minister of the town."[39] Another of the central issues that Jackson identified as contributing to the accusation of witches was that of anomalous women, including those who were considered to have too much power, who failed to submit to patriarchal cultural expectations, and who deviated from the traditional performance of their domestic roles as wives and mothers. For example, Jackson explains that Sarah Good "was a woman whose reputation was already doubtful. She was poor and probably half-crazy, and she wandered with her ragged children from door to door, begging for food and shelter and cursing those who denied her," while Sarah Osborne was "a respectable woman, but one who had acquired the reputation of being strange."[40] Women with power or those who resisted control, both inside the home and in the larger community, were considered a problem, and in addressing this issue, Jackson connects women's roles, the domestic sphere, and the larger cultural context for her young readers, presenting a complicated and contentious issue in a narrative they could understand and relate to, through the central position of homes, families, and children within her account of the Salem witch trials.

Magic, witchcraft, and the domestic space are key themes in Jackson's novels as well, with houses and the supernatural of central importance in *The Sundial* (1958), *The Haunting of Hill House* (1959), and *Castle*. The exploration of domestic witchcraft is particularly significant in the protective magic of *Castle*, and in the Blackwood sisters' reputation as witches at the novel's conclusion. Merricat, the younger of the two Blackwood sisters, is very particular about the rituals of her family's home and the land surrounding it. Merricat's fundamental perceptions of the world are grounded in magical belief, as "every event is an omen of either good or bad luck,"[41] and Merricat considers herself the only person capable of countering or influencing the outcome. Merricat provides the reader with the very specific litany of her and her sister Constance's days and routines, as well as guidelines for what she is and isn't allowed to do: "I was allowed to carry cups and saucers and pass sandwiches and cakes, but not to pour tea,"[42] and "I was not allowed to handle knives, but when [Constance] worked in the garden I cared for her tools, keeping them bright and clean."[43] It is necessary for Merricat to exert her influence and control on the house and the land which surrounds it in order to keep her and her sister safe. As Lenemaja Friedman explains of Merricat, "To ward off evils, she has a habit of nailing objects to a tree, perhaps a book, a watch chain, or a scarf. She also buries objects—her blue marbles, or a doll, or the bag of silver dollars—to achieve her desire or to act as powerful antidotes to evil."[44] In doing so, Merricat is taking everyday objects and investing them with creative magical power, using these to claim control of and work to protect the Blackwood home, her, and her sister Constance. These rules must be strictly adhered to if all is to be right in the Blackwood home and the sanctity of the domestic sphere assured, protecting the Blackwood sisters from the dangers of the outside world, including the hateful villagers and later, covetous Cousin Charles. Merricat and Constance are two women who are largely on their own, despite the presence of infirm Uncle Julian. This independence, coupled with their wealth, aligns them closely with the kind of women who were most often accused of witchcraft during the Salem witch trials[45] and makes the Blackwood sisters and their home vulnerable to the villagers and the patriarchal power structures that oppose this unconventional femininity.

In addition to the "safeguards"[46] she has established around the property and her ritualistic performance of what she is and isn't allowed to do, Merricat also relies on magic words, deciding one morning that "I would choose three powerful words, words of strong protection, and so long as those great words were never spoken aloud no change would come."[47] This is part of a long tradition of words, witchcraft, and women's power. According to Jane Kamensky, during the Salem witchcraft hysteria, "the witch's speech revealed the full destructive potential of the female voice,"[48] signaling the uncontainable and the uncontrollable. Kristen J. Sollée adds that "female speech can be a space of resistance,"[49] a refusal to be silenced, and a means of challenging and dismantling the status quo. Both of these potentially magical uses of language are evident in *Castle*. The words hold power only if they are spoken by Merricat and no one else, which makes her choice of words particularly significant. In addition to speaking the words aloud, Merricat must also consume them, taking them into herself to keep them safe. The first word she chooses is "melody," which she wrote "in apricot jam on my toast with the handle of a spoon and then put the toast in my mouth and ate it very quickly. I was one-third safe."[50] She decides on "Gloucester" as her second word, as being "strong, and I thought it would do ... [though] no word was truly safe when Uncle Julian was talking."[51] Merricat's third and final word is "Pegasus" and having decided it, she "took a glass from the cabinet, and said the word very distinctly into the glass, then filled it with water and drank."[52] Two of these words (melody and Pegasus) invoke music and magic and having consumed them, Merricat feels relatively safe. Tellingly, it is the word that is associated with the literal outside world (Gloucester) that leaves Merricat feeling most uncertain, and while she identifies the word itself as "strong," it remains the least incorporated and controlled of the three, a word that Uncle Julian could inadvertently invoke, compromising Merricat's power and protection.

While protecting her and her sister from the outside world is Merricat's driving concern, these patterns, repetitions, and words also serve to protect the home and family from Merricat, whose destructive potential was realized most dramatically in her poisoning of the rest of the Blackwood family. Though Merricat doesn't seem to be plagued by guilt for the deaths of the vast majority of her family, she polices herself and her behavior stringently, even when the need to do so no longer exists, as when Merricat tells Constance that she isn't allowed to enter Uncle Julian's bedroom, despite the fact that Uncle Julian has died and Constance has given Merricat permission.[53] In this doubling, Jackson provides readers with a protagonist who is undeniably powerful, while simultaneously terrified of and vigilant against the destruction that power may cause to her, her home, and those she loves, specifically Constance. Friedman notes Merricat's complex and at times contradictory nature, arguing that Merricat is "despite her great crime, sympathetic and likeable. Though in one sense horrifying, she is believable, capable of both intense love and intense hate … She is seemingly intelligent and yet totally mad. Because she does not trust people, she relies wholly on magic objects she hopes will ward off evil. What she does, she regards as necessary for survival."[54] Merricat's love for Constance is just as overwhelming as the hate she felt for the rest of her family on the night she poisoned them, and both have the potential for incredible destruction. Merricat's perspective, steeped as it is in her wholehearted belief in superstition and magic, shapes the daily lives of the Blackwood sisters and demarcates the boundaries of their interactions with the outside world. In using her magic to protect the house, Merricat keeps Constance contained and the sisters together, with Constance catering to Merricat's whims and desires. Merricat does not want to share Constance and cannot stand to be denied, as demonstrated in her poisoning of her family, and her policing of the domestic boundaries keeps her life and home just the way she wants them, an insular world in which she holds both creative and destructive power.

While Merricat's thinking and relationship to the home are overtly magical and ritualistic, Constance's is more benignly domestic. Constance's life revolves around food: she tends her garden, cooks for Merricat and Uncle Julian, and adds to the Blackwood women's cache of cans and preserves in the cellar. Food, individuals' relationships with it, and its larger significance are complex in *Castle*. Merricat poisoned her family after being sent to bed with no dinner. Constance is an excellent cook, though she is widely believed to be her family's poisoner, an assumption she never publicly denies or corrects. In addition, just as Merricat uses protective magic to secure the boundaries of their property, Constance's cooking is a domestic witchcraft of its own, keeping Merricat happy and contained, through Constance's preparation of the foods Merricat likes and requests. Just as on the night she poisoned her family, when Merricat is unhappy and unfed, she becomes dangerously destructive: she asks Constance for "a cake with pink frosting ... With little gold leaves around the edge,"[55] and shortly after this request is denied by Cousin Charles, Merricat sets his bedroom on fire. Food is central to the dynamics of the surviving Blackwood family, as Constance's cooking revolves around what Merricat wants and what Uncle Julian can eat. Cousin Charles disrupts this delicate balance, just as he upends everything else in the Blackwood home, chiding Constance for doting on Uncle Julian and spoiling Merricat by giving in to her every request. While Merricat used poison to destroy her family and impose her own will, for Constance, food is a means of creation and sustenance, both in feeding the body and moderating Merricat's behavior, and Constance's attention to detail and the love she puts into its preparation keep the home and family in check just as significantly as Merricat's ritualistic maintenance of its borders.

At the novel's conclusion, Merricat and Constance are hidden within their shattered home, and the villagers who helped destroy it now view them as akin to fairy tale witches, simultaneously terrified of and fascinated by the Blackwood sisters. The villagers have attacked and attempted to destroy the Blackwood women, but following Merricat and Constance's survival, the sisters become a force to be feared and paid tribute. This takes the form of food offerings the villagers leave outside the Blackwood sisters' door, an extension of the centrality of food throughout the novel, including Constance's relationship with food as form of benign domestic witchcraft in dramatic contrast with Merricat's fixation on what is and is not safe to eat. The villagers "sometimes ... brought bacon, home-cured, or fruit, or their own preserves, which were never as good as the preserves Constance made. Mostly they brought roasted chicken; sometimes a cake or pie, frequently cookies, sometimes a potato salad or coleslaw."[56] These offerings are sometimes accompanied by notes of apology and are often critiqued or even remade by Constance before being consumed, in an interaction that draws the lines of power and penance between the villagers and the Blackwood sisters. The villagers' whispered apologies and gifts of food "are their expressions of guilt for their witch hunting, but also the expression of fears toward the Blackwood sisters. By becoming completely invisible, instead of surrounding themselves with the awe-inspiring walls and gates, the Blackwood sisters finally gain power over the villagers."[57]

Prior to the destruction of the Blackwood home, the villagers were powerless to control or contain the Blackwood women, though this did not stop them from engaging in a campaign of insults, harassment, and intimidation, as Merricat endures in her trip to the village in the novel's opening chapter. However, in becoming invisible and removing themselves entirely from the scope of the villagers' influence, Merricat and Constance "rapidly gain a reputation as supernatural beings, 'ladies' who live in the darkness, who see and hear everything, evoked by parents to frighten children into obedience, but also as a source of numinous dread for adults."[58] Through this transformation, they become simultaneously dehumanized ("supernatural beings") and heightened in their gentility ("ladies"), both more and less than individual women, more uncontainable and uncontrollable than the villagers had ever dreamed they could be when they had the Blackwood women in their clear sight. In this moment, Merricat and Constance wrest the ability to craft their own narrative and identities from the villagers, finding power in their previous exclusion, as "*both* girls have now embraced wholeheartedly the sinister image that the villagers have always imposed upon them."[59] In her representation of Merricat—and later in the witch-y reputation of both Blackwood sisters—Jackson explores the potential danger and the subversive power of food, magic, and witchcraft. This new sense of power includes their control of the domestic space of the Blackwood home as well. Merricat's ritualistic protections have failed and the house has burned, largely as a result of Merricat's inability to control her own destructive impulses, starting the fire when she knocks Cousin Charles's pipe into the wastebasket. However, Merricat and Constance carve out a home for themselves within the ruins, centralized in the kitchen that has served as the site of so many conversations and conflicts. Constance finds food the villagers didn't destroy, reestablishing her control of the domestic space with armloads of preserves carried up from the cellar, rejoicing in "Vegetable soup ... and strawberry jam, and chicken soup, and pickled beef."[60] Just as Constance reclaims the domestic space of the kitchen, Merricat reframes her world once more through magic and imagination, shaping the house around her as she wishes it to be as she claims a tablecloth as her dress and tells Constance that "We are going to be very happy,"[61] a pronouncement that leaves no room for argument. Constance and Merricat remake the home around them and their occupation of it in this new image of themselves and the villagers' fear of them, embracing the mystery and potential danger of their presence and power.

Regardless of whether Jackson was really a practicing witch, the influence of magic and witchcraft resonates throughout her work, from her domestic writing and *Witchcraft* to her haunting final novel, *Castle*. Reading Jackson's work through the lens of magic and witchcraft provides readers with a unique insight to Jackson's perspective and worldview, regardless of how authentically she embodied that particular role. Whether or not the witchcraft itself is real, Jackson's use of its conventions in her writing and her life highlight the ways in which the everyday can take an unexpected turn at any moment, that power can be claimed and agency employed in any setting, and that despite the larger cultural impulse to define and categorize, there is great magic in resisting, in remaining indefinable and uncontainable.

Notes

1. Quoted in Ruth Franklin, *Shirley Jackson: A Rather Haunted Life* (New York: Liveright, 2016), 217.
2. Shirley Jackson, "The Real Me," in *Let Me Tell You: New Stories, Essays, and Other Writings*, ed. Laurence Jackson Hyman and Sarah Hyman Dewitt (New York: Random House, 2015), 357.
3. Judy Oppenheimer, *Private Demons: The Life of Shirley Jackson* (New York: Fawcett Columbine, 1989), 189–90.
4. Franklin, *Shirley Jackson*, 258.
5. Ibid.
6. Oppenheimer, *Private Demons*, 140.
7. Darryl Hattenhauer, *Shirley Jackson's American Gothic* (Albany, NY: State University of New York Press, 2003), 10.
8. Franklin, *A Rather Haunted Life*, 261.
9. Emily Temple, "Shirley Jackson: Possibly a Witch, Definitely Played the Zither," *Literary Hub*, August 8, 2018, https://lithub.com/shirley-jackson-possibly-a-witch-definitely-played-the-zither/.
10. Ruth Franklin, "Shirley Jackson Wasn't Actually a Witch, or Was She?" *Literary Hub*, September 28, 2018, https://lithub.com/shirley-jackson-wasnt-actually-a-witch/.
11. Bernice M. Murphy, "Introduction," in *Shirley Jackson: Essays on the Literary Legacy*, ed. Bernice M. Murphy (Jefferson, NC: McFarland, 2005), 12 (my emphasis).
12. Ibid., 12.
13. Malcolm Gaskill, *Witchcraft: A Very Short Introduction* (Oxford: Oxford University Press, 2010), 1.
14. Oppenheimer, *Private Demons*, 139.
15. Shirley Jackson, "Experience and Fiction," in *Come Along with Me: Classic Short Stories and an Unfinished Novel*, ed. Stanley Edgar Hyman. (1968; repr. New York: Penguin Classics, 2013), 219.
16. Franklin, *A Rather Haunted Life*, 262.
17. S. T. Joshi, "Shirley Jackson: Domestic Horror," in *Shirley Jackson: Essays on the Literary Legacy*, ed. Bernice M. Murphy (Jefferson, NC: McFarland, 2005), 188.
18. Dara Downey, "Not a Refuge Yet: Shirley Jackson's Domestic Hauntings," in *A Companion to American Gothic*, ed. Charles L. Crow (Hoboken, NY: John Wiley, 2013), 294 (emphasis in the original).
19. Ibid., 294.
20. Zoë Heller, "The Haunted Mind of Shirley Jackson." *New Yorker*, October 17, 2016, https:// www.newyorker.com/magazine/2016/10/17/the-haunted-mind-of-shirley-jackson.

21 Roberta Rubenstein, "Writer, Housewife, Witch." *Women's Review of Books*, 34, no. 3 (2017): 19.
22 Oppenheimer, *Private Demons*, 189.
23 Rubenstein, "Writer, Housewife, Witch," 18.
24 Shirley Jackson, *Raising Demons* (1957; repr. New York: Penguin, 2015), 168.
25 Ibid., 158.
26 Ibid., 161 (emphasis in the original).
27 Ibid., 162 (emphasis in the original).
28 Ibid., 165.
29 Jackson, "Experience and Fiction," 219.
30 Shirley Jackson, *The Witchcraft of Salem Village* (New York: Random House, 1956), 47–8.
31 Franklin, *A Rather Haunted Life*, 356.
32 Oppenheimer, *Private Demons,* 192.
33 Jackson, *The Witchcraft of Salem Village*, 3.
34 Franklin, *A Rather Haunted Life*, 357.
35 Jackson, *The Witchcraft of Salem Village*, 30–1.
36 Ibid., 150.
37 Ibid., 167.
38 *The Witchcraft of Salem Village* is also notable in the larger cultural context of McCarthyism in which Jackson was writing. As Jackson herself noted in considering the book, "The main trouble will lie in making the book *not* a comment on the present day; the parallels are uncomfortably close" (qtd. in Franklin 357, emphasis in the original).
39 Jackson, *The Witchcraft of Salem Village*, 30.
40 Ibid., 46.
41 Lenemaja Friedman, *Shirley Jackson* (Boston: Twayne, 1975), 138.
42 Shirley Jackson, *We Have Always Lived in the Castle* (1962; repr. New York: Penguin Classics, 2006), 24.
43 Ibid., 42.
44 Friedman, *Shirley Jackson*, 138.
45 Chiho Nakagawa, "How to Make a Witch—Shirley Jackson and Femininity." *Foreign Literature Research*, 28, no. 63 (2009): 68–9.
46 Jackson, *We Have Always Lived in the Castle*, 41.
47 Ibid., 44.
48 Jane Kamensky, "Female Speech and Other Demons: Witchcraft and Wordcraft in Early New England," in *Spellbound: Women and Witchcraft in America*, ed. Elizabeth Reis (1998; repr. Lanham, MD: SR Books, 2004), 27.
49 Kristen J. Sollée, *Witches, Sluts, Feminists: Conjuring the Sex Positive* (Berkeley, CA: ThreeL Media, 2017), 80.

50 Jackson, *We Have Always Lived in the Castle*, 44.
51 Ibid.
52 Ibid., 46.
53 Ibid., 126.
54 Friedman, *Shirley Jackson,* 137.
55 Jackson, *We Have Always Lived in the Castle*, 100.
56 Ibid., 139.
57 Nakagawa, "How to Make a Witch," 73.
58 Downey, "Not a Refuge Yet," 300.
59 Ibid., 300 (emphasis in the original).
60 Jackson, *We Have Always Lived in the Castle*, 115.
61 Ibid., 136.

References

Downey, Dara. "Not a Refuge Yet: Shirley Jackson's Domestic Hauntings," in *A Companion to American Gothic*, ed. Charles L. Crow, 290–302. Hoboken, NJ: John Wiley & Sons, 2013.
Franklin, Ruth. *Shirley Jackson: A Rather Haunted Life*. New York: Liveright, 2016.
Franklin, Ruth. Via W.W. Norton. "Shirley Jackson Wasn't Actually a Witch, or Was She?" *Literary Hub*, September 28, 2018 (accessed on November 14, 2018). https://lithub.com/shirley-jackson-wasnt-actually-a-witch/.
Friedman, Lenemaja. *Shirley Jackson*. Boston: Twayne, 1975.
Gaskill, Malcolm. *Witchcraft: A Very Short Introduction*. Oxford: Oxford University Press, 2010.
Hattenhauer, Darryl. *Shirley Jackson's American Gothic*. Albany, NY: State University of New York Press, 2003.
Heller, Zoë. "The Haunted Mind of Shirley Jackson." *New Yorker*, October 17, 2016 (accessed on November 14, 2018). https://www.newyorker.com/magazine/2016/10/17/the-haunted-mind-of-shirley-jackson.
Jackson, Shirley. *The Witchcraft of Salem Village*. New York: Random House, 1956.
Jackson, Shirley. *Life among the Savages*. 1953. Reprint, New York: Penguin Classics, 1997.
Jackson, Shirley. *We Have Always Lived in the Castle*. 1962. Reprint, New York: Penguin Classics, 2006.
Jackson, Shirley. "Experience and Fiction," in *Come Along with Me: Classic Short Stories and an Unfinished Novel*, ed. Stanly Edgar Hyman, 219–30. 1968. Reprint, New York: Penguin Classics, 2013.
Jackson, Shirley. *Raising Demons*. 1957. Reprint, New York: Penguin Classics, 2015.

Jackson, Shirley. "The Real Me," in *Let Me Tell You: New Stories, Essays, and Other Writings*, ed. Laurence Jackson Hyman and Sarah Hyman Dewitt, 357. New York: Random House, 2015.

Joshi, S. T. "Shirley Jackson: Domestic Horror," in *Shirley Jackson: Essays on the Literary Legacy*, ed. Bernice M. Murphy, 183–98. Jefferson, NC: McFarland, 2005.

Kamensky, Jane. "Female Speech and Other Demons: Witchcraft and Wordcraft in Early New England," in *Spellbound: Women and Witchcraft in America*, ed. Elizabeth Reis, 25–52. 1998. Reprint, Lanham, MD: SR Books, 2004.

Murphy, Bernice M. "Introduction," in *Shirley Jackson: Essays on the Literary Legacy*, ed. Bernice M. Murphy, 1–21. Jefferson, NC: McFarland, 2005.

Nakagawa, Chiho. "How to Make a Witch—Shirley Jackson and Femininity." *Foreign Literature Research*, 28 (2009): 63–84.

Oppenheimer, Judy. *Private Demons: The Life of Shirley Jackson*. New York: Fawcett Columbine, 1989.

Rubenstein, Roberta. "Writer, Housewife, Witch." *Women's Review of Books*, 34, no. 3 (2017): 18–19.

Sollée, Kristen J. *Witches, Sluts, Feminists: Conjuring the Sex Positive*. Berkeley, CA: ThreeL Media, 2017.

Temple, Emily. "Shirley Jackson: Possibly a Witch, Definitely Played the Zither." *Literary Hub*, August 8, 2018 (accessed on November 14, 2018). https://lithub.com/shirley-jackson-possibly-a-witch-definitely-played-the- zither/.

7

Homemaking for the Apocalypse: Queer Failures and Bunker Mentality in *The Sundial*

Jill E. Anderson

Survival in the nuclear age is a personal responsibility touching every American family. Make sure you take part. ... A prepared family builds a prepared nation. Civil defense is an American tradition.
—RETROSPECT, TELEVISION SERIES, 1961

Things will be different afterward ... Everything that makes the world like it is now will be gone. We'll have new rules and new ways of living. Maybe there'll be a law not to live in houses, so then no one can hide from anyone else, you'll see.
—SHIRLEY JACKSON, "THE INTOXICATED," 1949

When Aunt Fanny sets about preparing her home for the imminent apocalyptic event portended by her long-deceased father, she orders so many supplies to be brought via truck to the Halloran mansion that the home's other inhabitants notice "it was almost immediately clear that there was not going to be room enough in the storage basements."[1] Aunt Fanny and her companions choose the library as the next logical storage space, and as they load cans of peaches, milk, olives, soup, and spaghetti onto the bookshelves, they take the books to the barbeque pit to be burned (after all, they "are not made of candy," as Fanny points out).[2] When Orianna Halloran, Fanny's sister-in-law, complains, "Surely we are entering a land of milk and honey," Fanny retorts, "I don't really think we'll need to supply our own food. ... It only seemed perhaps, at first—while things are growing back, you know, and before we are quite *used* to the new ways—of course there *will* be a period of adjustment."[3] The preparation continues as Fanny, "mindful of Robinson Crusoe," adds a grindstone, tools, shotguns, hunting knives, a Boy Scout survival handbook, and first aid supplies to the apocalyptic stockpile.

But Shirley Jackson's 1958 novel *The Sundial* concludes the night *before* the apocalypse is set to take place, thus not only disrupting the novel's straightforward timeline but also never granting the audience a chance to see the "time of adjustment" or whether the family's stockpiling of supplies was ultimately necessary or advantageous. *The Sundial* is a rare bird in the apocalyptic genre in that it is *pre*-apocalyptic, tracing the time *up to* the event but not following it. The rhetoric of fallout, post-nuclear survival, and preparation circulated widely in the period Jackson wrote and published the novel, so Fanny's obsession with preparation situates *The Sundial* within the national fallout shelter debate as well as the larger, cultural context of nuclear anxieties during the period. "Homemaking for the apocalypse," a phrase I assign to the set of domestic rituals and practices specific to bunker mentality, includes shelter building and stockpiling with its implicit participation in consumerism, with a view toward an unimaginable yet definite future. Homemaking for the apocalypse also embraces containment of one's own home space, protection against outside influences, and a healthy paranoia toward suspicion of one's neighbors. Enabled and reinforced by the atomic anxieties of the early Cold War, this set of practices simultaneously plays up the queer failings of bunker mentality and the very presence of fallout shelters by emphasizing the futility of nuclear preparation. Susan Sontag describes this futility in her 1965 essay "The Imagination of Disaster" in which she argues that the "continual threat of two equally fearful, but seemingly opposed, destinies: unremitting banality and inconceivable terror" caused Americans in the Atomic Age to prepare for total disaster in ways that felt familiar and comfortable to them.[4] "These twin specters," as Sontag calls them, played on "the unbearably humdrum ... by an escape into exotic dangerous situations which have last-minute happy endings. But another one of the things that fantasy can do is to normalize what is psychologically unbearable, thereby inuring us to it."[5] In these terms, homemaking for the apocalypse helped habituate bomb-anxious Americans to the terrors of total destruction by replicating narratives of normative domesticity.

Bunker mentality and "bomb shelter abundance," to borrow Tom Engelhardt's terms, permeate *The Sundial*, since "national security and insecurity were merging in the home" in the period.⁶ The Hallorans' home comes to represent "an anxiety-ridden garrison state" in which "the worlds of consumer arcadia and global fear ... coexisted."⁷ When Fanny points out that "We will have to build shelters eventually, of course," she initiates the bunker mentality present in the novel, one predicated on dominant discourses of the fallout shelter and nuclear preparation and perceptions of time and inheritance that ultimately queer the domestic narrative and challenge the perceived stability of normative domestic practices that circulated widely in the early Cold War period.⁸ Alongside her disordered inheritance, Fanny's entrenchment in the bunker/mansion represents the embodiment of her strangeness and inability to reconcile the past with the present and future, causing her homemaking to be ultimately nonproductive. In the pivotal, revelatory scene of the novel, as she winds her way through the outdoor maze, looking for the statue of her mother and hearing the voice of her father, perpetually concerned with her ailing brother's health, we see a woman who has lived a life so closed off from "everything else" that her greatest fear is the continuance of a world filled with "everything else." The apocalyptic prophesy from her father seems a convenient device for Fanny, and it enables all the queer domestic, apocalyptic practices of the novel.

In situating the novel historically and dealing directly with issues of anxiety and preparation, I argue that Jackson's critique of the queer failings of this type of domestic, preparatory practice play against the "disciplining norms"⁹ that align narratives of success with a restrictive model of living. As Jack Halberstam contends in *In a Queer Time and Place*, embracing failure sanctions narratives of resistance, marked by their "subjugated knowledge" that allows people to "resist mastery" by "investing in counterintuitive modes of knowing such as failure and stupidity" and "privileg[ing] the naïve or nonsensical."¹⁰ These "oppositional pedagogies" allow for creative and differently generative ways of encountering the world that Halberstam argues should be recognized as fully legitimate. Fanny's prediction actually initiates a number of queer "failures" in the novel: the subjugated, yet powerful, knowledge of Fanny's prediction which becomes the novel's queer, disciplining norm; her anti-patriarchal vision of the future, which further secures and sanctions her "spinsterhood"; a perception of time that eschews progress and biological family and instead formulates inheritances that lie outside of the accepted circulation of goods; an affective domain within the home in which emotions and reactions run in unexpected, counterproductive ways; and a home space in which queer domestic practices circulate freely, running counter to the accepted, fixed, normative, dominant domesticities of the Cold War. Fanny goes off-line once again when she adopts her father's voice and the authority of the patriarchy he represents.

Never a mother, no longer a daughter, and soon not even a sister to any living relative, result in Fanny never having a "had a life" in any conventional sense. But Fanny's off-line sense of family relations begins when she becomes the father, the potentate and seer of the household. This is why the prophecy itself, which I quote at length here, is so important, because it meshes the voicing of the past with the embodiment of the future:

> Frances, there is danger. Go back to the house. Tell them, in the house, tell them, in the house, tell them that there is danger. Tell them in the house that in the house it is safe. The father will watch the house, but there is danger. Tell them. ... The father comes to his child and says gently that within himself there is no fear; the father comes to his child. Tell them in the house that there is danger. ... From the sky and from the ground and from the sea there is danger; tell them in the house. There will be black fire and red water and the earth turning and screaming; this will come. ... When the sky is fair again the children will be safe; the father comes to his children who will be saved. Tell them in the house that they will be saved. Do not let them leave the house; say to them: Do not fear, the father will guard his children. Go into your father's house and say these things.[11]

The repetition of "in the house" evokes the idea that the *only* safe place in the world is *in the house*. Also, by taking on his voice and installing what she deems as the productive bunker mentality of the home, Fanny simultaneously embraces and refuses "repro-time" or the "the time of inheritance" which emphasizes that "values, wealth, goods, and morals are passed through family ties from one generation to the next."[12] Ironically, only two sentences are devoted to a description of the apocalyptic events and another to its aftermath. The language of the proclamation is decidedly biblical (with its repetition of words like "father," "children," and "saved"). But when pressed by a villager whether Armageddon is coming, Orianna's companion Miss Ogilvie states, "I think that's different. ... I mean, the *rest* of you ..." Miss Ogilvie's hesitant observation signals something significant: the Hallorans and their hangers-on are appropriate enough to be saved, but to what end?

Additionally, the prophecy focuses on continuing the insularity of the Halloran's bunker/mansion. The proclamation also represents Aunt Fanny's way of not becoming "dislodged" from the home, a concern earlier in the novel when Orianna declares she is going to do some "housekeeping." Significantly, "Tell them in the house" can be read two ways: with the emphasis on "tell them" and "say these things," as the imperative in which the voice commands Aunt Fanny to simply return to those inhabiting the house to share the news; and with the emphasis on "in the house," as the command to return to the house, and, inside the house, "say these things." The latter explanation seems to be more pertinent because, despite the fact that she does warn everyone—"I want to tell you ..."—the proclamation initiates Fanny's entrenchment in the bunker/mansion.

Of course, we cannot say with certainty that the apocalyptic disaster that grounds the actions in *The Sundial* is a coming nuclear attack. The novel does not specify a time or place, but when Aunt Fanny receives the apocalyptic revelation from her father, it sounds vaguely like a H-bomb being dropped: "From the sky and from the ground and from the sea there is danger ... There will be black fire and red water and the earth turning and screaming."[13] In the preface of her posthumous short story collection, *The Magic of Shirley Jackson* (1966), Stanley Edgar Hyman states that Jackson's "fierce visions of dissociation and madness, of alienation and withdrawal, of cruelty and terror ... are a sensitive and faithful anatomy of our times, fitting symbols for our distressing world of the concentration camp and the Bomb."[14] Hyman's observation provides an important reminder of the historical context of Jackson's work, thus leading to her nuanced and sometimes alarming critques of Cold War America. According to Ruth Franklin, Jackson actually began the novel just after Eisenhower's reelection in 1956 and finished right before the USSR's launch of *Sputnik* in the summer of 1957—before the official implementation of the National Fallout Shelter Policy. But, as Franklin also notes, "apocalypse was in the air, quite literally," and while critics were puzzled by *The Sundial*'s symbolic apocalypse, many guessed that it had to do with "hell bombs and space platforms bristling with atomic artillery and ... [other] stylish nightmares of the day" or an "H-Hour of an apocalyptic D-Day approaches."[15]

Read through the lens of midcentury atomic paranoia, the "contagion of belief," to borrow John G. Parks's term is an apt description for preparation for nuclear survival.[16] I argue that the Federal Civil Defense Administration's (FCDA) preparation suggestions, which I discuss in detail later, were, if nothing else, an exercise in contagious belief—belief that one's preparations and stockpiling and bunkering could, in the worst case, allow one's family to survive a total disaster, and it was a belief circulated nationwide. Parks, referencing the apocalyptic tones of *The Sundial*, suggests that the novel centers primarily on "the nature of belief, with the way desperate people grasp a belief and make it their truth, with how belief and madness combine and lead to desperate behavior, with how belief is a form of madness itself, making people into grotesques."[17] "The question of belief is a curious one," the novel's narrator notes after Fanny has relayed the apocalyptic message to the rest of the household, "... in all the world there is not someone who does not believe in something. It might be suggested, and not easily disproven that anything, no matter how exotic, can be believed by someone."[18] The bunker/mansion becomes pivotal in the way the Hallorans and their hangers-on shape their beliefs, since in its American gothic mode the home also comes to symbolize "an image of authoritarianism, or imprisonment, or of 'confining narcissism' ... a growing obsession with one's own problems; a turning inward instead of a growing outward."[19] Rather than affording its inhabitants all the affluence and prosperity promised to postwar Americans, the mansion seems to close around its inhabitants, creating a vacuum of intention where nothing matters but what happens inside.

At its heart, *The Sundial* is a domestic narrative, but one that deviates from earlier domestic fiction that "feature[s] a self-consciousness about the home's physical space and the project of homemaking" to embrace "a politics of domestic instability, particularly emphasized through its distinctive domestic spaces and conclusions."[20] This instability, Kristin Jacobson explains, is a hallmark of "neodomestic fiction" and manifests through a practice of "'renovation' or 'redesign', the active construction and (re)design of the (conventional) domestic sphere and its concomitant effects on community and the self."[21] *The Sundial* is a neodomestic novel in its embrace of instability through its mundane actions, as the characters in the novel attempt to renovate their homespace for an unimaginable end time. Despite the fact that the bomb is never mentioned in the novel, Richard Pascal argues that the "obsession" with apocalypse actually stems from "the socially sanctioned impulse to retreat to 'American miniatures,' or small, exclusive enclaves of communal, familial, and individual sanctuary from the claims of the larger social universe" along with "some vague but fervently dreamt of communal fulfillment implicit in its originating image of itself as a New World."[22]

But even as Fanny's apocalypse appears to be more biblical in some sense, with the resulting world called a "Garden of Eden," a "brave new world," a "bright world," and a "green world," she actually manages to instill a fearful faith in her family that reconstitutes not only the kind of future available to this queer family but also the sort of ecological imperatives necessary for living after the apocalyptic events. It is a world seemingly returned to the pre-contact, New World (to invoke the mythos of Henry Nash Smith's famous *Virgin Land*): "Fresh, untouched, green, lovely. Untrammeled, except by ourselves. A lifetime of warmth and beauty and fertility. The kind of life and world people have been dreaming about ever since they first began fouling this one," as Fanny imagines.[23] It is an idealized version of the world that not only removes the possibility of other survivors but seemingly ignores any sort of residual fallout. Apart from the "period of adjustment" Fanny mentions to Orianna, there is no plan here. Each member of the household goes on Fanny's faith and proceeds bunkering in a way that would have made any Atomic Age FCDA official proud.

The security and stability that the Atomic Age home afforded after the upheaval of the Second World War was vital to dominant domestic ideologies of the day. In her groundbreaking study of the American family during the Cold War, Elaine Tyler May argues "domestic ideology emerged as a buffer" against communism and nonconformity, and it "ultimately fostered the very tendencies it was intended to diffuse: materialism, consumerism, and bureaucratic conformity."[24] Domestic containment or the "self-contained home" was the answer to security in the Atomic Age, and since the "American way of life" was distinctly capitalist in nature, official policies reaffirmed the centrality of the home: "Domestic containment was bolstered by a powerful political culture that rewarded its adherents and marginalized its detractors. More than merely a metaphor for the cold war on the home front, containment aptly describes the way in which public policy, personal behavior, and even political values were focused on the home."[25] May further notes, in her 2017 book *Fortress America: How We Embraced Fear and Abandoned Democracy*, a uniquely American domestic mythos meant that "privacy offered the possibility of internal fortification" (specifically in white, middle-class, heteropatriarchal suburbia), making the private home a space to "enjoy the fruits of postwar prosperity" at the same time "families could cultivate the virtues of independent citizenship that bolster both individual autonomy and national strength."[26]

Part of this domestic mythology arrived with the adoption of the US government's National Fallout Shelter Policy in 1958, which came after years of study and debate about how to survive a nuclear attack on American soil and signaled the establishment of a dominant discourse on shelter stockpiling and individualized civil defense. In a public address given in 1961, President Kennedy touted the fallout shelter as the nation's "survival insurance" and argued that "common prudence demands that we take all necessary measures to protect our homes, our institutions, and our way of life, so that they can survive should an enemy thrust war upon us."[27] Linking individual action with the survival of a collective "way of life" meant placing a nation's survival in the hands of private families. To reinforce official fallout shelter policy, the FCDA had to take into account the effects of radioactive fallout, the decreasing viability of evacuating population centers during an attack, private industry's willingness to develop and sell consumer goods related to shelter stockpiling, as well as advances in the delivery method of bombs from the USSR.

To this end, the FCDA had been testing aboveground nuclear weapons at their American Energy Commission proving grounds in Yucca Flat, Nevada, since 1951. Civil defense tests like Operation Doorstep and Operation Cue specifically addressed the effect of hydrogen bombs on "typical" American homes. In what became known as Survival Town, homes were stocked with various foodstuffs and filled with mannequins dressed as "Mr. and Mrs. America" set up in a number of domestic scenarios (reading the paper by the picture window, in a family group at the dining room table, asleep in an upstairs bedroom). Survival Town's purpose was to test the viability of private fallout shelters. Officials concluded that simple basement shelters that could be obtained relatively cheaply should contain a two-week supply of provisions and would mean the continuing survival of one's own family. The FCDA happily circulated the results of these tests widely via carefully edited evening television programs, newsreels, illustrated booklets and pamphlets, and multiple spreads in both *Time* and *Life*.

Since the development of the Fallout Shelter Policy shifted responsibility for nuclear preparation and survival from government entities to private citizens and communities, it reinforced the mythos of the contained, well-ordered, stable home space. The National Shelter Survey was implemented in 1961 (the same year the USSR tested Tsar Bomba, the most powerful single H-bomb ever detonated in the world), and it assessed the individual household's apocalyptic preparedness. Homemakers who participated received manuals like *Personal and Family Survival*, which argued that shelters "are the principle means of protection," allowing "tens of millions, who otherwise would die from the effects of radiation, to live. Their survival, in healthy condition, would help ensure the survival of the Nation."[28] Homemakers could earn a Home Preparedness Award to display in their front window after sending away for a Home Preparedness Workshop Kit, submitting to a home inspection by a civil defense official, and completing a required twenty-item "Readiness Requirement" checklist. The checklist included ensuring fallout shelters were stocked with a fourteen-day supply of food and water as well as recreational activities to keep up shelter survivalists' morale. "Alert today, alive tomorrow" and "It pays to get ready while your thinking is steady" became the mottos of the FCDA in the mid-1950s, as the government launched a massive advertising campaign to inform US citizens that surviving a nuclear attack could be as simple as preparing one's own shelter and stocking it with supplies.

Although today we dismiss the fallout shelter as a kitschy symbol of Cold War domestic anxieties, shelter stockpiling was a serious business at the height of the Atomic Age. In 1962, after years of research and development, the United States Department of Agriculture introduced what became known as the Doomsday Cracker, a biscuit made of bulgur wheat, which could be prepared as a "soft gruel" for children and the elderly or "may be crumbled and eaten with milk and sugar, served with a hot sauce such as chili or spaghetti sauce, or added to soup, like barley or rice."[29] Nabisco advertised its own All-Purpose Survival Biscuit the same year. The biscuit resembled a saltine and could be made more palatable by adding water. General Mills developed a portable meal kit known as Multi-Purpose Foods (MPF), a two-week supply of nutritionally dense canned food that families could order via mail, that was "compact—inexpensive—pre-cooked—ready to use—and virtually non-perishable as long as it is sealed in its container." The government even marketed and distributed Emergency Drinking Water in huge, sealed cans, and an empty 17-½ gallon drum could be reused as a commode, as the instructions on the container detail.

Popular home shopping companies like Sears and Roebuck set up civil defense window displays in their stores, showcasing the latest in shelter supplies, including first aid kits and sanitary facilities, while actresses portraying famed home baker Betty Crocker visited grocery stores to promote the FCDA's "Grandma's Pantry" program. When the FCDA developed "Grandma's Pantry" in order to associate shelter stockpiling with the homey readiness of Grandma's house, they "[b]orrowed an idea from Grandma's long years of experience in taking care of her family. ... the theme is: 'Grandma's Pantry Was Ready—Is Your Pantry Ready in Event of Emergency?'"[30] The program primarily targeted women, since a "responsible American woman" does not "gamble with the safety" of her family, neighbors, or country.[31] The program also invoked the Second World War home front to emphasize the necessity for civilian participation:

> You would hardly blame others for failing to provide food, clothing, and shelter for your family. ... If the women in this country will prepare with courage and determination, we will have the civil defense we need to be strong—and each woman who gives her time and effort to civil defense will be doing her part to keep the forces of communism in check, to prepare us against attack, and to help keep the peace.[32]

By elevating mundane, domestic responsibilities to a national responsibility and reinforcing normative gender roles for American women, the FCDA managed to implicate women in the survival of not just their own (white, middle-class, able-bodied, normal-looking) families but also the nation. The "centrality of ideal and real families to the privatization of defense" was both a "blessing and curse" for the government, since "family-centered preparedness looked benign" and seemed "more domestic than militaristic," according to Laura McEnaney.[33] By imbuing citizens with this level of domestic regimentation, officials "were asking citizens to share the fear, which, as planners knew, was not a human emotion easily shaped and controlled."[34] Also embedded within the fallout shelter narrative is the idea that able-bodied, white, middle-class heteropatriarchal families were the most desirable candidates for survival, but only if they were able to act according to preparation suggestions and come out of these situations unscathed and with a positive attitude, both in general and toward fallout shelters. Shelter life was, according to official discourse, meant to replicate life aboveground, with normative gender and family roles playing out, and life continuing as "normally" as possible.

For this reason, emotional management became one of the main concerns for shelter survival, since having to inhabit a fallout shelter, "would be terrible beyond imagination and description," as *Fallout Protection*, a booklet from 1961 explains: "But there is much that can be done to assure that it would not mean the end of the life of our Nation."[35] Chuck West, in his bestselling *Fallout Shelter Handbook,* advises that "[a] calm, optimistic, sympathetic, but unemotional acceptance of the situation will help considerably."[36] Fallout shelter manuals encouraged shelter survivalists to stock their spaces with board games and toys particularly for restless children. One radio promotion even recommended that tranquilizers were an essential shelter item: "By all means, provide some tranquilizers to ease the strain and monotony of life in a fallout shelter. A bottle of 100 should be sufficient for a family of four. Tranquilizers are not a narcotic, and are not habit-forming."[37] That well-known "careful fellow" Bert the Turtle from the *Duck and Cover* cartoon, which was shown in schools nationwide, sought emotional management by advising children that remaining calm by being prepared and practicing duck-and-cover drills were the best bets for surviving a bomb that could come at any time: "You might be eating your lunch when the flash comes, duck and cover under the table. Then if the explosion makes anything in the room fall down, it won't fall on you. Getting ready means we will all have to be ready to take care of ourselves. The bomb might explode when there are no grownups near."[38]

These official government policies that reinforced questions about emotional management and turned preparation over to households contributed to what Kenneth Rose labels "shelter morality" in his 2001 book *One Nation Underground*. Rose recalls that, while the government touted the necessity and viability of the private shelter to national civil defense policy, Americans rejected the policy because of the expense, the lack of guaranteed protection from radioactive fallout, along with the "troubling moral aspects of shelters," which included "questions about personal ethics and relationships with one's neighbors, as well as questions of national identity and the ultimate morality of the kind of world that would be created by nuclear exchange."[39] Besides just stockpiling, Fanny enacts a new type of morality in her insular, little world, offering an exclusionary mode of belief in which she argues, "humanity being for all practical purposes at an end, the kind of moral disapproval which has been so necessary up until now will be wholly unnecessary; *we*, after all, will not need to learn to behave ourselves."[40] She is seemingly rejecting the *rejection* of shelter morality, instituting and embracing her system of doing things. The suggestion here is that, even while accepting bunker mentality as part of her homemaking for the apocalypse, she is even more interested in setting herself apart from her peers. Because of this, the Hallorans' preparations include barricading the home, covering windows and doors to block the world outside, and excluding certain people. Orianna urges her family to "think of ourselves ... as completely isolated. We are on a tiny island in a raging sea; we are a point of safety in a world of ruin."[41] As their apocalyptic preparation makes them more insular, they become concerned with repopulating the world, but even that has its moral quandaries. With all possible patriarchs removed from the line of inheritance, they are free to imagine alternative family formations.

As the desexualized, bumbling, ineffectual spinster, Fanny seeks to finally disrupt the rightful paths of inheritance with her apocalyptic predictions, to unseat the established patriarchy of her family, and to maintain the insularity of the Halloran's homespace in opposition to an outer world inhabited by people of lesser "breeding." They "were charged with the future of humanity," since "the world outside was ending" and everyone not in the bunker/mansion would perish.[42] When Fanny declares, "Humanity, as an experiment, has failed," she initiates her own voice as authority, while, at the same time, making note that they would "emerge safe and pure ... into a world clean and silent, their inheritance."[43] With Lionel dead and Richard, Fanny's elderly brother, certainly incapable, the only men suitable for reproduction left are Essex, the librarian who dutifully burns books, and the captain. When Orianna composes the list of thirteen rules for their new world, she includes that "mates" will be arranged by Mrs. Halloran and "indiscriminate coupling will be subject to severe punishment."[44] Furthermore, "it is expected that all members of the party will keep in mind their positions as inheritors of the world, and conduct themselves accordingly," Orianna dictates.[45] Additionally, she advises, as the night of August 31 approaches,

> This is final. ... We have no time now, and certainly no patience, for hysteria or panic. We have all known about this coming day and night for many weeks, and we know, too, what we shall see tomorrow morning. Any one of you ... who provokes or indulges in an emotional outburst, will be shut in a closet and kept there by force.[46]

That is, in this figuration, there is a "right" way to act, and that includes following the rules of reproductive inheritance.

But given these reproductive imperatives, Fanny and the other Hallorans are squarely outside of normative, reproductive desires. "In the conventional family home," Sara Ahmed points out in *Queer Phenomenology: Orientations, Objects, Others*:

> what appears requires following a certain line, the family line that directs our gaze. The heterosexual couple becomes a "point" along this line, which is given to the child as its inheritance or background. The background then *is not simply behind the child*: it is what the child is asked to aspire *toward*. The background, given in this way, can orientate us toward the future: it is where the child is asked to direct its desire by accepting the family line as its own inheritance. There is pressure to inherit this line, a pressure that can speak the language of love, happiness, and care, which pushes us along specific paths.[47]

The Hallorans' lines of inheritance are messy, out of order, and encompass many possible paths. For one thing, Fancy, Lionel's daughter and heir to the home after her grandmother, Orianna, dies, falls neatly into the path of normative desires, of wanting to inherit the family home. So strong is her orientation to this "right" path that she explains, "When my grandmother dies, I am going to smash my doll house. I won't need it any more," and she periodically leaves grandmother-like voodoo dolls stuck with needles—symbols of Orianna's demise—around the home.[48] But inheritance is complicated, as Ahmed points out: "Indeed, the word inheritance includes two meanings: to receive and to possess. In a way, we convert what we receive into possessions, a conversion that often 'hides' the conditions of having received, as if the possession is too simply 'already there.'"[49] The methods by which Fancy is planning on receiving the home are questionable at best. Inheritance relies on the demise of her grandmother, something she and her mother actively wish to hasten. Toward the end of the novel, the "right path" of inheritance is partially enacted as Fancy metaphorically and literally takes up her grandmother's crown after Orianna has been pushed down the stairs (incidentally, the same stairs on which her own son met his demise) to her death.

However, Fancy, who is described as "subnormal" by Fanny, desires to inherit the Halloran mansion even as she is a queer child, growing "sideways," to use Kathryn Bond Stockton's term: "something related but not reducible to the death drive; something that locates energy, pleasure, vitality, and (e)motion in the back-and-forth of connections and extensions that are not reproductive."[50] Fancy worries that she has missed her childhood, growing up among adults in the isolated family mansion, and she offers what might be the most mature and sanest response to the novel's apocalyptic prophecy:

> Aunt Fanny keeps saying that there is going to be a lovely world, all green and still and perfect and we are all going to live there and be peaceful and happy. That would be perfectly fine for me, except right here I live in a lovely world, all green and still and perfect, even though no one around here seems to be very peaceful or happy, but when I think about it this world is going to have Aunt Fanny and my grandmother and you and Essex and the rest of these crazy people and my mother and what makes anyone think you're going to be more happy or peaceful just because you're the only ones left?[51]

As Fancy confirms, for everyone's concern about futurity and inheritance, life trajectories matter greatly. Fanny's trajectory is marred by disappointment and an eschewal of the present. Because "time inhabits all living beings, is an internal, indeed constitutive, feature of life itself, yet it is also what places living beings in relations to simultaneity and succession with each other insofar as they are all participants in a single temporality, in a single relentless move forward,"[52] Elizabeth Grosz suggests we "revel in the untimely" and "affirm the value of the nick, the cut, or rupture" of temporality as a way of understanding the way humans "straddle the past and the future without the security of a stable and abiding present."[53] Aunt Fanny "revels in the untimely," eschewing the stability of her family life for a strange dalliance with death and her past as well as the future of the mansion and the outside world. Part of this is because homemaking for the apocalypse requires her to imagine a time outside of time, but her attempt to ground herself in a reality to which she can adhere has her remaking the world in an image she can understand.

The mansion, then, as fallout shelter and repository for the new world's remaking, is meant to "contain everything" and to be set up in opposition to the "other world, the one the Hallorans were leaving behind."[54] The bunker/mansion "will become a kind of shrine, for our children and for *their* children," as "they will have no thought of houses, and a roof will become to them synonymous with an altar," as Fanny imagines.[55] In this way, Fanny projects a vision of the future that encompasses the bunker/mansion and imbues it with a ritual importance—everything ordered and predictable. But the only object in the house that is "badly off center" and deviates from the careful symmetry the elder Mr. Halloran created is the eponymous sundial, which bears the inscription WHAT IS THIS WORLD?[56] The inscription itself comes from "The Knight's Tale" in Chaucer's *The Canterbury Tales*, and that no one understands its meaning, including Mr. Halloran, who believes the saying is "a remark about time," is telling. However anyone interprets its inscription, though, the sundial remains off center. Time, in moments of apocalyptic anxieties, is often lived in strange, unimaginable fits and starts, often arrested but seemingly looking toward an unquestioning future.

Part of this arrested time lies in a separate apartment in the home, a place Fanny's long-dead mother decorated to her taste and which has remained fairly untouched in the decades since her mother's death. Fanny calls it her "dollhouse" and lovingly keeps the space as a kind of shrine, not to her mother exclusively, but to the girl that Fanny used to be, when she was merely Frances without the label of the spinster aunt. Fanny's dollhouse echoes Fancy's dollhouse. Fanny coaxes her young protégé upstairs, telling her, "I want to show you something no one has seen for many years."[57] With anxiety, Fanny realizes the importance of "a kind of continuity, a way of establishing one strong direct line from the first Mrs. Halloran to Fancy."[58] Fancy labels the apartment "funny" and "strange," and Fanny creates a tableau with her as mother and Fancy as "little Frances." From her own mother's chair, Aunt Fanny attempts to re-narrate the family's history and insert herself into the marriage plot:

> My darling Frances will grow up to be a lovely woman, tall and fair, and someday she will marry him and they will have strong and happy and handsome children of their own. But my son Richard will never marry; he will stay with his mother always, standing by his father, so I will always have a strong wise man on either side of me.[59]

She keeps photos of her mother there that track the trajectory of her shortened, "tragically swift" life—girl, bride, mother. Her obsessive fixation on her mother's short life reflects her value for "other" temporalities. The other temporalities are always bound up in Aunt Fanny's position within the Halloran mansion, articulating what I will call her sense of disordered inheritance. The apartment, moreover, plays no role in Fanny's pre-apocalyptic stockpiling, lying outside the reasonable intentions of their preparations. It is, in a sense, dead space, off-line with the rest of the home's purpose but part of the bunker narrative, nonetheless, because it represents yet another form of stockpiling for her. She shores up her possessions around her, unable to cope with the outside world, radioactive or not.

That the publication of Jackson's most renowned novel, *The Haunting of Hill House*, followed *The Sundial* seems no conincidence. Both novels deal with how groups of people become entrenched in a home and how that isolation can, for all intents and purposes, drive the occupants to a state of heightened paranoia, thereby shaping their rememberance of the past and how they proceed into the future. As I have argued elsewhere, in *Hill House*, domestic practices enable acts of storytelling for the protagonist, Eleanor, that give her imaginative alteratives to the life laid out for her by normative, white, middle-class social forces.[60] Her stories and the queer domestic practices in which she engages are also her way of imagining a future time in which she is fulfilled and happy, but this projection ultimately fails because she merely replaces ensconcement in one home for another equally haunted and destructive one. The major difference between Eleanor's and Fanny's outcomes lie in their world-building. Eleanor, in loneliness and suffering from some kind of mental lapse, destroys only herself; Fanny seemingly sacrifices the entire world, save the chosen few, to her apocalyptic prophecy. Fanny's vision is static, fixed to a past that is non-productive, and projecting into a future we cannot see. Her stockpiling and entrenchment in the bunker/mansion serves only her vision of the shortcomings of her family and humanity, and becomes the enduring legacy of a failed Atomic Age bunker mentality. Homemaking for the apocalypse is her attempt at controlling her narrative, but it is a narrative which does not contain a successful, meaningful end. And much like Eileen, the 17-year-old main character of Jackson's 1949 short story "The Intoxicated," from which this chapter's second epigraph comes, neither Eleanor nor Fanny can imagine the same world existing after the disasterous ends they each anticipate. They shore up their own defenses—Eleanor by ending her own life, Eileen by terrifying a partygoer with her apocalyptic predictions while innocently sketching out her Latin homework at the kitchen table, and Fanny by stockpiling and preparing—but they all come to naught. As Eileen states, moments before she is dismissed outright as a mere "kid," "I don't really think [the world's] got much future ... at least the way we've got it now."[61] In words wise (and haunting) beyond her years, Eileen seems to answer the sentiment painted over the stairway in the Halloran bunker/mansion: WHEN SHALL WE LIVE IF NOT NOW?

Notes

1. Shirley Jackson, *The Sundial* (New York: Penguin Press, 2014), 105.
2. Ibid., 107.
3. Ibid., 106.
4. Susan Sontag, "The Imagination of Disaster," *Commentary* (October 1, 1965): 42. It is a position echoed by Arlene Skolnick, who argues in *Embattled Paradise: The American Family in an Age of Uncertainty* that the "contrasting visions" of the 1950s set up the idealized family life portrayed in pop culture against the "nightmare vision" that filled the pages of playwrights and novelists of the period.
5. Sontag, "The Imagination of Disaster," 42.
6. Tom Engelhardt, *The End of Victory Culture: Cold War America and the Disillusioning of a Generation* (Amherst: University of Massachusetts Press, 1998), 107.
7. Ibid., 87.
8. Jackson, *The Sundial,* 106.
9. This is a concept adapted from Jack Halberstam's *The Queer Art of Failure.*
10. J. Jack Halberstam, *In a Queer Time and Place: Transgender Bodies, Subcultural Lives* (New York: New York University Press), 11–12.
11. Jackson, *The Sundial,* 26.
12. Halberstam, *In a Queer Time and Place*, 5. Elizabeth Freeman labels a similar sense of time "chrononormativity, or the use of time to organize individual human bodies toward maximum productivity" (3). Freeman also introduces a "chronobiopolitics," defined by "having a life" that is "event-centered, goal-oriented, intentional, and culminating in epiphanies or major transformations. The logic of time-as-productive thereby becomes one of serial cause-and-effect: the past seems useless unless it predicts and becomes material for a future" (5).
13. Ibid., 26.
14. Stanley Edgar Hyman, "Preface," in *The Magic of Shirley Jackson*, ed. Stanley Edgar Hyman (New York: Farrar, Straus, and Giroux, 1966), viii.
15. Ruth Franklin, *Shirley Jackson: A Rather Haunted Life* (New York: Liveright, 2016), 384; qtd. in Franklin, 398.
16. Ibid., 83.
17. John G. Parks, "Waiting for the End: Shirley Jackson's *The Sundial.*" *Critique: Studies in Contemporary Fiction*, 19, no. 3 (1978): 75. For an article that contextualizes other aspects of Jackson's apocalypticism, see also: Angela Hague, "'A Faithful Anatomy of Our Times': Reassessing Shirley Jackson." *Frontiers*, 26, no. 2 (2005): 73–96.
18. Jackson, *The Sundial,* 33.

19　Stephen King, *Dance Macabre* (New York: Berkley Books, 1983), 281. King also notes that he wrote *The Shining*, his own domestic horror story, "with *The Sundial* very much in mind" as "their inner world shrunk and turned inward."

20　Jacobson, *Neodomestic American Fiction*, 3.

21　Ibid., 29.

22　Richard Pascal, "New World Miniatures: Shirley Jackson's *The Sundial* and Postwar American Society." *Journal of American Culture*, 23, no. 3 (2000): 99.

23　Jackson, *The Sundial*, 144.

24　Elaine Tyler May, *Homeward Bound* (New York: Basic Books, 2008), 13.

25　Ibid., 16.

26　Elaine Tyler May, *Fortress America: How We Embraced Fear and Abandoned Democracy* (New York: Basic Books, 2017), 26.

27　John F. Kennedy, *John F. Kennedy, 1961: Containing the Public Messages, Speeches, and Statements of the President, January 20 to December 31, 1961* in *The Public Papers of the Presidents of the United States* (University of Michigan Library, 2005) (accessed November 15, 2018), 338. http://name.umdl.umich.edu/4730886.1961.001.

28　United States Government, Department of Defense, *Personal and Family Survival* (Washington, DC: Government Printing Office, 1966), 3.

29　United States Government, Department of Defense, *Annual Report of the Office of Civil Defense* (Washington, DC: Government Printing Office, 1962), 25.

30　United States Government, FCDA, *Grandma's Pantry Belongs in Your Kitchen* (Washington, DC: Government Printing Office, 1955), 1.

31　United States Government, FCDA, *Women in Civil Defense* (Washington, DC: Government Printing Office, 1952), 1.

32　Ibid., 20.

33　Laura McEnaney, *Civil Defense Begins at Home: Militarization Meets Everyday Life in the Fifties* (Princeton, NJ: Princeton University Press, 2000), 69.

34　Ibid.

35　United States Government, Office of Civil Defense, *Fallout Protection: What to Know and Do About Nuclear Attack* (Washington, DC: Government Printing Office, 1961), 7.

36　Chuck West, *Fallout Shelter Handbook* (New York: Fawcett, 1962), 50.

37　"If the Bomb Falls: A Recorded Guide to Survival," [Originally recorded 1961], YouTube video, 12:29, posted by PylonBureau, May 23, 2011 https://www.youtube.com/watch?v= 53Kh6aqkBT8.

38　*Duck and Cover*, [Originally recorded 1951], *National Archives and Records Administration* video, 9:15, https://archive.org/details/DuckandC1951.

39 Kenneth Rose, *One Nation Underground: The Fallout Shelter in American Culture* (New York: New York University Press, 2001), 10.
40 Jackson, *The Sundial*, 109.
41 Ibid., 209.
42 Ibid., 35.
43 Ibid., 37, 35–6.
44 Ibid., 172.
45 Ibid.
46 Ibid., 209.
47 Sara Ahmed, *Queer Phenomenology: Orientations, Objects, Others* (Durham, NC: Duke University Press, 2006), 90.
48 Jackson, *The Sundial*, 18.
49 Ahmed, *Queer Phenomenology*, 126.
50 Kathryn Bond Stockton, *The Queer Child: Or, Growing Sideways in the Twentieth Century* (Durham, NC: Duke University Press, 2009), 13.
51 Jackson, *The Sundial*, 147–8.
52 Elizabeth Grosz, *The Nick of Time: Politics, Evolution, and the Untimely* (Durham, NC: Duke University Press, 2004), 5.
53 Ibid., 14.
54 Jackson, *The Sundial*, 8.
55 Ibid., 109.
56 Ibid., 10.
57 Jackson, *The Sundial*, 163.
58 Ibid.
59 Ibid., 164.
60 See Jill E. Anderson, "The Haunting of *Fun Home*: Shirley Jackson and Alison Bechdel's Queer Gothic Neodomesticity," in *Shirley Jackson: Influences and Confluences*, ed. Melanie R. Anderson and Lisa Kröger (New York: Routledge, 2016), 142–59.
61 Shirley Jackson, "The Intoxicated," in *The Lottery and Other Stories* (New York: Farrar, Straus and Giroux, 2005), 5.

References

Ahmed, Sara. *Queer Phenomenology: Orientations, Objects, Others*. Durham, NC: Duke University Press, 2006.
Duck and Cover. [Originally recorded 1951]. *National Archives and Records Administration* video, 9:15. https://archive.org/details/DuckandC1951.
Engelhardt, Tom. *The End of Victory Culture: Cold War America and the Disillusioning of a Generation*. Amherst: University of Massachusetts Press, 1998.

Franklin, Ruth. *Shirley Jackson: A Rather Haunted Life*. New York: Liveright Publishing, 2016.
Freeman, Elizabeth. *Time Binds: Queer Temporalities, Queer Histories*. Durham, NC: Duke University Press, 2010.
Grosz, Elizabeth. *The Nick of Time: Politics, Evolution, and the Untimely*. Durham, NC: Duke University Press, 2004.
Halberstam, J. Jack. *In a Queer Time and Place: Transgender Bodies, Subcultural Lives*. New York: New York University Press, 2005.
Hyman, Stanley Edgar. "Preface," in *The Magic of Shirley Jackson*, ed. Stanley Edgar Hyman, vii–ix. New York: Farrar, Straus, and Giroux, 1966.
"If the Bomb Falls: A Recorded Guide to Survival." [Originally recorded 1961]. YouTube video, 12:29. Posted by PylonBureau, May 23, 2011 (accessed August 19, 2019). https://www.youtube.com/watch?v= 53Kh6aqkBT8.
Jackson, Shirley. *The Sundial*. 1958. New York: Penguin, 2014.
Jackson, Shirley. "The Intoxicated," in *The Lottery and Other Stories*, 3–8. New York: Farrar, Straus and Giroux, 2005.
Jacobson, Kristin. *Neodomestic American Fiction*. Columbus: Ohio State University Press, 2010.
Kennedy, John F. *John F. Kennedy, 1961: Containing the Public Messages, Speeches, and Statements of the President, January 20 to December 31, 1961. The Public Papers of the Presidents of the United States*, University of Michigan Library, 2005. http://name.umdl.umich.edu/4730886.1961.001.
King, Stephen. *Dance Macabre*. New York: Berkley Books, 1983.
May, Elaine Tyler. *Homeward Bound: American Families in the Cold War Era*, 1988. Revised ed., New York: Basic Books, 2008.
May, Elaine Tyler. *Fortress America: How We Embraced Fear and Abandoned Democracy*. New York: Basic Books, 2017.
McEnaney, Laura. *Civil Defense Begins at Home: Militarization Meets Everyday life in the Fifties*. Princeton, NJ: Princeton University Press, 2000.
Parks, John G. "Waiting for the End: Shirley Jackson's *The Sundial*." *Critique: Studies in Contemporary Fiction*, 19, no. 3 (1978): 74–88.
Pascal, Richard. "New World Miniatures: Shirley Jackson's *The Sundial* and Postwar American Society." *Journal of American Culture*, 23, no. 3 (2000): 99–111.
Rose, Kenneth. *One Nation Underground: The Fallout Shelter in American Culture*. New York: New York University Press, 2001.
Sontag, Susan. "The Imagination of Disaster." *Commentary* (October 1, 1965): 42–8.
Skolnick, Arlene. *Embattled Paradise: The American Family in an Age of Uncertainty*. New York: Basic Books, 1991.
Stockton, Kathryn Bond. *The Queer Child: Or Growing Sideways in the Twentieth Century*. Durham, NC: Duke University Press, 2009.
United States Government, Department of Defense. Department of Defense. *Annual Report of the Office of Civil Defense*. Washington, DC: Government Printing Office, 1962.
United States Government, Federal Civil Defense Administration. *Women in Civil Defense*. Washington, DC: Government Printing Office, 1952.

United States Government, Federal Civil Defense Administration. *Grandma's Pantry Belongs in Your Kitchen*. Washington, DC: Government Printing Office, 1955.

United States Government, Office of Civil Defense. *Fallout Protection: What to Know and Do About Nuclear Attack*. Washington, DC: Government Printing Office, 1961.

United States Government, Office of Civil Defense. *Personal and Family Survival*. Washington, DC: Government Printing Office, 1966.

West, Chuck. *Fallout Shelter Handbook*. New York: Fawcett, 1962.

8

Domestic Apocalypse in *The Sundial*

Christiane E. Farnan

Shirley Jackson's Cold War extremist satire *The Sundial* opens with the murder of the heir apparent, Lionel Halloran, and closes with the murder of Lionel's killer, his mother, the domestic despot, Orianna Halloran. The main structural focus of the 1958 novel—the isolated gothic Halloran family home—is placed within Jackson's familiar blend of fairy-tale-feudal style with a post–Second World War Americana landscape. As Bernice M. Murphy writes:

> Jackson's gothic mansions are clearly intended to represent modern-day versions of the traditional gothic castle ... Jackson's final novels all feature a mansion built by Victorian exemplars of American free enterprise, the new aristocracy in American life; and that her protagonists are all removed from the inhabitants and the locality in which they live ... symbolized by the actual physical barriers between them and the outside world.[1]

Halloran house, walled and gated like Jackson's Hill House and Blackwood Manor yet to come, stands castle-like in a position of detached power in relation to an economically dependent community. Built by Orianna's dead father-in-law Michael Halloran, whose "wealth is matched only by his ignorance and tastelessness,"[2] as a fantastical demonstration of patriarchal wealth, the house also contains within its tense walls the gendered fight for power and authority familiar to readers of *The Haunting of Hill House* (1959) and *We Have Always Lived in the Castle* (1962). As Michael T. Wilson argues, "Jackson's framework of philosophical horror in her exploration of the ineffable moment in the novel gains further power and subtlety, through ... the gendered nature of the Gothic narrative as an allegorical cautionary tale for women in general."[3]

However, while *Hill House* and *Castle* specify female characters' battles, both successful and unsuccessful, for self-autonomy in their largely male-controlled domestic environments, *The Sundial* begins with Orianna seemingly in firm command of Halloran house. But the narrative quickly exposes the fatal flaw in her authoritarian methodology. Orianna usurps the patriarchy by murdering Lionel, but rather than continuing to disrupt the hierarchical system, Orianna dons a crown and ruthlessly assumes primary power over the Halloran property and its inhabitants. Queens, Jackson informs us through this Atomic Age cautionary fairy tale, are no less socially destructive or dangerous than kings, and a matriarch is no guarantee of egalitarian domestic peace. However, Orianna's Cold War queen status is undercut not by the looming threat of nuclear bombs (metaphorically represented through apocalyptic hallucinations) but through the existence of additional rival domestic spheres within Halloran house. Orianna, to her own detriment, deigns neither to notice nor to rule her competitors' in-house fiefdoms despite the warning provided by grisly legend Harriet Stuart, a young local girl who assumed control over her own domestic queendom with a hammer.

While Orianna's regal gaze oversees Halloran house's chief domestic spaces, the two additional interior spheres she disregards are each controlled by a suspect in her own eventual murder: Orianna's sister-in-law, Fanny, and her 8-year-old granddaughter, Fancy. The sexually aggressive and hallucinatory Fanny has secretly reconstructed her long-dead parents' working-class apartment on the mansion's third floor where she plots against Orianna. On the second floor, Fancy happily anticipates her grandmother's death and plays tyrant with a luxurious dollhouse and the helpless dolls within, relishing her status as heir to the estate. Orianna not only ignores the danger brewing from this palace intrigue, but she also fails to heed the warning provided by a grisly source beyond the Halloran walls, the small empty village Stuart house. Harriet Stuart's bloody infamy combines with Orianna's filicide to evoke the legacy of ambitious deadly queens. Yet Orianna fails to heed the warning of her own actions and those of Harriet, who, having "taken up a hammer"[4] as a teenager, murdered the other four members of her family. Women, as revealed by history and characterized by fairy tales, have no qualms regarding the murder of family members to achieve political power and/or domestic control. However, Orianna fails to connect Harriet's family name with that of Mary, Queen of Scots, put to death by her own threatened cousin, Elizabeth I. Orianna's inability to perceive the danger she faces from Fanny and Fancy is even more striking considering the Stuart house is responsible for the majority of the village trade via ghoulish tourism. Blood-thirsty sightseers pave the way for the construction of Halloran house, deeply entwining the Stuart family slaughters with the Halloran's own violent cycle.

Darryl Hattenhauer has established that Jackson's representation of familial "abuses of power" serves to disrupt the myth of mid-twentieth-century idealized American domestic life, particularly "the notion that families make women more nurturing."[5] More specifically, Hattenhauer analyzes *The Sundial* as an allegorical satire of an American family who believe themselves chosen by God to push the restart button on America, to "take the virgin land (the New Eden, the new promised land) and create nature's nation (a new garden, a new frontier, a new paradise," but who make the mistake of packing "their old selves and history" into their (unrealized) plans for a new world.[6] I argue that Jackson particularly warns women against ideas both old and renewed; *The Sundial* not only disrupts the post–Second World War narrative of domestically fulfilled tranquil women with allusions to historically violent queens and female fairy-tale killers, but also warns American women against duplicating the destructive patterns of domestic authoritarian patriarchy, all the while acknowledging women as historically being violent.

The Sundial begins with the Halloran household's return from Lionel's funeral:

After the funeral they came back to the house, now indisputably Mrs. Halloran's. They stood uneasily, without any certainty, in the large lovely entrance hall, and watched Mrs. Halloran go into the right wing of the house to let Mr. Halloran know that Lionel's last rites had gone off without melodrama. Young Mrs. Halloran, looking after her mother-in-law, said without hope, "Maybe she will drop dead on the doorstep. Fancy, dear, would you like to see Granny drop dead on the doorstep?"[7]

Openly acknowledged as a homicide victim, Lionel's death triggers a seismic shift in the Hallorans' domestic order. Unrepentantly guilty of her son's murder, Orianna faces neither legal consequences for her crime nor legal impediments over her claim to home ownership. Jackson evokes both European royal history and medieval fairy tales as Orianna's blended Wicked Queen/Mother character murders her way to power. Halloran house "indisputably" now belongs to Orianna, despite the silent agreement which meets the widowed MaryJane's accusation that Orianna "pushed [Lionel] down the stairs" because "that nasty old woman couldn't stand it if the house belonged to anyone else."[8] Now that her son is dead, Orianna suspects no competition for she fatally perceives only men as competitors for the property, and Richard Halloran, Lionel's wheelchair-bound and demented father, cannot remember whether or not he has eaten dinner, let alone assume rule of a house and its inhabitants. Blind to the ambitions of the other women in her household, particularly Fanny and Fancy, Orianna makes a mistake in not recognizing the violent potential of her female family members. Orianna's failure to perceive murderous tendencies in other women is fatally shortsighted, especially since her own is not the most brutal female crime in the novel. Orianna's act of pushing her son down the stairs shrinks to near insignificance when compared to local legend Harriet Stuart's slaughter of her whole family. Harriet, a precursor to familicide poisoner Merricat Blackwood, "had one morning arisen unusually early in the Stuart house just outside the village, and taken up a hammer with which she murdered her father, her mother, and her two younger brothers, putting an abrupt end to the Stuart family tree." Although "Stuart" calls to mind two powerful queens who sought one another's death as a means to consolidate power, the historical association is lost on the villagers as well as on Orianna. Tried before her peers, Harriet is acquitted by a jury that refuses to acknowledge that a young girl could be guilty of such violence. Harriet enjoys a seemingly tranquil life in the family home, served and cared for by "an aunt who must sometimes have wondered if Harriet's hammer days were over."[9] Like Queen Elizabeth I, she makes no effort to fill the house with her own husband and children, even after her acquittal, but rules alone.

In one night of brutality, Harriet exposes the false notion of "the home" as a "site of safety and luxurious comfort that offered the nuclear family protection from the horrors of a politically fraught and rapidly changing world."[10] Instead, Jackson reveals "the home" has always served as a potential site of blunt-instrument trauma and blood, revealing the superficial and flimsy protection offered by the concept of the private domestic sphere. Jackson makes clear that while a home or a castle may protect a family from the violence of the outside world, it offers no protection from those already inside the walls. The cultural sanctification of the home also shields the perpetrators of domestic violence, be they man or woman. The more refined villagers look upon Harriet's slaughter of her family with distaste rather than horror as they profit from Harriet's ghoulish fame. Indeed, the violence leads to the village's financial security as Harriet's regional fame draws a "small regular stream of tourists" who spend money at the previously defunct Carriage Stop Inn as well as the eclectic village shops. The opportunity "to sell a little something to tourists" enables the elderly shopkeepers to "keep their own small businesses,"[11] since the only other available customers live in Halloran house. In this way, the small village countenances domestic violence in exchange for financial security, an invisible cycle that continues through the construction of Halloran house and Orianna's own eventual homicidal rise to power.

The automatic association of rule, or authority, with ownership is clearly what establishes Orianna's command of Halloran house. Orianna assumes she is the owner, and since no last will and testament is read nor any other legal paperwork revealed, her assumption becomes de facto law. Richard Halloran may remain the legitimate owner of the mansion, yet the "invalid ... imprisoned in a wheelchair"[12] is dismissed and rendered powerless in a novel where the noncorporeal figure of his own dead father carries more authoritative weight than Richard's still-living self. Orianna simply helps herself to the house much as her dead father-in-law, the ghostly apocalyptic prophet Michael Halloran, once helped himself to a neighboring farmer's land by building a wall around it and daring the farmer to "try and take it back."[13] The other remaining household members range from uneasy to angry in light of Orianna's ascension to power, but none of them dispute that Mrs. Halloran now possesses and controls the house, and therefore the inhabitants as well. Nor do they dispute the assumption that a house and its inhabitants require a possessor and controller, much as a kingdom requires a king, or, in Orianna's case, a queen. Most importantly, no one points to Orianna's gender as a reason to prevent her from behaving in the cruel patriarchal manner of Michael: presumptive, dominant, and ruthless. Orianna's tyrannous monarchy is protested only along class lines since commentary regarding Orianna's unsuitability is aimed at her lower-class origins, not her sex, and even these comments solidify Mrs. Halloran's connection to Michael, a self-made man who learned etiquette from books.

Even Aunt Fanny, Richard's elderly spinster sister, who will spend the next half-year sniping about her sister-in-law's working-class origins, reluctantly admits, "I was not brought up to take orders, Orianna, but I suppose you are mistress here now."[14] Daughter-in-law MaryJane limply seethes over her lost position in the Halloran mansion, now that she is no longer "a wife, and beloved helpmeet," but she does not protest the inevitability of Orianna's reign. Even as MaryJane bewails her daughter Fancy's fate as a "fatherless orphan," she acquiesces to the general perception that Mrs. Halloran now owns the house and will continue to do so until she "drop[s] dead on the doorstep."[15] Interestingly, no one foresees Mrs. Halloran experiencing a slow decay of body or power like her husband, but only her keeping tight control over the house until an abrupt death.

Orianna's pleasure in her new power is evident in the manner in which she speaks of Lionel's death as both "refreshing and agreeable"[16] and the sensual delight she takes in inspecting the estate immediately following Lionel's funeral. Mrs. Halloran "caressed with her soft steps the fine unyielding property she walked upon" and thinks, "this is all mine," as she "savor[s] the sweet quiet stone and earth and leaf and blade of her holding."[17] As the other members of the household automatically equate Orianna's power with ownership, she equates ownership with intense passion. Orianna's emotions call to mind Queen Elizabeth I's declaration of her marriage to England, as though the state of owning and controlling a house were circumstances with which she had fallen in love: "Now I own the house, she thought, and could not speak, for love of it."[18] The reader glimpses a younger, newly married Orianna in flashback as she frankly confesses to young Richard that she married him not for love but for his "father's money ... and the house."[19] Jackson's novel was published near the peak of the post–Second World War housing craze, and in Michael and Orianna's warped point of view, the house becomes synonymous with the Halloran's increasing power rather than merely providing shelter and comfort for one's family. Reminiscent of Hugh Crain, Michael builds a fairy-tale house that kills his wife, who dies from literal displacement as Halloran house transforms the powerful family into House of Halloran. In her turn, Orianna kills her son, Michael's grandson, to usurp the House of Halloran's seat of power.

Orianna's murder of Lionel within the castle-like grotesque setting of Halloran house further alludes to ambitious historical queens, but the feudal setting and Orianna's frequently remarked upon lower-class origins also call to mind poor fairy-tale mothers and stepmothers who kill children to consolidate family resources. Orianna's dream of Hansel and Gretel is Jackson's most blatant invocation of the child-killing cottage wife, but *The Sundial* also evokes another Grimm tale, "The Children Living in a Time of Famine," in which a poverty-stricken woman tells her daughters, "I will have to kill you so that I will have something to eat." The daughters evade a cannibalistic death by invoking the End of the World ("Judgment Day") and go to sleep "so soundly that no one could awaken them" while "the mother left and not a soul knows where she is."[20]

Lower-class Orianna's willingness to sacrifice her family to control Halloran house reveals the dark side of the single-family housing craze of the Cold War in which suddenly affordable suburban homes were advertised with the promise that "A man's home is his castle."[21] As Stephanie Coontz outlines in *The Way We Never Were*, "housing exploded after the war ... [e]ighty-five percent of the new homes were built in the suburbs, where the nuclear family found new possibilities for privacy and togetherness."[22] In *The Sundial*, Jackson exposes the inherent dangers of domestic privacy and togetherness through a woman who molds her brand of matriarchy in the cast of the patriarchy she overthrew, thus, as Angela Hague argues, "indict[ing] ... the 1950s nuclear family and suburban lifestyles and destabili[zing] the 1950s paradigm of containment and security in a variety of ways."[23] Jackson substitutes the suburban middle-class king with a self-crowning queen, yet doubles down on the dangerous rhetorical associations of *home* and *castle* which "promote secrecy of the violence within the home,"[24] thus warning women against replicating this old method of patriarchal control reborn in Cold War suburbia.

Orianna's regime quickly becomes authoritarian as she maintains rigorous suburban isolation and conformity. When she declares that a "thorough house cleaning is necessary,"[25] she is not implying mopping floors or beating dust from the draperies, but instead sweeping out and rearranging Halloran house's current inhabitants. Orianna destroys her nuclear family, "the most salient symbol"[26] of American prosperity, and reveals her scheme to pare the loosely connected household of seven down into a new twisted parody of the American suburban family of four: herself (an avaricious, murderous woman), Richard (a physically and mentally emasculated man), Aunt Fanny (a sexually aggressive, elderly spinster), and Fancy (a spying, gloatingly cruel child). Unrelated household members such as Essex, employed to catalog the house's library (a euphemism for his position as Orianna's hired lover), and Miss Ogilvie, supposedly young Fancy's governess but actually Richard's barely remembered mistress, and even MaryJane, the new widow, are all deemed superfluous and firmly directed toward new living arrangements. Reducing their human worth to her own understanding, monetary value, she provides "nest egg" and "settlement" funds for all. Orianna directs Essex upon a "path" away from the house toward "scholarship;" Miss Ogilvie is informed that she will be placed "into a little boarding house;" and MaryJane will be returned to the "little apartment" from whence she came. Blood relative Aunt Fanny, who grew up in Halloran house, is to be dismissed to a long unused portion of the mansion, as Orianna invokes the Tower of London by cruelly asking, "Do you recall the tower, Fanny?" before adding, "I daresay that people in this house years from now will begin to talk of the haunted tower,"[27] as though Fanny's presence in the house will become insubstantial and phantasmal. Only Fancy is deemed valuable enough to remain by Orianna's side, and as the heir apparent to the House of Halloran, Fancy becomes both an object within Orianna's controlled property and the future assurance of continued matriarchal reign. "Fancy is mine, too, now," Orianna declares, "Someday everything I have will belong to Fancy, and I think to keep Fancy with me."[28] Thus, Orianna simultaneously claims ownership of her granddaughter, while dismissing MaryJane's maternal authority as inconsequential in light of her need for an heir to the throne.

Young Fancy neither mourns the loss of her father nor objects to the threatened exile of her mother, but delights in her position as Orianna's heir. A fast learner, Fancy models herself after Orianna and demonstrates her flair for domestic dominance by torturing the dolls within her luxurious dollhouse. Rather than learning housewifery or mimicking childcare, Fancy practices ownership and control. "When my grandmother dies, no one can stop the house and everything from being mine," says the queen-in-training as she defies Ms. Ogilvie and Aunt Fanny's instructions regarding appropriate bedtimes. Fancy shares her grandmother's pleasure in household materials, conveniences, and appliances, as she exults, "I have my beautiful little doll house with real doorknobs and electric lights and the little stove that really works and the running water in the bathtubs."[29] Fancy also shares her grandmother's propensity for tyranny, slyly giggling after leaving one of "the little dolls ... lying in the little bathtub with the water really running." Just as Orianna dispenses decrees to her living household, so Fancy practices on her own domestic captives. "When I put them to bed they have to go to bed," Fanny remarks, pointedly not in bed herself. Happily anticipating Orianna's death throughout the novel, Fancy understands that her dollhouse, and the dolls within, are mere training tools, and announces, "When my grandmother dies, I am going to smash my dollhouse. I won't need it anymore."[30] Fancy understands that, upon Orianna's death, she will have a larger house and larger dolls with which she can do as she likes, because she has inculcated the patriarchal authoritarian codes adopted by Orianna. Distracted by Fancy's End of the World visions and foreseeing her death as a far distant point in the post-apocalyptic world, Orianna recklessly promises Fancy the "gold crown," never considering that Fancy may realize she can "smash" her grandmother rather than her dollhouse to claim domestic authority over the household as well as over the surrounding village.

In line with the worst characteristics of patriarchal capitalism, Orianna assumes her wealth and property invest her with the right to manage her chosen heir as well, a presupposition that goes undisputed in the household. Richard Pascal argues that Mrs. Halloran's "accession" to "full command … signals the possibility of a radical transformation of the gender hierarchy in American communal life," but maintains that her reign "is no less a tyranny than the system it has supplanted." However, Pascal claims that Jackson constructed Orianna along the postwar Freudian infused model of the castrating mother, wielding "insidious maternal power."[31] I maintain that Jackson does the opposite—she warns women not to mimic the patriarchy and not to fall back upon their own violent impulses as the means to assume and to maintain domestic agency. Orianna may be a matriarch, but she demonstrates no maternal characteristics, either positive, or those identified as negative in the postwar decades in which "all women, even seemingly docile ones, were deeply mistrusted."[32] Orianna does not castrate her son; she kills him. She does not smother Fancy with too-cloying damaging love; she ignores her. She does not treat her younger lover, Essex, as though he is a child; she has sex with him and then tries to get rid of him—like a stereotypical mid-twentieth-century businessman firing his secretary as a means of breaking off their affair.

To underscore the fallacy of adopting patriarchal methods, Orianna's dismissal of Miss Ogilvie, Essex, and Fanny, meant to "solidify her usurpation,"[33] is itself usurped by a visitation of the original family patriarch, her dead father-in-law, Michael. Much as the daughters in Grimm's "The Children Living in the Time of Famine" evoke Judgment Day to evade their cannibalistic mother, Fanny's ghostly vision warns of an apocalypse to circumvent eviction. In distinctly 1950s nuclear terms, Michael foretells: "From the sky and from the ground and from the sea there is danger; tell them in the house. There will be black fire and red water and the earth turning and screaming; this will come."[34] As Pascal makes clear, nowhere in this novel about nuclear families in the decade of heightened nuclear threat does the word "bomb" appear, "a decisive indication that atomic anxiety is not the basic source of the apocalyptic mentality that pervades the characters' thoughts."[35] Indeed, the anxiety is generated by their threatened exile by Orianna instead of nuclear war. Initially met with skepticism, Fanny's vision is quickly accepted as truth once those household members facing banishment are informed the vision includes the words: "Do not let them leave the house."[36] It quickly becomes "fact" that the inhabitants of Halloran house will be the only survivors of the forthcoming global annihilation and, therefore, the predetermined origins of a New World utopia, a parody of the way 1950s "popular culture turned ... suburban families into capitalism's answer to the Communist threat."[37] Additional household members arrive in the form of Orianna's old friends (from her old life of questionable respectability), and Orianna reluctantly expands her campaign of law and order to include plans for a large household within an empty burnt world. Orianna has trapped herself in her continuation of hierarchical control. In order to preserve her own authority, Orianna must acknowledge the greater patriarchal system and accede to Michael's posthumous power. Fanny, in a stroke of self-preserving genius, has gone over Orianna's head and exposed the fault line Jackson runs through the queen's rule. Orianna, consumed by her need to take advantage of the End of the World scenario, not only fails to create a new method of rule but also is distracted and fails to perceive Fanny and Fancy's own plots and ambitions.

The Sundial reveals that women's failure to develop a new egalitarian form of domestic governance to replace the old patriarchal model will result in historically familiar violent scenarios. Orianna's more strident dictatorial actions increasingly are met with derision and anger and such authoritarian efforts begin to have less effect. The household slowly realizes that Orianna's position of authoritative privilege requires their submissive acquiescence. Instead, Aunt Fanny's snide remarks regarding Orianna's lower-class upbringing grow more frequent, and the self-appointed queen answers the taunts by ordering herself a symbol of nobility and power to make her authority more visual and commanding. As doomsday draws near, a mail-order crown arrives amid the vast influx of survival supplies, and Orianna appears at dinner wearing the "gold band" with a self-satisfied demeanor. "'I expect you will soon be accustomed to seeing me wear a crown,' she said amiably down the dinner table. 'After all, it is not the least of the adjustments we will be called upon to make.'" However, Orianna's need for a royal prop makes it all too clear that her reign is coming to a quick end. Newcomer Gloria's precognitive talent (reading the post-apocalyptic future in a mirror) has transformed her into the most skilled, and therefore the most valuable, household member, and her frank criticism of Orianna's crown, "you look like a damned fool" and a "crazy old lady," is not retracted in fear of Orianna's power, but because Gloria, a "guest"[38] has merely made an error of etiquette. Orianna's futile attempt to reaffirm her previously unchallenged authority further weakens her position. Once the unquestioned queen, her coronation achieved through murder, Orianna's mail-order crown only emphasizes her dwindling power as the apocalypse draws near. Manipulated by Fanny to embrace the dead Michael's alleged word as Gospel, Orianna is surrounded by former obedient subjects who now anticipate a world devoid of broad government, economic, and social systems. In a last effort, Orianna turns to the only patriarchal system left upon which she may capitalize, religion.

Orianna's lack of vision regarding a new system of domestic governance is her most significant failure. Once the world ends, all that will remain is the Halloran household, yet Orianna is unable not only to create a new order for the New World, but she harkens back even further to borrow from ancient biblical authority. Orianna composes a variation of the Ten Commandments pertaining to final doomsday preparations and prescribed social behaviors required once The First Day heralds the dawn of the New World. Orianna's document threatens that: "ANY DEVIATION FROM THESE RULES WILL BE SUBJECT TO PUNISHMENT."[39] The rules authorize Orianna's control over every aspect of the survivors' lives: food, clothing, and all physical conduct with particular attention paid to sexual relationships. Underlying all is the constant threat of violent repercussions. Beginning with the silly tin-pot tyrant decree, "No one except Mrs. Halloran may wear a crown,"[40] the commands grow more severe as it reveals Orianna's New World order will mimic God's harsh omnipotent rule over Adam and Eve in the oldest of New Worlds, the Garden of Eden. "Mates," the document reads, "will be assigned by Mrs. Halloran. Indiscriminate coupling will be subject to severe punishment." Tellingly, much in the way the crown reveals Orianna's insecurity regarding the hollowness of her rule, the document's allusion to an otherworldly higher authority is meant to infuse the survivors with fear and to inspire them to obedience lest they be exiled from the New World as were Adam and Eve: "A proud dignity is recommended, and extreme care lest offense be given to supernatural overseers who may perhaps be endeavoring to determine the fitness of their choice of survivors."[41] Orianna's Old Testament tone and her insinuation that she will replace Fanny as the conduit between these "supernatural overseers"[42] and the survivors begets expected violence. Once Fanny reads Orianna's commandments, her realization that Orianna has effectively excised her from the position as Halloran house prophet triggers an intense reaction, causing her to become "angrier than she had ever been before in her life."[43] Orianna's failure of vision includes not just her inability to see a different kind of future for her family but also her inability to see that Fanny is as likely to kill her as not.

Through Fanny, Jackson demonstrates the immense difficulty of transforming the old patriarchal domestic order into a new egalitarian system. Transformation, Jackson implies, is not merely the matter of crowning a less naturally authoritarian leader but also of understanding the overwhelmingly complicated pull of the patriarchal past. Fanny, whose thwarted attempts to assume a position of equal importance with that of Orianna bring her to the boiling point, has built a secret domestic space on the top floor of Halloran house. Within "the big attic room," which she had "always known" to be the "core" of Halloran house, Fanny has painstakingly reconstructed the four rooms of her parents' working-class apartment. A shrine to her dead mother, the apartment is filled with the first Mrs. Halloran's beloved saved-for domesticities: a solidly-built sofa, beds and chairs, a phonograph and records, everyday dishes and "company china," kitchen linens, the "neat, intricately crocheted spread,"[44] hairbrushes and clothes. Within the order of the economical but comfortable apartment, the first Mrs. Halloran is revealed to be a superb domestic manager and planner, a true partner to her husband as he too worked for their future, completing a "mail order education."[45] Fanny worships her dead mother's domestic labor through ritualized object placement and playacting, but her stance toward her father's memory is more complicated.

In the main rooms of Halloran house, Fanny borrows her father's authority through prophecy. Within the secret apartment, by contrast, she stokes her resentment by remembering how the abruptly spectacularly wealthy Michael ended his wife's evident pleasure in "planning and saving to re-furnish the children's bedroom" once he "cancelled all her plans by deciding on the big house."[46] Fanny's mother's precisely arranged apartment, the symbol of her value as Michael's partner, is abandoned once he becomes unimaginably wealthy and "could think of nothing better to do with his money than set up his own world." Halloran house does indeed become "his" world, as "Mr. Halloran had insisted arrogantly that the big house be complete down to every slightest detail before he brought his wife there," and the first Mrs. Halloran has no say regarding the massive construction or the ridiculously ornate and hideous decor: "a great deal of silver, a great deal of gold, much in the way of enamel and mother-of-pearl."[47] Severed not just from her cherished apartment, but, more importantly, from her job as a literal homemaker, she dies while asking her new maids if her old furniture is safely stored. *The Sundial* is filled with the "violence" and "terror" Coontz perceives "beneath the polished facades of many 'ideal' families," but Jackson's novel also underlines the "simply grinding misery that only occasionally came to light."[48] Fanny's mother is not pushed down the stairs, or battered with a hammer. She dies of unhappiness once Michael erases her family role as homemaker. Fanny's secret lifelong mourning over her mother's death is revealed only when she invites Fancy into her clandestine lair and attempts to sway her niece to become heir to her secret space rather than Orianna's heir to the estate. Despite her sorrow and resentment toward Michael, Fanny is no more able to break away from the patriarchal traditions than is Orianna.

Aunt Fanny draws Fancy into the attic, telling "herself vaguely that it was a kind of continuity, a way of establishing one strong direct line from the first Mrs. Halloran to Fancy." Answering Fancy's confused questions about the space, Aunt Fanny tells her, "It's my dollhouse," before saying, "My mother's house,"[49] thus conflating both her and Fancy's privately controlled spaces into one. Furthering the amalgamation, Fanny insists that she and Fancy are "dolls"; and Fanny assumes the doll identity of her mother "wearing a yellow dress," while she places Fancy on a footstool and tells her, "You must be me, little Frances."[50] Fanny is so inculcated in the patriarchal model that she still envisions herself and Fancy as toy objects under the control of an invisible power, and Fanny's futile efforts to place Fancy under her in the dollhouse hierarchy further reveal her inability to visualize a new social order. Fanny is no more able to resist controlling Fancy's behavior than Orianna is able to resist controlling her household, or Fancy is able to resist controlling her actual dolls. Unable to playact any parent–child relationship other than the one she herself experienced, Fanny channels the authoritarian identity that destroyed her mother's domestic haven and integrates absolute obedience with love, telling Fancy she is "not allowed to touch things" before announcing, "We are a very happy family and we love each other dearly." The strange interaction ends with Fancy "turning uncomfortably on the footstool" and "moving toward the door,"[51] a clear rejection of her aunt's mimicry of the domestic domination which killed her mother. Fancy's rejection of Fanny's offering of her secret fiefdom is what makes it most likely that Fancy kills Orianna. Fancy, like Orianna, adopts the patriarchal model of violent usurpation and clearly prefers manipulating others over pretending to be a doll in the attic.

As the End of the World draws near, Orianna dreams of a solitary life in a timeless fairy-tale forest cottage. Equipped only with "one cup" and "one plate,"[52] Orianna has only herself for whom to care and no worries regarding the needs or desires of others. She is neither ruler, nor ruled. Her peaceful life is rudely interrupted by greedy children who begin stuffing themselves with the raw materials of her cozy cottage. Orianna, "feeling the roof being eaten away from over her head," chases the children away as they tell outrageous lies about her attempts to cannibalize them, casting her in the role of the cruel fairytale Queen/witch/mother. Jackson presents Orianna in a remarkably sympathetic light throughout the dream. Even when minding her own business in a tiny woodland cottage, Orianna is blamed for attempting to maintain her solitude, for she can think of no other way than to lock up the naughty children "until they promise to go away."[53]

Orianna's attempt to control the greedy dream children fails, as do all her attempts to control the members of Halloran house. Jackson's book ends not with an apocalypse, but with the failed Queen Orianna meeting the same fate as her son. "*Some*body pushed her down the stairs,"[54] Mrs. Willow insists, trying to summon some collective outrage, but the attempt soon dissipates amid general disinterest. Fancy, the heir, happily dons the crown. As the remainder of the self-identified survivors gather in the drawing room to await the apocalypse, the real question is not whether the holocaust will occur, but through what mode the household will govern itself as The First Day dawns. Minus their resident autocrat, the group's harmonious regard for one another's comfort and welfare veils tensions running below the surface as three women, having learned nothing from Orianna's lack of ingenuity and creativity, position themselves as competitors to rule over one another in the New World with the same old ideas. Fanny, who drinks too much and hallucinates, abstains from the proffered wine, all the better to keep a strategic head. Fancy, who now wears the crown, has not smashed her dollhouse, but has bequeathed it instead to Gloria in a clever move. Fancy effectively establishes Gloria as a rung beneath herself in the chain of inheritance, while ensuring the old patriarchal hierarchy will remain in the New World as she, Orianna's killer, disarmingly twirls under the Old World crown, saying only, "I like dancing in it."[55]

Notes

1. Bernice M. Murphy, "The People of the Village Have Always Hated Us," in *Shirley Jackson: Essays on the Literary Legacy*, ed. Bernice M. Murphy. (New York: MacFarland, 2005), 114.
2. Darryl Hattenhauer, *Shirley Jackson's American Gothic* (Albany: State University of New York Press, 2003), 139.
3. Michael T. Wilson, "'Absolute Reality' and the Role of the Ineffable in Shirley Jackson's *The Haunting of Hill House*." *Journal of Popular Culture*, 48, no.1 (2015): 120.
4. Shirley Jackson, *The Sundial* (New York: Penguin: 1958), 71.
5. Hattenhauer, *American Gothic*, 6–7.
6. Ibid., 137, 148.
7. Jackson, *The Sundial*, 1.
8. Ibid., 2.
9. Ibid., 70.
10. Brittany Roberts, "Helping Eleanor Come Home: A Reassessment of Shirley Jackson's *The Haunting of Hill House*." *The Irish Journal of Gothic and Horror Studies*, 16 (Autumn 2017): 74.
11. Jackson, *The Sundial*, 74.

12 Ibid., 4.
13 Ibid., 198.
14 Ibid., 5.
15 Ibid., 2.
16 Ibid., 14.
17 Ibid.,11.
18 Ibid.
19 Ibid.
20 The Brothers Grimm, "Children in the Time of Famine," in *The Grimm Reader: Classic Tales of the Brothers Grimm*, ed. and trans. Maria Tatar (New York, Norton, 2010), 317–18.
21 Deborah Nelson, *Pursuing Privacy in Cold War America* (New York: Columbia University Press, 2003), 85.
22 Stephanie Coontz, *The Way We Never Were: American Families and the Nostalgia Trap* (New York: Basic Books, 2016), 10.
23 Angela Hague, "'A Faithful Anatomy of Our Times': Reassessing Shirley Jackson." *Frontiers: A Journal of Women's Studies*, 26, no. 2 (2005): 82.
24 Alison Towns, Peter Adams and Nicola Gavey, "Silencing Talk of Men's Violence Towards Women," in *Discourse and Silencing: Representation and the Language of Displacement*, ed. Lynn Theismeyer (Philadelphia: John Benjamins, 2003), 47.
25 Jackson, *The Sundial*, 14.
26 Coontz, *The Way We Never Were*, 11.
27 Jackson, *The Sundial*, 14–15.
28 Ibid., 15.
29 Ibid., 17.
30 Ibid., *The Sundial*, 17–18.
31 Richard Pascal, "New World Miniatures: Shirley Jackson's *The Sundial* and Postwar American Society." *Journal of American Comparative Cultures*, 23, no. 3 (2001): 98.
32 Coontz, *The Way We Never Were,* 15.
33 John G. Parks. "Waiting for the End: Shirley Jackson's The Sundial." *Critique* XIX, no. 3 (1978): 74–88.
34 Jackson, *The Sundial*, 26.
35 Pascal, "New World Miniatures," 98.
36 Jackson, *The Sundial*, 25.
37 Coontz, *The Way We Never Were*, 13.
38 Jackson, *The Sundial*, 185.
39 Ibid., 171.
40 Ibid., 172.

41 Ibid., 171–2.
42 Ibid., 173.
43 Ibid., 174.
44 Ibid., 160.
45 Ibid., 161.
46 Ibid., 162.
47 Ibid., 8.
48 Coontz, *The Way We Never Were*, 16.
49 Jackson, *The Sundial*, 163.
50 Ibid., 164.
51 Ibid., 163–4.
52 Ibid., 101.
53 Ibid., 101–2.
54 Ibid., 215 (emphasis in the original).
55 Ibid., 222.

References

The Brothers Grimm. "Children in the Time of Famine," in *The Grimm Reader: Classic Tales of the Brothers Grimm*, ed. and trans. Maria Tatar, 317–18. New York: Norton, 2016.
Coontz, Stephanie. *The Way We Never Were: American Families and the Nostalgia Trap*. New York: Basic Books, 2016.
Hague, Angela. "'A Faithful Anatomy of Our Times': Reassessing Shirley Jackson." *Frontiers: A Journal of Women's Studies*, 26, no. 2 (2005): 73–96.
Hattenhauer, Darryl. *Shirley Jackson's American Gothic*. Albany: State University of New York Press, 2003.
Jackson, Shirley. *The Sundial*. New York: Penguin Books, 1958.
Murphy, Bernice M. "The People of the Village Have Always Hated Us," in *Shirley Jackson: Essays on the Literary Legacy*, ed. Bernice M. Murphy, 104–26. New York: MacFarland, 2005.
Nelson, Deborah. *Pursuing Privacy in Cold War America*. New York: Columbia University Press, 2003.
Pascal, Richard. "New World Miniatures: Shirley Jackson's *The Sundial* and Postwar American Society." *Journal of American Comparative Cultures*, 23, no. 3 (2001): 81–103.
Parks, John G. "Waiting for the End: Shirley Jackson's The Sundial." *Critique*, XIX, no. 3 (1978): 74–88.
Roberts, Brittany. "Helping Eleanor Come Home: A Reassessment of Shirley Jackson's *The Haunting of Hill House*." *The Irish Journal of Gothic and Horror Studies*, 16 (2017): 67–93.
Towns, Alison, Peter Adams, and Nicola Gavey. "Silencing Talk of Men's Violence Towards Women," in *Discourse and Silencing: Representation and the*

Language of Displacement, ed. Lynn Theismeyer, 43–77. Philadelphia: John Benjamins, 2003.

Wilson, Michael T. "Absolute Reality and the Role of the Ineffable in Shirley Jackson's *The Haunting of Hill House*." *Journal of Popular Culture*, 48, no. 1 (2015): 114–23.

9

"I May Go Mad, but at Least I Look Like a Lady": The Insanity of True Womanhood in *The Sundial*

Julie Baker

Shirley Jackson is well known for her gothic female protagonists who suffer from psychological illnesses and are imprisoned within the depths of their madness. Such is the case for Aunt Fanny, from Jackson's *The Sundial* (1958), as she illogically interprets her auditory hallucinations as prophetic encounters with her deceased father who both warns of an impending apocalypse and promises the arrival of a new utopic society. Jackson's portrayal of Aunt Fanny as mad is particularly significant in light of the disparaging historical view casting women as "psychiatrically impaired—whether they accept or reject the female role—simply because they are women."[1] While a cursory glance at Aunt Fanny seemingly points to Jackson's endorsement of this pervading conception, a closer reading reveals that Jackson subversively implicates culture at large for a woman's potential for insanity. Aunt Fanny's extreme allegiance to the patriarchal conception of True Womanhood becomes the source of her madness, particularly as "manlessness" bars her from full participation in this crippling performance of femininity.[2] In turn, Aunt Fanny's fixation upon a new world order, which she believes offers her the possibility of fully satisfying the requirements of True Womanhood, results in her eventual physical and psychological entrapment.

The Sundial, despite being marketed as a "stunningly creepy novel" in implicit comparison to *The Haunting of Hill House* (1959),[3] is far removed from the horror genre and is more closely aligned with comedic satire. Jackson's most recent biographer, Ruth Franklin, writes that *The Sundial* is "perhaps Jackson's funniest novel."[4] Yet, just as current publishers marketing *The Sundial* misread the work's mood, many contemporaneous reviewers also misunderstood the novel, evidenced in one reviewer's reading of it as a "bizarre tale with an enigmatic ending."[5] Viewing the humor as coincidental or mere entertainment, however, glosses over Jackson's skillful use of the device as a means of subtly providing social commentary, particularly regarding women's position within society. In an analysis of Jackson's most well-known humorous works, *Raising Demons* (1957) and *Life among the Savages* (1953), critic Nancy Walker posits, "below the surface of the humor are significant signs of restlessness and unease,"[6] which is equally true of *The Sundial*. While pioneering feminist Betty Friedan openly criticized Jackson's seeming acceptance of the domestic role within her humor writing and labeled her reductively as one of the "Housewife Writers,"[7] Walker counters this perception, arguing that though "muted," the "hostility" within Jackson's humor is "undeniably present."[8] Walker's reading of Jackson's use of humor is clearly demonstrated within Jackson's comical sketch in *Savages* detailing her encounter with a clerk upon arriving at the hospital in labor with her third child:

> "Name?" the desk clerk said to me politely, her pencil poised.
>
> "Name," I said vaguely. I remembered, and told her.
>
> "Age?" she asked. "Sex? Occupation?"
>
> "Writer," I said.
>
> "Housewife," she said.
>
> "Writer," I said.
>
> "I'll just put down housewife," she said.[9]

In this scene, Jackson subtly criticizes the patriarchal expectation relegating women to the position of homemaker through the use of a facetious tone. Such a limited view of women's social roles during Jackson's time period was in part driven by the effects of the "'back-to-the-kitchen' movement of the late 1940s and early 1950s," urging women to return to the home and leave the workforce they were previously encouraged to join as part of wartime efforts.[10] Popular media outlets aided in the movement's agenda through showcasing "the joys of housewifery," which was believed to be "the easiest way to re-order society" upon the conclusion of the Second

World War.[11] So it was that "by the mid-1950s, women had been safely relocated in the 'private' sphere of domesticity and in many ways excluded from the social production of meaning."[12]

Barbara Welter's "The Cult of True Womanhood," which details antebellum conceptions of the American woman, came riding in on the "headwinds of the feminist seventies" as her study of the past spoke to the present.[13] Welter describes that the "true woman's place" within the cult's framework is thought to be "unquestionably by her own fireside—as daughter, sister, but most of all as wife and mother,"[14] and feminist critics began to categorize True Womanhood into four tenants of "piety, purity, domesticity, and submissiveness."[15] Considering the post–Second World War presentation of femininity depicted by the mass media as the "virtuous, passive woman who would not eclipse her husband,"[16] the antebellum expectation of the True Woman continued to thrive in America. Welter's awareness of the perpetuation of the cult of True Womanhood within her own time is evident in her final footnote referencing Friedan's seminal work, *The Feminine Mystique*, which she asserts "challenges the whole concept of True Womanhood as it hampers the 'fulfillment' of the twentieth-century woman."[17]

Friedan's definition of the "feminine mystique"—her term serving as a shorthand for the patriarchal expectations placed upon women in the post–Second World War era—mirrors the ethos of True Womanhood as women realized their femininity when finding "fulfillment only in sexual passivity, male domination, and nurturing maternal love."[18] Critic Daniel Horowitz summarizes Friedan's global analysis in *The Feminine Mystique* of women's position within society following the Second World War:

> She asserted that in the aftermath of World War II, a series of factors came together to encourage women to seek fulfillment as wives and mothers and avoid pursuing careers, professionalism, or politics. This happened, she noted, even though an increasing proportion of women were working outside the home. She identified a shift from a prewar emphasis on individuality and careers to a postwar equation of fulfillment with the role of housewife and motherhood. She accused popularizers of Freudianism, but not Freudian therapy itself, of giving a scientific gloss to old notions that "women are animals, less than human, unable to think like men, born merely to breed and serve men," when they were not busy envying or hating them.[19]

Friedan asserts that "fulfillment as a woman had only one definition for American women after 1949—the housewife-mother,"[20] which aligns with True Womanhood as described by Welter, and Friedan too understands the power the past can hold over the present and future: "And so the feminine mystique began to spread through the land, grafted onto old prejudices and comfortable conventions which so easily give the past a stranglehold on the future."[21]

It is no mistake that Jackson imbues Aunt Fanny with an acceptance of traditional femininity touted by the culture at large during this post–Second World War time period in an effort to mirror—and ultimately critique—Jackson's own social reality, anticipating analyses by second-wave feminist critics like Welter and Friedan. Critic Roberta Rubenstein writes that "several critics have specifically highlighted Jackson's proto-feminist impulses by focusing on her representations of female characters who are oppressed within patriarchy,"[22] which arguably stemmed from Jackson's own lived experience of enacting the role of the "housewife-mother" described in her loosely autobiographical works like *Savages*. Franklin posits that Jackson's position as both an "important writer who happened also to be—and to embrace being—a housewife, as women of her generation were all required to do" created a "tension" within her life that serves to "animate all of Jackson's writing."[23] Franklin further suggests that Jackson's work accordingly addresses the conflict between her "devotion to her children" that "coexists uneasily with her fear of losing herself in domesticity."[24]

Yet despite her fears regarding the domestic life, Jackson struggled with periods of agoraphobia that ironically resulted in her inability to leave her home:

> Something new and unpleasant had begun to happen every time she tried to leave the house. She would begin to shake, her legs would give way, and everything would start spinning. If she did not go inside right away, she feared passing out ... She suffered from delusions that even she recognized were irrational: she was afraid to go into the post office, for instance, because she believed the postmaster thought she was crazy ... Eventually her anxiety was no longer associated only with leaving the house: anything could trigger a panic attack, even the phone ringing.[25]

This experience of crippling anxiety plays out in Jackson's fiction in which protagonists like Aunt Fanny suffer from psychological disorders that entrap them—often within their homes—despite their longing for freedom. Jackson wrote in her personal diary that "insecure, uncontrolled, i [sic] wrote of neuroses and fear and i think my books laid end to end would be one long documentation of anxiety."[26] Interestingly, Jackson views this anxiety not as an inhibition to her writing but as a source of creative fodder, continuing in her diary that "if i am cured and well and oh glorious alive then my books should be different. who [sic] wants to write about anxiety from a place of safety?"[27]

Considering Jackson's intensive focus upon anxiety in her work, it is no wonder her husband and prominent literary critic of his time, Stanley Edgar Hyman, describes her work as "neurotic modern fiction."[28] Jackson's mother, with whom she had a caustic relationship, picked up on these themes as well and was critical of Jackson's focus upon "demented girls."[29] But for Jackson, it seems her greatest comfort and escape from societal pressure—particularly in communities where she and Stanley "hardly fit in and their neighbors let them know it"[30]—was found through her writing where she could safely explore her plethora of anxieties. Enmeshed within her exploration of fear, however, is an examination of her own hopes and longings. Franklin posits that Jackson "was consumed with the idea of leaving Stanley" and "of creating a new home for herself" in which "her fantasies are of leaving alone."[31] In homage to this "fantasy of total independence," Jackson wrote in her diary, "writing is the way out."[32] Tellingly, this theme of freedom experienced through the creation of fiction is expressed within many of her works, including *The Sundial*: though Aunt Fanny never takes up a pen and paper, her authoring of a supposed utopic world allows her to retreat from her otherwise inescapable reality and encounter a hope previously absent from her life within the Halloran mansion.

Jackson's authorial voice, however, encompasses not only the concerns of "unhappy housewives" but captures her sensitivity to other societal currents roiling around her that influenced women's lived experience within post–Second World War America.[33] Critic Marta Caminero-Santangelo writes that Jackson became part of "a startling and unprecedented flurry of writing by American women" depicting the madwoman in works published after 1945,[34] a trend driven in part by the newfound national attention given to psychiatric reform following the return of veterans from the Second World War requiring mental health services.[35] In her study, Caminero-Santangelo considers works by writers like Eudora Welty and Toni Morrison, in addition to Shirley Jackson, highlighting these authors' identification of the "connections between psychology as a means of social control and the regulation of gender roles," as well as their awareness that "explanations of madness looked to family structures."[36] In particular, mainstream physicians of the time blamed women for the perpetuation of "mental instability … throughout the country" due to insufficient mothering resulting in childhood trauma, which they argued later developed into psychiatric illness in adulthood.[37]

To offset this outcome, these same physicians argued that women should embrace a femininity rooted in True Womanhood. In doing so, they asserted that women protected their own mental health—and thus were in a position to serve as better wives and mothers—considering that a "dissatisfaction with their natural domestic role" was viewed to be "the source of women's deep-seated neurosis."[38] This idea of women's innate housewife–mother proclivity also became the central premise to the "traditionalist" argument fixated upon "woman's reproductive capacity and sees in motherhood woman's chief goal in life, by implication defining as deviant women who do not become mothers."[39] Not surprisingly, these mainstream physicians warned of the dangers of unwed women, who they suggested "posed an enormous psychic threat to the social fabric."[40]

Considering the cultural condemnation of the single, childless woman during "this period, marked by the feverish postwar pursuit of domesticity and the 'traditional' nuclear family,"[41] Caminero-Santangelo points out a common theme within works by women writers like Jackson in which female protagonists' madness is "connected with manlessness"[42]; this was likely due in part to the reality that during this post–Second World War era "female manlessness was a serious cultural issue sometimes linked explicitly with madness in popular discourse."[43] Historically, society has scorned the unmarried, single woman considering the interconnectedness "between feminism, women's independence and spinsterhood,"[44] and unwed women have been depicted by culture at large as "vicious and destructive creatures" due to their sexually "thwarted desire."[45] Yet, within the texts that Caminero-Santangelo considers, the source of the protagonist's insanity is not the condition of manlessness per se, which would imply an inherent need in a woman for a husband; rather that the woman who has "strayed outside the prescribed notions of womanhood" by not entering into both marriage and motherhood is condemned by society to an ostracized, Othered position.[46] Writers like Jackson are aware that "social definitions of gender could draw lines of inclusion and exclusion," and, when "taking up the representative space of the 'manless madwoman,' these women writers reveal it to be a social production."[47] Thus the distinction between the madwoman and the manless woman demonized by her society become inseparable. As Caminero-Santangelo suggests, the manless woman's insanity—particularly in works by women writers like Jackson—signifies that though "aberrance from the feminine role may well indicate resistance to it … these writers depict madness as the *end* of any such resistance and as the signal that society has successfully reinscribed its definitions of femininity" upon the woman.[48]

Aunt Fanny is representative of such madness stemming from an extreme allegiance to the patriarchal conception of True Womanhood in an effort to remedy her situation as the socially ostracized manless woman. Her desire for a traditional heterosexual romantic relationship is most clearly demonstrated within her bumbling pursuits of Essex and Captain Scarabombardon, two of the male residents within the Halloran mansion. She knocks and pleads at Essex's bedroom door, begging dejectedly, "Essex, please let me in?"[49] while Essex ignores her and envisions himself "enclosed in the tight impersonal weight of a coffin" that he sees as preferable to coupling with Aunt Fanny.[50] Aunt Fanny later initiates a pursuit of Captain Scarabombardon, pleading with him in a comedic moment: "I'm only forty-eight years old." But the Captain's reaction is similar to Essex's in his decision "to shove all the furniture in the room against the door and lean on it" if needed in an effort to keep Aunt Fanny at bay.[51] Aunt Fanny's daydream further illustrates her desire to resolve the problem of her manlessness through establishing a relationship with Essex:

> Roses, she thought: I would like to give Essex a rose. She put her head gently back against the marble bench, tears on her cheeks, and listened to the drops of water singing as they went down the fountain ("Frances, I have waited for you so long ..." "Impatient, Essex?" "Impatient? Say rather mad ... burning ..."). She stirred, and smiled, and lifted her hand in tender protest.[52]

Aunt Fanny's pursuits of the male household members—and particularly her daydream—additionally point to her thinly veiled sexuality, which she attempts to repress in an effort to further adhere to the expectations of True Womanhood. Sandra M. Gilbert and Susan Gubar write, "It is debilitating to be *any* woman in a society where women are warned that if they do not behave like angels they must be monsters,"[53] and Aunt Fanny recognizes this reality: if she does not act the part of the angelic, asexual woman, she would suffer the consequence of further demonization by society as a sexual monster. While it is understood that Aunt Fanny's imagined "tender protest" to Essex's "burning" sexual desire is disingenuous, Aunt Fanny is aware that she must convey the ability to harness raging masculine desires in accordance with the cult of True Womanhood viewing men as "by nature more sensual" than women.[54] Alarmingly, however, True Womanhood is revealed to have infiltrated her psyche to the point in which, even within her private reveries, she engages in self-censorship. Welter writes of True Womanhood: "Purity was as essential as piety to a young woman, its absence as unnatural and unfeminine. Without it she was, in fact, no woman at all, but a member of some lower order."[55] As a manless woman, Aunt Fanny's open expression of sexuality would incur judgment and subsequent classification as subhuman. Even married True Women were expected to be passive and responsive to their husbands' sexual advances rather than to initiate them. Welter notes, "The marriage night was the single great event of a woman's life, when she bestowed her greatest treasure upon her husband, and from that time on was completely dependent upon him, an empty vessel, without legal or emotional existence of her own."[56] Thus, within the pinnacle moment of consummation, True Womanhood mandates the erasure of the woman's personhood so as to be fully subsumed by her husband.

Through this erasure of a woman's personhood, powerlessness is ultimately at the core of True Womanhood as women are forced to "exchange submission for protection" in response to their "conditions of public powerlessness and economic dependency."[57] Especially true is the madwoman's powerlessness due not only to her position as a woman but her societal Otherness as well. Ironically, however, Gilbert and Gubar have set the trajectory for feminist critics to popularly read madness as a form of subversive power,[58] asserting in *The Madwoman in the Attic* that madwomen are "fiercely independent characters who seek to destroy all the patriarchal structures."[59] In actuality, their stance mirrors popular historical perceptions of women's madness as "some sort of willed stubbornness,"[60] and even "a power grab rather than a genuine illness."[61] Unlike Gilbert and Gubar and many other feminist critics, however, Caminero-Santangelo does not view the madwoman as imbued with "secretly subversive power,"[62] reading madness instead as "an illusory self-representation of power that offers an *imaginary* solution to the impasse. As an illusion of power that masks powerlessness, madness is thus the final removal of the madwoman from any field of agency."[63] When applying Caminero-Santangelo's interpretation of madness to Aunt Fanny, her experience of powerlessness is apparent in her actions like her "little cough" used to announce her presence in a room rather than her voice.[64] Her passive-aggressive manner further evidences her powerlessness, which renders her incapable of "a single, definite, clear-cut, unembellished act."[65] Even Aunt Fanny, aware of her Othered position, self-deprecatingly says of herself "you know perfectly well that Aunt Fanny is not one to worry over."[66]

In the absence of a husband figure, Aunt Fanny's subscription to male authority in the form of her deceased father is the very definition of an "imaginary solution" as readers are aware she is not in actual communication with her father; instead, her effort to conform to social expectations and ameliorate her Otherness in light of her inability to procure a husband evidences a rupture in her sanity that places her upon a descent into madness. Evidence exists in the text that points to the contrast between her imagined and actual father, which is supportive of Aunt Fanny's auditory hallucinations as delusion. While she believes she hears her imagined father say, "The father comes to his child and says gently that within himself there is no fear," readers later learn of her father's cruelty—and his express ability to inspire fear in others—in the villagers' description of him as a man who "comes raging out with his gang of bullies."[67] Aunt Fanny also intuits this asymmetry between the two versions of her father despite not consciously acknowledging this disparity when she reflects aloud to her paternal auditory hallucination, "you were never so kind to me before."[68] Thus, Aunt Fanny's confabulated interaction with her deceased father can be read as emanating from her psyche fractured by societal pressure requiring women to participate in matrimony and motherhood from which she has been excluded.

Stemming from this supposed encounter with her father, Aunt Fanny gains the ability to enact submission to male headship required within a True Womanhood framework. While her resurrected relationship with her father is never hinted at as incestuous, she subordinates herself to him as she has done in childhood and as a husband figure would require of her in the context of marriage. Historian Gerda Lerner points out that while "the male children's subordination to the father's dominance is temporary ... until they themselves become heads of households ... The subordination of female children and of wives is lifelong. Daughters can escape it only if they place themselves as wives under the dominance/protection of another man."[69] In the absence of a husband, Aunt Fanny submits to the male authority figure of her father. While men are to be "the movers, the doers, the actors," women are to be "the passive, submissive responders,"[70] which is replicated within Aunt Fanny's situation. She is the passive recipient of her father's message urging action, and her fear of her father illustrates her submissiveness and subordinate position to him. She cries and states that "he will be angry" with her, following her realization that upon fainting she has not immediately delivered his initial message to the others. She tries "to be exact" once she begins relating details of her encounter with her father, all the while "wringing her hands" and suggesting her dread of the consequences she might incur should she even unwittingly alter details.[71] Aunt Fanny's anxiety-riddled actions imply her own awareness of her inferior position in relation to her father's supremacy.

Yet Aunt Fanny's "imaginary solution" to not only her condition of manlessness but her powerlessness is evidenced within her achievement of appropriated authority permissible within the context of True Womanhood. She casts her belief in a prophetic new world to the other household members not as the madness that it is but as evidence of an inherent piety, which results in her eventual withdrawal to "her own fireside" within the domestic sphere of the Halloran mansion.[72] Of the four pillars of True Womanhood, Welter identifies that "religion or piety was the core of woman's virtue" and "belonged to woman by divine right, a gift of God and nature." As such, the woman "would be another, better Eve, working in cooperation with the Redeemer, bringing the world back 'from its revolt and sin.'"[73] Yet piety within True Womanhood is not valued for its own sake but is, in part, lauded by a patriarchal society as it confines the woman within the home, which Welter describes: "One reason religion was valued was that it did not take a woman away from her 'proper sphere,' her home. Unlike participation in other societies or movements, church work would not make her less domestic or submissive, less of a True Woman."[74]

While Aunt Fanny does not demonstrate piety in a classical Judeo-Christian sense, she works to display her propensity for elevated spirituality as a prophetess leading those within her household toward a new Eden. She warns in Old Testament language that the world as they know it "has been a bad and wicked and selfish place,"[75] and—as the "better Eve"—provides her household with a plan for redemption in her urgings to retreat into the mansion. Her visions serve to demonstrate her "naturally religious" nature supposed to be innate within the True Woman,[76] which Aunt Fanny alludes to: "It is as though something I had known all my life, and believed without ever really knowing what it was—some lovely, precious secret had suddenly come into the open. When my father spoke to me he only reminded me of what I had always known, and forgotten."[77] Within this declaration, Aunt Fanny affirms her inherent religiosity residing within her all along like a dormant seed that only required an epiphany from her father to awaken her inner prophetess.

Aunt Fanny continues to openly reflect upon her moral superiority stemming from her claims of an innate religiosity in an effort to further solidify her sense of illusory power, which ironically illuminates to an even greater extent the madness upon which her assertions are predicated. She reflects that while "she did not know why these extraordinary messages had been sent through her own frail self," she delivers self-affirmations as she "believed without question that the choice had been good."[78] Aunt Fanny labels herself as one of the "chosen people" to be saved,[79] thereby elevating herself above the vast majority of society and using such language to equate herself with the biblical story of the Israelites as God's chosen people. Additionally, in her mind, her own sanctification is possible to the point of experiencing earthly perfection as predicted in her foretelling that "evil, and jealousy, and fear, are all going to be removed from us" within the new world.[80] Her sense of newfound moral superiority is most evident in her statement to her domineering and controlling sister-in-law, Orianna: "There are many areas of refinement not possible to one of your background. One area of refinement ... is—if you will permit me to put a name to it—the supernormal. *There* you must allow *me* superiority ... "[81] Only following her initial vision is she for once depicted as "regally" walking by Orianna and Essex,[82] which is a wholly new manner of carrying herself in a house where she previously had no authority.

Aunt Fanny's preparations for entrance into her supposed new world also point to her newfound religiosity. Her participation in domestic tasks plays an integral role in the True Woman's "great task of bringing men back to God."[83] By physically preparing for the impending apocalypse, Aunt Fanny literally readies her household to satisfy and potentially meet "the beings who created" the world.[84] Her brief exit from the Halloran mansion is made in an effort to purchase necessary supplies to sustain them as they enter into the forthcoming utopia. She goes to the "hardware store" and also stops at "the grocery and then the little shop where Mrs. Martin sold her jams and jellies and yard goods and an occasional pie upon order."[85] Aunt Fanny determines what is to be shipped to the Halloran mansion, and "on a very bright clear morning ... the first of Aunt Fanny's preparations arrived, the result of her shopping in the village and her orders sent to the city."[86] Aunt Fanny is later depicted coordinating the interior of the home as she orders "the deliverymen ... to carry out bushel baskets of books" to make room for her purchases to be stored in the library.[87] Through seemingly trivial details in the text, Aunt Fanny's domestic endeavors showcase the spiritual foundation upon which homemaking is established.

Aunt Fanny's belief in the arrival of a new universe is the final aspect of her illusory solution as a madwoman to both her manlessness and Otherness; considering the possibility of marriage and motherhood that exist within her version of a utopia, she believes full participation within True Womanhood to be achievable in this new world. Her maternal hopes are apparent when she addresses the household to "'remember, our little group must include builders and workers as well as—' she blushed faintly—'the mothers of future generations.'"[88] Though not stated explicitly, the implication of Aunt Fanny's blushing is her expectation of becoming a matriarch meant to establish, as she frames it to the household earlier, "a new race of mankind."[89] And in this world, flawlessness is attainable, which mirrors the "perfect female" conception at the core of the tenants of True Womanhood.[90] Aunt Fanny explains that "evil, and jealousy, and fear, are all going to be removed from us,"[91] and she promises that they will be "free of pain and hurt" once they "survive the catastrophe" on par with the burning destruction of Sodom and Gomorrah.[92] The world Aunt Fanny describes is also a classically feminine one. She labels it as a "lovely" place,[93] and one that will be filled with "purity" and "cleanliness,"[94] all suggestive of attributes of True Womanhood latent in Aunt Fanny's psyche from which her utopic vision emanates.

But Aunt Fanny is not blind to the possibility of the madness underscoring her imaginary solution to her manlessness and Otherness in her purported paternal visions and claims of knowledge regarding a utopic world to come. In the very moment when she first perceives her father calling her name, Aunt Fanny questions what she is hearing and, importantly, decides that "it is worse if it is not there; somehow it must be real because if it is not real it is in my own head; unable to move, Aunt Fanny thought: It is real."[95] To recognize her auditory hallucinations would mean to recognize her own madness and, most importantly, result in her inability to pursue True Womanhood, as madness is not allowed of the feminine "lady." Aunt Fanny's focus upon conformity to True Womanhood, which ironically means succumbing to her own madness in an attempt to ignore its presence, is most apparent immediately preceding her vision with her father as statues become animate and warm to her touch as if made of flesh:

> I must control myself. She forced herself to sit up primly on the edge of the marble bench, repressing firmly the nausea she felt at its warm pressure, and she smoothed the black linen of her dress across her lap, and tucked in her hair, which had somehow come loose, and crossed her ankles decently, and took her black-edged handkerchief from her bosom and dried her eyes and wiped away the dampness and grime from her face. Now, she thought; I may go mad, but at least I look like a lady.[96]

When analyzing gendered performances, True Womanhood can be viewed as "a sedimentation of gender norms" that "produces the peculiar phenomenon of a ... 'real woman' or any number of prevalent and compelling social fictions."[97] Even in the midst of a psychotic break, Aunt Fanny absurdly—and comically—adheres to conventions of True Womanhood, evidenced in her insistence on performing a socially accepted femininity in her fixation upon acting the part of a "lady." It is in this moment that True Womanhood and madness are most overtly linked with one another in *The Sundial*, and Aunt Fanny's delusional state is acutely depicted in her hypersensitivity to her own performance as a lady, even at the cost of her own sanity.

If madness signals "the final removal of the madwoman from any field of agency,"[98] it is important to observe that Aunt Fanny does not retreat just anywhere with her group of followers but specifically withdraws into the home, which is the space women are relegated to within the context of True Womanhood. Franklin suggests the following regarding the appearance of the house within Jackson's work:

> As her career progressed and her personal life became more troubled, her work began to investigate more deeply the kinds of psychic damage to which women are especially prone. It is no accident that in many of these works, a house—the woman's domain—functions as a kind of protagonist, with traditional homemaking occupations such as cooking and gardening playing a crucial role in the narrative.[99]

The psychic damage women experience when imprisoned within their homes is particularly explored within *The Sundial* by considering True Womanhood's oppressive and maddening effects upon Aunt Fanny. Appropriately, the Halloran mansion is rendered as a gothic home that brings the genre's preoccupation with "women who just can't seem to get out of the house" to the forefront.[100] This physically sprawling structure is described as having "twenty windows to the left wing ... and twenty windows to the right" with a "great door in the center" that is "double,"[101] which mirrors the castle found in the traditional gothic.[102] But more important than the physical properties of the Halloran mansion are the psychological implications of the gothic home symbolizing the True Woman's confinement within the domestic sphere, the home representing "a set of boundaries that have an all-too-specific origin in the social and economic institutions of patriarchy and their psychological consequences for women."[103] Despite the barriers symbolized by the gothic home, it is not just "a place of danger and imprisonment," but, paradoxically, it can be a "place of security and concord."[104] This contradictory experience is captured in Aunt Fanny's view of the mansion as a waypoint of safety to shield her from the apocalypse, while the house in reality serves to entrap her and remove her entirely from "the social production of meaning."[105] Such tension is most clearly apparent when Aunt Fanny believes she hears her father instruct her to "tell them in the house that there is danger,"[106] a statement laden with double meaning.

Aunt Fanny interprets the message to mean danger lurks outside the walls of the mansion, but the reader intuitively understands that—quite literally—danger is within the house for Aunt Fanny in her loss of social influence.

Regarding the psychological consequences of patriarchal structures imposed upon the True Woman confined within the domestic sphere, Gilbert and Gubar suggest the following:

> It seems inevitable that women reared for, and conditioned to, lives of privacy, reticence, domesticity, might develop pathological fears of public places and unconfined spaces … such afflictions as anorexia and agoraphobia simply carry patriarchal definitions of "femininity" to absurd extremes, and thus function as essential or at least inescapable parodies of social prescription.[107]

Considering Aunt Fanny's entrapment within the Halloran mansion, agoraphobia can certainly be viewed as an aspect of the "psychic damage" she suffers at the hands of patriarchy in taking True Womanhood to "absurd extremes." Aunt Fanny ensures a complete severance from the outside world in her instructions to "cover the window and doors" of the mansion on the supposed final night before the apocalypse "lest the screams of the dying reach our ears and touch us with compassion."[108] Orianna gives voice to this disconnection from the outside world, telling the other household members that "we must think of ourselves … as absolutely isolated. We are on a tiny island in a raging sea."[109] In the final night before the destruction of the world and following Orianna's murder, those within the Halloran mansion continue to enact a separation from the outside world as "all together, they pushed the great chest across the doorway, laughing together because it was their last chore."[110] And while the novel ends before the characters reach the day of the expected apocalypse, the reader knows that the end of the world is not imminent and, instead, those inside the Halloran mansion will remain with Aunt Fanny as ineffectual prisoners shut off from the actual world around them.

As others within the Halloran mansion begin to follow Aunt Fanny's lead resulting in extreme isolation, she counterintuitively experiences a newfound sense of purpose and belonging, despite the realization of the "servants and villagers" that Aunt Fanny's "fine aristocratic mind was slipping rapidly into imbecility."[111] Caminero-Santangelo points out, "Here lies a contradiction: madness begins to provide a sense of community, while sanity for the manless woman denies it."[112] The narrator alludes to the madness sweeping through the entire household with Aunt Fanny as its source, suggesting, "anything, no matter how exotic, can be believed by someone."[113] Aunt Fanny, who cannot conform to the classical definition of a True Woman without a husband, has found acceptance by predicting an apocalypse and utopia to come. As Essex observes, "if I can bring myself to believe in Aunt Fanny's golden world, nothing else will ever do for me; I want it too badly."[114] Orianna is equally infatuated with this "golden world," admitting to the others that "I will not be left behind when creatures like Aunt Fanny and her brother are introduced into a new world. I must plan to be there."[115] Aunt Fanny's utopia speaks to the human desire for perfection and—arguably even more desired—power. Thus, against all odds, Aunt Fanny steadily secures a group of followers and thereby a sense of belonging in a world that she otherwise experiences ostracism within as a manless woman, yet with dire consequences: her madness results in her final severance from the outside world through her complete entrapment "in the 'private' sphere of domesticity."[116]

Aunt Fanny's experience of entrapment is most acutely depicted in her literal embodiment of the "disenfranchised" madwoman in the attic,[117] which occurs in *The Sundial*'s "big attic room" scene.[118] Within this "dollhouse,"[119] as Aunt Fanny terms it, she engages in role play of her mother who serves as Aunt Fanny's prototypical model of True Womanhood in her mother's achievement of both marriage and motherhood. Aunt Fanny has recreated the setup of the apartment she occupied with her parents before the construction of the Halloran mansion using the original furnishings stored within the attic space. In light of the fact that the "first Mrs. Halloran died without ever seeing the greater part of the furnishings in the big house" following an illness, Aunt Fanny regards this wing of the house as a representation of her mother's true home.[120] As Aunt Fanny shows Fancy, a young Halloran family member, her dollhouse, she "opened the door with a flourish, as though she were her mother welcoming a guest."[121]

Aunt Fanny continues to enact her True Woman-motherhood within this attic scene, informing Fancy that they themselves are the dolls in the dollhouse and specifying, "I am the mother, wearing a yellow dress," and "You must be me, little Frances."[122] She reiterates to Fancy that within her attic dollhouse, she becomes a mother: "I am my mother and I am always thinking about my darling children."[123] Finally, Aunt Fanny verbalizes her desire to adhere to True Womanhood while acting the part of her mother, stating, "My darling little Frances will grow up to be a lovely woman, tall and fair, and someday she will find a man who is as good as her father, and she will marry him and they will have strong and happy and handsome children of their own."[124] Considering Aunt Fanny has not achieved this goal determined for women by society and perpetuated in many cases by their mothers, she resorts to playing a married matriarch within her dollhouse that temporarily resolves her exclusion from marriage and motherhood. The text reveals that Aunt Fanny has even contemplated retreating entirely into the dollhouse, experiencing in her madness an extreme isolation from not only the outside world but even those within the Halloran mansion: "If Aunt Fanny had cared to, she might have dropped from sight altogether into this apartment in the big house, might have left the others behind and gone into the apartment and closed the door, and stayed."[125] Thus, within this moment, madness is not depicted as a female protagonist's means of claiming a newfound sense of authority but results instead in her experience of powerlessness and the erasure of personhood to a profound degree.

The Sundial deserves much greater critical attention than what it receives considering Jackson's exploration of feminist themes in relation to patriarchy, True Womanhood, and madness through the character of Aunt Fanny. Jackson draws upon humor not just for entertainment but also as a means of subtly examining the substrates of society constraining women through the continued iterations of True Womanhood. Furthermore, during a time in which women were held responsible for their own psychological disorders, Jackson bravely places the locus of women's madness upon patriarchal society within The Sundial; importantly as well, she reveals madness to be a consequence for even those women like Aunt Fanny who most desire to fully participate within hegemonic structures. Caminero-Santangelo writes that "Art ... has the potential power to work against myth—that is, against repeated stories which have hardened into 'barriers'—by offering an alternative understanding of reality,"[126] and Jackson's exploration of insanity does just that as the madwoman is revealed to be one who is not so much trapped within her own psyche but ultimately imprisoned within the strictures of society. Considering Jackson's view that "writing is the way out,"[127] The Sundial serves as not only a means of Jackson's escape of her own world through fiction but also provides readers with an avenue of beginning to transcend the clutches of patriarchy. Through the novel's careful analysis of the detrimental effects of restrictive social structures forced upon women, Jackson spurs readers toward thoughtful evaluation of the world they live in and, more importantly, the world they want to live in.

Notes

1   Phyllis Chesler, *Women & Madness* (New York: Doubleday, 1972), 115.
2   Marta Caminero-Santangelo, *The Madwoman Can't Speak: Or Why Insanity Is Not Subversive* (Ithaca: Cornell University Press, 1998), 54.
3   Shirley Jackson, *The Sundial* (New York: Penguin, 2014), see blurb on back cover.
4   Ruth Franklin, *Shirley Jackson: A Rather Haunted Life* (New York: Liveright, 2016), 387.
5   John Barkham, "The End of the World," *Saturday Review Syndicate* (n.d.): n.p., quoted in Ruth Franklin, *Shirley Jackson*, 398.
6   Nancy Walker, "Humor and Gender Roles: The 'Funny' Feminism of the Post-World War II Suburbs," *American Quarterly*, 37, no. 1 (1985): 99.
7   Ibid., 99.

8   Ibid., 102.
9   Shirley Jackson, *Life among the Savages* (New York: Quality Paperback Book Club, 1998), 67–8.
10 Walker, "Humor and Gender Roles," 98.
11 Floriane Place-Verghnes, *Tex Avery: A Unique Legacy, 1942–1955* (Eastleigh: John Libbey, 2006), 98.
12 Caminero-Santangelo, *The Madwoman Can't Speak*, 94.
13 Mary Louise Roberts, "True Womanhood Revisited." *Journal of Women's History*, 14, no. 1 (2002): 150.
14 Barbara Welter, "The Cult of True Womanhood: 1820–1860." *American Quarterly*, 18, no. 2 (1966): 162.
15 Nancy A. Hewitt, "Taking the True Woman Hostage." *Journal of Women's History*, 14, no. 1 (2002): 156.
16 Place-Verghnes, *Tex Avery*, 99.
17 Welter, "The Cult of True Womanhood: 1820–1860," 174.
18 Betty Friedan, *The Feminine Mystique* (New York: W.W. Norton, 2013), 35.
19 Daniel Horowitz, *Betty Friedan and the Making of* The Feminine Mystique: *The American Left, the Cold War, and Modern Feminism* (Amherst: University of Massachusetts Press, 1998), 2.
20 Friedan, *The Feminine Mystique*, 36.
21 Ibid., 35.
22 Roberta Rubenstein, "House Mothers and Haunted Daughters: Shirley Jackson and Female Gothic." *Tulsa Studies in Women's Literature*, 15, no. 2 (1996): n.p.
23 Franklin, *Shirley Jackson,* 5.
24 Ibid., 9.
25 Ibid., 469.
26 Qtd. in Franklin, *Shirley Jackson,* 477.
27 Ibid.
28 Qtd. in Franklin, *Shirley Jackson,* 217.
29 Ibid., 37.
30 Franklin, *Shirley Jackson,*162.
31 Ibid., 478.
32 Qtd. in Franklin, *Shirley Jackson,* 479.
33 Judith Evans, *Feminist Theory Today: An Introduction to Second-Wave Feminism* (London: Sage Publications Ltd., 1995), 1.
34 Caminero-Santangelo, *The Madwoman Can't Speak*, 4.
35 Ibid., 5–6.
36 Ibid., 9, 53.
37 Ibid., 54.

38 Ibid.
39 Gerda Lerner, *The Creation of Patriarchy* (New York: Oxford University Press, 1986), 17.
40 Caminero-Santangelo, *The Madwoman Can't Speak*, 54.
41 Ibid., 10
42 Ibid., 54.
43 Ibid., 10.
44 Margaret Jackson, *The Real Facts of Life: Feminism and the Politics of Sexuality c 1850–1940* (London: Taylor & Francis, 1994), n.p.
45 Sheila Jeffreys, *The Spinster and Her Enemies: Feminism and Sexuality 1880–1930* (North Melbourne: Spinifex Press, 1997), 97–8.
46 Caminero-Santangelo, *The Madwoman Can't Speak*, 93.
47 Ibid., 54–5.
48 Ibid., 55.
49 Jackson, *The Sundial*, 18.
50 Ibid.
51 Ibid., 117.
52 Ibid., 24–5.
53 Sandra M. Gilbert and Susan Gubar, *The Madwoman in the Attic: The Woman Writer and the Nineteenth-Century Literary Imagination* (New Haven: Yale University Press, 2000), 53.
54 Welter, "The Cult of True Womanhood: 1820–1860," 155.
55 Ibid., 154.
56 Ibid., 155.
57 Lerner, *The Creation of Patriarchy*, 217–18.
58 Caminero-Santangelo, *The Madwoman Can't Speak*, 1.
59 Gilbert and Gubar, *The Madwoman in the Attic*, 78.
60 Caminero-Santangelo, *The Madwoman Can't Speak*, 76.
61 Barbara Ehrenreich and Deirdre English, *Complaints and Disorders: The Sexual Politics of Sickness* (Old Westbury: Feminist Press, 1974), quoted in Caminero-Santangelo, *The Madwoman Can't Speak*, 76.
62 Caminero-Santangelo, *The Madwoman Can't Speak*, 4.
63 Ibid., 11–12.
64 Jackson, *The Sundial*, 5.
65 Ibid., 27.
66 Ibid., 5.
67 Ibid., 26, 198.
68 Ibid., 26.
69 Lerner, *The Creation of Patriarchy*, 218.

70 Welter, "The Cult of True Womanhood: 1820–1860," 159.
71 Jackson, *The Sundial*, 32.
72 Welter, "The Cult of True Womanhood: 1820–1860," 162.
73 Ibid., 152.
74 Ibid., 153.
75 Jackson, *The Sundial*, 37.
76 Welter, "The Cult of True Womanhood: 1820–1860," 153.
77 Jackson, *The Sundial*, 38
78 Ibid., 36.
79 Ibid., 38
80 Ibid., 37.
81 Ibid., 39.
82 Ibid.
83 Welter, "The Cult of True Womanhood: 1820–1860," 162.
84 Jackson, *The Sundial*, 37.
85 Ibid., 77.
86 Ibid., 105.
87 Ibid., 106.
88 Ibid., 81.
89 Ibid., 36.
90 Welter, "The Cult of True Womanhood: 1820–1860," 169.
91 Jackson, *The Sundial*, 37.
92 Ibid., 38.
93 Ibid., 108.
94 Ibid., 38
95 Ibid., 26.
96 Ibid., 23–4.
97 Judith Butler, *Gender Trouble* (New York: Routledge, 1999), 178.
98 Caminero-Santangelo, *The Madwoman Can't Speak*, 12.
99 Franklin, *Shirley Jackson*, 3.
100 Eugenia DeLamotte, *Perils of the Night: A Feminist Study of Nineteenth-Century Gothic* (New York: Oxford University Press, 1990), 10.
101 Jackson, *The Sundial*, 9.
102 Kate Ferguson Ellis, *The Contested Castle: Gothic Novels and the Subversion of Domestic Ideology* (Chicago: University of Illinois Press, 1989), x.
103 DeLamotte, *Perils of the Night*, 27.
104 Ellis, *The Contested Castle*, x.
105 Caminero-Santangelo, *The Madwoman Can't Speak*, 94.

106 Jackson, *The Sundial*, 26.
107 Gilbert and Gubar, *The Madwoman in the* Attic, 54.
108 Jackson, *The Sundial*, 100.
109 Ibid., 209.
110 Ibid., 220.
111 Ibid., 105.
112 Caminero-Santangelo, *The Madwoman Can't Speak*, 90.
113 Jackson, *The Sundial*, 33.
114 Ibid., 42.
115 Ibid., 41.
116 Caminero-Santangelo, *The Madwoman Can't Speak*, 94.
117 Gilbert and Gubar, *The Madwoman in the* Attic, xxxvi.
118 Jackson, *The Sundial*, 157.
119 Ibid.
120 Ibid.
121 Ibid., 163.
122 Ibid.
123 Ibid.
124 Ibid., 164.
125 Ibid., 162.
126 Caminero-Santangelo, *The Madwoman Can't Speak*, 68.
127 Qtd. in Franklin, *Shirley Jackson*, 479.

References

Butler, Judith. *Gender Trouble*. New York: Routledge, 1999 (accessed December 29, 2019). http://search.ebscohost.com.marshall.idm.oclc.org/login.aspx?direct=true&db= nlebk&AN=70541&site=ehost-live.

Caminero-Santangelo, Marta. *The Madwoman Can't Speak: Or Why Insanity Is Not Subversive*. Reading Women Writing Series, ed. Shari Benstock and Celeste Schenck. Ithaca: Cornell University Press, 1998.

Chesler, Phyllis. *Women & Madness*. New York: Doubleday, 1972.

DeLamotte, Eugenia. *Perils of the Night: A Feminist Study of Nineteenth-Century Gothic*. New York: Oxford University Press, 1990 (accessed August 17, 2017). http://search.ebscohost.com.marshall.idm.oclc.org/ login.aspx?direct=true&db= nlebk&AN=143698&site=ehost-live.

Ellis, Kate Ferguson. *The Contested Castle: Gothic Novels and the Subversion of Domestic Ideology*. Chicago: University of Illinois Press, 1989.

Evans, Judith. *Feminist Theory Today: An Introduction to Second-Wave Feminism*. London: Sage, 1995 (accessed January 15, 2019). http://search.ebscohost.com.

marshall.idm.oclc.org/login.aspx?direct=true&db=nlebk&AN=716910&site=ehost-live.
Franklin, Ruth. *Shirley Jackson: A Rather Haunted Life*. New York: Liveright, 2016.
Friedan, Betty. *The Feminine Mystique*. New York: W.W. Norton & Company, 2013.
Gilbert, Sandra M. and Susan Gubar. *The Madwoman in the Attic: The Woman Writer and the Nineteenth-Century Literary Imagination*. 2nd ed. New Haven: Yale University Press, 2000.
Hewitt, Nancy A. "Taking the True Woman Hostage." *Journal of Women's History*, 14, no. 1 (Spring 2002): 156–62 (accessed November 21, 2018). https://doi.org/10.1353/jowh.2002.0020.
Horowitz, Daniel. *Betty Friedan and the Making of* The Feminine Mystique: *The American Left, the Cold War, and Modern Feminism*. Amherst: University of Massachusetts Press, 1998 (accessed June 20, 2019). http://search.ebscohost.com.marshall.idm.oclc.org/login.aspx?direct=true&db=nlebk&AN=13853&site=ehost-live.
Jackson, Margaret. *The Real Facts of Life: Feminism and the Politics of Sexuality c 1850–1940*. London: Taylor & Francis, 1994 (accessed November 5, 2018). https://books.google.com/books?isbn=113574971X.
Jackson, Shirley. *Life among the Savages and Raising Demons*. New York: Quality Paperback Book Club, 1998.
Jackson, Shirley. *The Sundial*. New York: Penguin, 2014.
Jeffreys, Sheila. *The Spinster and Her Enemies: Feminism and Sexuality 1880–1930*. North Melbourne: Spinifex Press, 1997 (accessed November 5, 2018). https://books.google.com/books?isbn=1875559639.
Lerner, Gerda. *The Creation of Patriarchy*. New York: Oxford University Press, 1986.
Place-Verghnes, Floriane. *Tex Avery: A Unique Legacy, 1942–1955*. Eastleigh: John Libbey Publishing, 2006 (accessed January 04, 2019). https://books.google.com/books?isbn=0861966597.
Roberts, Mary Louise. "True Womanhood Revisited." *Journal of Women's History* 14, no. 1 (Spring 2002): 150–55 (accessed September 16, 2018). https://doi.org/10/1353/jowh.2002.0025.
Rubenstein, Roberta. "House Mothers and Haunted Daughters: Shirley Jackson and Female Gothic." *Tulsa Studies in Women's Literature*, 15, no. 2 (Fall 1996): 309–31 (accessed October 23, 2018). http://link.galegroup.com/apps/doc/H1420078278/LitRC?u=ashl71426&sid=LitRC&xid =8286d937.
Walker, Nancy. "Humor and Gender Roles: The 'Funny' Feminism of the Post-World War II Suburbs." *American Quarterly*, 37, no. 1 (Spring 1985): 98–113 (accessed November 18, 2018). https://www.jstor.org/ stable/2712765.
Welter, Barbara. "The Cult of True Womanhood: 1820–1860." *American Quarterly* 18, no 2 (Summer 1966): 151–74 (accessed June 2, 2017). http://www.jstor.org/stable/2711179.

10

Insisting on the Moon: Shirley Jackson and the Queer Future

Emily Banks

Throughout Shirley Jackson's fiction, domestic, familial spaces become perilous for the women confined within their walls. Her protagonists are not, however, intent on escaping their confinement; rather, they reimagine and recreate the structures surrounding them, redefining the parameters of kinship and repurposing the domestic as a shelter from the outside world. The domestic rebellions Jackson crafts suggest a radical claim—that women cannot simply escape patriarchal structures, but must destroy and reinvent them. By examining Jackson's two best known novels, *The Haunting of Hill House* (1959) and *We Have Always Lived in the Castle* (1962), through the lens of queer futurity and world-making, I argue that her work dramatizes the difficulty of imagining life beyond the patriarchal domestic structure but also evokes the vision of a possible queer future, achievable only through the destruction of traditional concepts of lineage and production. Using the moon and stars as metaphors, Jackson envisions a queer future that seems impossible, but considering she was writing at the beginning of the space age, may be closer than we imagine. In both novels, Jackson's protagonists resort to extreme, violent actions in pursuit of nontraditional family structures: Eleanor takes permanent residence in a haunted house and Mary Katherine murders her family to create her ideal domestic life with her sister. Although neither of these narratives initially seems optimistic, both protagonists do, in a way, get what they want. Through hyperbolic scenarios of fantasy fulfillment, Jackson asserts the necessity of radical, destructive change if women are to free themselves from the traditional heteropatriarchal family structure and create a new future.

In "Sex in Public," Lauren Berlant and Michael Warner conceive of queer culture as "a world-making project" in which "world" indicates the inclusion of "more people than can be identified, more spaces than can be mapped beyond a few reference points, modes of feeling that can be learned rather than experienced as a birthright."[1] In *Hill House* and *Castle*, Jackson's interplanetary metaphors allude to this kind of world-making practice as her protagonists attempt, with varying degrees of success, to reconceive of the spaces they inhabit and the relational ties that constitute their family structures. Their "worlds" are ultimately both domestic and cosmic; rather than escaping the feminized space of the home, they reclaim it, creating self-sustaining spaces that reject masculine intrusion. "The queer world," in Berlant and Warner's illustration, "is a space of entrances, exits, unsystematized lines of acquaintance, projected horizons, typifying examples, alternate routes, blockages, incommensurate geographies."[2] The haunted homes Jackson crafts embody this queering of physical space— the off-kilter angles of Hill House and the deconstructed remains of the Blackwood mansion provide suitable structures for the task of reworking traditional domesticity for the queer future. In keeping with the gothic literary tradition, Jackson's novels establish a parallel between the state of the home and the state of the family. While this move typically works to illustrate the disturbing deterioration of a family line—as in Poe's "The Fall of the House of Usher"—Jackson uses the gothic home to connote the queer possibility of destroying and reimagining traditional family structures. In *Hill House*, uncanny architecture signifies new possibilities of identification for the unmarried, childless Eleanor, while, in *Castle*, Merricat destroys her familial home to recreate it as a space in which she can live out her queer fantasy. For both protagonists, the gothic home becomes a refuge from societal expectations and a means of resisting the compulsion of heteronormative futurity.

In *Hill House*, Eleanor Vance inhabits, in many ways, the literary trope of the childless spinster. Living off the goodwill of her relatives, she is marked by her marital status as inferior and unnecessary within her family. After years of caring for her dying mother, a responsibility that fell to her as the unmarried daughter, she lives with her sister's family, a member of the class Margaret Fuller deemed "despised auxiliaries."[3] While women made significant strides towards independence in the first half of the twentieth century, in the 1950s, when Cold War tensions accelerated the postwar emphasis on traditional family values and homosexuality was increasingly visible and increasingly policed, unmarried women were viewed with renewed suspicion.[4] To introduce Eleanor's character, Jackson informs us that, "The only person in the world she genuinely hated, now that her mother was dead, was her sister. She disliked her brother-in-law and her five-year-old niece, and she had no friends." Her bitterness, Jackson explains, results from "the eleven years she had spent caring for her invalid mother," which were "built up devotedly around small guilts and small reproaches, constant weariness, and unending despair."[5] Eleanor, who, at 32, has given up on pursuing her own desires, embodies the resentment of women who failed to find their place within the postwar family ideal. The expectation that, not having started a family of her own, she must remain tethered to an inferior role within her birth-family hinders her self-development, rendering her isolated and purposeless.

As Eleanor prepares for her journey to Hill House, she argues with her sister and brother-in-law about taking the family car. To justify their refusal, they repeatedly cite the possibility of "poor little Linnie" getting sick and needing a doctor, with the implicit accusation that she is selfish for making such a request.[6] This reasoning emphasizes their underlying belief that, as a childless spinster, Eleanor has less of a natural claim to the car although the sisters share it legally. Her financial equality is meaningless in the face of the persistent societal belief that unmarried, childless women are inherently less valuable than wives and mothers. By defying her sister and taking the car anyway, Eleanor refuses this logic, committing the culturally abhorrent crime of putting herself before the symbolic child. She violates what Lee Edelman calls "the social consensus" that an appeal on behalf of children is "impossible to refuse."[7] Like Edelman's "*sinthomosexual*" who "assert[s] itself against futurity, against its propagation," Eleanor departs for Hill House in defiance of family values and heteronormative futurity.[8] She not only eschews marriage and motherhood personally, but also expresses disdain for the institution of family by unapologetically despising her relations—children included.

The disdain for family is more tangible in *Castle*, as Mary Katherine (or "Merricat") literally destroys her family. In a pertinent parallel between the novels, the opening scene of *Castle* depicts Merricat's hatefulness, emphasizing the extension of this sentiment to children. Having ventured to the village, she describes how she "would have liked to come into the grocery some morning and see them all, even the Elberts and the children, lying there crying with the pain and dying"[9]—an attitude undoubtedly related to the intense agoraphobia Jackson developed toward the end of her life.[10] By specifying the inclusion of children in her murderous fantasy, Merricat rejects the cultural norm of protecting children at all costs, exemplifying Edelman's provocation that "*queerness* names the side of those *not* 'fighting for the children.'"[11] Her constant conflict with taunting youths throughout the novel paints her as a *sinthomosexual* figure in that she lives (literally and figuratively) on the outskirts of the reproductive future and is suspected of posing a danger to children. While both protagonists initially embody Edelman's model of queer anti-futurity through their refusal to accept society's adoration of procreation and childhood, they expand this paradigm, as the novels unfold, by envisioning new, antinormative possibilities for futurity.

Eleanor's solitary road trip to Hill House, away from her family, allows her to begin imagining a future outside the norm. Her drive, in which the road "turned and dipped, going around turns where surprises waited," signals the possibility of deviation from the expected, linear path. Eleanor experiences a queering of space and temporality as she narrates, "Time is beginning this morning in June ... but it is a time that is strangely new and of itself."[12] Following Jack Halberstam's theorization of queer subjects who "will and do opt to live outside of reproductive and familial time," Eleanor's sense of altered time and space as she approaches Hill House signals the promise of queer potentialities opening up for her.[13] When she arrives, Eleanor enters a home that defies geometry. Dr. Montague explains to his volunteers that, in Hill House, "every angle is slightly wrong ... Angles which you assume are right angles you are accustomed to, and have every right to expect are true, are actually a fraction of a degree off in one direction or another."[14] Hill House is uncanny in the Freudian sense, the familiar image of a home rendered horrifying by slight alteration.[15] Sara Ahmed, in *Queer Phenomenology: Orientations, Objects, Others*, defines "Queer orientation" as "those things that don't line up, which by seeing the world 'slantwise' allow other objects to come into view," and, while Hill House's odd angles make the structure uncanny, they also reveal, for Eleanor, the possibility of new experience.[16] The house is further cast as a queer space when Theodora compares it to "any good girls' camp" and "a boarding school I went to for a while,"[17] referencing spaces commonly suspected by early sexuality theorists of harboring and spreading female homosexuality.[18] Upon entering this environment, Eleanor begins to discover her own identity; on her first night, she thinks, "I am the fourth person in this room; I am one of them; I belong."[19] The very act of seeing herself as "the fourth person," indicating individuality and wholeness, is radical for Eleanor whose previous existence was peripheral to her family's needs.

Jackson exaggerates Eleanor's process of self-identification as the group engages in playful banter, pretending to deduce each other's identities by process of elimination; Eleanor determines, "And you are Theodora ... because I am Eleanor," while Theodora tells Luke, "Doctor Montague has a beard ... so you must be Luke."[20] Their game suggests the extent to which selfhood is developed in relation to those around us; for Eleanor, it promises the possibility of redefinition, a new identity made viable by a new relational web apart from her family. The fluid sense of identity they cultivate as they declare themselves "A courtesan, a pilgrim, a princess, and a bullfighter" enables her to begin reimagining herself.[21] Throughout the novel, she frequently makes childlike observations such as, "I have red shoes," which dramatize her delayed development of a sense of self. By cataloguing individual attributes—"I dislike lobster and sleep on my left side and crack my knuckles when I am nervous and save buttons"—she attempts to shape an understanding of herself as "a complete and separate thing."[22] Only in the haunted house, with its offset lines and angles, can she conceive of claiming an individual identity. As an unmarried, and implicitly queer, woman, Eleanor's role in her family is apparitional, at once confined and invisible. In Hill House, she becomes visible by entering a world of apparitions; a haunted space is, after all, one in which the invisible make their presence known.

As the group falls into their evening routine of gathering around the sitting room fireplace, they emulate a familial rhythm that suggests for Eleanor the tantalizing possibility that family may be created rather than inherited. We soon learn that the conflict between inheritance and queer familial production is deeply woven into Hill House's mythology. The story of the Crain family's eldest sister, an unmarried woman who "took a girl from the village to live with her, as a kind of companion" and caused familial strife when she left Hill House to the younger woman illustrates the violence of heteronormative society when disrupted by relational bonds that fall out of line with marriage and heredity.[23] As Dr. Montague explains, "The companion insisted that the house was left to her, but the younger sister and her husband maintained most violently that the house belonged legally to them and claimed that the companion had tricked the older sister into signing away property," a dispute which recalls Eleanor's earlier argument with her sister.[24] As Eleanor's sister assumes full ownership of their car, the younger Crain sister believes heredity and marital status entitle her to the house even when legal documents say otherwise. The companion's claim is disputed because her community fails to recognize two women cohabitating, a bond that falls outside the family line, as a legitimate relationship. By killing herself in the house, she becomes part of the haunting, simultaneously refusing to leave and making it uninhabitable for those who would deny her claim to it.

Eleanor later expresses to Theodora, "You keep thinking of the little children ... but I can't forget that lonely little companion, walking around these rooms, wondering who else was in the house."[25] That she relates to the companion foreshadows the novel's ending and strengthens the connection between the two stories. Shortly before killing herself, Eleanor asserts, "Hill House belongs to *me*," reiterating the companion's sentiment and rejecting Luke's legal claim on the house.[26] This occurs after Luke appears to usurp Eleanor's role as Theodora's companion when she finds them "leaning against a tree trunk and talking softly and laughing" by the brook where the two women had, earlier, imagined an idyllic sisterhood.[27] They begin treating Eleanor like a child who cannot outgrow her fantasy world—or the dream of a queer future—and Luke's claiming of Theodora is linked, for Eleanor, to his legal ownership of Hill House. By repeating the companion's gesture of ownership, Eleanor asserts her right to remain in the queer space of the house, and thus her right to a queer future.

In *Castle*, Jackson again uses a subversive domestic structure to symbolize the potential for a queer future. After murdering most of her family, Mary Katherine ultimately succeeds in shutting out societal influence to build a future cohabitating with her beloved sister Constance in domestic bliss. Like *Hill House*, the later novel challenges traditions of inheritance, envisioning a future in which women can sustain themselves without masculine interference or the goal of reproductive futurity. Rather than finding her place in a preexisting haunted house, like Eleanor does, Merricat, through violence and destruction of property, fashions her own ideal domestic space. After Merricat has killed their parents, she and Constance function blissfully together for the most part, but are still plagued by interactions with townspeople and necessary trips to the outside world. It is only after Merricat finishes the job, killing her already-damaged Uncle Julian—the last dying breath of the patriarchy—and radically altering their home with an act of arson, that the sisters make it to "the moon," thereby fulfilling her ultimate fantasy.

Much like Eleanor's plans for her future with Theo, Merricat's fantasy of a future with Constance is threatened by the intrusion of a man. While Luke successfully drives a wedge between Eleanor and Theo, making it clear to Eleanor that her fantasy of a queer future cannot exist in the world outside Hill House, Cousin Charles's interference in Merricat's plans is more short-lived. Charles's arrival briefly disturbs the sisters' relationship, as he makes Constance consider whether Merricat should be oriented toward a "normal" adolescence; she tells her younger sister, "We should have been living like other people. ... You should have had boy friends" before laughing at the absurdity of the idea.[28] Unlike Eleanor, Merricat succeeds in driving away this threat to her primary relationship by destroying the property from which he hopes to profit. Notably, the two male transgressors, Luke Sanderson and Charles Blackwood, both enter the text through the structure of inheritance—Luke is the heir to Hill House, and Charles is hoping to capitalize on the deaths in the Blackwood home. The heteronormative notion of inheritance, the "family line" to which Ahmed refers, is a roadblock in the protagonists' quests for a queer future. Merricat is ultimately victorious when she destroys her family's inheritance, diminishing its capitalist value and repurposing the family home as a space for her own queer desires. Her rejection of the heteronormative, inherited future is explicit when she looks through her father's jewelry box, relating, "I would not touch the ring; the thought of a ring around my finger always made me feel tied tight, because rings had no openings to get out of, but I liked the watch chain, which twisted and wound around my hand when I picked it up."[29] Rejecting the ring and the predestined future it entails, she prefers the malleable watch chain, which represents her ability to change and mold temporality, determining her own future.

The queering of structures and futurity in Jackson's novels is bolstered by her allusions to and subversions of familiar narratives. The ending of *Hill House* mirrors the common narrative of lesbian tragedy, but subverts it to suggest an alternative to this fate. As Amanda H. Littauer discusses in her article "Someone to Love," lesbian pulp novels of the 1950s, one of the primary media through which queer women and girls could access non-pathologizing depictions of women's same-sex desire, almost exclusively ended tragically. This was related to the claim promoted by Caprio and others "that lesbians could never sustain healthy intimate partnerships" and were "doomed to unhappiness because their sexual relationships were necessarily unstable and ephemeral."[30] In his reading of the novel, George Haggerty posits that Hill House halts the erotic progression of Eleanor and Theodora's relationship "by revealing the deeply buried guilt Eleanor feels about her mother's death," and that Eleanor "gives in to the voices calling her because she feels in her heart that she does not deserve the freedom she has started to feel."[31] Hill House, in this reading, operates as a queer space and a space of recurrent trauma. It allows Eleanor to imagine a new paradigm of relations, but punishes her, or prompts her to punish herself, for her emerging desires. This duality reflects the conflict between the queer future symbolized by the companion's relationship with the eldest Crain daughter and the hegemony of the heteropatriarchal family line enforced by her sister and by the looming presence of Hugh Crain's paternal cruelty.

The trope of lesbian tragedy in *Hill House* is depicted as a haunting when the companion's suicide repeats itself in Eleanor's. In this way, the novel illustrates how real patterns form from repeated tropes, and the power of representation to affect queer lives. After Theodora has dismissed Eleanor's visions of queer domestic life, the only conclusion she can imagine is death. Still, if we believe in the novel's ghosts, we might read Eleanor's suicide as a happy, or at least fulfilling, ending: defying the demands of her fellow visitors, she asserts a permanent claim over Hill House, where she is able to envision a queer future. She, like Ms. Crain's companion, refuses to relinquish the house to its rightful—in the legal, patriarchal, and heteronormative sense—owners. Perhaps Eleanor, who has previously stated that she "can't picture any world but Hill House," is asserting her claim to a queer future by rejecting the real, heteronormative world in favor of the haunted house.[32] While Jackson engages with the narrative structure of lesbian tragedy, the supernatural possibilities of *Hill House* belie a hope that queer fantasy can indeed find its place.

In *Hill House*, we learn that part of Eleanor's torturous duty as caretaker for her mother entailed reading "Love stories" aloud to her, which indicates that her escape from maternal oppression is also an escape from the romantic narratives that were forced upon her.[33] The image of Eleanor stuck in a room with her dying mother reading romances to her rather than pursuing her own desires indicates the suppression of her fantasy life by the normative storyline pushed on her as part of familial duty. Throughout the novel, though, the love story Eleanor keeps returning to is Shakespeare's decidedly queer *Twelfth Night*—her repeated refrain, "Journeys end in lovers meeting," is originally spoken by Feste, the play's Fool.[34] After the twins Viola and Sebastian, separated by a shipwreck, each become love objects, while in drag, for a member of the same sex, *Twelfth Night* concludes with a neat fix: the twins' sexes are revealed, and Olivia and Orsino each easily transfer their attractions to the twin of the opposite sex. This all-too-easy conclusion comically ignores the fact that twins are not merely the same person with different genitals, and dismisses the genuine attraction Olivia and Orsino felt for a person of the same sex in different clothes, attaching the expected heteronormative marriage plot to what is ultimately a very queer narrative.

In *Hill House*, Eleanor's delayed psychosexual journey is catalyzed by her attraction to a female playmate, a phase that women are expected to grow out of. By the end of the narrative, Theodora has outgrown, or tired of, her childlike affection for Eleanor, and appears, in the psychoanalytic terms of the time, to reach the phase of heterosexual maturity by transferring her attraction to Luke. As in *Twelfth Night*, the love story's queer potential is quickly dismissed in its normative conclusion. But Jackson refuses to conclude *Hill House* with such any easy solution, and Eleanor's love for Theodora cannot be transferred to a proper recipient. Rather, upon realizing her fantasy ending cannot come to fruition in the normative world, she chooses Hill House, a structure that, through its design, subverts expectations of direction and orientation. Within the gothic setting, Jackson's allusions to and subversions of romantic stories suggest the need for queer alternatives to the expected narratives and conclusions of romance.

Throughout *Castle*, Jackson similarly signals the revision of heteronormative expectations by invoking and subverting fairy tale motifs. Merricat sees Constance as "a fairy princess," portraying her in drawings "with long golden hair and eyes as blue as the crayon could make them, and a bright pink spot on either cheek."[35] As the novel's title suggests, she does not dream of being whisked away by a prince, but rather knows that the "castle," or fairy-tale ending she desires, has always been her life with her sister. While the traditional happy ending is intrinsically bound to the acquisition, through marriage, of wealth, Merricat's fairy tale culminates in the purposeful disavowal of capital, with the monetary value of the sisters' property obliterated. The rubble of the Blackwood home is distinctly gendered, as generations of bridal dowries are destroyed, and the only clothing left in the house belongs to the now late Uncle Julian.[36] As Constance dons his clothes while Merricat opts for a modified tablecloth, the sisters engage in a kind of drag performance, redefining their identities and roles for their newly new deconstructed domicile. Though Constance initially regrets that her sister must be "dressed in a tablecloth like a rag doll," Merricat calls the new garment "a robe" and dances in it, convincing Constance to appreciate their modest fate as a fairy-tale ending.[37] By referring to Constance's new attire as "the skins of Uncle Julian," Merricat emphasizes their drag performance as a conquest.[38] Their sartorial inhabiting of traditional gender roles in this scene mimics the quick fix of *Twelfth Night* alluded to in *Hill House*, but Jackson highlights the subversive violence of the performance as the sisters play dress up in the ruins of normative order. Their performance evokes Judith Butler's theorization of drag as a means of deconstructing binary gender by revealing the extent to which *all* gender is performative, and also gestures toward the utopian performativity José Muñoz describes in *Cruising Utopia: The Then and There of Queer Futurity*.[39] Revising the idea of queerness as a "a stage" in normative development, Muñoz asserts the power of "a stage" in the sense of a performance which "is imbued with a sense of potentiality."[40] The performative manner in which the sisters begin their new life signals the potentiality they discover in the rewriting of old narratives and their ability to create new roles for themselves in their own queer fairy tale. The gothic home is Merricat's enchanted castle and the stage upon which her fantasies play.

In addition to reimagining the gothic home, Jackson puts a unique spin on the gothic theme of maternal loss and, in doing so, critiques the psychoanalytic assumptions from which it is typically produced. In *Queer Gothic*, Haggerty describes "the erotics of maternal loss" as an essential element of queer gothic literature in which the mother is positioned as "an originary loss" that "forecloses same-sex bonds in favor of brutal and brutalizing gendered alternatives."[41] Both *Hill House* and *Castle*, however, deviate from this model in that the protagonists are women who have, directly or otherwise, killed their mothers. In Eleanor's case, her guilt over her mother's death and her positive feelings about it convince her that the death was her fault, while Merricat has no evident qualms about her matricide. Rather than longing for the lost feminine erotic connection of the absent mother, Jackson's protagonists must destroy the mother before they can seek new, less toxic feminine erotic connections. The mothers in these novels are agents of heteronormative, patriarchal control as Jackson critiques the power dynamics of the mother–daughter relationship, favoring, instead, sisterly bonds that enable alternative modes of production and sustenance.

In a crucial scene from her drive, Eleanor observes a little girl refusing to drink milk from a glass in a diner because it is not decorated with stars like the one she has at home, and she quietly advises, "Don't do it … insist on your cup of stars; once they have trapped you into being like everyone else you will never see your cup of stars again."[42] Eleanor's reaction to the little girl builds on Jackson's depiction of her psychological childishness, as she relates to the child rather than to her mother, and hints at her traumatic history of familial repression—Eleanor sees the family as a trap that will eventually consume the girl's individual identity as it did hers. Given her implicitly toxic relationship with her mother, Eleanor's inner monologue demonstrates her resentment at having been trapped by familial pressures into an attempt at social conformity and at having relinquished, or lost touch with, her primary desires. While the parents are permissive in this instance, Eleanor's unspoken advice warns that such a loss is inevitable, if the girl does not constantly and fiercely guard herself against it.

Read alongside sexuality theories, rooted in works by Freud and Havelock Ellis, that reemerged in Frank Caprio's 1954 *Female Homosexuality* and pervaded popular culture in the 1950s, the milk scene depicts the repression of queer childhood impulses. As Littauer details, Caprio's text as well as contemporaneous articles in publications like the *Washington Post* promoted the idea that "young women who chose not to build their lives on the cornerstones of postwar social life—marriage and motherhood—were stunted in their psychosexual development," linking lesbian desire to immaturity and implying that such feelings should be left in childhood.[43] The idea of stunted psychosexual development is evident in Jackson's portrayal of Eleanor, but this scene implies that it is the stifling of Eleanor's true desires, not her failure to grow into a heteronormative lifestyle, that hinders her progress. The cup of stars is a fascinating metaphor in that it contains milk, an emblem of maternal nourishment. Roberta Rubenstein writes, "The very fact that Eleanor never possesses such a cup but makes it hers in imagination ... betrays her distance from and longing for maternal nurturance."[44]

I would argue, though, that the milk signifies not continued dependence on the maternal, but separation from it. The child drinking cow's milk from a cup emphasizes that she has been weaned from her mother's breast, while the cup represents a fetish, a new object of attachment to which the child has transferred her erotic energies. That the milk is still a feminine form of nourishment represents a deviation from the psychoanalytic norm of the female child transferring object choice from mother to father; the cup, an attachment to a new feminine source, represents a queer object choice. As a cup of *stars*, it signifies the unreachable, a fantasy only a child can truly believe in and which, Eleanor knows, she will undoubtedly be steered away from by parental discipline. The child's desire is dismissed as frivolous in the same way lesbian desire was, at the time, dismissed as immaturity. This scene sheds light on the protagonist's resentment of her mother's constant oppressive presence, for which she blames the suppression of her primary fantasies.

In *Shirley Jackson: A Rather Haunted Life*, Ruth Franklin provides an in-depth discussion of Jackson's experiences with her own overbearing mother.[45] Her struggle to resist her mother's constant critical advice, especially as it pertained to her body and fashion sense, is certainly visible in Eleanor's unsuccessful efforts to create an individualized self after her mother's death, and I agree with Rubenstein's claim that this personal history manifests in Jackson's portrayal of identity-consuming maternity in *Hill House*, as "the mother's absence becomes a haunting presence that bears directly on the daughter's difficult struggle to achieve selfhood."[46] Through her formative years, Eleanor is attached to her mother's dying body, and her "inability to face strong sunlight without blinking" after her mother's death implies a toxic womb-space that produces death rather than life and entraps the daughter, forcing a continued dependence that makes it difficult for her, as much as she despises it, to live outside of it.[47] After her mother's death, as Rebecca Munford observes, "she is further denied a full adult subjectivity by her infantilizing sister and brother-in-law with whom she lives, sleeping in the nursery."[48] This image exemplifies the lasting effects of her mother's tyrannical presence; emerging from the metaphorical toxic womb, she is unequipped to live independently.

While Clare Kahane claims Eleanor's relationship with Theodora—a stronger, independent woman who, in her real life, lives with another woman–"recreates the terms of Eleanor's relation with her mother, making overt the hidden force of her longing and hatred," I believe it is crucial to consider the extent to which their bond more closely resembles one of sisterhood.[49] Kahane writes that, as the two begin sharing a bed and clothing, "Theodora's lesbianism demonstrates the adult implications of remaining bound within a mother-daughter relationship—erotically bound, that is, to a woman."[50] Eleanor's feelings for Theodora may be connected to maternal melancholia, but a stronger reading observes how their relationship offers an alternative to maternal erotics. As their bond develops, Eleanor and Theo do not emulate a mother–daughter relationship but rather see themselves as little girls or "cousins" frolicking on idyllic picnics.[51] Their childlike play recalls portrayals of lesbianism as an erotic continuation of friendships between young girls; as Littauer writes, the claim that "women who desired other women were psychologically immature, frozen in a state of permanent adolescence" was central to discourse on female homosexuality Americans encountered in newspapers, paperbacks, and magazines in the 1950s and shaped the way many young women came to understand their sexual preferences.[52]

In Hill House, Eleanor experiences as an adult the youthful erotic attachment, which, according to contemporaneous expectations of psychosexual development, she should have encountered and outgrown in prepubescence. That Eleanor's desire for Theodora manifests in this manner emphasizes the absence of representation for same sex desire between psychologically mature women at the time—the only queer connection Eleanor can conjure is regressive, resembling play between young cousins more than an adult relationship. As Franklin details, Jackson was personally affected by an intense and "tempestuous" relationship with a female friend, Jeanou, of whom she wrote in her journal: "everyone, even the man i loved, thought we were lesbians," which prompted her decision to "write stories about lesbians and how people misunderstood them."[53] While Jackson denied the association of her novels with lesbianism, her experience of emotionally fraught female friendship undoubtedly informed her portrayal of Eleanor's relationship with Theodora.[54] Given Jackson's difficult relationship with her own mother, the emotionally complex relationships between women she portrays in *Hill House* and *Castle* envision feminine intimacy without the hierarchal control of the toxic maternal relationship. While her own sister relegated her to the nursery, Eleanor seeks, in Theodora, a female relation she can essentially grow up with, discovering herself through shared fantasies and confidences. Ahmed literalizes the idea of "sexual orientation" by understanding queerness as falling out of line, in the sense of a line associated with inheritance and familial progression; "The 'hope' of the family tree," she writes, "is that the vertical line will produce a horizontal line, from which further vertical lines will be drawn." Within this value system, children are "'brought into line' by being 'given' a future that is 'in line' with the family line."[55] Eleanor's attraction to Theodora falls outside the proverbial line as she develops backwards, away from reproduction and towards the non-procreative erotics of childhood.

Hill House, where lines that appear straight are subtly angled, enables Eleanor to reconceptualize what relationships can define kinship. Rather than reinscribing the maternal relationship, the queer female sexuality Jackson presents undoes the maternal, replacing it with the lateral, non-hierarchal bonds of sisterhood, which operate outside the timeline of normative development and reproduction. In *Castle*, the replacement of maternal with sisterly bonds is much more overt: Merricat has literally killed her mother and replaced her with her sister, who cares for her without wielding power or enforcing discipline. For both protagonists, the death of their mothers allows them to explore erotic connections with other women without the hierarchal structure of the maternal relationship; rather than killing their fathers to marry their mothers or vice versa, they kill their mothers to marry their sisters.[56] The disturbance of the family structure by matricide and a reconstruction of familial bonds in both novels exemplify what Ahmed describes as falling out of line.

Merricat's childlike behavior also illustrates how familial trauma can result in halted development and resistance to continuing the familial line. While Eleanor struggles to develop a sense of self and to imagine a livable future in the wake of her familial trauma, Merricat has a clear vision of the domestic life she wants to create, but can conceive of creating it only through extreme violence. Throughout *Castle*, Jackson hints at the cause of Merricat's animosity toward her family, describing disciplinary action taken against her as a child. Constance relates, "Merricat was always in disgrace. I used to go up the back stairs with a tray of dinner for her after my father had left the dining room. She was a wicked, disobedient child."[57] In her fantasies,

Merricat imagines her parents saying things like, "Mary Katherine, we love you" and "Mary Katherine must never be punished. Must never be sent to bed without her dinner."⁵⁸ Her rewriting of reality emphasizes her lingering resentment toward her punishments and her familial treatment as a bad child, unworthy of love. To imagine a queer future, both protagonists must reimagine their childhoods. Eleanor begins to act out a more pleasurable childhood with Theodora as a playmate, though her progress is stymied by her mother's constant pull. Merricat's fantasies of a rewritten childhood allow her to envision the kind of familial love and acceptance she desires, which she solicits from her sister. The implication of disciplinary trauma in *Castle* reiterates the attitude towards parental control Jackson suggests in the "cup of stars" scene in *Hill House*. Parental discipline, in these novels, suppresses the fantasy lives of children, training them to mold their desires into the traditional heteronormative structure. By murdering the disciplinary actors, her parents, Merricat preserves her childlike insistence on the possibility of a fantastic future.

In *Hill House* and *Castle*, Jackson depicts a resistance to futurity—in Eleanor's death and Merricat's destruction of the family line—but she simultaneously illustrates new possibilities for productivity that deviate from the standard of *re*productivity. Alongside destruction, these texts contain an impulse for collection and preservation. In addition to complicating Edelman's concept of queer anti-futurity with her visions for an antinormative future, Jackson pushes against it by conceiving of alternative ways to collect, preserve, and produce that deviate from both heteronormative and capitalist standards. Through the motif of preserves, Jackson imagines a feminist and queer future that rejects reproduction as its means, focusing instead on survival by hiding from, shutting out, and protecting oneself from the outside world. Eleanor collects mentally, taking the objects she admired or imagined on her journey to Hill House and using them to build a fantasy of the private home she pretends to have, which she describes to Theo, "White curtains ... little stone lions on each corner of the mantle ... a white cat and my books and records and pictures" and, of course, "a blue cup with stars painted on the inside."⁵⁹ Her vision for a solitary domestic life consists of "dusting the lions" that guard her steps "each morning and patting their heads good night," eating dinner alone in a "long, quiet dining room" with "radishes from the garden, and homemade plum jam," and having townspeople bow to her because "everyone was proud of [her] lions."⁶⁰ Her fetishization of objects in these imaginings suggests an alternative to reproduction in that she tends to them as one might care for children. The objects represent her independence. By imagining curating a space for herself, she can develop a self-image, and her care for the objects represents care for herself. The jam and radishes she includes articulate her desire for a self-sustaining life in which she collects, produces, and preserves rather than reproducing and purchasing.

In *Castle*, Merricat infuriates cousin Charles by burying heirlooms in the yard. Her mistreatment of valuables implies an investment in a different kind of future, one in which the sisters may be truly independent from men and masculine institutions, including capitalism. Merricat operates outside the economic structures that assign monetary value to objects, embodying for Charles what Ahmed calls a *bad debt*.[61] Additionally, the sisters keep cans of preserves in their basement, which are mentioned frequently throughout the text. Lynette Carpenter understands the familial preserves as emblematic of "the legacy of the Blackwood women," in contrast to the monetary legacy of the Blackwood men—with the exception of the girls' mother, whose preference for the masculine inheritance of wealth marked her as a necessary casualty of Merricat's rebellion.[62] The cans survive the looting of the townspeople and emerge unscathed as the sisters sort through the rubble of their inheritance. The china, silverware, and linen brought into the home by generations of Blackwood brides are scattered and destroyed, but Constance's preserves prevail, signifying the necessity of self-preservation over the false belief in the power and sustainability of inheritance and the heteronormative marriage economy. Preservation is, in a sense, the opposite of reproduction, and, in *Castle*, the preservative future replaces the reproductive future. Preserves must, by nature, be shut tightly, as any interference from the outside world will ruin them. Similarly, Merricat and Constance opt to close themselves within their home, excluding the toxic influence of the outside world as an act of self-preservation.

Although the Blackwood sisters remain shuttered in what was once their familial home, Merricat's vision of futurity takes the form of interstellar imaginings, as she refers to their new life as living *on the moon*: "'I am so happy,' Constance said at last, gasping. 'Merricat, I am so happy.' 'I told you that you would like it on the moon.'"[63] Sustained by their store of preserves and the guilty generosity of the townspeople, Merricat and Constance claim a queer future. Only by fully destroying and reinventing the family structure are they able to do so—their "moon" is built on the ruins of their familial home and the disavowal of their inheritance and their designated roles within that domestic space.

Merricat's moon vision connects to Eleanor's hope that the girl she observes will "insist on [her] cup of stars."[64] In both cases, Jackson's otherworldly images connote the imaginary potential of childhood and indicate a vision for the future that surpasses existent social norms. Franklin writes, "The happy ending to their fairy tale requires a new definition of happiness, severed from the traditional marriage plot."[65] I would go even further, though—their happy ending is severed not only from the marriage plot but from the world itself. The moon and stars represent striving for something outside the known world, beyond the structures of human society. That Jackson's characters rely on this imagery to convey the potential for a future outside the heteropatriarchal structure indicates the extent to which Jackson saw that structure as inescapable, woven so tightly into the cultural fabric that to imagine a future that rejects it would be akin to planning a life on the moon.

Of course, Jackson published *Castle* in 1962, when the idea of space travel, and particularly a moon landing, was prominent in American consciousness. Franklin usefully contextualizes Jackson's relationship to space age rhetoric, writing that, as the "space race" began with the 1957 Soviet launch of *Sputnik I*, "enormous anxiety about new disasters that might rain down from the sky" permeated American culture.[66] Such a vision of catastrophic disaster is certainly visible in the ending of *Castle*, as is the simultaneous excitement regarding space travel and terror of the nuclear potential that arose alongside interstellar adventure. Jackson portrays the two going hand in hand: the destruction of the current world and the possibility of discovering something new. The familial structure of Merricat's upbringing is so oppressive that, rather than simply planning to move away, she envisions escaping the world itself, intuiting that any earthly place will be bound by the same patriarchal structures and traditions that made her family life unbearable. Jackson's novels are pessimistic in that they locate alternatives to the harmful traditional structure of family in essentially unreachable places, but also hopeful in the suggestion that, if we maintain and *insist upon* our ability to imagine something else, we can undo the cultural structures that keep us earthbound.

As Eleanor's cup of stars and Merricat's moon fantasy imply, Shirley Jackson represents the queer future as a radical world-making, a complete rejection of the patriarchal and heteronormative structures so widespread that their absence can be imagined only through planetary departure. This desire for a new planet, though, manifests in the reality of her characters' lives through violence. Eleanor's suicide and Mary Katherine's homicides are acts that reject the reality of normative domestic life and the temporality that accompanies it. While it might seem difficult to read optimism into these novels, especially *Hill House*, both end with a sense of self-determination for women who resist the script of heteronormative futurity. That they must kill and, in Merricat's case, burn down a home to accomplish this suggests that crafting a queer future is essentially an impossible task within the bounds of legal and ethical conventions. While Jackson is clearly not advising women to kill themselves or their loved ones, she does imply that women's liberation can be achieved only through radical action that challenges some of the notions our society holds most dear. Women cannot, she indicates, merely escape the toxic, oppressive institutions of society; they must destroy them and create something new. Like landing on the moon, this task, for a feminist writing in the 1950s, seems, at the same time, out of reach and entirely possible. Through Eleanor and Merricat, Jackson asserts the need for radical reimaginings of domestic culture that look beyond the familiar to invent new spaces, new worlds, and new temporalities in which a livable queer future is imaginable.

Notes

1. Lauren Berlant and and Michael Warner, "Sex in Public." *Critical Inquiry*, 24, no. 2 (Winter 1998): 558 (accessed November 26, 2019), https://www.jstor.org/stable/1344178.
2. Ibid., 558.
3. Margaret Fuller, *Woman in the Nineteenth Century* (New York: Dover Publications, [1845] 1999), 51.
4. John D'Emilio and Estelle B. Freedman, *Intimate Matters: A History of Sexuality in America* (Chicago: University of Chicago Press, 2012), 388.
5. Shirley Jackson, *The Haunting of Hill House* (New York: Penguin Books, 1959), 3.
6. Ibid., 7.
7. Lee Edelman, *No Future: Queer Theory and the Death Drive* (Durham: Duke University Press, 2004), 2.
8. Ibid., 33.
9. Shirley Jackson, *We Have Always Lived in the Castle* (New York: Penguin Books, 1962), 9.
10. Ruth Franklin, *Shirley Jackson: A Rather Haunted Life* (New York: Liveright, 1923), 469.
11. Edelman, *No Future*, 3.
12. Jackson, *Castle*, 12.
13. Jack Halberstam, *In A Queer Time & Place: Transgender Bodies, Subcultural Lives* (New York: New York University Press, 2005), 10.
14. Jackson, *Hill House*, 77.
15. Sigmund Freud, "The Uncanny," in *The Standard Edition of the Complete Psychological Works of Sigmund Freud Vol. XVII (1917–1919): An Infantile Neurosis and Other Works*, ed. James Strachey (London: Hogarth Press, 1957), 219.
16. Sara Ahmed, *Queer Phenomenology: Orientations, Objects, Others* (Durham: Duke University Press, 2006), 107.
17. Jackson, *Hill House*, 31–2.
18. Carroll Smith-Rosenberg, *Disorderly Conduct: Visions of Gender in Victorian America* (New York: Oxford University Press, 1986), 276–7.
19. Jackson, *Hill House*, 43.
20. Ibid., 43.
21. Ibid., 45.

22 Ibid., 60.
23 Ibid., 56.
24 Ibid., 57.
25 Ibid., 75.
26 Ibid., 181 (emphasis in the original).
27 Ibid., 159.
28 Jackson, *Castle*, 82.
29 Ibid., 76.
30 Amanda H. Littauer, "'Someone to Love': Teen Girls' Same Sex Desire in the 1950s United States," in *Queer 1950s: Rethinking Sexuality in the Postwar Years*, ed. Heike Bauer and Matt Cooke (Basingstoke: Palgrave Macmillian, 2012), 72.
31 George Haggerty, *Queer Gothic* (University of Illinois Press, 2016), 144; 147.
32 Jackson, *Hill House*, 111.
33 Ibid., 62.
34 William Shakespeare, *Twelfth Night* (London: Bloomsbury Arden Shakespeare, 2008), II, iii, 42.
35 Jackson, *Castle*, 20.
36 Ibid., 135.
37 Ibid., 136–7.
38 Ibid., 137.
39 Judith Butler, *Gender Trouble: Feminism and the Subversion of Identity* (New York: Routledge, 1990), 211–12.
40 José Esteban Muñoz, *Cruising Utopia: The Then and There of Queer Futurity* (New York: New York University Press, 2009), 99.
41 Haggerty, *Queer Gothic*, 30.
42 Jackson, *Hill House*, 15.
43 Littauer, "Someone to Love," 69–70.
44 Roberta Rubenstein, "House Mothers and Haunted Daughters: Shirley Jackson and the Female Gothic," *Tulsa Studies in Women's Literature*, 15, no. 2 (Autumn, 1996): 318 (accessed November 25, 2019). https://www.jstor.org/stable/464139.
45 Franklin, *Shirley Jackson*, 23–5.
46 Rubenstein, "House Mothers and Haunted Daughters," 311.
47 Jackson, *Hill House*, 3.
48 Rebecca Munford, "Spectral Femininity," in *Women and the Gothic: An Edinburgh Companion*, ed. Avril Horner and Sue Zlosnik (Edinburgh: Edinburgh University Press, 2016), 126.
49 Clare Kahane, "The Gothic Mirror," in *The (M)other Tongue: Essays in Feminist Psychoanalytic Interpretation*, ed. Shirley Nelson Garner, Clare

Kahane, and Madelon Sprengnether (Ithaca: Cornell University Press, 1985), 341.
50 Ibid., 342.
51 Jackson, *Hill House*, 38.
52 Littauer, "Someone to Love," 61.
53 Franklin, *Shirley Jackson*, 61–2.
54 Ibid., 63.
55 Ahmed, *Queer Phenomenology*, 83.
56 In this sense, the novel bears an interesting resemblance to the internationally prominent 1933 case of the Papin sisters, two French maids commonly believed to share an incestuous sexual relationship after murdering their employers, as discussed in Lacan's "Motives of Paranoic Crime." While it is unclear whether Jackson derived inspiration directly from this case, her characterization of the Blackwood sisters certainly plays upon the depiction of lesbians as incestuous murderesses which, as Karen Boyle discusses in "Revisiting the Papin Case," was central to public reception and retellings of the incident.
57 Jackson, *Castle*, 35.
58 Ibid., 96.
59 Jackson, *Hill House*, 64.
60 Ibid., 12.
61 Ahmed, *Queer Phenomenology*, 86 (my emphasis).
62 Lynette Carpenter, "The Establishment and Preservation of Female Power in Shirley Jackson's We Have Always Lived in the Castle." *Frontiers: A Journal of Women Studies*, 8, no. 1 (1984): 35 (accessed October 23, 2019), https://www.jstor.org/stable/3346088.
63 Jackson, *Castle*, 145.
64 Jackson, *Hill House*, 15.
65 Franklin, *Shirley Jackson*, 450.
66 Ibid., 384.

References

Ahmed, Sara. *Queer Phenomenology: Orientations, Objects, Others*. Durham: Duke University Press, 2006.

Berlant, Lauren, and Michael Warner. "Sex in Public." *Critical Inquiry*, 24, no. 2, "Intimacy" (Winter 1998): 547–66 (accessed November 26, 2019). https://www.jstor.org/stable/1344178.

Boyle, Karen. "Revisiting the Papin Sisters: Gender, Sexuality and Violence in *Sister my Sister*." *South Central Review*, 19, no. 4 (2002): 103–18 (accessed November 20, 2019). https://www.jstor.org/stable/3190138.

Butler, Judith. *Gender Trouble: Feminism and the Subversion of Identity.* New York: Routledge, 1990.
Carpenter, Lynette. "The Establishment and Preservation of Female Power in Shirley Jackson's *We Have Always Lived in the Castle.*" *Frontiers: A Journal of Women Studies*, 8, no. 1 (1984): 32–8 (accessed October 23, 2019). https://www.jstor.org/stable/3346088.
D'Emilio, John, and Estelle B. Freedman. *Intimate Matters: A History of Sexuality in America.* Chicago: University of Chicago Press, 2012.
Edelman, Lee. *No Future: Queer Theory and the Death Drive.* Durham: Duke University Press, 2004.
Franklin, Ruth. *Shirley Jackson: A Rather Haunted Life.* New York: Liveright, 2016.
Freud, Sigmund. "The Uncanny," in *The Standard Edition of the Complete Psychological Works of Sigmund Freud Vol. XVII (1917–1919): An Infantile Neurosis and Other Works*, ed. James Strachey, 217–56. London: Hogarth Press, 1957.
Freud, Sigmund. *Three Contributions to the Theory of Sex.* Trans. A. A. Brill. Washington, DC: Nervous and Mental Health Disease Publishing Company, 1920. Project Gutenberg, February 8, 2005, EBook #14969 (accessed September 19, 2019). http://www.gutenberg.org/files/14969/14969-h/14969-h.htm.
Fuller, Margaret. *Woman in the Nineteenth Century.* New York: Dover Publications (1845) 1999.
Haggerty, George. *Queer Gothic.* Champaign: University of Illinois Press, 2006.
Halberstam, Jack. *In a Queer Time & Place: Transgender Bodies, Subcultural Lives.* New York: New York University Press, 2005.
Jackson, Shirley. *The Haunting of Hill House.* New York: Penguin Books, 1959.
Jackson, Shirley. *We Have Always Lived in the Castle.* New York: Penguin Books, 1962.
Kahane, Clare. "The Gothic Mirror," in *The (M)other Tongue: Essays in Feminist Psychoanalytic Interpretation*, ed. Shirley Nelson Garner, Clare Kahane, and Madelon Sprengnether, 334–51. Ithaca: Cornell University Press, 1985.
Lacan, Jacques. "Motives of Paranoiac Crime: The Crime of the Papin Sisters." *Le Minotaure*, 3–4 (December 1933). *Lacan Dot Com* (accessed October 12, 2019). http://www.lacan.com/papin.htm#1.
Littauer, Amanda H. "'Someone to Love': Teen Girls' Same-Sex Desire in the 1950's United States," in *Queer 1950s: Rethinking Sexuality in the Postwar Years*, ed. Heike Bauer and Matt Cooke, 61–7. Basingstoke: Palgrave Macmillan, 2012.
Munford, Rebecca. "Spectral Femininity," in *Women and the Gothic: An Edinburgh Companion*, ed. Avril Horner and Sue Zlosnik, 120–35. Edinburgh: Edinburgh University Press, 2016.
Muñoz, José Esteban. *Cruising Utopia: The Then and There of Queer Futurity.* New York: New York University Press, 2009.
Rubenstein, Roberta. "House Mothers and Haunted Daughters: Shirley Jackson and the Female Gothic." *Tulsa Studies in Women's Literature*, 15, no. 2 (Autumn, 1996): 309–31 (accessed November 25, 2019). https://www.jstor.org/stable/464139.

Shakespeare, William. *Twelfth Night*. London: Bloomsbury Arden Shakespeare, 2008.
Smith-Rosenberg, Carroll. *Disorderly Conduct: Visions of Gender in Victorian America*. New York: Oxford University Press, 1985.

11

Shirley Jackson's Merricat Story: Conjugal Narcissism in *We Have Always Lived in the Castle*

Richard Pascal

All cat stories start with the statement "My mother, who was the first cat, told me this," and I lay with my head close to Jonas and listened. There was no change coming, I thought here …. The days would get warmer, and Uncle Julian would sit in the sun, and Constance would laugh when she worked in the garden, and it would always be the same. Jonas went on and on ("And then we sang! And then we sang!") and the leaves moved overhead and it would always be the same.[1]

To Mary Katherine Blackwood, "Merricat" in Shirley Jackson's *We Have Always Lived in the Castle* (1962), there is something very comforting about the stories told by her pet cat Jonas. The content of this cat story goes unrecorded, though, for what is most important about it to Merricat is the reassurance it conveys of sameness and eternal recurrence, as signified by the never varying opening statement and what appears to be an equally formulaic refrain bespeaking everlasting contentment: "And then we sang! And then we sang!" More reassuringly still, the stories are not actually told by Jonas the cat. They are created by and ascribed to him by his human alter ego, Merricat, thereby ensuring that they reflect unfailingly her own needs, desires and centrality. Her favorite fantasy, as we come to learn, conjures up an otherworldly lunar setting where everything is safe and all needs are provided for effortlessly, and where there are wondrous things created by her fancy—"cat furred plants and horses dancing with their wings"[2]—and she and her beloved older sister live in blissful togetherness. Though her actual world doesn't quite replicate the moon fantasy, in her imperturbable narcissism she loves to intermingle her daydreams with her lived experience, such that the unpredictable and confrontational aspects of the latter may be obscured and even dispelled—and her world will be, or seem, an emanation of herself. Life, for her, is a cat story conjured into actuality, as nearly so as she can arrange it to be. It is she who is the true first cat, the maternal creator who magically elicits order, comfort, security, and feline self-satisfaction from the resistant chaos of lived experience.

So riveting and entrancing is the Merricat story that eventually she even persuades her more balanced sister Constance that the two of them have indeed transported themselves to a fairy-tale castle or a very close facsimile thereof; and readers may be hard pressed not to follow the two sisters at least part way into her spellbound fantasy world and accept her spellbindingly subjective account of how that castle came to be.[3] The narrative in which she is the central figure, however, though told by her, is not a perfect cat story, for there are alien intrusions. It is, rather, a fantasy marred by incursions of the actual. Just as unwelcome visitors at times intrude upon the real domain in which Merricat's tightly guarded melding of fantasy and actuality is situated, the ancient estate of her Blackwood family forebears, so too do textual indicators of the hazards of credulous assent to her escapist mental household naggingly interject themselves. *Castle* explores the implications of determining to live as an adult child, in defiance of familial and social pressures as well as basic reality checks from the world beyond the ego— ironically, the very social world, postwar America, that has encouraged such solipsistic individualism. It is a psychological narrative about one narcissist's attempt to enslave reality to the whims of fantasy, and, with the help of some homicide and arson and chilling amorality, largely getting away with it. But it is also, more broadly, about the society that encourages such intense selfishness through the recasting of domestic myths and templates into a child's "let's pretend" space of insular atemporality. In the figure of Merricat, the traditional American veneration of "home, sweet home" is both subverted and preserved as, essentially, "self, sweet self." Consequently, the new domestic space she creates does away with the nuclear family in its standard configuration by compressing it into a monogendered pairing dominated by a child-self that has usurped the patriarchal role.

Merricat is a powerful raconteur, and, as readers, we can feel as bounded by her vision as Constance feels bounded by the grounds of the estate. In varying degrees that sense of containment is inherent in the very form of the first-person narrative. David Copperfield, Huckleberry Finn, and Holden Caulfield all limit and slant our apprehension of their experiences and their milieus, even as we strive, at the behest of carefully arrayed textual prompts, to see more than they do. Merricat, however, is extreme in her egocentricity, policing her subjective realm rigorously. Unlike many other first-person narrators, she makes no effort to apprehend aspects of actuality that are literally beyond her grasp; rather, she is intent upon transforming what of it she permits herself to behold, and barring from awareness all that she cannot. The result is that she is all but entirely uninterested in the world beyond her carefully tended and virtually conterminous personal and domestic domains. Other than as a necessary source of the basic means of life, she could not care less about her neighbors in the local community, or that grand abstraction "society."

Her intense egocentricity advances its claim on the totality of the reader's attention and imagination in the opening paragraph of her account:

> My name is Mary Katherine Blackwood. I am eighteen years old, and I live with my sister Constance. I have often thought that with any luck at all I could have been born a werewolf, because the two middle fingers on both my hands are the same length, but I have had to be content with what I had. I dislike washing myself, and dogs, and noise. I like my sister Constance, and Richard Plantagenet, and Amanita phalloides, the death-cup mushroom. Everyone else in my family is dead.[4]

Her tone here is a curious blend of the dispassionately informative mode of a schoolchild's "report" and the impishly confessional. As though writing in accord with a prescribed model, she presents in a series of simple declarative sentences the most essential introductory information about who she is and what she is like. The one sentence that is syntactically complex is the musing interjection that expresses her desire to have been born a werewolf, and her readiness to admit to such an unconventional inclination seems disarmingly chatty and personal, a less than serious claim intended to ingratiate herself with the reader. Her professed acceptance of the limits of her "luck," moreover—of the degree to which uncontrollable circumstance has failed to favor her lupine proclivity—seems at first similarly jocular, as do her professed likings for Richard Plantagenet and the death cup mushroom, *amanita phalloides.*

She presents herself initially, then, if not exactly as a charmer in the usual sense, as a cool narcissist disarmingly sure of her power to sustain a listener's interest. Any disquiet a first-time reader might have been tempted to feel about being subsumed within the viewpoint of a narrator thus willing to introduce herself is likely to be both ameliorated and enhanced by the remainder of the chapter, a tense account of her shopping expedition to the nearby town. As she goes about her weekly errands, its residents make the trip an ordeal. She is subjected to coldness, stage-whispered taunts, overt insults, and even a degree of physical intimidation from the town bully. She endures all without giving her antagonists the satisfaction of seeing her cry, object, or even hurry very much, by retreating as fully as possible into the fortress of her mind through psychological ploys familiar to children and adolescents: narrowly focusing on the precise path she must follow; imagining that she is somewhere more pleasant; pretending that the immediate situation is only a game; and conjuring up fantasies of inflicting suffering and death on the townspeople who seem especially hostile. It is first-person narration at its most riveting, and the well calculated aim is to facilitate unguarded empathy from the reader. By the end of the first chapter, when she has finally returned to the safe haven of her home, her characteristic conception of social interaction as an irremediable conflict between self and hostile social Other has been virtually thrust upon the reader as a sine qua non for engagement with Merricat's world.

Yet, as is the case with many first-person fictions, the novel has been carefully crafted to gesture toward alternative perspectives that undermine, or at least call into question, the accuracy and reliability of the narratorial account. One such textual whisper is audible in the very certitude of Merricat's assessments of other people: she does not doubt that all are awful, other than her adored Constance and the mentally incapacitated old Uncle Julian. Throughout the first chapter, the impression she provides of the townspeople's unrelenting hostility seems credible, if only because it is a convention of first-person narrative that speech utterances are reported faithfully, as though the narrator is a neutral transmitter, a human microphone. And the townspeople do indeed say terrible things to Merricat, and behave, in some cases, nastily. Her defense against the abuse is to withdraw mentally, as far as possible, to her lunar fantasy, thereby keeping the taunts at bay. But, in addition to that understandable and innocuous psychological tactic, she also conjures up visions of excruciating suffering being visited upon her tormenters, the vividness and cruelty of which are breathtaking: "I always thought rot when I came to the row of stores; I thought about burning black painful rot that ate away from inside, hurting dreadfully. I wished it on the village";[5] "They saw me at once, and I thought of them rotting away and curling up in pain and crying out loud; I wanted them doubled up and crying on the ground in front of me";[6] "Their tongues will burn, I thought, as though they had eaten fire. Their throats will burn as the words come out and in their bellies they will feel a torment hotter than a thousand fires."[7] The motivation that inspires the exaggerated brutality of these imaginings goes well beyond the understandable impulse of an otherwise defenseless subject to endure uninvited verbal abuse. In their extremity, they reveal a Merricat who delights in the fantasy of exerting her superiority to others by extorting from others the homage of pain. There is, that is to say, an imperious and callous ego informing the narration of the shopping trip to the village, putting the reader on alert: Merricat's reporting, far from dispassionate, may be distortive.

As the novel progresses, dissonances are discernible at times between what is said in Merricat's presence or what the reader gets as her interpretation of what she hears. In the following chapter, for example, when the extremely reclusive Constance remarks casually that she herself might someday venture into the village, Merricat asserts that she knows she is being teased, even though nothing in Constance's choice of words suggests so. Not long thereafter Constance reiterates her intent—"Someday I'll go"—and Merricat, "chilled" because this time she senses the seriousness of the assertion, has to alter her previous judgment and acknowledge that Constance may indeed wish to reestablish relations with the community.[8] She is sufficiently flexible in her thinking to make the adjustment, but not to draw the conclusion that her thinking tilts perpetually toward the wishful, the self-absorbed, and the distortive.

Such dissonances accrete. A neighbor, Helen Clarke, has visited regularly in an effort to provide emotional support for the Blackwood women, especially Constance. When she and a friend arrive for tea and Constance is moderately effusive with her chatting, Merricat observes privately, "She was talking a little too much and a little too fast, but no one noticed it but me,"[9] inadvertently inviting the reader to question her assessment of her sister's behavior. And when Helen expresses her long-standing regard for Constance and consequent concern for the well-being of one so young and lovely living in such shrouded seclusion, Merricat remarks that the visitor could not see how Constance withdrew from such words. But Constance does not withdraw, and though Merricat is quick to realize the implication of her sister's signs of receptivity—"Constance had looked as though suddenly, after all this time of refusing and denying, she had come to see that it might be possible, after all, to go outside"[10]—she displays no capacity for entertaining the suggestion that Constance's apparent complacency with regard to her reclusive existence belies an underlying desire to engage once more with people other than Merricat.

In short, Merricat can discern aspects of her experience that impinge threateningly upon her desired constructions of it. Her capacity to peer outside of those constructions, however, comes to seem so limited and so self-interested that her reliability as an observer is severely compromised, and throughout the remainder of the narrative, the reader has been cautioned, her views must be critiqued in the light of contravening textual hints that seep into her reporting. Perhaps the clearest indication of her narratorial unreliability is the account of a fantasy she entertains about her place in the family hierarchy as a child:

"Mary Katherine would never allow herself to do anything wrong; there is never any need to punish her."

"I have heard, Lucy, of disobedient children being sent to their beds without dinner as a punishment. That must not be permitted with our Mary Katherine."

"I quite agree, my dear. Mary Katherine must never be punished. Must never be sent to her bed without her dinner. Mary Katherine will never allow herself to do anything inviting punishment."

"Our beloved, our dearest Mary Katherine must be guarded and cherished. Thomas, give your sister your dinner; she would like more to eat."

"Bow all your heads to our adored Mary Katherine."[11]

Clearly such a scenario is fanciful in the extreme. Constance has mentioned that Merricat was often banished from the dinner table, but even without that cautionary textual hint, the ludicrously glaring narcissism of her reminiscence here renders it suspect and serves as a warning to the reader: do *not* bow your head to Merricat's highly charged reporting.

Merricat's extreme egocentricity is most apparent in her ever more cloying attachment to the sister whom she reveres. As the considerably older sibling, Constance seems initially to have assumed the role of a doting parent to Merricat, although by the end of the narrative, it is Merricat who is clearly the dominant parent figure in basic respects. Their affection for one another is certainly sisterly as well, in the figurative sense as in the literal, to a degree that seems obsessive. They live in what appears to be blissful harmony, with Constance happily assuming the role of loving maternal homemaker, the angel in the kitchen, and Merricat that of the beloved child who cannot be expected to do much more than play: "'Did you really forget your boots?' Constance said. She tried to frown and then laughed. 'Silly Merricat.' 'Jonas had no boots. It's a wonderful day.'"[12] Such loving interchanges are the norm for the sisters. They never quarrel, and always seem delighted by one another, as their personalities, quite different, are perfectly synchronized. Sunlight is always expected, as familial love is always in the air.

Children do develop crushes on older siblings and playmates, of course. Constance was the one member of Merricat's family who was unfailingly sympathetic to her, even perhaps to the point of spoiling her, and certainly to the point of shielding her from legal reprisal for homicide that she committed when she was a child. The reclusiveness of the sisters' lifestyle suits Merricat's possessive love perfectly, enabling her to have Constance almost entirely to herself. As we've seen, when outsiders call, she is tense with jealousy, and, with a child's affinity for effective mischief, she devises ways to shorten their visits. Constance is ever indulgent toward her, assuming all responsibility for domestic chores and thus allowing her to pass her days in idle play.

The indulgent older sister of her childhood has clearly taken on the role of an ideal mother figure who focuses almost all of her permissive love and attention on Merricat. The slightly deranged Uncle Julian is also served and coddled by Constance, but in his addled feebleness he offers no significant competition for her affections.

But there is more: the older Merricat's nervousness over signs that Constance is growing restless in her severely restricted circumstances indicates that her love has become more than merely sisterly or childishly adulatory. "When I was small," she tells us, "I thought Constance was a fairy princess. Even at the worst time she was pink and white and golden, and nothing had ever seemed to dim the brightness of her. She was the most precious person in my world, always."[13] Yet Merricat's romantically hued feelings about her indulgent older sister did not wane with the passing of her childhood; rather, although still childish, even when she is 18, they have become charged with erotic ardor. "I love you, Constance," she says, several times, apropos of nothing in particular, as a child or a dreamy lover might, and Constance responds in kind, albeit somewhat patronizingly.

But the fairy princess older sister has metamorphosed, in Merricat's eyes, into an object of romantic desire, securely embedded in a narcissistic fantasy of total and unwavering loyalty to the adoring subject. Constance must not be permitted to be *in*constant. Absolute dedication to the egocentric subject is a familiar demand that children impose upon those they adore, of course: as the price of their adulation, they crave to *be* adored. But it is also one of the defining attributes of romantic lovers, and, as the narrative progresses, it becomes apparent that the Blackwood sisters are emotionally entranced with one another. They banter at times like young lovers, and eventually (as discussed later) their mutual attachment comes to have lesbian overtones. And as mentioned previously, Constance was the one member of Merricat's family who was unfailingly sympathetic to her, even perhaps to the point of spoiling her, and certainly to the point of shielding her from legal reprisal for homicide.

Competition for the love of the princess does arrive, however, in the person of Cousin Charles, who is only a few years older than Constance and who is clearly interested in winning her over to his own self-centered vision of how the household should be administered. It isn't certain that his intentions are romantic, but they are definitely predatory in that he wants to assume control over the affairs and, especially, the wealth of the household. His behavior toward Constance is crude and largely bumbling in its pretense of charm, and quintessentially male, in Merricat's eyes at least. Merricat immediately associates him with the father whom she had detested to the point of committing patricide, and, as though unwittingly complicit in her role casting, he blithely assumes the dominant position in the house as though his status as the only able-bodied male left in the extended family endows him with that right. And Constance proves to be susceptible. When he holds forth to her with stentorian assertiveness on "What Must be Done," especially as regards the strange younger sister, she begins to succumb to his appeal to normality as the larger social world conceives of it. Merricat, threatened with the possibility not only of losing Constance's love and attention, but even of being sent away, sets her mind to the ousting of him from the household she thinks of as her world exclusively.

The contest of wills between Merricat and Charles, who quickly comes to detest her as a nuisance and an obstacle, takes on to some extent the trappings of a jousting match between rivals for the affection of the princess. The weapons, initially, are verbal. Merricat tries her standard tactics of remaining relatively unresponsive when Charles addresses her, and of referring ominously to the lethal properties of the *amanita phalloides* when she does speak. He is undaunted, however, and threatens her with what she most fears—the loss of Constance's love and devotion: "What would cousin Mary do if Constance and Charles didn't love her?"[14] She counters by attempting to rid the premises of him through witchcraft of her own idiosyncratic devising. As she associates Charles with her late father, and as he also has made efforts to assume that role by appropriating some of the late Mr. Blackwood's possessions, she nails a gold watch chain that had belonged to her father to a tree and hides an expensive scarf and a box of silver dollars in the woods. Charles, furious over these relatively innocuous pranks, threatens her openly with punishment, thus precipitating what proves to be her final and victorious act of retaliation, the act of arson that sets the old house ablaze and vanquishes the intruder.

Merricat's resort to the practical magic of arson does more than rid the field of her rival: it creates the conditions that allow her to claim Constance as her fair prize more fully and exclusively than before. In the aftermath of the fire, Uncle Julian, who dies, has also been banished from the household. Julian was hardly a rival of significance, but his very presence and his demands upon Constance as a petulant invalid meant that Merricat's centricity had been at least somewhat compromised. More significantly still, the conflagration wreaks the desired magic on Constance, who, traumatized by the catastrophe, relinquishes her burgeoning desire to reengage with the outside world, and becomes emotionally dependent on Merricat exclusively. It is bliss to Merricat, and her euphoric response to the radically altered relationship with her sister is reflected in her imaginative impression of the charred and partially destroyed family home: "Above us the stairs were black and led into blackness or burned rooms with, incredibly, tiny spots of sky showing through. ... I could feel a breath of air on my cheek; it came from the sky I could see, but it smelled of smoke and ruin. Our house was a castle, turreted and open to the sky."[15] The past tense verb here, "was," is deceptive if one overlooks the context. What it signifies is a very fresh past: the house has only just been, she implies, transformed through ruination into the most appropriate dwelling place in which to secure her fantasy of having Constance all to herself in a place that is secure against all outside intrusion. For where else but in a turreted castle does one live happily ever after with one's beloved princess? It is easy to miss the implication—and most commentators have—that the Blackwood home does not appear as the "castle" of the title until after the fire. The designedly puzzling "always" appears to suggest otherwise—that the family has inhabited the mansion for many generations. And so it has. But that mansion was never a "castle" until its transformation through conflagration disrupts long established family traditions. Merricat's "always" is not faithful reporting; it is wishful thinking at its best.

What Merricat's account of the fire's effect on the Blackwood family home indicates, then, is the refashioning of domestic arrangements accreted down through the years and their replacement with atemporality, a space beyond sequential time that never was or will be in the real world. The transition does not happen entirely smoothly. Initially, the sisters experience some trauma, as indicated by Merricat's admission that on the day after the fire she thought that they had come back through "the wrong gap in time ... or the wrong fairy tale."[16] It is a nervous moment; the wrong fairy tale would not seem to be the stuff of wish fulfillment fantasies. But her capacity for subsuming the particularities of the actual within the dreaminess of fantasy is not thwarted for very long, and the wrong fairy tale still *is* a fairy tale, at least as far as Merricat is concerned, especially as the change, she realizes, may offer an opportunity for revising and reenvisioning—and most importantly for insulating—her world. She has her princess sister all to herself, and what is left of the old house is not merely salvageable, but susceptible to a sort of magical transformation. As the sisters collect what they can in an effort to tidy up, they strive to reimpose a degree of order and familiarity upon the charred and strewn remains of their family home site.

The old house is not the same, nor are the domestic patterns of the sisters. Both have been divested of some features that tied Constance and Merricat to the community and to their own family lineage. The Italian staircase that had been a source of pride to the town is charred into a mass of twisted wood; the seldom-used drawing room has been largely gutted. And the sisters have determined to withdraw even more fully than before into the protective confines of what is left. They never entertain Helen Clarke, their one regular visitor, again, and Merricat abandons her weekly shopping expeditions to the town. They create new daily patterns of domestic living to replace the old ones, and most significantly, they lead their lives almost entirely indoors, hiding quietly when townspeople come occasionally to view the site of the catastrophe, to gawk at the strange ladies, and to leave food. Merricat has the tense wrong: literally, they *come to live always in* the castle. It is their sole habitat for all futurity, not merely a home place.

And as such, the newly alwaysed castle becomes the site of what so many fairy tales end with: a climactic happily-ever-after marriage, or whatever idyllic union of lovers is to serve as its alternate in the Merricat-inspired world refashioned from the ruins of the old domestic arrangements. In their castle, they set up their own version of housekeeping, as might many other young couples in love who have committed themselves totally to a long life together under the same roof. It is, in retrospect at least, an inevitable development, for marriage, the veneration of it, has been a subtly insinuated motif from early on in the narrative. After introducing herself, Merricat was quick to contextualize her peculiar mode of individuality within a Blackwood tradition founded upon possessions garnered through successive generations of marital alliances: "Blackwoods had always lived in our house, and kept their things in order; as soon as a new Blackwood wife moved in, a place was found for her belongings, and so our house was built up with layers of Blackwood property weighting it, and keeping it steady against the world."[17] Subsequently, it becomes apparent that the special room that the sisters maintained in pristine condition but rarely used, with its conspicuous "wedding cake trim at the tops of the walls,"[18] is a shrine to Blackwood matriarchy, but more broadly to the traditional state of matrimony, and a social order that has valorized it so highly.

For Merricat, all this represents a kind of honeymoon: she and Constance, she believes, are finally living in the (honey)moon world of her favorite escapist fantasy, her personal fairy tale that she has always resorted to as a means of distancing immediate reality. It had served her well as such a mental refuge when she endured the ordeal of shopping in the village; as the villagers shouted insults, she defended herself against humiliation by retreating to her favorite daydream. But even when safe in the confines of the family home, she often fantasizes about that lunar domestic space that would improve upon actuality. "On the moon," she has told her sister Constance prior to the life-changing conflagration, "we have everything. Lettuce, and pumpkin pie, and Amanita phalloides. We have cat furred plants and horses dancing with their wings," and Constance replies, with a touch of condescension, "I wish I could go to your moon."[19] It seems a wistful response at the time, but, in effect, she eventually does. After the fire, Merricat says, "I am thinking we are living on the moon, but it is not quite as I supposed it would be," and in the altered circumstances, Constance's reply is more respectful: "It is a very happy place, though."[20]

Most tellingly, by the latter stages of the narrative, it seems evident that the relationship of the sisters may well have an erotic dimension. Immediately after the fire, Merricat takes Constance to her special hiding place in the bushes, "freshened, so that it would now be pleasant for Constance" (160), where they are literally to sleep together. While there is no direct indication of an active sexual liaison, she pushes Constance "gently until she sat down"[21] on a carefully prepared bed of leaves—a distinct hint of conjugal consummation, irrespective of whether or not physical lovemaking ensued. We are left to wonder at what the deeper reaches of that night wrought, as the chapter ends like an old-fashioned Hollywood movie fade-out that insinuates more than it is willing to disclose. But to dwell too greatly on the possibility of incestuous lovemaking can be to miss the more important point: sexual or not, the bedding of Constance is nuptial. It is Merricat's way of undermining the traditional mold of marriage that had welded generations of the Blackwood family together, and, at the same time, preserving it for the foreseeable future. With the banishment of Cousin Charles, marriage in the traditional sense also has been banished from the Blackwood realm. And yet, curiously, the tradition as such is retained: the old home is to be inhabited, domesticated, by an intimate liaison of two individuals who are committed to one another till death do them part. It is a radically conservative refashioning of matrimony, a carefully bounded transgressiveness.

Certainly, the new matrimony is strikingly monogendered; men have been eliminated from Merricat's world, and Constance's. The eradication of the male—and patriarchal—element from the home site is such a remarkable stroke of gender cleansing that several commentators have seen it as the novel's most fundamental concern and implication—patriarchy vanquished, it would appear, the female lovers will thrive in perfect harmony, or at least happy symbiosis.[22] Thus construed, Jackson's early 1960s novel can legitimately be regarded as a harbinger of the feminist critiques and social movements that emerged shortly thereafter. But to highlight strongly the novel's savagely wry critique of long-standing gender myths and the social arrangements deriving from them may be to obscure its fuller thrust. The Blackwood sisters' new domestic arrangement is more than a rebellion against patriarchal oppression; it amounts, more widely, to a repudiation of the iconic midcentury model of the nuclear family as heteronormative and oriented toward the rearing of children. Even in the early stages of the narrative there are hints of a nuclear normativity gone awry. From the start, as Roberta Rubenstein notes, the Blackwood household, embracing the two sisters and their feeble uncle, constitutes an "ironic nuclear family: an incapacitated and dependent male figure, a housebound maternal figure ... and a child who lives in a fantasy world sustained by magical thinking."[23] By the end, however, the model has been revised and pared down still further: the male figure has been replaced by the female child who has achieved the domestic dominance that Cousin Charles could not, and the maternal figure has become even more housebound and compliant. It is still "nuclear," a small family sequestered cozily away from the wider social world. But its refashioned normativity is, so to speak, abnormal in being supernormal. The remaining Blackwoods have condensed their familial relationship and domestic arrangement into an almost parodic embodiment of midcentury society's revered social unit, the nuclear family: they are to one another children, parents, siblings and spouses—all rolled into two.

So too with the refashioned household's ties to the wider community. It has transformed into a bizarre version of the home unto itself that American society so valorized in the postwar years, discrete yet socially dependent.[24] The local community, of course, has mostly been horrible to the sisters. We are shown that in the opening chapter, as previously discussed, and the full fury of their collective malice is dramatized in the mobbish behavior that occurs in the immediate aftermath of the fire. Not only do the townspeople destroy whatever they can lay hands on, they also subject the two frightened young women to a humiliating verbal assault. Given the lengths which their malice and vindictiveness are shown to reach, it seems little wonder that the sisters subsequently withdraw as fully as they can from all social intercourse. The reimagined Blackwood family of two repudiates even the few faint connections it had maintained for some years after Merricat's dinner table familicide. Merricat no longer goes on her weekly shopping trip to town, and no visitors are permitted to enter the castle.

As it turns out the repudiation is one-sided. Food and provisions are left on the doorstep for the reclusive sisters, providing vital supplies. In one instance, a nameless man knocks lightly on the door and says, "I hope you can hear me, Miss Blackwood. I broke one of your chairs and I'm sorry."[25] The kindness and concern of the Clarkes, too, are made apparent. They alone were resistant to the mob frenzy when it was at its height, and they return more than once after the crisis has passed to offer their assistance to the sisters. And the baskets of food, and further apologies, keep appearing. As gestures of expiation, they are, in this regard, far from token, because before much time passes, the sisters, having severed all ties with the larger social network, depend on them for their very sustenance. Constance in a small (and very amusing) way tacitly acknowledges the civility of the community's efforts when she insists on returning a basket with the linen napkin washed and folded because, she says, "What would she think of me?"[26]

Such gestures of concern and repentance make not the slightest impression on Merricat's stony obliviousness, however. She reports them without indicating, even in passing, that she regards them as they are clearly intended to be regarded. Her adamant refusal to be social, much less civil, amounts to a turning away almost entirely from the extrafamilial network of the local community and of, fundamentally, the very notion of polity as a social value. Its extremity, in this regard, is both striking and telling—the novel's slyest indication that its broadest target is postwar American social norms and values. Consider that, by the novel's end, Merricat has attained the middle-class security of a completely insular home that is, for her, a site of unrestrained emotional power; fully prepared meals—fast food, in effect—are delivered daily by anonymous and self-effacing service personnel; within the home, her emotional needs are serviced by a devoted, happily subordinate (or so she thinks) spouse; and she believes she inhabits an atemporal realm in which nothing she loves can change or die. (As Darryl Hattenhauer astutely observes, "one of Merricat's defenses for maintaining her obsession with time is to deny it.")[27]

But she is a spoiled child still—her adult-seeming iron reign over the household notwithstanding—which is, as Jackson insinuates in many of her writings, a characteristically American ideal. In the postwar era, many commentators suggested, the nation had become a "filiarchy," in which domesticity and many social mores and arrangements centered upon the figure of the perfect, and perfectly imperious, child.[28] Shirley Jackson's contribution to that insight (if such it was) was apparent even in the playful titles of her two books about her own experiences as a parent, *Life among the Savages* and *Raising Demons*, and appeared more darkly in the figure of 10-year-old Fancy, the aspiring household monarch (and murderess) of *The Sundial*. *Castle* goes farther still in suggesting that the obsession with perfect parenting masked a desire on the part of adults to be that ideal child. Hence the brilliance of the figure of Merricat: she is an infantile adult, embodying an extreme of self-seeking individualism. In the end, the reconfigured family that is also a refashioned marital alliance in *Castle* signifies multiplicity and only superficially; its underlying tie that binds is the will of the individual ego for dominance over others—a frightful Gothic Thing that has always been going bump in the night and now, in the person of Merricat, has emerged more openly. Both the romance and the sisterly togetherness of her superficially happy final arrangement with Constance are deceptive, for she has made Constance an underling to serve only her in a domestic capacity that is as closely aligned with the inner sphere of her ego and its imaginings as possible. The newly revamped Blackwood household is singular, a spoiled child's fantasy of living effortlessly in a fairytale world. The castle is purely private. It is Merricat.

The novel, however, is no such fairy tale. Merricat's insistence upon a saccharine happily ever after ending at the close of the text—"Oh Constance ... we are so happy!"[29]—fails to ring true to what the foregoing pages have discreetly implied about her accession to the domestic throne, and what that upheaval of the conventional familial structure says about the state of American society more broadly. While Merricat's highly subjective narration often seems to banish the ego abashing checks and balances of society and champion the private property of resolutely policed selfhood, through Shirley Jackson's strategic textual insinuations, it reflects and savagely parodies social trends widely prevalent in the America of its time. "When people remarked on the stability of marriage in the 1950s and early 1960s," Stephanie Coontz has pointed out, "they were actually standing in the eye of a hurricane."[30] The conjugal relationship of two sisters imagined in Jackson's 1962 novel appears, in retrospect, portentous in that regard. Moreover, it is not enough to say, as many commentators have done, that the sisters' final arrangement inverts the ideals of conventional domesticity.[31] For the inversion (if such it is) only caricatures the model concisely summed up by Edward Shorter in *The Making of the Modern Family*: "In its journey into the modern world the family has broken its ties with the kinship network, community, generations past and future. It has separated from the surrounding community, guarded now by high walls of privacy. It has cast off its connections with distant kin, and has changed fundamentally even its relationship to close relatives."[32] Shorter's generalization casts its net widely, as befits a study in social history; but it could easily serve as a summation of the situation of the "family" left to inhabit the Blackwood home by the end of *Castle*.

At the novel's close, the sisters are totally concealed from the prying eyes of the townspeople who regularly appear to bask nervously in the presence of the shrine to hermetic selfness that the Blackwood home has become and to provide obeisant sustenance for it. The castle and its occupants are nervously revered entertainment, like Shirley Jackson's great modern gothic thrillers. But the visitors, the townspeople, the society, are still more susceptible to the voyeur gaze, and the sisters entertain themselves by peering through the blinds they have constructed and commenting with amusement on those emissaries from the wider social network. Thus too, *We Have Always Lived in the Castle*, carefully camouflaged as gothic escapism, looks outward upon its readers' world, casting its eye critically on predominant aspects of middle-class American life as communally mythicized and therefore in some degree actually experienced. Shirley Jackson's final novel may have enchanted readers over the years with its apparent summons to shun society beyond the home and the self by seeing things largely as Merricat sees them. There is indeed seductive cat magic in it, and lunar allure. But by so compellingly conjuring into narrative Merricat's fanciful world, by confining us to her perspective while teasing us to see beyond it, it finds ways to do what Merricat herself would most emphatically rather not. It glances searchingly backward, outward, and even inward, at what she has ostensibly shunned—and, more broadly, at the baroque variations upon American domestic ideals that were lurking in the sunny home spaces of the postwar era.

Notes

1 Jackson, Shirley, *We Have Always Lived in the Castle* (New York: Viking, 1962), 76–7.
2 Ibid., 92.
3 Stuart Woodruff, for example, accepts almost uncritically Merricat's vitriolic view of the local community and of Constance's bliss over ultimately being confined to a housebound existence with only her sister for company. See Stuart C. Woodruff, "The Real Horror Elsewhere: Shirley Jackson's Last Novel," *Southwest Review*, 52, no. 2 (Spring 1967), 160–1. Lynette Carpenter allows that "[readers'] sympathy with Merricat remains uneasy," but claims that there is only one point at which Merricat's perceptions seem "limited." See Carpenter,

"The Establishment and Preservation of Female Power in Shirley Jackson's *We Have Always Lived in the Castle*," *Frontiers*, VIII, no. 1 (1984): 160–1. Roberta Rubenstein, more sensibly, refers to Merricat's "skewed vision of the world;" however, her commentary largely accepts that vision as reliable with regard to the wider community and the threat it poses to the Blackwood sisters. See Rubenstein, "House Mothers and Haunted Daughters: Shirley Jackson and the Female Gothic." *Studies in Women's Literature*, 15, no. 2 (Fall, 1996): 320.

4 Jackson, *We Have Always Lived in the Castle*, 1.
5 Ibid., 9.
6 Ibid., 22.
7 Ibid., 2.
8 Ibid., 30.
9 Ibid., 37.
10 Ibid., 38–9.
11 Ibid., 139.
12 Ibid., 177.
13 Ibid., 28.
14 Ibid., 113.
15 Ibid., 176–7.
16 Ibid., 168.
17 Ibid., 2.
18 Ibid., 33.
19 Ibid., 108.
20 Ibid., 195.
21 Ibid., 160.
22 See, for example, Karen J. Hall, "Sisters in Collusion," in *The Significance of Sibling Relationships in Literature*, ed. Jo Anna Stephens Mink and Janet Doubler Ward, 118–19 (Bowling Green: Bowling Green State University Press, 1993); Roberta Rubenstein, "House Mothers and Haunted Daughters: Shirley Jackson and the Female Gothic." *Studies in Women's Literature*, 15, no. 2 (Fall, 1996): 324–5.
23 Rubenstein, "House Mothers and Haunted Daughters," 319.
24 Elizabeth Brake has argued persuasively that the twentieth-century's reigning marital ideal of a "dyadic" relationship in which the two partners become disproportionately entranced with one another to the virtual exclusion of all other emotional ties was a modern aberration as, "historically, marriage integrated the couple into the community." Elizabeth Brake, *Minimizing Marriage: Marriage, Morality, and the Law* (New York: Oxford University Press), 87–96.
25 Jackson, *We Have Always Lived in the Castle*, 202.
26 Ibid., 203.

27 Darryl Hattenhauer, *Shirley Jackson's American Gothic* (New York: SUNY Press, 2003), 183.
28 The literature on the postwar era's fascination with the figure of the spoiled child is extensive. See, for example, Mary Cable, *The Little Darlings: A History of Child Rearing in America* (New York: Scribner's 1975), 163–81; J. Ronald Oakley, *God's Country: America in the Fifties* (New York: Dembner Books, 1986), 123; and Ann Hulbert, *Raising America: Experts, Parents, and a Century of Advice About Children* (New York: Knopf, 2003), 208–28.
29 Jackson, *We Have Always Lived in the Castle*, 214.
30 Stephanie Coontz, *Marriage, a History: From Obedience to Intimacy or How Love Conquered Marriage* (New York: Viking Press, 2005), 8.
31 See, for example, James Egan, "Sanctuary: Shirley Jackson's Domestic and Fantastic Parables," *Studies in Weird Fiction*, no. 6 (Fall, 1989): 23.
32 Edward Shorter, *The Making of the Modern Family* (New York: Basic Books, 1975), 3.

References

Brake, Elizabeth. *Minimizing Marriage: Marriage, Morality, and the Law*. New York: Oxford University Press, 2012.
Carpenter, Lynette. "The Establishment and Preservation of Female Power in Shirley Jackson's *We Have Always Lived in the Castle*." *Frontiers*, 8, no. 1 (1984): 32–8.
Coontz, Stephanie. *Marriage, a History: From Obedience to Intimacy or How Love Conquered Marriage*. New York: Viking Press, 2005.
Egan, James. "Shirley Jackson's Domestic and Fantastic Parables." *Studies in Weird Fiction*, no. 6 (Fall 1989): 15–24.
Hall, Karen. "Sisters in Collusion," in *The Significance of Sibling Relationships in Literature*, ed. Jo Anna Mink Stephens and Janet Doubler Ward, 110–19. Bowling Green: Bowling Green State University Press, 1993.
Hattenhauer, Darryl. *Shirley Jackson's American Gothic*. New York: SUNY Press, 2003.
Jackson, Shirley. *We Have Always Lived in the Castle*. New York: Viking, 1962.
Oakley, J. Ronald. *God's Country: America in the Fifties*. New York: Dembner Books, 1986.
Rubenstein, Roberta. "House Mothers and Haunted Daughters: Shirley Jackson and the Female Gothic." *Studies in Women's Literature*, 15, no. 2 (Fall 1996): 309–31.
Shorter, Edward. *The Making of the Modern Family*. New York: Basic Books, 1975.
Woodruff, Stuart C. "The Real Horror Elsewhere: Shirley Jackson's Last Novel." *Southwest Review*, 52, no. 2 (Spring 1967): 152–62.

12

My House Is My Castle: On the Mutually Enabling Persistence of Familial Devotion and Defunct Economies in Shirley Jackson's *We Have Always Lived in the Castle*

Allison Douglass

Some of the eeriest scenes in Shirley Jackson's *We Have Always Lived in the Castle* (1962) come at quiet, loving, domestic moments, when nothing in particular is happening beyond the everyday goings-on of life at the Blackwood manor. Inside, Constance, Julian, and Mary Catherine Blackwood cohabitate as the sole surviving members of a family that was mostly decimated in a grisly mass murder carried out by its youngest member, the then 12-year-old Mary Catherine, or Merricat. The novel's sunny passages stand out, providing the most unsettling chills, despite the presence of other, more easily explainable horrors. When we learn the details of the family's morning routine, full of consideration and acts of kindness, we are ill at ease. Constance arranges Uncle Julian's tray, gives him hot milk in a "jug painted with yellow daisies," and trims his toast "so it would be tiny and hot and square."[1] She and her sister plan the menu for the day, thinking of what they'll harvest from the garden—maybe radishes, dandelion greens, carrots, and rhubarb.

Why are these scenes of domestic tranquility so strange? I would argue this is because tranquility for the Blackwoods unerringly equates with isolation and stasis. Merricat desperately seeks stasis throughout the story, with every suggestion of change or intrusion causing her to feel "chilled." For these characters, domestic tranquility means being *left in peace* so they can carry on living just as they always have. A home supposedly establishes a small corner of the world that is only yours, where only your family has access. What kind of domestic peace can there be without walls? What slithering horrors would take advantage of any breach in them, any broken window or faulty latch, in order to enter and enjoy the bounty you've stored up inside? But security can be taken too far. Houses keep us safe, but only insomuch as we stay inside them, allowing nothing to cross their thresholds, and we can't stay inside forever. People come and go from their houses. They move away, on to new phases of their lives and new challenges. And why shouldn't they? Not everything outside is harmful: though the unknown might be frightening, we've got to encounter it to learn. Moreover, not everything inside is necessarily wholesome. The home is constructed to cordon off a space for its inhabitants that outside influences cannot reach, but we actually experience our homes' barriers as permeable.

The Blackwoods, however, do not come and go from their home as most people do. They have shut themselves inside so thoroughly that their lives have calcified. The result is that these characters seem stuck out of time, failing to mature, or even move into the modern era. Their home is reminiscent of a forgotten past when (some) houses were castles, and their inherited wealth bestows on the family a courtly economic mind-set reminiscent of feudalism. At the beginning of the novel, this frozen-in-time feeling of stasis is exemplified particularly in Merricat, whose psychological development appears to have stalled at the age of 12, simultaneously with the story's original parricidal event. The enclosed space of this house has been sealed too long, and things inside have begun to turn rancid. And yet, the family stays indoors with no desire to escape the fetid air. It's a live burial in the sense described by Eve Sedgwick, where the enclosure "derives its horror not from the buried person's loss of outside activities (that would be the horror of dead burial), but from the continuation of a parallel activity that is suddenly redundant."[2] Live burial is so disturbing because the spaces both inside and outside the tomb are full of life, but the space inside has been unnaturally cut off from the rest of the world. The twist in Jackson, though, is that this burial is a willing one. It's as if, at the end of "The Fall of the House of Usher," Roderick had opened Madeline's crypt to find her alive, but perfectly content and smiling, asking him to shut the door again.

This desire for isolation and stasis should not be read as some bizarre quirk of the Blackwoods, but rather as representative of the outdated social, political, and economic systems reflected in the imagery of the gothic past that this novel draws on. Jackson's depiction of shut-up, claustrophobic domesticity built on wealth by inheritance (suggesting gothic images of medieval, landed courtliness) contrasts with contemporary capitalist images of prosperity proliferated in the 1960s, wherein private spaces were made to signify happiness through acts of consumerist exchange. Through the Blackwoods, Jackson investigates what makes closed-off spaces, both small- and large scale, work at a level of feeling. And what perpetuates the kind of toxic isolationism sought by the Blackwoods on an emotional level is very simple: houses. The peace and safety ensured to us by these enclosures suggest that everything *out there* is inescapably opposed to everything *in here*, but the idea of enclosure promises that its walls will keep the two at a distance. The failure of this promise that the home's interior will be peaceful and stable is foundational to the gothic in America: it's what underlies the trope of the haunted house,[3] an image which violates the pervasive cultural ideal of home ownership as an important measure of personal happiness and prosperity.

The conceptualization of home as a tool for keeping *us* safe from *them* hinges on our love of what's inside our houses and on our love of one another. For home to retain its meaning, the value we place on its interior must be maintained, whatever it consists of. We see the drive to preserve domestic love emphasized at the end of *Castle*, after the Blackwood house is in ruins, destroyed by fire, and its inhabitants rendered destitute. Surely, nothing is left in that house to entice the Blackwood sisters to remain; but still they stay, holed up in the corner of the structure that hasn't fallen down around them, making tea. Within the life they've inherited, where the only safety they know to look for is inside their house, danger, death, and ruin have only one possible response: further retreat inward. The novel ends on the line, "Oh Constance, we are so happy,"[4] and the sincerity of that statement exemplifies the novel's off-putting tone, uttered as it is from within the castle's wrecked, vine-covered walls. Tranquility and contentment are disturbing when they exist in an unlivable space so marked by a history of violent destruction. However, the sisters must remain happy because domestic bliss is a necessary component of the structure of their lives and their economic positioning.

Gothic literature is obsessed with the failure of progress, the failure of the rejected past to fall away, and Jackson's novel offers a very particular answer to that classic gothic problem. In this story, the bizarre continuation of the courtly economic mind-set of the Blackwoods is presented as a *by-product* of their domesticity. The nature of the isolationist, identity-based family structure that undergirds their domestic life guarantees an uncritical commitment to that which makes it up, no matter how defunct or harmful. The Blackwood sisters will treasure their preserves even if they are poisonous. They will dust their mother's Dresden dolls even if they hated her enough to murder her. They will live in their house even though it is in charred ruins. Their unfettered love for their morning routine guarantees it.

Constance, Merricat, and Julian experience "domestic bliss" in their home, but details of their past surface revealing that the family these people are so devoted to has been full of strained relationships and toxicity. The novel presents the possible maltreatment of the sisters in their past as a mystery, centered around the eerie scene where Merricat plays house, imagining a family dinner with everyone still alive. That scene depicts the family expressing repeated outpourings of love for Merricat, and the reader is left to wonder whether this scene is disturbing because it is an invention, a smoothing over of the children's actual mistreatment, or whether it is disturbing because it is true, and this is the kind of loving scene that Merricat responds to with homicide. Whatever the real nature of the family's past, whether its hostility originates in its older generation, younger generation, or both, its internal dynamics continually prove to be full of distress. One such revelation comes when we learn that, after Merricat murdered her family, Constance helped her to conceal the crime, telling the police in a moment of passion at odds with her usual kind placidity that her relatives deserved to die.[5] Think, too, of the arrival of the deeply hated Charles to the Blackwood home; that character—perceived as a monster by the story's narrator—is compared immediately to the sisters' deceased father as if he were a returning ghost. The sisters' murdered brother is described as possessing "many of his father's more forceful traits of character,"[6] and their mother is figured as cold and distant, not allowing them to play in their elegant house. Uncle Julian, too, tells stories of having to continually prove his and his wife's pliable helpfulness to the dead Blackwoods to keep his place in the household.

The oddest part about these hints at a troubled past, though, is how, despite all these seeming resentments, felt deeply enough to inspire murder, Constance, Merricat, and Julian's fond attachment to family, to one another, and to those same deceased relatives *persists*. Despite her horror at seeing Charles, the seeming ghost of her father, Merricat cherishes her father's gold watch. Despite their mother's distance, Merricat and Constance keep her elegant drawing room spotlessly maintained with ritual reverence. But Julian, perhaps, most vividly demonstrates the disconnection between the dark reality of the Blackwoods' family life and their continued enjoyment of it. Despite the certainty that one of these women attempted to murder Julian, he continues to live with them, to be cared for by them, and to accept food from them every day, seemingly without fear. When she poisoned her family, Merricat made sure to keep Constance safe—not so with Julian, who should have died along with everyone else. Julian understands how close he came to death at his nieces' hands. We know this because he takes copious notes on the subject, recording the history of what happened to his family on that night, and refers to his own survival as an intervention of fate. One explanation for Julian's continued trust of his nieces could be that he is aging and unable to fully understand his predicament. After precisely recounting the story of the murder early in the novel, Julian demonstrates bewilderment, asking Constance, "Didn't it really happen?"[7]

However, his confusion is not simply the result of a deteriorating mind. Julian's frequent confusion, instead, seems to result from his inability to reconcile his own contentment with his simultaneously held acute awareness of the violence in his domestic environment. Julian can explain with precision every detail from the day of the murders and seems to fully grasp how damning those details are in a judgment of Constance. He recounts her quick washing of the arsenic-laced sugar bowl before the arrival of the police, saying, "you will allow that it was not a felicitous moment to wash a sugar bowl. The other dishes used at dinner were still on the table, but my niece ... scrubbed it thoroughly with boiling water. It was a curious act."[8] In this moment, as in many others, Julian reveals his consciousness of both what is happening around him and what it implies about his family. Yet, Julian greatly enjoys the recording and the telling of this family history, performing it as entertainment for their rare visitors. He sees the import of the evidence but refuses to acknowledge the conclusion he must draw or feel its weight. This character's confusion does not come from age; rather, it comes from burying his head in the sand. He asks whether the event really happened not because he has forgotten, but because he is full of a double awareness that he cannot render comprehensible. His whole happiness is built on Constance and Merricat, but they are also a source of danger to him. In the face of these conflicting truths, he, along with his nieces, ignores the troubling reality of his circumstances and chooses instead the far more pleasant path of enjoying his life uncritically.

The uncritical acceptance of and contentment with the interior life of one's home-place, the phenomenon I'm describing with the Blackwoods, can develop in any structure that attempts to create a closed system through isolation. Ludwig von Bertalanffy, the groundbreaking thinker in general systems theory, describes closed social systems, which are inner-directed and reject transactional states, as being subject to a kind of entropy similar to that of closed physical systems, being characterized by "conservatism and conformism, defending the 'system' as is, conceptually neglecting and hence obstructing social change."[9] The manor, then, parallels larger social and economic forms of isolationism. But this relation between family structure and social structure is not just representative; it is also real. Individual actors in economic structures cannot be conceived without the unit of the household,[10] and the idea of the nation as the domestic, in contrast to the foreign, is built on the ability of citizens to feel an "at-homeness"[11] inside a large geopolitical boundary. Many systems create structure and coherence using the same logic as kinship relations by naturalizing a sense of identity within a group that stabilizes the system inside, while defining that interior in opposition to something outside. In other words, insular family structures, like other kinds of identity-based structures, derive their coherence from their ability to place that which is "not us" outside, in distinct opposition to "us."

Castle presents the two distinct parts of this operation. First, family acts here as a unifying social force. Immanuel Wallerstein explains in his text *World-Systems Analysis: An Introduction* that the family is the "primary socializing agency" of all systems, and its work of regulating identity and social rules serves to maintain the coherence of a household for the purposes of economic stability, despite whatever inequalities might exist within that household.[12] This unifying force is at work in the Blackwood family, where group identity is maintained relentlessly. The other side of this operation, though, is the definition of the group in opposition to its *constitutive outside*, in the Derridean sense, where "the constitution of an identity is always based on excluding something and establishing a violent hierarchy between the resultant two poles."[13] Just as nationalism is built around hostility toward enemies,[14] the only thing the Blackwoods feel more deeply than their love of home is their hatred of their neighbors. And structures like these, built on the separation of the unit from that which does not belong to it, require fortifications. On the large scale, those fortifications can look like border walls, while on the small scale, they can look like the stone walls of houses.

This critique of the Blackwoods, though, does not equate to a critique of *all* familial structures and their parallel systems. The family should be seen as exemplifying systems that so fully invest in their own structures that their borders become impermeable and their members immobile. This is what border studies refers to as an *enclave* community, and such calcified systems are usually imagined as counter to the trends of modernity and as potentially harmful, creating stagnation within the group and illogical distrust of anything beyond its walls.[15] So, when family is conceived as the Blackwoods are, as a source of identity, and as a cohesive group distinct from outsiders, it behaves much as intense nationalism behaves, and it is this mindset that I am characterizing when I use the term *toxic isolationism*. The Blackwoods conceive of themselves in contradistinction to all others, thinking of any day they have to leave their home as a "terrible day."[16] As a result, they are committed to one another by nature, in spite of the poisonous qualities of their internal dynamics, and their committed domesticity proves the root of their demise. It is for this reason that the most loving scenes in the novel are the most off-putting, because they seem, for the Blackwoods, inevitable. Their entire way of life is built around their domesticity, and, for them, it must remain no matter the horrors that have taken place.

Thinking of domestic love as a stabilizing, structural force is one way to approach a critical conversation about Shirley Jackson's domestic settings. *Castle* exemplifies her repeated interest in the ways in which homes are cordoned off from the outside world, and what that can mean for women. Dara Downey explores this tendency in her essay "Not a Refuge Yet: Shirley Jackson's Domestic Hauntings." In this piece, Downey thinks through Jackson's obsession with "enclosed domestic space," positing that Jackson negotiates the home's "tendency to vacillate between functioning as a refuge or a prison ... [articulating] the fear that the spaces inhabited by her female protagonists are not merely beyond their control, but are themselves controlling these isolated, beleaguered women."[17] Downey argues that Jackson's characters engage with domestic tasks in such a way that they become magical rituals, and the housekeeper's work is aligned with the practice of witchcraft. These characters wage a battle against disorder through housework, forbidding malevolent spirits entry and creating a space of safety within. This figuration, Downey suggests, empowers the work of women and allows them to carve out their own environments in a world that is often hostile toward them.[18] Certainly, this vision of housework can be traced in *Castle*, where Merricat and Constance are obsessive about their rituals of "tidying," which are paralleled with Merricat's other, more explicitly magical rituals for warding off intruders.

These rituals do possess the power Downey describes, palpably constructing a space that belongs to these women alone. In their house, the sisters build a life that is secure and, in many ways, happy. But their safety comes at a price, because these rituals build and reinforce conceptual borders that do more than simply isolate. The boundaries around the Blackwood home may protect the sisters from a hostile world, but they also heighten and extend that hostility by preventing empathy from developing between the Blackwoods and their neighbors. The connection between the home's protective bounds and the hostility of the people outside is clearest during the fire scene, when the Blackwoods' neighbors express their animosity by breaching the family's carefully constructed security, using rocks to break open the house's windows and to invade.

The imagery of domestic ritual Jackson creates is complicated further when viewed in light of the contemporary rhetoric around consumerist domesticity in post–Second World War America, where women were constantly bombarded by images encouraging them to update their potions and technologies for domestic serenity. Downey's interpretation of *The Haunting of Hill House* emphasizes "the almost irresistible lure of home and all that it stands for, the possibility of both safety and self-determination that contemporary domestic ideology insisted came automatically with ownership."[19] The domestic imagery proliferated in *Castle* was similarly saturating women's lives in the early 1960s, but the models of domestic tranquility typically offered to women were driven by a consumerism that was about exchange rather than isolation. The imagery surrounding domestic ritual has mixed implications. Although we may see ritual's power in achieving independence and autonomy, we must also recognize the anxieties that Jackson explores through those same rituals that focus on the other qualities of buttressed, enclosed spaces for their inhabitants. How does this particular domestic enclosure speak to contemporary consumerist messages about the home, when its residents so loathe outsiders that they assiduously avoid having to buy or sell with strangers?

The specific quality of the Blackwood home's domestic interior is articulated through the novel's most prevalent domestic imagery: food. The food symbols in *Castle*, like all aspects of this home, are about isolationism, and about the Blackwoods' need to retain control. They perceive food that comes from inside their walls as wholesome, while anything from outside is figured as dangerous, but Jackson comments on this vision of domesticity by showing that, for the Blackwoods, the real poison originates inside the property. If the Blackwoods could, they would vastly prefer to live off of the food they produce themselves, fully independent from trade and, most importantly, from dependence on others. They seek a completely self-sustaining domestic enclosure.

The Blackwoods' need for enclosure relates to the gothic obsession with the *Other*. If the gothic is interested in the fear attached to unfamiliarity, food imagery has often served as a vehicle for that conversation, and in *Castle*, Jackson uses depictions of food and eating to play with those existing gothic narratives. Lorna Piatti-Farnell, in her examination of food horror in films, explains:

> There is a certain unavoidable Otherness about the very process of eating. Food, an external, foreign matter, enters our bodies. In order to gather nourishment, we must process it, assimilate it: in short, we must make it part of ourselves. While eating is commonplace, and foods can be either known or unknown, there is a layer of unfamiliarity that is intrinsic to consumption: when food is outside of our bodies, it is inevitably "not us," it is something that—conceptually and physically—does not belong to us.[20]

In this novel, where food is the central element of a domestic structure all about maintaining internal order, this concept of consumption as the integration of Otherness bears consideration. The Blackwoods do everything they can to limit the Otherness of what they eat by endeavoring to limit that consumption to their own garden and preserves. The opening scene filled with anxiety in the novel shows Merricat taking her dreaded weekly trip to the store, a chore she abhors among other reasons because it reveals her dependence on outsiders for things her family cannot grow, like meat and eggs. Within an American system, reliance on trade for survival would ordinarily be assumed, but the Blackwoods operate almost totally outside the economy of buying and selling. They cannot always do so, though, when it comes to sustenance. In this novel of isolation, where magical and physical barriers are erected again and again, those barriers are repeatedly breached because food must be allowed to pass.

Viewing the novel's focus on food this way illuminates how familial affections in this house are bred out of a system of enclosure where that which is inside the manor's boundaries is automatically considered good, trustworthy, and orderly despite the fact that Jackson makes it clear that the domesticity this family values so highly is poisonous. Jackson describes the family's shining rows of preserves in their cellar: "All the Blackwood women had taken the food that came from the ground and preserved it, and the deeply colored rows of jellies ... stood side by side in our cellar and would stand there forever, a poem by the Blackwood women."[21] This inherited and internal sustenance is a source of extreme pride for Merricat—this food was grown and maintained inside their walls, by their own family, and has remained there ever since. However, the passage immediately continues: "Each year Constance and Uncle Julian and I had jam or preserve or pickle that Constance had made, but we never touched what belonged to the others; Constance said it would kill us if we ate it."[22] Because the family cherishes these stores, they've kept them past the point of rotting.

The deep valuing of food is figured alongside its potential toxicity throughout the novel. Piatti-Farnell discusses the way images of food in the gothic are always tinged with an element of risk-taking. Because, in eating, one integrates foreign bodies into one's own, the act is one of trust, where "individuals are often 'at the mercy' of the cook."[23] This novel, with its many poisons, continually highlights the paired risk and trust in acts of eating. In that context, the Blackwoods' love of growing their own food speaks to the family's isolationism. Piatti-Farnell elaborates in her discussion of food horror:

> It concerns not only the obvious risks of being physically damaged by the food, in terms of poisoning and all its associations, but also the socio-cultural, and, to some extent, psychic notion that the wrong food might "damage" us as cultural entities: that is to say, that eating the "wrong" foods would challenge our identities and our sense of self ... The classification of "edible" inevitably creates categories of disgust and revulsion, and sediments those reactions of mistrust and even fear that are at the heart of food horror.[24]

The Blackwoods avoid food from outside because they deeply hate and fear integrating anything other than their inheritance into themselves. However, the "wrong food," the food that actually kills in this home, is always their own.

By looking at these food images in the novel, we also begin to see an elaboration of the connections Jackson makes between the small-scale isolationism of this household that is a microcosm of larger social forces, specifically economic ones. The domestic and food imagery is always paired with economic ideas, usually anachronistic ones, tied to feudal European economies. The Blackwoods obsess over the treasure trove that is their pantry, and this novel deliberately figures sustenance as wealth. Merricat says to Constance, "You bury food the way I bury treasure," and the cellar of preserves is described visually as a vault, with its "deeply colored" jellies in their jewel tones of "maroon and amber and dark rich green." The way the Blackwoods store up and protect this wealth demonstrates a courtly relationship to both family and money regularly portrayed in gothic traditions.

Jackson takes pains to emphasize throughout her novel that this family's domesticity is an inherent facet of how they relate to the world, and that this way of relating is built into their antiquated class positioning, which reads as a relic, out of place in the small American town where the novel is set. For Jackson, these two modes of being embodied by the Blackwoods—domestic and economic—enable one another's persistence. Economic class is at the forefront of *Castle* from its first chapter. On the opening page, Merricat describes her home by saying that it has "a solid foundation of stable possessions" and that the family has always lived in their "castle." This focus on old wealth is directly connected to land, property, and lineage. On that same first page, Merricat describes the periodic entrance of new Blackwood wives and dowries into their home, "so [their] house was built up with layers of Blackwood property weighting it, and keeping it steady against the world,"[25] a description that calls to mind landed gentry. This focus is distinctly gothic and comes with a built-in critique: the gothic has always been obsessed with pastness, and the saturation of the genre with images of castles, knights, and ladies has traditionally been tied to the political systems those signs invoke, political systems explicitly built on hierarchies of familial inheritance and protected by fortified battlements. Jackson's gothic juxtaposes references to courtliness with their settings, which are resolutely "American" in their folksy, unpretentious aesthetics, so that the Blackwoods' stately mansion appears not to belong to the town where it sits.

Jackson's vision of this castle on a hill fits awkwardly into its small-town setting because the concept of the castle is inconsistent with our rosiest ideas about American identity. America theoretically rejects the undemocratic nature of monarchal systems, along with their castles, yet old-money American dynasties resembling that of the Blackwoods live on. The conflict between the Blackwoods and "American" ideals surfaces when the family members talk about their neighbors in town as "commoners," and Merricat imagines that "the Rochester house and the Blackwood House and even the town hall had been brought [to the village] perhaps accidentally from some far lovely country where people lived with grace."[26] In gothic traditions, references to antiquity address the fearful potential failure of cordoning off the past and the present. Eric Savoy writes that "the gothic tendency in American culture is organized around the imperative to repetition, the return of what is unsuccessfully repressed."[27] Specters in this tradition represent the resurfacing of supposedly defunct problems of the past in the face of American myths of progressive rationalism, and in *Castle*, the Blackwoods are a resurfacing of a form of economic life at odds with modernity. The failure of these people to stay behind in Europe, or to die out, is key.

Even in early English Gothicism, the focus on such families and castles critiques their outdated values. The gothic recreates an imitative medieval aesthetic for exactly this purpose. Gary Kelly describes it as a critique of aristocracy that "suggests that court culture and values are somehow 'not English,' [and] depicts the courtly as shallow, ineffectual in the long run, and doomed to fail in the face of bourgeois values."[28] This generic, class-based critique is heightened in the American gothic, where references to economic pastness mark a distinction, not just between courtly and bourgeois values, but between "old" and "new" worlds, in a place where national identity is tied to Enlightenment-era concepts of progress, democracy, and rationalism explicitly defined against monarchy and its trappings. The gothic, especially in America, doesn't just reject antiquated values, though. It expresses a fear of their resurgence, and of the potential failure of Enlightenment ideals. Jerrold Hogle puts it this way:

> The beginnings of both America and its Gothic fictions [arise] from the ideological tug-of-war in the "bourgeois, Protestant mind" ... "between the drive for economic power" that pulls people back towards Old-World forms of domination in new guises, on the one hand, "and the need for cultural autonomy," on the other, that could make the New World and its rising classes more progressive than the Old with its ruling orders and myths, by which the American experiment is still attracted, and thus haunted, in trying to overthrow them.[29]

In an America whose identity is one of the frontier, democracy, and open borders, the obsession with the walled past visible in American gothic texts betrays the ways that national identity is forever obstructed by its own history and cultural progenitors, shaped inescapably by the patterns of domination and exclusion that are its inheritance and palpable reality.

It is important to note that *Castle* does not simply make a distinction between an oppressive upper class, as a relic of the past, and a distinctly American, democratic middle class. Rather, Jackson contrasts class structures that include affluence, but of different kinds. This story provides multiple representations of wealth, but the wealth of other characters has a distinctly capitalist quality, focused on trade and the generation of *new* money. These other families are described in terms of money, value, production, and exchange as opposed to the emphasis on maintaining inheritance and lineage that we see in the Blackwoods. The Blackwoods associate with other well-to-do families, including the Clarkes, the Carringtons, and the Shepherds, but those other families have built "*new* lovely homes,"[30] and while the Blackwoods' wealth lies in their inheritance of land, the Carringtons' wealth comes from industry. They are rich because they own the paper mill in town. Even the Blackwoods' use of their land is at odds with capitalist goals. When Merricat encounters farmers in the village, they suggest that they could get rich farming the Blackwood land, which the family has allowed to lie fallow, emphasizing once again the focus on value-accumulation by everyone other than the sisters.

The ultimate representation of American capitalism in the novel comes from an estranged branch of the Blackwood family in the form of cousin Charles Blackwood, who invades the manor. Charles constantly evaluates the net worth of the house and its objects and is interested primarily in getting his hands on the family's safe. This moneygrubbing quality (in Merricat's view) makes him the novel's villain, setting up the drama of the plot as a conflict between two ways of viewing wealth. Charles's interest in monetary exchange shows the value he places on economic mobility. He treats property as a way of interacting with the world and improving his position within it, while Merricat's interest in the preservation of her family's accumulated property shows the value she places, conversely, on economic security and stability. She treats property as something to be accumulated and protected as a way of maintaining her position in the world rather than advancing it. Though Merricat disdains Charles's fixation on money, she constantly worries about the various physical and symbolic borders of the family property, continually testing the padlock and constructing her magical boundaries. Though this obsession with security may not appear on its surface to be economic in nature, it is so for the Blackwoods. Merricat's mother connected the family's seclusion directly to their economic positioning: "The highway's built for common people … and my front door is private,"[31] and Merricat's internalized attitude toward privacy is directly connected to her mother's. Just after this, Merricat reminisces:

> When I was small I used to lie in my bedroom at the back of the house and imagine the driveway and the path as a crossroad meeting before our front door, and up and down the driveway went the good people, the clean and rich ones dressed in satin and lace, who came rightfully to visit, and back and forth along the path, sneaking and weaving and sidestepping servilely, went the people from the village.[32]

It is the economic contrast between Merricat's desire to guard the family property from others and Charles's interest in the liquid value of the estate that plays out when Charles, furious, finds that Merricat has nailed her father's gold watch to a tree in a ritual of protection. His way of imagining value and hers are both on display when he brandishes this object, meant by Merricat to ward off the "sneaking and weaving" of poor outsiders, and says, "Connie this thing's made of *gold* ... what a hell of a way to treat a valuable thing. We could have sold it ... It's worth money."[33]

Jackson sets up this distinction between the Blackwoods and those around them as two different orientations toward class and wealth. But the important point for my argument is that, by contrast, the *family* does not view its focus on property as being about wealth at all, but about their love of one another. Merricat scorns what she perceives as the townspeople's jealousy of their monetary wealth. She "knew they talked about the money hidden in [the] house, as though it were great heaps of golden coins and Constance and Uncle Julian and I sat in the evenings, our library books forgotten, and played with it, running our hands through it and counting and stacking and tumbling it, jeering and mocking behind locked doors."[34] To Merricat, this vision of the Blackwoods as dragon-like hoarders of cash is a complete misreading. We get a sense of what the "correct" reading would be in the Blackwoods' eyes by noting how every mention of their wealth is immediately connected to some cherished family member of theirs. The opening of the novel focuses on the dowries of the various Blackwood wives as establishing the economic weight and security of the Blackwood home. But for Constance and Merricat, their dishes are more consciously connected to the long line of women who preceded them in stewardship of the house. Each time the sisters prepare a meal, the plates, cups, saucers, and jugs being used are described in loving detail, and each time they are connected to the ancestor who brought them into the home. And again, we see that the sisters cherish these items in a straightforward way, despite the women's complex relationships with their family, and with that china: they still use the sugar bowl that once contained fatal arsenic, though, of course, it has been "thoroughly washed."[35]

The pairing of economics and domesticity in *Castle* manifests in its food imagery. The Blackwoods do not sit at night running their fingers through piles of golden coins, but they do jealously guard the contents of their food-vault, even when it is full of poisonous rot. Considered in economic terms, these are people who accumulate, pass down, and protect their wealth internally, not people who generate or trade it. The Blackwoods' patterns of domestic life are built around the food they eat and the china they use. These items are theirs by inheritance and are connected deeply in their minds to their family, reinforcing every day their investment in one another. For them, this is the correct understanding of their wealth, and the focus others place on their cash is absurd. The larger economic systems that the Blackwoods represent work this way as well, because the people within them are so willing to love and trust what is internal—nation and family— to the exclusion of all outsiders, who conversely must be hated.

Everything about the Blackwoods—their poisonous familial dynamics, resistance to modern economic thought, and terror of change—feels like a gothic fantasy out of sync with its historical moment, and their story is frustrating. Why won't these people just move on, as they have every reason to, and as it seems Constance wants to? Why won't they simply walk out of their crypt? But we know, too, that the sweep of history does not always trend toward progress, and that the longing for borders, enclosure, and nationalism are actually contemporary issues. With this family, Jackson explores the continued life of people and problems that feel like anachronisms, whose resurgence surprises us, and offers that their illogical continuation can be founded, simply, on the powerful desire for domestic love.

The twist at the end of the novel is that this toxic isolationism resulting in the failure of the past to die off is part of a *reciprocal* process. Some readers might interpret the tension between the Blackwoods and everyone around them as a product of Merricat's imagination, but the events of the novel belie that idea. The deep-seated hatred of the family for everyone else turns out to be mutual, and though the Blackwoods begin their own destruction from within, starting the fire that brings down their home, the villagers finish it off, raiding and vandalizing the ruins of the manor. The Blackwoods and their neighbors have made monsters of each other, and the process of demonization has not just made the Blackwoods into hermits. It has made these "outsiders" into more cruel and destructive versions of themselves. These neighbors are not isolated as the Blackwoods are, but they have undergone the same process of identity formation, using the Blackwoods as their own "others."

I began by asking why peace and tranquility are so disturbing in the context of this novel and offering that it is because in *Castle*, peace means seeking isolation, resulting in a stasis that stunts development. As I conclude, I'd like to pose another question: how have these people so successfully *achieved* stasis? This question is ever-present in *Castle*, as we wonder how these characters have managed to go so long without confronting the world beyond their gates, how Merricat has remained crystallized in her 12-year-old mind-set, and moreover, how this aristocratic family even came to inhabit such a typical American town. How have they resisted the pull of modernity's tide? The novel's final chapter compounds these questions, after Constance and Merricat barricade themselves in a corner of their ruined home, renouncing even the small methods of contact they once had with surrounding civilization, making survival seem practically impossible.

The answer *Castle* gives is this: the Blackwoods want to stay in their home despite its terrible past and uninhabitable state because of their domestic love, but they are ultimately only able to survive because their "enemies" keep them alive. Despite the repugnance the Blackwoods' neighbors show them through the course of this story, and despite their gleeful vandalizing of the manor, these same people sustain the sisters after their house's ruin, quite literally feeding them by leaving foodstuffs at their doorstep. This turn of events feels unexpected in a novel that so fully invests in the mutual separation and mistrust of these two groups. But their neighbors keep the Blackwoods alive because the two groups depend on rejecting one another to understand themselves. This structural reciprocity accounts for the final chapter in the novel, as the sisters are converted from people into stories. As plantlife grows around what's left of the manor, it is now "barely recognizable as a house," and Merricat tells us that "no one ever saw our eyes looking out through the vines."[36] The two sisters in this final passage are nothing more to their neighbors than a legend, a cautionary tale starring a pair of witches: "You can't go on those steps ... if you do, the ladies will get you." Even so, the people in town continue to bring the fabled sisters their baskets of eggs. The Blackwood sisters survive because they serve a purpose. What stories do we tell about ourselves that demand foils in the shape of monsters? And how does our desire for those monsters prompt us to feed and give life to parts of our culture that we theoretically reject? How have we kept regressive ideologies alive in our stories, telling them again and again, and leaving behind on their doorsteps casseroles we've made for them, lovingly?

Notes

1 Shirley Jackson, *We Have Always Lived in the Castle* (New York: Penguin, [1962] 2006), 43.
2 Eve Kosofsky Sedgwick, *The Coherence of Gothic Conventions* (New York: Methuen, 1980), 20.
3 Eric Savoy, "The Face of the Tenant: A Theory of American Gothic," in *American Gothic: New Interventions in a National Narrative*, ed. by Robert K. Martin and Eric Savoy (Iowa City: University of Iowa Press, 1998), 12.
4 Jackson, *We Have Always Lived in the Castle*, 146.
5 Ibid., 37.
6 Ibid., 34.
7 Ibid., 32.
8 Ibid., 36.
9 Ludwig von Bertalanffy, *General System Theory: Foundations, Development, Application* (New York: George Braziller, 1968), 196.
10 Immanuel Wallerstein, *World-Systems Analysis: An Introduction* (Durham: Duke University Press, 2007), 32.
11 Amy Kaplan, "Manifest Domesticity." *American Literature*, 70, no. 3 (1998): 581.
12 Wallerstein, *World-Systems Analysis*, 37.
13 Chantal Mouffe, *The Return of the Political* (London: Verso, 1993), 141.
14 Ibid., 66.

15 Bryan Turner, "The Enclave Society: Towards a Sociology of Immobility," *European Journal of Social Theory*, 10, no. 2 (2007): 288.
16 Jackson, *We Have Always Lived in the Castle*, 1.
17 Dara Downey, "Not a Refuge Yet: Shirley Jackson's Domestic Hauntings," in *A Companion to American Gothic*, ed. by Charles L. Crow (Hoboken, NJ: John Wiley & Sons, 2014), 290.
18 Ibid., 295.
19 Ibid., 291.
20 Lorna Piatti-Farnell, *Consuming Gothic: Food and Horror in Film* (London: Palgrave Macmillan, 2017), 4.
21 Jackson, *We Have Always Lived in the Castle*, 42.
22 Ibid., 42.
23 Piatti-Farnell, *Consuming Gothic*, 12.
24 Ibid., 12–13.
25 Jackson, *We Have Always Lived in the Castle*, 1.
26 Ibid., 6.
27 Eric Savoy, "The Face of the Tenant: A Theory of American Gothic," in *American Gothic: New Interventions in a National Narrative*, ed. by Robert K. Martin and Eric Savoy (Iowa City: University of Iowa Press, 1998), 4.
28 Gary Kelly, "Social Conflict, Nation and Empire: From Gothicism to Romantic Orientalism." *Ariel: A Review of International English Literature*, 20, no. 2 (1989): 6.
29 Jerrold E. Hogle, "The Progress of Theory and the Study of the American Gothic," in *A Companion to American Gothic*, 1st ed., ed. Charles L. Crow (Hoboken, NJ: John Wiley & Sons, 2014), 6–7.
30 Jackson, *We Have Always Lived in the Castle*, 3.
31 Ibid., 18.
32 Ibid.
33 Ibid., 77.
34 Ibid., 7.
35 Ibid., 36.
36 Ibid.,146.

References

Bertalanffy, Ludwig von. *General System Theory: Foundations, Development, Application*. New York: George Braziller, 1968.

Downey, Dara. "Not a Refuge Yet: Shirley Jackson's Domestic Hauntings," in *A Companion to American Gothic*, 1st ed., ed. Charles L. Crow, 290–302. Hoboken, NJ: John Wiley & Sons, 2014.

Hogle, Jerrold E. "The Progress of Theory and the Study of the American Gothic," in *A Companion to American Gothic*, 1st ed., ed. Charles L. Crow, 3–14. Hoboken, NJ: John Wiley & Sons, 2014.

Jackson, Shirley. *We Have Always Lived in the Castle*. New York: Penguin (1962) 2006.

Kaplan, Amy. "Manifest Domesticity." *American Literature*, 70, no. 3 (1998): 581–606.

Kelly, Gary. "Social Conflict, Nation and Empire: From Gothicism to Romantic Orientalism." *Ariel: A Review of International English Literature*, 20, no. 2 (1989): 3–18.

Mouffe, Chantal. *The Return of the Political*. London: Verso, 1993.

Piatti-Farnell, Lorna. *Consuming Gothic: Food and Horror in Film*. London: Palgrave Macmillan, 2017.

Savoy, Eric. "The Face of the Tenant: A Theory of American Gothic," in *American Gothic: New Interventions in a National Narrative*, ed. Robert K Martin and Eric Savoy, 3–19. Iowa City: University of Iowa Press, 1998.

Sedgwick, Eve Kosofsky. *The Coherence of Gothic Conventions*. New York: Methuen, 1980.

Turner, Bryan. "The Enclave Society: Towards a Sociology of Immobility." *European Journal of Social Theory*, 10, no. 2 (2007): 287–303.

Wallerstein, Immanuel. *World-Systems Analysis: An Introduction*. Durham: Duke University Press, 2007.

13

Flipping Hill House: The Netflix Renovation of Shirley Jackson's Landmark Novel

Jessica R. McCort

In October 2018, Netflix released its streaming series revising Shirley Jackson's 1959 novel, *The Haunting of Hill House*. While Jackson's book considered the interactions between a group of strangers brought together under the guise of an anthropologist studying "supernatural manifestations," the Netflix series instead focuses its attentions on an estranged family dealing with the residue of their residence in a haunted mansion some twenty-six years after they fled the house in the middle of the night.[1] The show's creators flip the premise of the original tale by also flipping the premises. Here, the main characters Hugh and Olivia Crain are house-flippers by trade, and Hill House is the last and largest residence they must renovate and sell before they can build their "Forever House," a unique dream home designed by Liv, who is an architect. Netflix's Hill House, however, has other plans for the Crain family. The series creatively reimagines the design of the original Hill House as something altogether new, while also shoring up the novel's foundational interests in domestic and psychic drama. This chapter seeks to unravel the palimpsest that is the Netflix *Hill House*, considering how the series' intersections with Jackson's novel reveal ongoing cultural anxieties about female experience.

Both Jackson's *Hill House* and the Netflix revision concentrate on the aftermath of familial experience and childhood in relation to what

American society has had to say about the American family when each text was created. More particularly, the monstrous feminine and the monstrous maternal become central focal points in each version. In her study of the portrayals of monstrous women over time (from the witch trials to recent films), Barbara Creed notes that "when woman is represented as monstrous it is almost always in relation to her mothering and reproductive functions," and that the many faces she wears include "the archaic mother; the monstrous womb; the witch; the vampire; and the possessed woman."[2] The monstrous females who emerge in Jackson's novel and the Netflix revision are obsessively coded as maternal or victims of the maternal—devouring, tricky, and possessed.[3] In what follows, I will first lay out the ways in which Jackson builds the monstrous feminine into the walls of her fictional house and the experiences of her largely stunted female characters. Then, I will turn my attentions to how Netflix built upon that foundation, focusing on how this version, in many ways, produces a vision of maternity and motherhood that is just as damning as the one offered by Jackson by exploiting current cultural anxieties regarding working mothers, absentee and over-present mothers, and helicopter parenting. The Netflix revision uses many of the tropes of monstrous femininity to construct a deeply disturbing portrayal of contemporary mothering that both critiques and reentrenches cultural definitions of what it means to be a "good" mother. It also considers what happens to children when the connection to that mother is severed. Through this, I hope to continue to demonstrate the lasting importance of Jackson's work to the foundations of American horror and the texts that she continues to inspire, and to show some of the ways in which contemporary domestic horror continues to grapple with the ghosts of its past.

Upon its publication in 1959, Jackson's *Hill House* was part of a rising wave of terrifying texts that sought to investigate the dark side of the American family and home, which had stood entrenched at the center of the nation's domestic ideology since the country's inception. Rhetorical concentration on the importance of the American family to national security was nothing new. However, focus on the conventional family was heightened greatly after the Second World War, and this focus continued throughout the 1950s and into the 1980s, even as many sought to challenge its constructs and traditions. Jackson's novel, like numerous films and books that would follow, exploited the anxieties many white middle-class Americans in particular were experiencing as they struggled to build lives that echoed in some fashion the spectacle of the perfect American family regularly trotted out on television and in domestic fiction, popular magazines, and film.[4]

Participating in what would come to be defined as "domestic horror," Jackson often explores "the oppressive, the threatening, the perverse, and the sickening flip side" of American family life, especially for girls and women.[5] Her investigations regularly center on the "average" American home, inserting the gothic tradition into rooms that seem very much like the ones her readers and viewers might have inhabited. She also uses horror tropes to deconstruct what were often ideally portrayed in the public sphere as loving, positive familial relationships. In her consideration of domestic horror, Gina Wisker explains that the genre, "particularly contemporary *women's* domestic horror[,] exposes the contradictions and potential/ real unpleasantnesses of domestic settings and relationships, nuclear and extended families, marriages, and parenting."[6] She further notes that this type of fiction "focuses in particular on the non-nurturing home as a site for horror, on parents and monster children."

Jackson's Hill House is a nonnurturing home haunted by the spirits of debate surrounding the role of middle- and upper-middle-class white women in American society during the 1940s and 1950s. As Jackson came of age, the American mother and American girls were central figures in public discourse. Following the Depression and World Wars I and II, political figures, doctors, psychologists, and scholars placed renewed emphasis on family life as a means of reentrenching mainstream American values, and a particular stereotype of the American mother and her children emerged within the rhetoric they espoused as important signifiers of the nation's renewed promise.[7] During this period, the role of housewife and mother was encouraged in the public sphere as the primary function of middle- and upper-middle-class white women in America.[8] Furthermore, these women's daughters were to learn from their mothers' examples.[9] Through the lens of Hill House as a nonnurturing home, Jackson considers the ways in which women's personal experiences as daughters negatively influenced their perception of their own identity. Above all, the house that she constructs demonstrates the ways in which conservative patriarchal control warps all of those who operate under its smothering architecture.

As her novel opens, Jackson unlocks the doors to a structure that is "born bad," but one that has also, over time, grown in strength by serving as a receptacle for the pain, rage, and suffering of its inhabitants.[10] The book's opening lines immediately personify the house, establishing it as both insane and isolated: "Hill House, not sane, stood by itself against its hills, holding darkness within; it had stood so for eighty years and might stand for eighty more."[11] This personification is extended when the novel's protagonist, Eleanor Vance, first sees the house outside of her imagination. Jackson, through Eleanor's vision, describes it as "vile," "diseased," "evil," "arrogant and hating," and provides an extended description of the house as alive:

> No Human eye can isolate the unhappy coincidence of line and place which suggests evil in the face of a house; and yet somehow a manic juxtaposition, a badly turned angle, some chance meeting of roof and sky, turned Hill House into a place of despair, more frightening because the face of Hill House seemed awake, with a watchfulness from the blank windows and a touch of glee in the eyebrow of a cornice.[12]

Moreover, Hill House is introduced as a place that has been lying in wait, patiently biding its time until the arrival of new prey. When Eleanor, that prey, steps foot onto the house's veranda, she imagines the place "c[oming] around her in a rush," seeing herself as "enshadowed" in its dark embrace.[13] From this point forward, the house is described as heavy, its structure and its hills pressing down on the people within. It also is depicted as having a vampiric sort of "reputation for insistent hospitality," refusing to allow its visitors/inhabitants to leave once they cross the home's threshold.[14] Early on, Theodora notes, "All the time I'm here I'm going to be terrified, … thinking one of those hills will fall on us," and Eleanor replies, "They don't fall on you. They just slide down, silently and secretly, rolling over you while you try to run away."[15] This personification lends the house a great deal of power and intent; it becomes a character in its own right, suggesting that houses are much more than places we inhabit. They are places that absorb our energy and take on lives of their own.

These early depictions of the house's exterior initially conjure a more masculine countenance for the mansion, and Jackson does emphasize throughout that the house's vileness springs from the paternal. As she unfolds the mansion's history, she focuses heavily on its original owner, Hugh Crain, and his oppressive control of his offspring, exemplified by the book of guidance he leaves behind that is graphic, violent, and signed in his own blood. This heavy-handedness is symbolized by the home's weighty, deeply traditional décor, as well as the gigantic statue of the man and his daughters that spans the entire wall of the house's drawing room: "it's a family portrait, you sillies. Composite. … that figure in the center, that tall, undraped—good heavens!—masculine one, that's old Hugh, patting himself on the back because he built Hill House, and his two attendant nymphs are his daughters."[16] Furthermore, in her telling of Hugh Crain's tale, Jackson concentrates on the familial decline that spirals downward from his failed attempt to construct a "dynasty" through real estate. His daughters become deeply estranged from one another and fight over the inheritance of the mansion, and the house eventually falls into outside hands, disrupting Crain's plans for continued patriarchal rule. Dr. Montague connects the house's off-kilter design to the off-kilter nature of Hugh Crain's mind, and Jackson, continuing the metaphor of the house as the man, encourages readers to imagine it as Eleanor's suitor. Eleanor thinks repeatedly of the line "Journeys end in lovers meeting," suggesting that she senses a romantic, sexual connection between herself and the mansion.

These more patriarchal aspects of Hill House are indeed threatening and dangerous, but in the end they prove not as unnerving as the threads of feminine monstrosity that emerge within Hill House's walls. The mansion's exterior and its more public-facing spaces are brutalist, statuesque, and grandiose, but its insides are more often coded as stereotypically female and are redolent of the body. In her discussion of the monstrous-feminine, Creed notes that the "symbolization of the womb as house/room/cellar or any other enclosed space is central" to horror iconography. Furthermore, Creed observes, "Behind the quest for identity ... lies the body of the mother represented through intra-uterine symbols and devices. Here, the body/house is literally the body of horror, the place of the uncanny where desire is always marked by the shadowy presence of the mother."[17] Hill House is personified from the very first pages, and its interior is riddled with intrauterine symbols and devices linked to entrapment. Mazelike and claustrophobic, the house seems comprised of concentric circles that squeeze inward on the characters and force the cracks in their personalities to open, its interior passageways suggesting entrails designed to consume and dissipate the lives of its inhabitants. The downstairs rooms are dark, the curtains drawn to block out any external light. When the characters try to open any doors or windows, they soon find them all closed again shortly thereafter, as if they had never been opened. The rooms in the very center of the house have no exterior walls, and thereby, no windows. These interior rooms, in which the characters spend most of their time, heighten the perception that the house was designed to keep secrets. "The prevailing mood of *The Haunting of Hill House*, the spell of the book that so many readers find hard to shake," notes Laura Miller, "is one of physical and psychic claustrophobia."[18]

At first, Jackson describes the interior spaces as rather cold, hard, and unwelcoming. When the characters first enter the parlor that they use as a center for their operations (a space that lies at the dead center of the house), for example, Jackson notes that the room is not "cozy" and that "it had an unpleasantly high ceiling, and a narrow tiled fireplace which looked chill in spite of the fire which Luke had lighted at once; the chairs in which they sat were rounded and slippery."[19] However, the interior of Hill House, in other of its more domestic aspects, is very inviting, especially for the main character, Eleanor. Getting ready for bed, she notes, "The blue bed was unbelievably soft. Odd, she thought sleepily, that the house should be so dreadful and yet in many respects so physically comfortable—the soft bed, the pleasant lawn, the good fire, the cooking of Mrs. Dudley."[20] Part of the house's strangeness is that it is at once off-putting and hardened and uncomfortably plush and devouring, all characteristics that Jackson connects to the maternal:

> "It's all so motherly," Luke said. "Everything's so soft. Everything so padded. Great embracing chairs and sofas which turn out to be hard and unwelcome when you sit down, and reject you at once ...—and hands everywhere. Little soft glass hands, curving out to you, beckoning—... Perhaps ... the single most repulsive aspect is the emphasis upon the globe."[21]

While one might think of such characteristics as desirable—warmth, softness, luxuriousness—Jackson portrays them as unwelcoming, dangerously globular and womb-like, lulling the characters to sleep or into dreamlike states that are threats to their self-awareness and safety. Luke, one of the heirs to Hill House, further describes the mansion as a "mother house," "a housemother, a headmistress, a housemistress," connecting its ambivalently soft/hard duality to female oversight. This theme is amplified in Mrs. Montague's session with the planchette, in which the words "Mother" and "Home" are beckoningly and insistently repeated.[22]

Hill House's manifestation of the maternal in the threatening, but attractive supernatural suggests a complicated understanding of the mother–daughter relationship, presenting the mother as at once desirable and dangerous, and inescapable. In this paradigm, the mother *is* the house, akin to the Monster House in the children's film of the same name; mothering becomes a murderous trait that results in forever stilted, ghostly childhood.[23] One could argue that part of the reason Eleanor wants to remain at Hill House is that her relationship with her mother, while negative, was dangerously symbiotic throughout her life. She hears her mother's voice calling her in the house; she hears what she thinks is her mother knocking on the walls; she's overwhelmed by a vision of a happy family playing on the lawn; she smells, in the library, a scent that reminds her of her mother's grave. Importantly, one of the most haunted, and coldest, spaces in Jackson's house is the nursery, a room that she describes as "the heart of the house" – "musty and close," at once both cold and stiflingly warm, with an "air of neglect."[24]

Just as readers can sense from the novel's opening that Hill House is not an ideal home, it also becomes readily apparent that all Eleanor wants is a home. Eleanor is house-hunting in Jackson's book, looking for a new place to settle because she feels unaccepted or unwanted everywhere else. At the age of 32, Eleanor finds herself thoroughly displaced and unwanted, sleeping on a cot in her niece's room after the death of her invalid mother. For eleven years prior to that, Eleanor was her mother's sole caretaker, which left her sad, angry, and reclusive. Jackson describes her as almost mole-like, afraid of the sunlight, "reserved and shy."[25] Prior to that, her father had died and left her alone under the influence of her mother, and Jackson is careful to portray Eleanor's mother as a woman who refused to grow into adulthood herself, declining into a bitter, physically ill state that exempted her from becoming a mature adult.

On the way to Hill House, Eleanor conjures up in her imagination several different homes she contemplates making her own, heightening the reader's sense that what Eleanor really longs for is belonging and a place where she feels loved and comfortable. She first considers the possibility of wandering forever, but quickly turns her attentions to other fairy-tale-like places that she sees and then imagines herself inhabiting: a "vast house" with stone lions on the main street in a town she passes through, a gateway protected by pink and white oleanders complete with a handsome prince, a "tiny cottage buried in a garden."[26] Tellingly, none of these places are even remotely *real*, suggesting that Eleanor has no real sense of what her life might look like outside of her past and her miserable present. The place that will accept her is Hill House—an outdated, outmoded, deadened place that will freeze her forever in its hardened womb in her daughterly, disenfranchised state.

Jackson noted, to herself at least, that Hill House was, in fact, Eleanor. As Darryl Hattenhauer explains in *Shirley Jackson's American Gothic*, "Jackson wrote in her notes, as if she discovered this point while reading her drafts, 'Eleanor IS house' … that Eleanor is 'ALL DISTORTED *LIKE HOUSE*.' By the end of the novel, … It turns out that the house's foundation and construction allegorize Eleanor's psychological foundations."[27] Jackson shows readers that these psychological foundations were planted askew from the very start, leading to an adult woman who cannot function outside of the very limited space her family and her society has imagined for her. In her depiction of Hill House, down to her use of a child's face on the doorknocker, Jackson calls into question the actions of parents who use their children as servants to their existence, whether that be to uphold the masculinity of Hugh Crain or to support the failed and unhappy existence of Eleanor's mother. Despite its fantastical appearance as a house outside of the "real world," Hill House ultimately serves as a symbol of the very real suffering and smothering that is rooted in the family dynamic symbolized by the grand family home; for Eleanor, becoming part of the house's body is a dangerous thing indeed, as it suggests the complete loss of her identity. Whatever is walking in Hill House at the novel's end walks alone, just as it did at the novel's opening. This suggests that while Eleanor thought she was being accepted into the house's maternal or romantic embrace, whichever the reader views her as ultimately choosing, she was actually tricked into offering up her own life to continue the house's existence.

Jackson amplifies this by developing the reader's view of the house as a great mouth, set upon devouring its inhabitants, riffing on themes focused on the cannibalism of young women in literary precedents from the fairy tale to the zombie story. Eleanor notes, "I am like a small creature swallowed whole by a monster, she thought, and the monster feels my tiny little movements inside."[28] This portrayal of the house as a hungry body forces the reader to question the dangerous influence of houses in general on women's lives. The very concept of a house devouring a young woman is alarming, suggesting that it's not just haunted houses that consume the identities and life force of the young women who live in them. It also turns the womb into a stomach, complicating the metaphor described earlier; whereas the womb is typically a space that offers up life, Hill House is a perpetual womb that devours the life force of the daughter it refuses to relinquish.

In this, Jackson's Hill House, depicted at once as womb, as mouth, as monster, as suitor and father, becomes a complicated symbol for anxieties about the family, maternal influence, and the patriarchy circulating in the culture at the time. Perhaps Dr. Montague describes it best when he muses, "Essentially, ... the evil is the house itself, I think. It has enchained and destroyed its people and their lives, it is a place of contained ill will."[29] Montague's words are backed up by Jackson's description of the haunted place in her notes on the novel: "The house *is* the haunting (can never be un-haunted)."[30] For Jackson, Hill House is a fantasy space that allows Eleanor to escape from the drudgery of her childhood and young adult life, only to find herself unable to escape the fantasy and consumed by reality's maw. As Christine Junker notes in her essay on "domestic tyranny" in Jackson's work, "The idea that the house is a malevolent force that, in particular, harms the female inhabitants is borne out by the history of the house, in which nearly all the women who live there are driven to madness and/or suicide."[31] In her imagination of Hill House's murderous tendencies, Jackson seeks to demolish a dangerous, albeit much idolized literary landmark—the American family home. But at the end of the book, the house still stands, the mausoleum for a multitude of women, suggesting the ongoing, nefarious power of this symbol in late-1950s America. Furthermore, Jackson makes it clear that there's not really any meaningful existence for Eleanor to be had outside Hill House. As Melanie R. Anderson describes in her reading of gender in the novel, "Eleanor has no place in the outside world other than in subservience. Her life has been paused since she had to be her mother's caretaker; she has no career; she has no home; she feels that she has no future outside of the fairy-tale narratives that she daydreams."[32] Jackson argues that the path of wife and mother was not opened up to Eleanor, there was indeed no path. In this, Jackson's novel equates the haunted house with the young woman who has been nurtured into a pitiful existence—isolated, alone, and sick.

The newest iteration of Hill House emerges in a time that has seen a return of the mother and the American family and home to political debates about national security and success. Following the political turmoil in the wake of the 2016 election, public discourse has pushed the mother and the American family into the center again. The maternal body, for example, has become a fierce battleground as debates over abortion continue to rage. A strong backlash against the feminist movement has arisen, the rhetoric regarding the dangers of feminist thinking echoing that which erupted during the 1960s and 1970s. Scholars have recently noted that many of the same "motherhood myths" that limited women's ability to achieve power in the workplace during the 1950s and 1960s continue to persist: "recognizing the pervasive justifying function of motherhood myths may help understand the psychosocial barriers faced not only by women who are mothers, but by women as a whole since 'women are [still] expected to become mothers sooner or later.'"[33] Female identity is still persistently bound up in the maternal, and women themselves belabor how to manage their self-perception in relationship to their children. They continue to try to understand where the boundaries between their own identities and those of their children lie, as is evidenced in such articles as Leslie J. Davis's "Motherhood Gave Me an Identity Crisis" published in the *Washington Post*: "You can't separate the mother from the child or the child from the mother. Without the mother, the child would not exist. Without the child, the mother would not exist. And if we lose ourselves, our children also lose us."[34] Despite this persistent rhetorical onslaught upholding motherhood as most important in their lives, many women are nonetheless expected to simultaneously manage careers outside the home and seamlessly run their households when they leave their jobs at the end of the day.[35] Just as Jackson's vision of Hill House exploited the anxieties of motherhood and female identity prevalent during her time, Netflix's construction of a new Hill House likewise depends upon cultural anxieties regarding working mothers, absentee and over-present mothers, and helicopter parenting for the strength of its metaphors. It also demonstrates that women continue to deal with many of the same stereotypes that their foremothers confronted decades ago and that a gendered view of "the American way" doggedly persists.

Netflix's Hill House shares many characteristics with Jackson's house. It is opulent and concentric, but looks more like a wheel, with a central hub that serves as the entrance way and spokes that go off into the rest of the house. This is visualized in the series by a large entryway that has hallways extending outward, along with one grand central staircase leading to the second floor. Just as Jackson's Hill House is personified, the house in the series is portrayed as something that is alive—with bones, a heart, veins, arteries, and a mind. The mother in the series, Olivia, often makes use of this metaphor. "You know, a house is like a person's body," she says. "The walls are like bones. The pipes are veins. It needs to breathe. It needs light and flow. And it all works together to keep us safe and healthy inside."[36] The upstairs living space is marked by a long hallway lined with closed doors leading to the children's and parents' bedrooms, suggesting that the family is one unit, albeit a disconnected one. Situating viewers in haunted house iconography of the past, the interior spaces are filled with heavy, dark woodwork, and the rich colors of Victoriana. Amplifying this connection to prior haunted places, the show's opening montage portrays the interior of the house as a maze, connecting it to the mazelike spaces in Jackson's mansion, Stanley Kubrick's hotel in his version of *The Shining*, and the gothic castles of the past.

The Netflix treatment of Jackson's *Hill House* also places familial strife and grief directly at the center of the story from the very start. Aida Edemariam points out in her early review of the series that it is a family drama: "It's clear from the initial episode that the programme makers intend to plumb all the ways in which Jackson suggests a haunting can be just as much about trauma, about memory and the unquiet unconscious as about the paranormal."[37] In this iteration, the main characters find themselves in Hill House's environs as house-flippers. In this, the show's creators make use of the current house-flipping craze to explore the economic tenuousness of home ownership and the cultural energy bound up in the purchase of a home. As evidenced by popular shows such as *House Hunters*, *Rent or Buy*, *My First Place*, and more, buying a home, in today's American cultural imagination, is a key component in achieving familial happiness. Through this, the show's creators place a great deal of emphasis on the family's healthfulness being intertwined with the house; the family's morale is connected to its upward mobility through successive and progressively better home ownership. The goal for the Crains, ultimately, is their Forever House, where the family can thrive, having never again to work or exist in a transient state. However, the Forever House, in the show, ultimately becomes a static place, putting pressure on the false perception in American culture that once a certain level of financial stability or success is achieved, people will no longer experience struggle or strife. Importantly, the Crain family's movement toward the Forever House is frozen in time, that dream never fully realized.

Despite the presence of two parents who seem exceptionally dedicated and thoughtful (unlike the distanced and distancing parents in Jackson's novel), the Crain family partly lacks a stable home life because the parents' professions keep them in a constant state of progress and forward movement. The parents also struggle from an apparent unwillingness to admit to sadness, despair, or struggle, with Hugh Crain especially presenting the attitude that everything can be "fixed" every time something goes wrong. After the trauma that unfolds in Hill House and the dream of the Forever House is dashed, the father rescinds his claims on the family and becomes an absentee parent; the children are raised by their aunt, rending an even deeper tear in the family's emotional fabric. Nonetheless, the Forever House that Olivia, the mother, was designing persists as an emblem of the once supposedly happy family. Exemplifying this, one of the Crain daughters, Shirley, keeps a model of the Forever House in her office. At the end of the episode "Open Casket," which focuses on Shirley's experience, the porch light in the model blinks twice to tell her it's time to come home, just as Olivia did when the children were little (the same happens for Nell when she pulls up in front of Hill House later in the series and sees the mansion's interior lights glowing warmly). This positions Hill House as the last place in which the family was whole. After the Crains leave, and with the death of Olivia, the family is forever broken.

Homing in on the theme that childhood trauma unmanaged results in traumatized adulthood, the series finds nearly all of the Crain children, when we first meet them in the present, displaced and disoriented in some way. Steven, estranged from his wife because she discovers that he has had a vasectomy because he refuses to have children, has been kicked out of his house and is staying in an apartment. Nell is in Los Angeles after the shocking death of her husband. Luke is in rehab after years of wandering and drug abuse. Theo is living in a guesthouse at Shirley's. Shirley is the only Crain sibling who could be viewed as having a real home, but her home is part funeral home and part domestic space, revealing that she is constantly living with one foot in the world of the dead (Shirley decided to become a funeral director after her experience with the undertaker at her mother's funeral and his ability to "fix" her mother—the word "fix" here could be taken to apply to her mother's broken body or to fixing her in time; in this, Shirley continues the emotional work of her father, the fixer). Furthermore, after their experiences in Hill House, each of the characters is presented as being walled off or disconnected from the other characters in some way. For example, when Nell calls her siblings when she really needs help, they all ignore her phone call or brush her fears aside. Interestingly, the house uses them, in one sense, against one another, but it also exploits their fears to make them reconnect with one another and become something resembling a real family again with some sense of connection (presumably, this effort is driven by the ghostly Olivia, who still wants her "kittens" to return home).

Building on the foundation Jackson constructed, Netflix's Hill House operates heavily on the idea that physical spaces retain the residue of the past. Stephen King describes this theory of the haunted house in *Danse Macabre*, explaining that such spaces might actually be "psychic batteries, absorbing the emotions that had been spent there." Furthermore, he notes that, according to this theory, the former inhabitants may have indeed passed on, but left behind a "residue" that could be harmful to the future inhabitants, in the vein of lead paint (or, in the iconography of this particular show, black mold).[38] The Netflix series, riffing just as much on *The Shining* as it does on Jackson's novel, relies on the idea that "the past *is* a ghost which haunts our present lives constantly."[39] In Netflix's Hill House, ghosts consistently erupt from the past into the present, coming out of the walls near where they experienced trauma or where secrets are buried, as in the bootleggers' basement, for example (which doesn't appear on any of the house's plans). They also unexpectedly appear in spaces that are far removed from the environs of Hill House. This is akin to King's use of this motif in *The Shining*, in which the young boy, Danny, can actually see the dark events of the past (and the future) on the hotel's walls and outside of them, and later in *Dr. Sleep*, in which Danny is visited by ghosts from the hotel in his new home. Furthermore, in *The Shining*, Danny's father, Jack, is duped by the ghosts of the past into nearly killing his son so that both can stay at the hotel forever and uphold its evil agenda. Scars from the past (and the future) also nearly convince Olivia, the mother, to destroy her children, but from an entirely different angle. While King emphasizes that the influence of toxic masculinity on his main character Jack is the destructive factor, for Olivia, her maternal instincts overpower all others, and the house convinces her that it would be best to keep all of her children together, under one roof, for eternity. Hill House's ghosts work to persuade her that it is dangerous to let her children grow into the outside world and that an early death that will keep them under her wing is the preferable option.

Whereas King's *The Shining* (which he has noted various times was deeply influenced by Jackson's *Hill House*) traced the demise of a young father by his demons, the Netflix series concentrates especially on the demise of a young mother by hers. Ultimately, the series pivots on forcing the viewer to question Olivia's maternal nature. She is indeed a loving and devoted mother, but that love and devotion is warped by her affiliation with this particular house and leads, eventually, to her murder of one of her own children and a neighbor, as well as her husband's suicide. Here, it is in some regard the house playacting the voice of the mother to call her child home, as in Jackson's novel; however, in Netflix's version, the mother herself becomes the dark supernatural force, possessed by the house, who, like a nefarious Pied Piper, nearly leads all of her children into an eternal existence within the house's walls. More importantly, the show considers the ways in which the demands of the house, along with the demands of motherhood, slowly disorder the mother's mental health. When the Crains first move into Hill House, Olivia Crain is portrayed as a beautiful, loving, intelligent, caring young woman. Her relationship with her husband seems solid. She takes time to interact with each of her children, and she listens to their fears and values them as individuals. As the show progresses and events unfold, the house uses all of its evil energies to unravel her sanity, which is revealed to be on the edge anyway as a result of constant work, constant mothering, financial strain, and more. To add to this, two of the younger Crain women in the show have jobs in which they care for other people or provide services to other people; while most of the men are presented as needy, egotistical, or distant, most of the women, particularly the Crain sisters, try to build connections and use their traumatic pasts to leave a positive mark on the world.

The creators of the series make it clear that Hill House is indeed haunted, hungry, and that it has power. They do not seem to suggest that the entities roaming Hill House are entirely figments of Olivia's mind or are created by her, as Jackson at least partly suggests in her novel. However, the show presents Olivia as easily influenced by the persuasive ghosts, mostly women, who reside therein, and she becomes a persuasive ghost herself. One of these ghosts in particular, a young woman named Poppy, exercises a great deal of power over Olivia's imagination. An insane "city" girl who was displaced to the country, Poppy whispers repeatedly to Olivia how much better things would be if Olivia would exert her maternal control. As Olivia works on the plans for the house and a mysterious black mold spreads throughout the property, her husband eventually finds that she has been drawing a miniscule blueprint of the Forever House throughout the plans of Hill House that echoes the mold's expanding path, suggesting that she now sees Hill House as her permanent home. Under the sway of the ghosts of the past, Olivia comes to find her vision of the Forever House and Hill House melded into one, and she decides to do whatever she must to keep her children frozen in time. Olivia is dismantled from a strong, seemingly independent young parent into a scattered, needy, and eventually murderous monstrous mother. The show suggests that her demise comes as a result of her being haunted by the women of the past, who manipulate her desire to care for and protect her children into making her think that murder is the only way to save them. The house consistently uses images of the dead twins, for example, to scare Olivia into taking action. Eventually, she tries to trick the twins and a young girl who lives near the property into drinking poison in a childish game of tea party. Tellingly, this game takes place in the nefarious Red Room, which stands at the heart of the series from the start.

One of the most striking features of the Netflix mansion that does not appear in Jackson's novel is the Red Room, its door locked and seemingly completely off-limits (akin to the door to the Other Mother's world in *Coraline*, *The Shining*'s Room 217, or the crypt of the husband's former wives in the fairy tale "Bluebeard"). To return to Creed's vision of womb-like or secret spaces in connection to the monstrous-feminine, she notes that "These intra-uterine settings consist of dark, narrow, winding passages leading to a central room, cellar or symbolic place of birth."[40] In one regard, the Red Room serves as a safe space for the mother and her children, each in their own way (the father, tellingly, never finds or uses this room). However, as one critic of the show notes, this room also functions as the belly of the house that digests the wishes of the home's inhabitants, amplifying the intersection between womb and mouth that is recognizable in Jackson's novel: "the house is really alive—more akin to the shark in Jaws than a standard haunted house. The Red Room (basically an evil version of the Room of Requirement from Harry Potter) functions as the house/monster's 'stomach.' It creates illusions tailored to each of the Crain siblings, luring them in and ultimately devouring them."[41]

Initially, the Red Room serves a different function for the mother and each of her children. For Steven, it is a game room; for Theo, it's a dance studio; for Nell, a toy room; for Luke, a tree house; and for Shirley, a living room. For the mother, it is a place for her to read and relax with her tea. But, while the space on the other side of the door seems initially to fulfill what the curious child (and parent) isn't getting from their current family, it is also the place that all of the aforementioned mold spreads from, which suggests that the house's feeding off of and excreting the family's fantasies is deeply dangerous. Its iconography, with its blood-red door and its tentacle-like mold, is deeply uterine, amplifying the symbolism of womb/mouth that Jackson had previously established. The room and its mold ultimately represent the destruction of the family, its decay from within prodded on by the ghosts of the past and fantasies of the ideal family. Of course, this destruction is fed by the evil that already lurks within the house. Many of Hill House's ghosts were destroyed by their own negative family experiences.

What the mold ultimately stands for is complicated. In one regard, it can be viewed as a tentacle from the past that drags down the future; the mold emerges from places in the house where bad things have happened—where a bootlegger died, where one of the previous owners walled himself up in the house. It could be viewed as the life and will of the house itself that destroys its inhabitants. Hill House undertakes a slow process of bleeding the Crain family dry financially; as the mold spreads, both parents worry about money. The mold, along with the former owner bricking himself up in the house's walls, could be read as indicative of the Crains' obsession with moving forward to the Forever House. But it also can be argued that the mold could represent the mental decay of a young woman trying to operate under the paradigms of the past and the expectations of the present, which she finds to be impossible. The mold, eventually, serves as a metaphor for what the loss of a parent, especially a mother, to madness and to apparent suicide can do to a child. The orphaned children's minds become haunted houses, and they are never able to achieve healthy adult existences because they have been stunted in their growth, much like Jackson's Eleanor.

Coming home in the Netflix series means something very different than it did in Jackson's novel. The return home seems to be something that is desired by the creators of the series (in the end, both Nell and Hugh Crain commit suicide in the house in order to remain with Olivia). In this, the end of the show, which some viewers found satisfying and some found disorienting and incongruent, hearkens back to the end of the first season of *American Horror Story*, which found the family, now dead, ensconced around the Christmas tree, forever part of the home that caused their demise. While the end of Jackson's novel focuses on an evil thing walking alone, the end of the show notes that whatever now walks in Hill House walks "together." This presents a weird reaffirmation of the traditional family dynamic at the very same time that it demonstrates its potential destructiveness. This could be because, as Arielle Bernstein notes in her review of the show,

> Throughout the series, the show makes the argument that it's better to see the terrifying last moments of someone we love over and over than to never see them at all again, and, that chasing these ghosts is an inevitable part of the human condition, as bleakly solid as the fact that one day each of us is going to die.[42]

Nonetheless, much like other horror texts that question the influence of the maternal, the series places what it means to be a "good" mother (a contemporary ghost in the house) at its center. The suggested answer is that being a good mother is impossible. Even when Olivia tries to do her best, she winds up a destructive force, even from beyond the grave. The children's and her husband's last memories of her from the night they left are as a deformed, crazed, murderous force lovingly bent on their destruction (much like Jack Torrance's possessed state in the close of *The Shining*).

Ultimately, both Jackson and the creators of the Netflix series use the nonnurturing home and horror symbolism of monstrous maternity to investigate psychological trauma, especially as it relates to familial upheaval, loss, grief, and oppressive parenting in all its various forms. For Jackson, the house exploits Eleanor's desire for belonging, for connection, for escape from her deadened reality that has resulted from an unfulfilling family life. In the Netflix version, the house exploits the Crain children's desire for closure, for reconnection to the lost mother. Neither Hill House ultimately becomes a home, even though some of the characters end up residing there for eternity. The houses erected in these two texts speak to preoccupations about the home and family in their time, complicating readers' and viewers' understanding of the ways in which we are influenced, and sometimes destroyed, by the spaces in which we reside and the people we are often forced to live with—and become. Furthermore, the Netflix series, despite being a re-visionary text created over fifty years after Jackson's novel, demonstrates that women continue to struggle under the weight of cultural imagery that often presents mothers in an unerringly negative light, as mad, dangerous, and killing. The contemporary domestic horror created in Netflix's *Hill House* fixates on a mother who, in short, can't win, because anything she does results in psychological struggle for the children who must navigate her care.

Notes

1 Shirley Jackson, *The Haunting of Hill House* (New York: Penguin, 2006), 1.

2 Barbara Creed, *The Monstrous-Feminine: Film, Feminism, Psychoanalysis* (New York: Routledge, 1993), 7.

3 As any brief survey of Jackson scholarship demonstrates, the importance of the monstrous mother to Jackson's vision of Hill House has already been well established. Laura Miller notes in her introduction to the Penguin Classics edition, for example, that "the specter of Eleanor's mother" haunts nearly every corner of the mansion and that "the most fearsome beast lurking in Hill House is Eleanor's stifled rage at her mother, her sister, her life, her self." Laura Miller, "Introduction," in *The Haunting of Hill House* (New York: Penguin, 2006), xxi. See also, for example, Roberta Rubenstein, "House Mothers and Haunted Daughters: Shirley Jackson and the Female Gothic." *Tulsa Studies in Women's Literature*, 15, no. 2 (1996): 309–31, https://doi.org/10.2307/464139; Lynne Evans, "'Help Eleanor Come Home': Monstrous Maternity in Shirley Jackson's *The Haunting of Hill House*." *Canadian Review of American Studies/Advance Online* (2019), https://doi.org/10.3138/cras.2018.015; and Ruth Franklin, *Shirley Jackson: A Rather Haunted Life* (New York: Liveright, 2016).

4   Examples of novels and films that followed in the wake of *The Haunting of Hill House*, for instance, include *Something Wicked This Way Comes* (novel: 1962, film: 1983), *Rosemary's Baby* (novel: 1967, film: 1968), *The Exorcist* (novel: 1971, film: 1973), *The Stepford Wives* (novel: 1972, film: 1975), *The Omen* (1976), *The Shining* (novel: 1977, film: 1980), and *Poltergeist* (film: 1982). Jackson's novel became a film in 1963.

5   Gina Wisker, "'Honey, I'm home!': Splintering the Fabrication in Domestic Horror," *Femspec*, 4, no. 1 (2002): 108. Domestic horror is one of America's lasting contributions to the gothic and horror genres, and its preoccupations have persisted into the present, with new permutations coming to the surface every year.

6   Ibid.

7   For more on this, see Catherine Driscoll, *Girls: Feminine Adolescence in Popular Culture and Cultural Theory* (New York: Columbia University Press, 2002).

8   Examples of such rhetoric include Adlai Stevenson's speech to the 1955 graduating class from Smith ("I think there is much you can do about our crisis in the humble role of housewife.") and John Bowlby's early 1950s declaration that "The provision of constant attention night and day, seven days a week and 365 days in the year, is possible only for a woman who derives profound satisfaction from seeing her child grow through babyhood, through the many phases of childhood, to become an independent man or woman, and knows that it is her care which has made this possible" (suggesting that any women who did not derive such profound satisfaction were somehow defective). See Stevenson, "A Purpose" and Bowlby quoted in Marga Vicedo, "The Social Nature of the Mother's Tie to Her Child: John Bowlby's Theory of Attachment in Post-War America." *The British Journal for the History of Science*, 44, no. 3 (2011): 405, https://doi.org/10.1017/S0007087411000318.

9   Jackson's son, Laurence Jackson Hyman, notes an incident that makes plain how Jackson faced opposition to her aspirations: "It was the 50s, and she lived in a community [in Vermont …] where women didn't generally work. When she went into the hospital to have my sister, and was asked what her occupation was, she said 'writer,' and the man who was checking her in replied: 'Well, I'll just put down housewife.'" See Rachel Cooke, "Laurence Jackson Hyman on His Mother Shirley: 'Her Work Is so Relevant Now …'; Shirley Jackson's Son Laurence on the Revived Interest in His Mother's Brilliantly Unsettling Tales of Suspense and Horror," *Observer*, December 12, 2016 (accessed June 3, 2019), https://www.theguardian.com/books/2016/dec/12/laurence-jackson-hyman-mother-shirley-jackson-dark-tales.

10 Jackson, *Hill House,* 50.

11 Ibid., 1.

12 Ibid., 24.

13 Ibid., 25.

14 Ibid., 48.

15 Ibid., 36.

16 Ibid., 79.
17 Creed, *The Monstrous-Feminine,* 54.
18 Miller, "Introduction," xv.
19 Jackson, *Hill House,* 42.
20 Ibid., 66.
21 Ibid., 154.
22 Ibid., 156, 142.
23 *Monster House,* directed by Gil Kenan (2006, Culver City: Columbia Pictures), 2006, DVD.
24 Ibid., 87.
25 Jackson, *Hill House,* 3.
26 Ibid., 15.
27 Darryl Hattenhauer, *Shirley Jackson's American Gothic.* (Albany: State University of New York Press, 2003), 159.
28 Jackson, *Hill House,* 29.
29 Ibid., 60.
30 Qtd. in Ruth Franklin, *Shirley Jackson: A Rather Haunted Life* (New York: Liveright, 2016).
31 Christine Junker, "The Domestic Tyranny of Haunted Houses in Mary Wilkins Freeman and Shirley Jackson." *Humanities,* 8, no. 2 (2019), 111, https://doi.org/10.3390/h8020107.
32 Melanie R. Anderson. "Perception, Supernatural Detection, and Gender in The Haunting of Hill House," in *Shirley Jackson, Influences and Confluences,* ed. Melanie R. Anderson and Lisa Kröger (London: Routledge, Taylor & Francis, 2016), 46.
33 Catherine Verniers and Jorge Vala, "Justifying Gender Discrimination in the Workplace: The Mediating Role of Motherhood Myths." *PLOS ONE,* 13, no. 1 (January 9, 2018): 3, https://doi.org/10.1371/journal.pone.0190657.
34 Leslie J. Davis, "Motherhood Gave Me an Identity Crisis: Solving It Was Simple, but It Wasn't Easy," *Washington Post,* October 4, 2018 (accessed July 10, 2019). https://beta.washingtonpost.com /news/parenting/wp/2018/10/04/motherhood-gave-me-an-identity-crisis-solving-it-was-simple-but-it-wasnt-easy/.
35 A simple query in any academic database returns numerous hits on books/articles with titles like *Making Motherhood Work: How Women Manage Careers and Caregiving* (2019) and "Work, Career, and Motherhood: The Outlooks and Dilemmas of Contemporary Women Professionals" (2018).
36 *The Haunting of Hill House,* episode 2, "Open Casket," directed by Mike Flanagan, aired October 12, 2018, on Netflix.
37 Aida Edamariam, "Agoraphobia and an Unhappy Marriage: The Real Horror behind *The Haunting of Hill House.*" *Guardian,* October 22, 2018 (accessed April 16, 2019). https://www.theguardian.com /books/2018/oct/22/

pure-fear-how-the-haunting-of-hill-house-opened-a-new-chapter-in-horror-netflix.
38 Stephen King, *Danse Macabre* (New York: Simon and Schuster, 2011), 280–1.
39 Ibid., 280.
40 Creed, *The Monstrous-Feminine*, 53.
41 Flora Carr, "When Is *The Haunting of Hill House* Season 2 Released on Netflix?" *RadioTimes.com*, May 13, 2019 (accessed May 20, 2019). https://www.radiotimes.com/news/on-demand/2019-05-13/the-haunting-of-hill-house-season-2-netflix-release-date-bly-manor-new-cast-story-trailer-plot/.
42 Arielle Bernstein, "How *The Haunting of Hill House* Conveys the Horror of Family; In the Intricately Terrifying Netflix Adaptation of Shirley Jackson's Classic Novel, a Family Is Torn Apart by the Supernatural but Also Each Other." *Guardian*, October 26, 2018 (accessed April 4, 2019). https://www.theguardian.com/tv-and-radio/2018/oct/26/haunting-hill-house-netflix-family-horror.

References

Anderson, Melanie R. "Perception, Supernatural Detection, and Gender in The Haunting of Hill House," in *Shirley Jackson, Influences and Confluences*, ed Melanie R. Anderson and Lisa Kröger, 35–53. London: Routledge, Taylor & Francis, 2016.

Anderson, Melanie R. "'Whatever Walked There, Walked Alone': What Is Haunting Shirley Jackson's Hill House?" *Journal of the Georgia Philological Association* (December 2009): 198–205.

Bernstein, Arielle. "How *The Haunting of Hill House* Conveys the Horror of Family." *Guardian*, October 26, 2018 (accessed April 4, 2019). https://www.theguardian.com/tv-and-radio/2018/oct/26/haunting-hill-house-netflix-family-horror.

Carr, Flora. "When Is *The Haunting of Hill House* Season 2 Released on Netflix?" *RadioTimes.com*, May 13, 2019 (accessed May 20, 2019). https://www.radiotimes.com/news/on-demand/2019-05-13/the-haunting-of-hill-house-season-2-netflix-release-date-bly-manor-new-cast-story-trailer-plot/.

Collins, Caitlin. *Making Motherhood Work: How Women Manage Careers and Caregiving*. Princeton: Princeton University Press, 2019.

Cooke, Rachel. "Laurence Jackson Hyman on His Mother Shirley: 'Her Work Is So Relevant Now …'; Shirley Jackson's Son Laurence on the Revived Interest in His Mother's Brilliantly Unsettling Tales of Suspense and Horror." *Observer*, December 12, 2016 (accessed June 3, 2019). https://www.theguardian.com/books/2016/dec/12/laurence-jackson-hyman-mother-shirley-jackson-dark-tales.

Cordeiro de Almeida, Viviane, and Carolina Maria Mota-Santos. "Work, Career and Motherhood: The Outlooks and Dilemmas of Contemporary Women Professionals." *Administração: Ensino e Pesquisa*, 19, no. 3 (2018): 583–605. doi:10.13058/raep.2018.v19n3.1119.

Creed, Barbara. *The Monstrous-Feminine: Film, Feminism, Psychoanalysis.* New York: Routledge, 1993.
Davis, Leslie J. "Motherhood Gave Me an Identity Crisis. Solving It Was Simple, but It Wasn't Easy." *Washington Post*, 2018 (accessed July 10, 2019). https://beta.washingtonpost.com/news/parenting/wp/2018/10/04/motherhood-gave-me-an-identity-crisis-solving-it-was-simple-but-it-wasnt-easy/.
Driscoll, Catherine. *Girls: Feminine Adolescence in Popular Culture and Cultural Theory.* New York: Columbia University Press, 2002.
Edamariam, Aida. "Agoraphobia and an Unhappy Marriage: The Real Horror behind *The Haunting of Hill House*." *Guardian*, October 22, 2018 (accessed April 16, 2019). https://www.theguardian.com/books/2018/oct/22/pure-fear-how-the-haunting-of-hill-house-opened-a-new-chapter-in-horror-netflix.
Evans, Lynne. "'Help Eleanor Come Home': Monstrous Maternity in Shirley Jackson's *The Haunting of Hill House*." *Canadian Review of American Studies/Advance Online* (2019). doi: 10.3138/cras.2018.015.
Flanagan, Mike, dir. *The Haunting of Hill House.* Season 1, episode 2, "Open Casket." Aired October 12, 2018, on Netflix.
Franklin, Ruth. *Shirley Jackson: A Rather Haunted Life.* New York: Liveright, 2016.
Hattenhauer, Darryl. *Shirley Jackson's American Gothic.* Albany: State University of New York Press, 2003.
Havrilesky, Heather. "The Possessed: Shirley Jackson's Vision of Haunted Womanhood." *Atlantic*, 2016 (accessed April 16, 2019). https://www.theatlantic.com/magazine/archive/2016/10/the-possessed/497513/.
Jackson, Shirley. *The Haunting of Hill House.* New York: Penguin, 2006.
Junker, Christine. "The Domestic Tyranny of Haunted Houses in Mary Wilkins Freeman and Shirley Jackson." *Humanities*, 8, no. 2 (2019): 107–20. doi:10.3390/h8020107.
Kenan, Gil, dir. *Monster House.* 2006; Culver City: Columbia Pictures, 2006, DVD.
King, Stephen. *Danse Macabre.* New York: Simon and Schuster, 2011.
Miller, Laura. "Introduction," in *The Haunting of Hill House.* New York: Penguin, 2006.
Rubenstein, Roberta. "House Mothers and Haunted Daughters: Shirley Jackson and Female Gothic." *Tulsa Studies in Women's Literature*, 15, no. 2 (1996): 309–31. doi:10.2307/464139.
Stevenson, Adlai. A Purpose for Modern Woman (1955) (accessed August 1, 2019). https://wwnorton.com/college/history/archive/resources/documents/ch32_04.htm.
Verniers, Catherine, and Jorge Vala. "Justifying Gender Discrimination in the Workplace: The Mediating Role of Motherhood Myths." *PLoS ONE*, 13, no. 1 (January 9, 2018): 1–23. doi: 10.1371/journal.pone.0190657.
Vicedo, Marga. "The Social Nature of the Mother's Tie to Her Child: John Bowlby's Theory of Attachment in Post-War America." *The British Journal for the History of Science*, 44, no. 3 (2011): 401–26. doi:10.1017/S0007087411000318.
Wisker, Gina. "'Honey, I'm home!': Splintering the Fabrication in Domestic Horror," *Femspec*, 4, no. 1 (2002): 108.

Zinoman, Jason. "Netflix's *The Haunting of Hill House* Is a Family Drama with Scares." *New York Times*, October 11, 2018 (accessed April 16, 2019). https://www.nytimes.com/2018/10/11/arts/television/netflix-the-haunting-of-hill-house-review.html.

CONTRIBUTORS

Jill E. Anderson is Associate Professor of English and Women's Studies at Tennessee State University. Her current book project is entitled *Homemaking for the Apocalypse: Domesticating Horror in the Atomic Age.*

Melanie R. Anderson is Assistant Professor of English at Delta State University. She is the author of *Spectrality in the Novels of Toni Morrison* (2013) and coauthor of *Monster, She Wrote: The Women Who Pioneered Horror and Speculative Fiction* (2019).

Julie Baker completed her MA in English at Marshall University in 2017. Her research interests include feminist and psychoanalytic analyses of American and gothic literature.

Emily Banks is a doctoral candidate at Emory University, where her research focuses on sexuality and the gothic in American women's literature.

Alissa Burger is Assistant Professor of English at Culver-Stockton College and author of *Teaching Stephen King: Horror, The Supernatural, and New Approaches to Literature.*

Michael J. Dalpe Jr. is a high school English teacher and an adjunct in The College of New Jersey's Women's, Gender, and Sexuality Studies Department.

Allison Douglass studies American culture after 1945 at the Graduate Center, City University of New York (CUNY), and focuses on rhetorical and performative tools of fun, "escape," and play.

Christiane E. Farnan is an associate professor at Siena College in Loudonville, New York, where she teaches American literature for the English Department and serves as codirector of the American Studies Program. Her research and teaching interests revolve around nineteenth- and twentieth-century American women writers, mapping technologies, and historical geography.

Ashley Lawson is Associate Professor of English and the director of the Honors Program at West Virginia Wesleyan College. She earned her PhD from the University of Nebraska–Lincoln and has published essays on Zelda Fitzgerald, Sarah Haardt Mencken, Estelle Faulkner, and Dawn Powell.

Jessica R. McCort is Assistant Professor of Composition and Rhetoric at Point Park University. McCort earned a PhD in English and American literature from Washington University in St. Louis and is the editor of a compilation of essays titled *Reading in the Dark: Horror in Children's Literature and Culture*.

Bernice M. Murphy is Lecturer in Popular Literature at the School of English, Trinity College, Dublin. She edited *Shirley Jackson: Essays on the Literary Legacy* (2005).

Richard Pascal has published several articles on Shirley Jackson's fiction and is currently a visiting fellow in the School of Literature, Languages and Linguistics at Australia National University. He has held visiting fellowships at the University of Canterbury in New Zealand and the University of New Mexico.

Luke Reid teaches in the English Department at Dawson College in Montreal.

L. N. Rosales is Lecturer in English at University of Nebraska–Lincoln. Her research interests include the gothic, detective fiction, and neo-Victorian literature and culture.

INDEX

adaptations 1, 2, 36, 38
"After You, My Dear Alphonse" 3, 34
"Afternoon in Linen" 34–5
agency 79, 89, 140, 156, 160, 210
  loss of 48, 62–3, 69, 72
  through magic 101, 102, 108
agoraphobia 20, 152, 161, 171
Agrest, Diane 86
Ahmed, Sara 123, 124, 172, 174, 180, 182
ambivalence
  about domestic space 13
  about domesticity in *New Yorker* fiction 28–31
  emotional 83
  mother–child 15, 78, 80, 82, 83, 88, 89
  about sexual desire 80
American Energy Commission 119
American Horror Story 236
anxiety/anxieties 63, 78, 115, 125, 157, 212 *see also* panic
  American 51, 54
  atomic/nuclear 3, 4, 114, 117, 141, 183
  Cold War 87, 114, 120
  cultural 53, 223, 224, 231
  domestic 12, 20, 44, 120
  female 3, 16, 19, 21, 32, 45, 55
  about home 20, 54, 55
  of Jackson, Shirley 12, 152–3
  around witchcraft 99
  about womanhood 80
  about women's participation in public realm 29
apocalypse *see also Sundial, The*
  domestic 133–45
  homemaking for the 3, 4–5, 113–26

  preparations for 114, 118–22
  prophecy about the 116–17, 124, 126, 140–1
architectural theory 78–9, 82, 86
architecture *see* domestic architecture
Atomic Age 87, 114, 118–19, 120, 126, 134

Bachelard, Gaston 79–80, 82, 89
belonging 4, 15, 43–4, 54, 161, 162, 228, 237 *see also Haunting of Hill House, The* (novel); "Honeymoon of Mrs. Smith, The"
Berlant, Lauren 170
Bernstein, Arielle 236
Bertalanffy, Ludwig von 209
biomorphism 87–8
Bird's Nest, The 2, 8, 9, 10, 15
  Morgen (Aunt) 15
Blackwood, Constance 15, 20, 104–8, 174, 180, 189, 190–201, 205, 207–9, 211, 217–18
  concealment of crime 208, 209
  cooking skills 106–7, 194
  domestic bliss, experience of 174, 207, 208
  drag performance 176–7
  "a fairy princess" 176, 195
  monogendered matrimony of 190, 198–9
  preserves 106, 107, 108, 181–2, 207–8, 212, 213–14
  as supernatural being 108
  townspeople, interactions with 174, 182, 192, 197, 200, 202, 217–19
Blackwood home 108, 197, 202, 208
  destruction of 108, 174, 176, 196–8
  domestic interior 212

protection of 104–5, 106, 107, 211–12, 216–17
refashioning of 108, 176, 197–8
tranquility in the 205–6, 207, 211, 218
Blackwood, Merricat 14, 16, 20, 136, 180–3, 189–202, 205–6, 208–9, 211–14, 216–19
an adult child 5, 190
affection for Constance 106, 194–5
Amanita phalloides (mushroom), liking for 191, 196, 198
contradictory nature of 106
destructive actions of 106, 107, 108, 170, 171, 174, 196–8
disciplining of 180–1, 194
domestic bliss, experience of 174, 207, 208
drag performance 176–7
egocentricity of 191, 194
fantasies of a rewritten childhood 180–1, 193–4
magic, resort to 105–6, 196
monogendered matrimony with Constance 190, 198–9
moon fantasy 174, 182–3, 190, 198
narcissism of 190, 191, 194
poisoning of family 106–7, 171, 174, 183
preserves 106, 107, 108, 181–2, 207–8, 212, 213–14
privacy, attitude toward 197, 200, 216–17
protection of Constance 104–7, 208
a raconteur 190–2
ritualistic protections 104–5, 106, 107, 211–12, 216–17
as "*sinthomosexual*" 171
a spoiled child 180, 194, 201
as supernatural being 108
townspeople, interactions with 174, 182, 192, 197, 200, 202, 217–19
Bracken, Peg 10
Brandeis, Irma 29
Breit, Harvey 98
bunker mentality 114–15, 116, 122, 126
Burke, Kenneth 2

Burke, Libbie 2
"Bus, The" 4, 60, 77, 79–82, 84, 90
  Harper, Miss 79–82
Butler, Judith 45, 177

Caminero-Santangelo, Marta 153, 154, 156, 161, 163
Canterbury Tales, The 125
capitalism 5, 140, 141, 182, 216
Caprio, Frank 175, 178
Carpenter, Lynette 7, 13, 14, 182
cartoons 29, 30, 122
Castle of Otranto, The 13
Caulfield, Holden 191
Cerf, Bennett 102
"Charles" 9, 10–11, 15–16, 65–6
  changing identities of children 15–16, 66
  Laurie 10–11, 65–6
child/children 4, 10, 15, 19, 22
  adult 5, 190 (*see also* Blackwood, Merricat)
  identity shifting by 15–16, 17, 66
  invasion of private space by 50, 51–2, 53, 66 (*see also* "Charles"; "Sorcerer's Apprentice, The")
  killing of 138, 140, 171
  magic, involvement in 101–2
  rebellion by 34–5
  subordination to father's dominance 157
  troublesome/disruptive 11, 66 (*see also* "Charles")
  uncanny 61–3, 64–6, 69
  and witchcraft 98, 101–4, 108
"Children Living in a Time of Famine, The" 138, 140
claustrophobia 65, 207, 227
Cold War 29, 118, 119, 133, 134, 170
  America 117
  anxiety 87, 114, 120
  domesticitiesof the 115
  housing craze of the 138
"Colloquy" 35
Come Along with Me 60, 100
"Come Dance with Me in Ireland" 34
conformity 5, 118, 138, 159, 178
consumerism 3, 114, 118, 211

consumption 11, 55, 99, 212
"Continued Humid" 30–1
Coontz, Stephanie 138, 143, 201
Copperfield, David 191
Corbusier, Le 86, 89
Corey, Mary F. 29, 30, 36
Creed, Barbara 224, 227, 235
Cruising Utopia: The Then and There of Queer Futurity 177
"Cult of True Womanhood, The" 4, 151, 155

Danse Macabre 233
Dark Tales 45, 47, 53
Davis, Leslie J. 231
destabilization 31–4, 35–6, 51, 54–5, 89, 138
destruction 46, 49, 114, 159, 161, 169, 207 *see also* violence
  of Blackwood family 106–7, 171, 181, 183, 218 (*see also We Have Always Lived in the Castle* (novel))
  of Crain family 235–6, 237 (*see also Haunting of Hill House, The* (TV series))
  in domestic spaces 50–3, 54–5, 108 (*see also* "Sorcerer's Apprentice, The")
  of the family idyll 31, 236
  of property 174
"Demon Lover, The" 12, 19
DeWitt, Sarah Hyman 1
domestic architecture 77–90 *see also* "Bus, The"; *Haunting of Hill House, The* (novel)
  childhood home 79–82
  and female body 77–9, 86–7 (*see also* female body)
  and female sexual desires 80–1
  and female sexuality, control of 78–9, 81, 86
  in gothic fiction 4, 11–15
  haunting parent 81, 84 (*see also* parenting)
  matrophobia 78–9, 83
  mother–child dynamic 78, 83, 88, 89
  and poetics of space 4, 77, 78, 79–80, 82

domestic gothic 59–72 *see also* "Charles"; "Intoxicated, The"; "Like Mother Used to Make"; "Men with Their Big Shoes"; "Renegade, The"; "Trial by Combat"; "Witch, The"
  classic tropes 59–60
  domestic failure 59, 64
  domestic invasion 59, 66–7, 68–72
  entrapment 60, 65, 69, 71–2
  horror 67, 70, 71, 72
  Jackson's style of 31, 37
  victims 59, 62, 65, 72
  violence in 63, 64–5, 66
domestic horror 224–5, 237
domestic humor 2, 3, 7–8
  females in male contexts, placing of 29–30
  and gothic fiction 8, 10, 13–14, 19, 21
  urban newcomers versus rural locals 12, 14–15
  women's escape from domesticity 19–21
domestic labor 68, 143
domestic love 207, 210–11, 218
domestic rituals 114, 211–12
domestic saga 8–9
domestic space(s) 4, 5 *see also* home/house
  ambivalence about 13
  destabilization in 31–4, 35–6 (*see also* "Trial by Combat"; "When Things Get Dark")
  destruction in 50–3, 54–5, 108 (*see also* "Sorcerer's Apprentice, The")
  fear in 31–2, 34
  love for 67–8 (*see also* "Like Mother Used to Make")
  magic within the 101–2, 103, 104, 108, 211
  maternalism and 78 (*see also* domestic architecture)
  privacy of 31–4, 35, 44–5, 50–2 (*see also* privacy, invasion of)
  as symbols of "rational" and "familiar" 31, 37
  as a trap 30–1, 44

INDEX

uncanny 31, 37, 77–80, 82, 85 (*see also Haunting of Hill House, The* (novel))
domestic tranquility 30, 31, 205–6, 207, 211, 218
domestic writing 13, 97, 98, 100, 104, 108
domesticity 9, 11, 50, 114, 151, 154
  consumerist 211
  entrapment in 2, 5, 21–2, 32, 44, 47–8, 101
  escape from 19–21, 47–8
  of family home 81 (*see also* family home)
  frustration of 16–17
  New Yorker magazine's portrayal of 30
  as power 44, 101
  and women's freedom, regulation of 35 (*see also* freedom)
Downey, Dara 211
dream(s)/dreaming 138, 144, 145, 197, 228
  day- 81, 84, 88, 89, 154–5, 190, 198, 230
  house/home 82, 89, 223
  interminable 79–80, 82, 90
  of a queer future 173 (*see also* queer future)
Duck and Cover 122

Edelman, Lee 171–2, 181
Edemariam, Aida 231
Egan, James 31
Egg and I, The 8
Elizabeth I, Queen 134, 136, 137–8
Ellis, Havelock 178
Ellison, Ralph 2
"Endless House" 88, 89, 90
Engelhardt, Tom 114–15
entrapment 66–7, 227
  domestic gothic 60, 65, 69, 71–2
  in domesticity 2, 5, 21–2, 32, 44, 47–8, 101
  within female body, fear of 60
  of men by women 30–1
  and migration from city to countryside 11–12
  in patriarchal systems 78 (*see also* patriarchy)
  physical and psychological 150, 152, 161, 162
estrangement 78, 82, 85, 89, 216, 223, 226, 232–3
"Experience and Fiction" 100, 102

"Fall of the House of Usher, The" 170, 206
fallout shelter 114–15, 117, 199–22, 125
Fallout Shelter Handbook 121
family/families 48–9, 63–5
  chronicles 10, 15–22 (*see also Life among the Savages*; *Raising Demons*)
  disciplinary trauma in 180–1
  entrapment in traditional structures 2, 5, 21–2 (*see also* entrapment)
  heteropatriarchal 121, 170
  home (*see* family home)
  life 3, 5, 21, 28, 98, 100, 101, 124, 183, 208, 224–5, 237
  migration of 8–9, 11–12
  nuclear 136, 138, 139, 141, 154, 190, 199, 225
  preparations for apocalypse 114, 118–22
  wartime impact on 32–4, 36, 52
  women's struggle in 3, 5, 19–21
family home 4, 133, 136, 229, 230
  anxieties related to 20
  childhood home 79–82
  destruction of 108, 174, 176, 196–8
  domesticity of the 81
  inheritance of 123–4
  personification of 13–14, 231
Fanny, Aunt 5, 122–3, 134–7, 139–45, 149–50, 152–63
  apocalyptic revelation 116–17, 124, 126, 140–1
  death of 162
  dollhouse of 125, 134, 139–40, 144, 145, 162
  domestic endeavors 158
  entrapment 150, 152, 161, 162

entrenchment in the bunker/mansion 115, 116
hallucinations, auditory 134, 145, 149, 156, 159
"imaginary solution" of 156, 157, 159
madness of 149, 154, 156–63 (see also True Womanhood)
manlessness of 149, 154, 155, 157, 159
moral superiority of 158
Otherness of 155–6, 159
powerlessness of 156, 157, 163
pursuits of male household members 154–5
reconstruction of parents' apartment 143
religiosity of 157–8
sexuality, veiled 155
spinsterhood 115, 122, 125, 137, 139
stockpiling of supplies 113–14
submission to father's authority 156–7
withdrawal into home 160–2
fantasy/fantasies 82, 84, 114, 171, 173–6, 178
cup of stars 169, 177–8, 181, 182–3
fulfilment 169–70
matrophobic horror 87–8, 89
moon 169, 174, 182–3, 190, 198
murderous 171
procreative 87
psychological 31
queer 170, 174, 175
of running away from home 19, 153
FCDA see Federal Civil Defense Administration (FCDA)
fear(s) 5 see also paranoia
Atomic Age 87
of children, mother's 15
in domestic spaces 31–2, 34
of entrapment within the female body 60
feminine, pervasive 47
of ineptitude 59
of mothers 78–9, 83
of nuclear apocalypse 3

Federal Civil Defense Administration(FCDA) 117, 118, 119–21
"Grandma's Pantry" 120–1
female body 77–80, 82
co-optation of 79–80, 86–7
entrapment withinthe 60
and patriarchal imagination 79–80
phobic response to the 79 (see also matrophobia)
Female Homosexuality 178
female identity 32–3, 83, 84, 87, 89, 230–1
Feminine Mystique, The 9–10, 151–2
femininity 51, 149
contempt for 28, 29–30
as maternal 87
metaphorization of 79 (see also "Bus, The")
monstrous 224 (see also monstrous feminine, the)
patriarchy and 80, 83, 105, 161
social expectationsof 47
traditional 151–2
in True Womanhood 153–4, 160
feminism 3, 154
Fern, Fanny 8
"Fine Old Firm, A" 3, 35
Concord, Mrs. 35
Friedman, Mrs. 35
Finn, Huckleberry 191
Flanagan, Mike (dir.) 1
"Flower Garden, The" 3, 11
Fortress America: How We Embraced Fear and Abandoned Democracy 119
Foucault, Michel 49
fragmentation 4, 28
Franklin, Ruth 1, 3, 21–2, 99, 100, 103, 117, 150, 178, 179, 182
Franks, Fred S. 13
freedom 35, 37, 48, 49, 152, 153, 175
Freud, Sigmund 178
Friedan, Betty 9, 10, 22, 150–2
Friedman, Lenemaja 15, 105, 106
Fuller, Margaret 170

Gaskill, Malcolm 99
gender 137, 154
  and agency, limitation of 48
  discrimination 5, 27–31
  dynamics in *New Yorker* fiction 28, 29, 32, 34, 37, 38
  hierarchy 140
  norms 79, 159–60
  performance 44, 45, 159–60, 177
  roles 37, 121, 153, 177
Gilbert, Sandra M. 155–6, 161
Good Housekeeping 3, 7, 8, 9, 60
gossip 14, 29, 44–5, 71
gothic, the 2, 3 *see also* domestic gothic
  American 77, 78, 117, 215, 229
  female 60, 78
  "home", concept of 11–15, 31–2, 37, 60
  matrophobic 78, 82, 87, 89
  relationship between housewife humor and 8, 10, 13–14
  space and architecture in 4, 11–15 (*see also* domestic architecture)
  split personalities 8, 10, 11
Gothicism 3, 215
Green, Fiona 36
Grosz, Elizabeth 79, 124
Gubar, Susan 155–6, 161

Haggerty, George 175, 177
Hague, Angela 138
Halberstam, Jack 115, 172
Hall, Joan Wylie 9, 15, 28, 37, 60
Halloran, Orianna 5, 114, 118, 133–45, 158, 161, 162
  death 123–4, 145
  murder of Lionel 133–8
  New World order 123, 142
  power over Halloran property 134, 135, 136–8
  preparations for apocalypse 116, 122–3, 142
  queen status of 134, 137, 141
  rearranging of inhabitants 138–9
Hangsaman 2, 9, 10, 17
  Arnold, Elizabeth 17–18
  "faculty wife, the" 17–18
  imaginary identity of children 16
  mother, ineffectual 15
  Tony 11
  Waite, Natalie 11, 16, 17
Hattenhauer, Darryl 8, 98, 135, 200, 229
haunted house(s) 1, 3, 5, 207, 231, 233, 235 *see also Haunting of Hill House, The* (novel)
  and identity of women 229, 230 (*see also* Vance, Eleanor)
  and the maternal body 4, 77–8
  orphaned children's minds as 236 (*see also* Vance, Eleanor)
  queering of physical space 169, 173, 174, 175
Haunting of Hill House, The (novel) 1–2, 4, 60, 82–90, 104, 126, 169
  architectural details 82–3, 85–6, 88, 172, 225–7
  belonging, desire for 15, 228, 237
  Crain, Hugh 85, 86–7, 138, 175, 223, 226, 229, 232, 236
  depersonalization, gothic 84, 85, 87–8
  female competition 84–5
  home, concept of 11–13, 77
  lesbian tragedy 175 (*see also* lesbianism)
  locals' clash with urban newcomers 14
  monstrous mother 82, 83–4, 86 (*see also* matrophobia)
  Montague, Dr. 84, 86, 88, 172, 173, 226, 230
  mother–daughter relationship 86, 177, 179, 228
  move from city to countryside 11–12
  parenting culture 83, 86 (*see also* parenting)
  Sanderson, Luke 82–4, 86, 172–4, 176, 227–8, 233, 235
  Theodora 84–6, 172–3, 175–6, 179–81, 226
  Vance, Eleanor (*see* Vance, Eleanor)
  womb-like interiors 87–8, 179, 228, 229–30 (*see also* womb)
Haunting of Hill House, The (TV series) 1–2, 8, 223–37
  Crain family 1, 5, 173, 232, 234, 236

Crain, Nell 232, 233, 235, 236
Crain, Olivia 223, 231–7
Crain, Shirley 1, 232, 233, 235
Crain, Steven 1, 232–3, 235
Forever House 223, 232, 234–5, 236
monstrous feminine, the 5, 224, 226–7, 235
monstrous maternity 224, 237
Red Room 235
H-bomb 117, 120
heteronormativity 5, 84–5, 173, 175
  heteronormative futurity 170, 171, 183
  and marriage 176, 182
  notion of inheritance 174
  nuclear family and 199
  parents as agents of 177, 181
Hinduism 53
Hogle, Jerrold E. 215
home/house *see also* domestic space(s)
  American 4, 30, 119, 224–5
  boarding house as 32–4
  as a danger zone 4, 31, 33, 136, 160
  family (*see also* family home)
  furniture 13, 33, 70, 82–3, 143, 154
  gothic 11–15, 31–2, 37, 160, 170, 177
  as a hegemonic system 47–8
  as a living entity 13–14, 231
  as prison 101, 117, 160, 211
  privacy of 31–4, 35, 44–5 (*see also* privacy, invasion of)
  renovation 15, 118, 223
  as a safe place/refuge 31, 35, 49, 101, 116, 211
  stability of the 30, 35, 36 (*see also* destabilization)
  as supernatural 79, 81, 85, 104, 175, 228
  as trauma site 136 (*see also* trauma)
  as womb replacement 80, 87–8, 227, 228 (*see also* womb)
homemakers *see* housewives/homemakers
homemaking 4, 68, 98, 114–15, 118, 122, 125, 126, 158, 160
homicide 106–7, 133–8, 138, 140, 171, 174, 183 *see also Sundial, The*; *We Have Always Lived in the Castle* (novel)
homosexuality 170, 172, 178, 179 *see also* lesbianism
"Honeymoon of Mrs. Smith, The" 43–5
  Jones, Mrs. 43, 44–5
  Smith, Mrs. 43–5
Horowitz, Daniel 151
horror 2, 3, 21–2
  domestic 224–5, 237
  in domestic gothic fiction 67, 70, 71, 72
  food 212–13
  matrophobic 87–8
  nonrecognition as 47
  of personal becoming public 46 (*see also* "Louisa, Please Come Home"; "Possibility of Evil, The")
  and societal limitations of women 45
  "weaponized civility" as 45
  of women as destructive force 52–3, 106, 107, 108 (*see also* "Sorcerer's Apprentice, The"; *We Have Always Lived in the Castle* (novel))
housekeeping 10, 17, 116, 198
housewives/homemakers 120, 143, 150, 194
  demeaning life of 10, 17
  and domestic danger, source of 30–1
  escape from domesticity 19–21, 47–8
  expectations on 4, 5, 8, 16, 65
  "faculty wife, the" 17–18
  humor 7–8, 9–10 (*see also* domestic humor)
  imprisonment of 101, 117, 160, 211
  magic, use of 101 (*see also* magic)
  middle-class 18, 101
  panic attacks of 12, 20, 152
  repetitive chores of 10, 17, 22
  rural 19–20
  traditional 34
How to Be Perfect 10
humor *see* domestic humor
"Hunger of Miss Burton, The" 30
Hyman, Laurence Jackson 1
Hyman, Stanley Edgar 36, 97, 100, 117, 152–3

I Hate to Cook Book, The 10
identity slippage 15–16, 17–18
"Imagination of Disaster, The" 114
In a Queer Time and Place 115
insanity 149, 154, 163 *see also Sundial, The*
instability 9, 31–2, 51, 118, 153
interlopers 34, 35, 36
"Intoxicated, The" 60–1, 62, 126
  Eileen 60–1, 126
invasion 4, 32, 51–3, 59, 66–7, 70
isolation 5, 63, 126, 138, 161, 162
  of the Blackwoods 206–10, 211–13, 218
  of women 8, 31–4
isolationism 209, 212, 213–14
  toxic 207, 210, 218

Jackson, Shirley
  anxieties of 12, 152–3
  biographical accounts 1, 12, 21, 36, 97, 99 (*see also Shirley Jackson: A Rather Haunted Life*)
  career development with the *New Yorker* 27–9, 36–8
  children of 1
  critics' opinion of workof 2–3, 7, 9, 27, 28, 60
  dynamic identity of 3, 5, 98, 99
  financial successof 8
  as a housewife/homemaker 3, 5, 7, 18, 98, 99, 101, 152
  husband of 36, 97, 100, 117, 152–3
  major themes of work 2–5, 13, 22, 28, 43, 98, 100, 104
  as a mother 3, 5, 7, 18, 98
  as narrator 10–12, 15–18, 20
  and *New Yorker* stories (*see New Yorker* (magazine); *New Yorker* (fiction))
  rejection of work of 37
  self-deprecation of 9
  social issues, stories on 3, 5–6
  as a witch 97–9 (*see also* magic; witchcraft)
  writing style 3, 28, 37–8, 133
Jacobson, Kristin 118

Joshi, S. T. 60, 100–1
Junker, Christine 230

Kahane, Clare 179
Kamensky, Jane 105
Kelly, Gary 215
Kennedy, John F. (President) 119
Kerr, Jean 8, 10
Kiesler, Frederick 88–9
King, Stephen 233–4
Kirkland, Caroline 8
"Knight's Tale, The" 125
Knopf, Alfred A. 97
Kröger, Lisa 2
Kubrick, Stanley 231

"Ladies in the Dark" 29–30
Leer, David Van 9, 10
Lerner, Gerda 156–7
lesbianism 175, 178, 179–80, 195 *see also Haunting of Hill House, The* (novel)
Let Me Tell You 1, 97
Life among the Savages 3, 9, 10, 21, 22, 98, 152 *see also* "Charles"
  changing identities of children 15–16
  comedy in 16–17, 150
  domestic saga, evolution of 3, 8, 9, 10
  Ellenroy, Mrs. 16
  home/house concept in 11, 12, 13–14
  Jannie 16
  local gossip 14
  mother–child ambivalence 15
"Like Mother Used to Make" 66–9
  Harris, Mr. 68–9
  Marcia 68–9
  Turner, David 67–9
Littauer, Amanda H. 175, 178, 179
Lobrano, Gus 37
Lottery and Other Stories, The 2, 10, 19, 31, 60
"Lottery, The" 2, 3, 7, 27, 32, 36, 46–7
"Louisa, Please Come Home" 44, 46–9
  Carol 48
  domestic yearning 47
  escape and return to domesticity 47–8
  Louisa 46–9, 50, 51, 52, 54, 55

INDEX

nonrecognition 47, 49
Paul 48, 49
Peacock, Mrs. 48
punishment for Louisa 49, 50
Taylor, Lois 48

McCort, Jessica R. 5
McDonald, Betty 8
McEnaney, Laura 121
Mademoiselle 9, 17
madness 5, 8, 16, 22, 153–63, 230, 236
  belief and 117
  and manlessness 149, 154, 155–7, 159
  removal of madwomen from field of agency 156, 160
  and witch trials 103
magic 4, 54, 97–8, 100–2, 104–8, 196, 202 *see also* supernatural, the; witchcraft
  black 97
  in domestic spaces 101–2, 103, 104, 108, 211
  metaphorical use of 98
  and power, claiming of 98, 101, 102, 105, 108
  protective 98, 104, 106
  of storytelling 100 (*see also* storytelling)
Magic of Shirley Jackson, The 117
Making of the Modern Family, The 201–2
Malamud, Bernard 2
marriage 48, 84, 85, 125
  New Yorker's views on 29, 30
  society's views on 17–18
  and True Womanhood 151, 154, 155, 156–7, 159, 162
matriarchy 134, 140, 159, 162 (*see also Sundial, The*)
matrophobia 78–9, 83
Matthews, Glenna 11
May, Elaine Tyler 118–19
"Men with Their Big Shoes" 70–2
  Anderson, Mrs. 70–2
  Hart, Mr. 71
  Hart, Mrs. 70–2
  Martin, Mrs. 71

mental disintegration 20–1
mental illness 17–18, 32
mental instability 9, 153
migration, urban to rural 8–9, 11–12, 63–4, 70
Miller, Laura 227
misogyny 31, 46–7
modernity 31, 35–6, 82, 210, 215, 218
monstrous feminine, the 5, 224, 227, 235
moon 169, 174, 182–3, 190, 198
Morrison, Toni 153
Moshfegh, Ottessa 47
motherhood 81, 82, 85, 101
  anxieties of 224, 231
  challenges of 15
  frustrations of 10, 17
  Jackson's representation of 5, 10, 15, 83
  "momism" 83, 87
  monstrous 82, 83–4, 86, 235
  mother–child ambivalence 15, 78, 80, 83, 88, 89
  patriarchal notion of 86
  powerlessness, feeling of 62, 64–5
  slapstick comedy of 10, 16–17
  and True Womanhood 151, 153, 154, 156, 159, 162
  uselessness, feeling of 11
"Motherhood Gave Me an Identity Crisis" 231
movies 1, 8, 53–4
MPF *see* Multi-Purpose Foods (MPF)
multiple personalities *see* split personalities
Multi-Purpose Foods (MPF) 120
Munford, Rebecca 179
Muñoz, José Esteban 177
Murphy, Bernice M. 2, 60, 99, 133
"My Son and the Bully" 9

narcissism 5, 46, 117–18, 190, 191, 194
  see also Blackwood, Merricat
National Fallout Shelter Policy 117, 119
Nemerov, Howard 2
Netflix series *see Haunting of Hill House, The* (TV series)

Nevada 119
New England 8, 11, 14, 16, 99
new world/New World 31, 35, 118, 123, 125, 135, 141, 142, 145, 149, 157–9, 162, 215
New York 12, 19–21, 49
New York City 8, 11, 19
New Yorker (fiction) 27–38
  destabilization in domestic spaces 31–4, 35–6
  and the domestic realm, ambivalence about 28–31
  female identity, crisis of 32–3
  and gender dynamics 28, 29, 32, 34, 37, 38
  gothic consciousness in 31–2
  interlopers 34, 35, 36
  "loony" style of Jackson 37–8
  Otherness 34
  social calls, conventional 34–5
  trademark themes 3, 28
  women's depiction in 29–31
New Yorker (magazine) 27–38
  career development of Jackson, impact on 27–9, 36–8
  contempt for femininity 28, 29–30
  context for publication of Jackson's stories in 31–2
  editoral staff 27, 28–9, 36–8
  gender discrimination 27–31
  golden age 36
  on marriage 29, 30
  readership 3, 27–8
  style 28, 36
Newman, Judie 84
normalcy 4, 44, 47, 55
Norton, W. W. 99
"Not a Refuge Yet: Shirley Jackson's Domestic Hauntings" 211
nuclear attack 117, 119, 120
nuclear family 136, 138, 139, 141, 154, 190, 199, 225
nuclear preparation 114, 115, 120
nuclear war 3, 4, 141

"On being a Faculty Wife" 17–18
One Nation Underground 122
Operation Cue 119

Operation Doorstep 119
Oppenheimer, Judy 16, 99–101, 103
Orpheus 49
Otherness 34, 155–6, 159, 212

panic 12, 19–20, 68, 123, 152
Panter-Downes, Mollie 30
paranoia 3, 5, 14, 32, 114, 117, 126
parenting 83, 201, 225
  helicopter 224, 231
  oppressive 86, 237
  patriarchal 86
Parks, John G. 46, 117
Pascal, Richard 5, 82, 118, 140, 141
Passon, Stacie 1
patriarchal system(s) 50, 55, 78, 141, 142
patriarchy 122, 152, 160, 174, 199, 230
  authority of 31, 115, 143, 156, 157
  escape from 4, 5, 163, 169
  and feminity 80, 83, 105, 161
  mimicking of 135, 138, 140
  between mothers and daughters 83–4, 86
  usurpation of 134, 140, 144, 190
Personal and Family Survival 120
Piatti-Farnell, Lorna 212–13
"Pillar of Salt" 19–21
  Margaret 21
Plant, Rebecca Jo 83
Please Don't Eat the Daisies 8
Poetics of Space, The 79–80
politics 31, 118, 151
"Possibility of Evil, The" 44, 45–7, 50, 53
  punishment for Strangeworth 45, 50, 55
  Strangeworth, Miss 44, 45–6, 50, 51, 52, 54–5
power 10, 51, 54
  destructive 106 (*see also* Blackwood, Merricat)
  domesticity as a form of 44, 101
  through homicide 106–7, 133–8, 171, 174, 183
  and magic 98, 101, 102, 105, 108
  usurpation of 134, 138
  women 4–5, 98, 101, 104, 105, 134

powerlessness 10, 62, 70, 107, 137, 155–6, 157, 163
privacy 119, 138, 202, 216
  of domestic space/home 31–4, 35, 44–5, 50–3
  invasion of 32–3, 44, 50, 51–2, 53, 66–7, 68–70
punishment 36, 45, 49, 50–1, 55, 66, 82, 123, 142, 175, 181, 194, 196

queendom 134, 135, 136, 137, 138, 139, 141, 142, 144–5
queer anti-futurity 171–2, 181
queer future 169–84 see also *Haunting of Hill House, The* (novel); *We Have Always Lived in the Castle* (novel)
  haunted houses and 169, 173, 174, 175
  queer culture 170
  queer fantasy 170, 174, 175
  queering of space 169, 170, 172, 173, 174, 175
Queer Gothic 177
Queer Phenomenology: Orientations, Objects, Others 123, 172

Raising Demons 3, 8, 9, 15–22, 97, 98
  anger and frustration of domesticity 16–17, 19
  Barry 20
  children's changing behavior 15, 16, 20
  comedy of motherhood and housekeeping 16–17
  "faculty wife, the" 17
  family trip/vacation 20–1
  gossip, local 14 (see also gossip)
  Jannie 20
  Laurie 20
  locals' clash with urban newcomers 14–15
  new home purchase 14
  psychological breakdown of the narrator 20–1
  Sally 16, 20–1, 101–2
"Real Me, The" 97
"Renegade, The" 11, 15, 63–5, 70
  Jack 64–5
  Judy 64
  Lady (dog) 63–5
  Nash, Mrs. 64
  Walpole, Mr. 65
  Walpole, Mrs. 15, 63–5, 69, 70, 71
  White, Mr. 64
reproduction 77, 81, 123, 153, 180, 181, 182
Road through the Wall, The 2, 97
"Rock, The" 60
Rogers, Deborah D. 78
Rose, Kenneth 122
Ross, Harold 28
Rubenstein, Roberta 78, 152, 178, 179, 199

Saarinen, Eero 87
Said, Edward 53
San Francisco 49
satire 133, 135, 150 see also *Sundial, The*
Savoy, Eric 214–15
Schorer, Mark 30
Second World War, post-American family life 5, 30, 224
  consumerist domesticity in 211
  housing in 133, 138
  New Yorker publications and readers 27–9
  women in 135, 151, 152, 153, 154
Sedgwick, Eve Kosofsky 206
"Sex in Public" 170
Shining, The 231, 233–4, 235, 237
Shirley Jackson: A Rather Haunted Life 1, 99, 178–9
Shirley Jackson: Essays on the Literary Legacy 2
Shirley Jackson, Influences and Confluences 2
"Shirley Jackson: Possibly a Witch, Definitely Played the Zither" 99
"Shirley Jackson Wasn't Actually a Witch, or Was She?" 99
Shorter, Edward 201–2
Smith, Andrew 59–60
social system(s) 21, 142, 209
solipsism 5 see also narcissism

256 INDEX

Sollée, Kristen J. 105
"Someone to Love" 175
Sontag, Susan 114
"Sorcerer's Apprentice, The" 44, 49–55
 destructionin domestic space 50–3
 intrusion into personal space 50, 51–2, 53
 Marian 50, 52, 54
 Matt, Miss 49–55
 "programmatic music" 54
 punishment for Miss Matt 50–1
 Raleigh, James 52
 Raleigh, Krishna 50–4
 reverse-Orientalism 53
 self-determinism of Miss Matt 50, 54
 violence 52, 53, 54
 xenophobia 53
spinsters 49, 50, 51, 54, 82, 115, 154, 170–1, 173 see also Fanny, Aunt; Vance, Eleanor
split personalities 8, 10, 11
stability 115, 118, 124, 201
 economic 210, 216, 232
 home as a symbol of 30, 35, 36
stars, cup of 169, 177–8, 181, 182–3
stasis 5, 206–7, 218
Stockton, Kathryn Bond 124
storytelling 100, 101, 102, 103, 126
suburbs/suburbia 5, 8–9, 30, 61, 119, 138, 139, 141
"Summer People, The" 11, 14
Sundial, The 2, 4–5, 15, 104, 113–26, 133–45, 149–63
 apocalyptic prophecy 116–17, 124, 126, 140–1
 bunker mentality 114–15, 116, 122, 126
 domestic containment 118–19
 egalitarian domestic governance, failure to develop 141–3
 entrenchment in the bunker/mansion 115, 116, 126
 Essex 123, 124, 139–40, 154–5, 158, 161–2
 Fallout Protection 121
 fallout shelter 114–15, 117, 199–22, 125
 families' role in survival efforts 114, 118–22
 Fanny, Aunt (*see* Fanny, Aunt)
 "Garden of Eden" 118, 142
 Gloria (guest) 141–2, 145
 Halloran, Fancy 123–5, 134–7, 139–41, 143–5, 162, 201
 Halloran, Lionel 123, 133–8
 Halloran mansion 113, 124, 126, 137, 153, 154, 157–8, 160–2
 Halloran, MaryJane 135, 137, 139
 Halloran, Michael 133, 137, 140, 141, 142, 144
 Halloran, Mrs. 123, 125, 135, 137, 140, 142–4, 162
 Halloran, Orianna (*see* Halloran, Orianna)
 Halloran, Richard 123, 125, 135–6, 137–9
 lines of inheritance of the Hallorans 123–4
 locals' clash with urban newcomers 14
 nuclear preparation 114, 115, 120
 nuclear survival 114, 117
 nuclear weapons 119
 Ogilvie 116, 139, 140
 power and authority, women's struggle for 133–7
 queen(s) 134, 135, 136, 137, 138, 139, 141, 142, 144–5
 Scarabombardon, Captain 123, 154
 stockpiling, shelter 113–14, 117, 119, 120, 121, 122, 126
 Stuart, Harriet 134–6
 True Womanhood 149–63 (*see also* True Womanhood)
supernatural, the 4, 98, 234 see also magic; witchcraft
 "beings" 108
 houses as 79, 81, 85, 104, 175, 228
 "manifestations" 223
 "overseers" 142
 and women trapped in patriarchal systems 78

Temple, Emily 99
"Third Baby's the Easiest, The" 18
threat(s) 50, 62, 66, 72, 81, 142, 154, 174
 to home 35–6, 104
 of nuclear bombs 114, 134, 141
 perceived 31–2, 104
"Tooth, The" 12, 19–21
Torrance, Jack 237
trauma 175, 177–8, 196, 197, 231–2, 233, 234
 childhood 153, 232
 disciplinary 180–1
 familial 180, 237
 home as site of 136
"Trial by Combat" 32–3, 69–70
 Allen, Mrs. 32–3, 69–70
 Johnson, Emily 32–3, 69–70
True Womanhood 149–63
 cult of 4, 151, 155
 feminine mystique 151–2
 femininity in 153–4, 160
 madness and manlessness 149, 154, 155, 157, 159
 marriage and 151, 154, 155, 156–7, 159, 162
 motherhood and 151, 153, 154, 156, 159, 162
 patriarchal conception of 149, 154
 pillars of 157–8
 as sedimentation of gender norms 159–60
Twelfth Night 176–7

Vance, Eleanor 11–13, 14, 83–9, 126, 170–83, 225–30
 belonging, desire for 228, 237
 caretaker for her mother 83–4, 170, 175–6, 228, 230
 childless spinster 170, 171
 cup of stars 177–8, 181, 182–3
 daydreaming of 84, 88, 89, 90, 230 (*see also* dream(s)/dreaming)
 depersonalization of 87–8
 first impressions of Hill House 12, 225–6, 227
 guilt of 88, 175, 177

 maternal haunting 83–6, 175, 179, 228
 permanent residence in Hill House 87–90, 169, 181
 psychosexual development 176, 178, 179
 relationship with Theodora 84–5, 175, 176, 179–80
 self-identification process of 172–3
 solitary road trip to Hill House 171, 172
 suicide 173, 175, 183
 unstable mind of 83, 85, 236
Vermont 12, 19
Vidler, Anthony 78
violence 46, 52, 143, 174, 209 *see also* destruction
 toward children 53, 54
 domestic 136, 138
 and domestic gothic 63, 64–5, 66
 by women 135–6, 142, 173, 177, 180, 183
"Visit, The" 60

Wagner-Martin, Linda 2
Walker, Nancy 8–10, 17, 150
Wallace, Diana 59–60
Wallerstein, Immanuel 210
Walpole, Horace 13, 63
Warner, Michael 170
wartime 29, 30–2, 53, 150
Way We Never Were, The 138
We Have Always Lived in the Castle (novel) 2, 4, 8, 15, 60, 98, 169, 174, 189–202, 205–19
 Blackwood, Charles (Cousin) 105, 107, 108, 174, 182, 195–6, 199, 208, 216
 Blackwood family 5, 106–7, 190, 199, 200, 210, 216
 Blackwood home (*see* Blackwood home)
 Blackwood, Mary Katherine (*see* Blackwood, Merricat)
 Blackwood sisters 98, 104–8, 182, 195, 199, 207, 219 (*see also* Blackwood, Constance; Blackwood, Merricat)

china of the Blackwood family
  182, 217
Clarke, Helen 193, 197
domestic love 207, 210–11, 218
food, importance of 106–8,
  212–14, 217
isolation of the Blackwoods 206–10,
  211–13, 218
Jonas (cat) 189–90, 194
Julian, Uncle 105–7, 174, 176–7, 192,
  195, 196, 205, 208–9, 213, 217
live burial of the Blackwoods 206
movie on 1
paranoia andresentment 14
preserves 106, 107, 108, 181–2,
  207–8, 212, 213–14
protectionof home by rituals 104–5,
  106, 107, 211–12, 216–17
tranquility in the Blackwood home
  205–6, 207, 211, 218
Welter, Barbara 151–2, 155, 157
Welty, Eudora 153
West, Chuck 121
"When Things Get Dark" 33–4
  Garden, Mrs. 33–4
  Hope, Mrs. 34
"Whistler's Grandmother" 35–6
Whittier, Gayle 46, 55
Wigley, Mark 79, 81, 86, 89
Wilson, Michael T. 134
Wisker, Gina 225
"Witch, The" 15, 61–3
  Johnny 61–3
witchcraft 4, 62, 97–108 *see also* magic;
  supernatural, the
  anxieties surrounding 99
  in children's literature 98, 101–4,
    108 (*see also Witchcraft of Salem
    Village, The*)
  domestic 104, 107 (*see also We Have
    Always Lived in the Castle* (novel))
  housework as 101
Witchcraft of Salem Village, The 98,
  102–4, 108
  Good, Sarah 104
  Osborne, Sarah 104
  Putnam, Ann 103
  Salem witch trials 102–5

Tituba 103, 104
witch hysteria 98, 102–3, 104
womanhood/Womanhood
  anxieties about 80
  patriarchal notions of 82, 149, 154
  True 149–63 (*see also* True
    Womanhood)
womb
  house as replacement for 80, 87–8,
    227, 228
  monstrous 224, 235
  as mouth 229–30, 235
  toxic 179
Womb Chair 87
women
  anxieties of 3, 16, 19, 20, 21 (*see also*
    anxiety/anxieties)
  entrapment in domesticity 2, 5, 21–2,
    32, 44, 47–8 (*see also* entrapment)
  heteronormative futurity, resistance
    of 170, 171, 183
  as homemakers 8, 10, 18–19, 120,
    143, 150, 194 (*see also* housewives/
    homemakers)
  identity (*see also* female identity)
    crisis of 32–3, 89, 178, 230–1
    fragmentation of 28
  middle-class 8, 16, 18, 101, 225
  migration from city 8–9, 11–12
  in *New Yorker* stories 28–31 (*see also
    New Yorker* fiction)
  and patriarchy 4, 5, 78, 135, 138,
    140, 151, 163, 169
  power 4–5, 98, 101, 104, 105, 134
  sexual desires of 80–1, 155
  struggles of 3, 5, 19–21, 34
  as symbols of "rational" and
    "familiar" 31
  uncanny 60, 82, 83
  unmarried 49, 50, 51, 54, 82, 154,
    170–1, 173 (*see also* Fanny, Aunt;
    Vance, Eleanor)
  violence by 135–6, 142, 173, 177,
    180, 183
*World-Systems Analysis: An
  Introduction* 210

Yagoda, Ben 36

www.ingramcontent.com/pod-product-compliance
Lightning Source LLC
Chambersburg PA
CBHW052112010526
44111CB00036B/1882